Death, Life and Laughter

C000056414

Birth, death and the rituals that take us from one to the other tell us a lot about humanity and our quest to understand ourselves. It is cross-disciplinary analyses of the life course that have generated the most profound insights into religion and spirituality, challenging the concepts and methods we commonly use to understand these universal aspects of human experience. Douglas Davies' work is a rare example of this kind of scholarship, challenging the boundaries that separate theology from the social sciences and that divide academia from public life. This book serves as a tribute to Davies' work and a critical commentary on the questions that arise from it. Featuring essays by renowned international scholars, this book brings cutting-edge research into conversation with ongoing debates about disciplinary difference and the nature of scholarship.

Mathew Guest has published widely on contemporary British Evangelicalism and on Christianity in general, addressing such topics as the sociology of spirituality, creationist belief and the reproduction and transmission of religious identities. His recent research has focused on the status of religion within university contexts. He has worked with Douglas Davies on several research projects and as a teaching colleague in Durham for the past fifteen years. With Douglas Davies, he has co-authored *Modern Christianity: Reviewing Its Place in Britain Today* (2000) and *Bishops, Wives and Children: Spiritual Capital across the Generations* (2007). He has also co-edited *Congregational Studies in the UK: Christianity in a Post-Christian Context* (with Karin Tusting and Linda Woodhead; 2004), *Religion and Knowledge: Sociological Perspectives* (with Elisabeth Arweck; 2012), is the author of *Evangelical Identity and Contemporary Culture: A Congregational Study in Innovation* (2007) and co-author (with Kristin Aune, Sonya Sharma and Rob Warner) of *Christianity and the University Experience: Understanding Student Faith* (2013).

Martha Middlemiss Lé Mon has worked with Douglas Davies on the UK case studies within the framework of two European research projects. The first, 'Welfare and Religion in a European Perspective', resulted in, among other projects, reports in one of the chapters in the volume *Welfare and Religion in 21st Century Europe: Volume 1 Configuring the Connections* (2010). It also provided the empirical material for her PhD thesis (supervised by Douglas Davies), later published as *The In-between Church: A Study of the Church of England's Role in Society through the Prism of Welfare* (2009). From the second project, the European Commission-funded 'Welfare and Values in Europe: Transitions Related Religion, Minorities and Gender', a number of project reports were produced and published online, as well as various articles, including 'Care and Career: A Value Conflict with a Woman's Face, Beliefs and Values' (forthcoming). She is currently engaged in research into values and family life in Sweden and is editing a volume (in Swedish) on Welfare and Religion.

Death, Life and Laughter

Essays on religion in honour of
Douglas Davies

Edited by
Mathew Guest
and Martha Middlemiss Lé Mon

Routledge
Taylor & Francis Group

LONDON AND NEW YORK

First published 2017
by Routledge
2 Park Square, Milton Park, Abingdon, Oxon OX14 4RN

and by Routledge
711 Third Avenue, New York, NY 10017

Routledge is an imprint of the Taylor & Francis Group, an informa business

British Library Cataloguing in Publication Data
A catalogue record for this book is available from the British Library

Library of Congress Cataloging in Publication Data
Names: Davies, Douglas James, honouree. | Guest, Mathew, editor.
Title: Death, life and laughter : essays on religion in honour of Douglas
Davies / edited by Matthew Guest and Martha Middlemiss Lé Mon.
Description: 1 [edition]. | New York : Routledge, 2016. | Includes
bibliographical references and index.
Identifiers: LCCN 2016027277 | ISBN 9781472427700 (hardback : alk.
paper)
Subjects: LCSH: Religion. | Davies, Douglas James.
Classification: LCC BL25 .D43 2016 | DDC 200—dc23
LC record available at https://lccn.loc.gov/2016027277

ISBN: 978-1-4724-2770-0 (hbk)
ISBN: 978-1-4094-5702-2 (pbk)
ISBN: 978-1-315-40402-8 (ebk)

Typeset in Sabon
by Book Now Ltd, London

MIX
Paper from
responsible sources
FSC
www.fsc.org   FSC® C013056

Printed and bound in Great Britain by
TJ International Ltd, Padstow, Cornwall

Contents

Contributors

Anders Bäckström is Professor Emeritus in the Sociology of Religion at the Faculty of Theology, Uppsala University, Sweden. His research has focused on Sweden and Europe, particularly focusing on questions of the 'new' visibility of religion in contemporary society, the role of religion in welfare systems, and the role of the church in Swedish society. He has led a number of international research projects in which Douglas Davies has been involved, including 'Welfare and Religion in a European Perspective' (2003–2006) and 'Welfare and Values in Europe: Transitions Related to Religion, Minorities and Gender' (2006–2009), and he initiated the ongoing research programme at Uppsala University, 'The Impact of Religion: Challenges for Society, Law and Democracy' (2008–2018). His publications include *Welfare and Religion in 21st Century Europe* (2010 and 2011; edited with G. Davie, P. Pettersson and N. Edgardh).

James A. Beckford, a fellow of the British Academy, is Professor Emeritus of Sociology at the University of Warwick and a former president of the Society for the Scientific Study of Religion. His main research interests are chaplaincies and relations between religion and the state. His publications include *Religion in Prison: Equal Rites in a Multi-Faith Society* (1998, with Sophie Gilliat), *Social Theory and Religion* (2003), *Muslims in Prison: Challenge and Change in Britain and France* (2005, with D. Joly and F. Khosrokhavar), *The SAGE Handbook of the Sociology of Religion* (2007, edited with N. J. Demerath III) and *Migration and Religion* (two edited volumes, 2015).

James G. Crossley is Professor of Bible, Culture and Politics in the Centre for the Social-Scientific Study of the Bible at St Mary's University, Twickenham, London. His main areas of research are first-century Palestine (especially the historical Jesus) and contemporary political understandings of the Bible. His recent publications include *Jesus and the Chaos of History: Redirecting the Life of the Historical Jesus* (2015) and *Harnessing Chaos: The Bible in English Political Discourse since 1968* (second edition, 2016).

Douglas Davies studied anthropology at Durham followed by initial research at Oxford's Institute of Social Anthropology. He also read Theology at Durham and subsequently held posts at Nottingham University, including that of professor in the Study of Religion. Since 1997 he has been a Professor at Durham University's Department of Theology and Religion. He has researched and published many monographs and edited volumes covering Mormonism, Death Studies, Anglicanism and theoretical issues in Religious Studies.

Valerie DeMarinis is Professor of Psychology of Religion at Uppsala University, Sweden; guest professor in Public Mental Health at the Department of Clinical Medicine and Public Health at Umeå University, Sweden; and consulting professor in Public Mental Health Promotion at the Innlandet Hospital Trust in Norway. Her research is primarily linked to an investigation of mental and physical health and its connections to cultural and existential information. She has published widely in the areas of addiction treatment, palliative care, transcultural psychiatry, youth and mental health, and women's health.

Hugh Goddard is Director of the HRH Prince Alwaleed bin Talal Centre for the Study of Islam in the Contemporary World at the University of Edinburgh. From 1984 to 2009, he worked in the Department of Theology and Religious Studies in the University of Nottingham, where he served initially as Lecturer in Islamic Theology and then Professor of Christian–Muslim Relations from 2004. He is the author of *Christians and Muslims: From Double Standards to Mutual Understanding* (1995), *Muslim Perceptions of Christianity* (1996) and *A History of Christian-Muslim Relations* (2000), as well as many articles on different aspects of Islamic Studies and Christian–Muslim relations.

Mathew Guest is Reader in the Sociology of Religion in the Department of Theology and Religion, Durham University. He has published widely on the sociology of Christianity in late-modern Western cultures, focusing especially on the evangelical movement and religion within university contexts. He is the author of *Evangelical Identity and Contemporary Culture: A Congregational Study in Innovation* (2007) and *Christianity and the University Experience: Understanding Student Faith* (2013, with Kristin Aune, Sonya Sharma and Rob Warner). Between 2001 and 2004, he worked alongside Douglas Davies on the 'Clergy and British Society' project, leading to their co-authored volume *Bishops, Wives and Children: Spiritual Capital across the Generations* (2007).

Christian Karner is Associate Professor in the School of Sociology and Social Policy at the University of Nottingham, and has been a research associate in the Center for Austrian Studies at the University of Minnesota. His research and wide-ranging publications focus on the (discursive) negotiations of ethnic, national, local and religious identities in the context of contemporary globalization, on memory studies and on urban sociology. His publications include *Writing History, Constructing Religion* (co-edited with James Crossley, 2005), *Ethnicity and Everyday Life* (2007), *Negotiating National Identities: Between Globalization, the Past and 'the Other'* (2011), *The Use and Abuse of Memory: Interpreting World War II in Contemporary European Politics* (2013, co-edited with Bram Mertens) and *The Commonalities of Global Crises* (2016, co-edited with Bernhard Weicht).

Seth D. Kunin is Professor and Deputy Vice Chancellor at Curtin University in Australia, having previously worked at the University of Aberdeen, Durham University and Nottingham University. His work has focused on the development and application of structuralist theory to religious traditions, including Judaism and the Church of Jesus Christ of Latter Day Saints. His publications include *The Logic of Incest: A Structuralist Analysis of Hebrew Mythology* (1995), *God's Place in the World: Sacred Space and Sacred Place in Judaism* (1998) and *Juggling Identities: Identity and Authenticity among the Crypto-Jews* (2009).

David Martin is Emeritus Professor of Sociology at the London School of Economics and an emeritus fellow of the British Academy. From 1986 to 1990, he was Distinguished Professor of Human Values at Southern Methodist University and was also attached to Boston University. He has published over 20 books on topics related to secularization, secularism, Pentecostalism, religious pacifism and violence, sociology and theology, and the sociology of music. His most recent books are *Religion and Power: No Logos without Mythos* (2014), *Ruin and Restoration: On Violence, Liturgy and Reconciliation* (2016) and *Recuperations, Recapitulations and Rebuttals* (forthcoming).

Martha Middlemiss Lé Mon is a researcher in the Sociology of Religion, and Director of the Uppsala Religion and Society Research Centre at Uppsala University, Sweden. In her research she has focused on issues of religion and welfare and in particular on the role of the Christian churches and faith-based organizations in a changing landscape of welfare provision in contemporary Europe. She has also researched and published on issues of gender and values in relation to religion. Between 2003 and 2008, she worked with Douglas Davies on the UK case studies for two European projects: 'Welfare and Religion in Europe' and 'Welfare and Values in Europe'. Her publications include *The In-between Church: A Study of the Church of England's Role in Society through the Prism of Welfare* (2009).

Eleanor Nesbitt is Emeritus Professor in the Religions and Education Research Unit, Centre for Education Studies, University of Warwick. Her ethnographic research has focused principally on religious socialization in Christian, Hindu and Sikh communities, and she has published widely on Hindu and Sikh tradition and on interfaces between education and religions. Her publications include *Interfaith Pilgrims* (2003), *Intercultural Education: Ethnographic and Religious Approaches* (2004), *Pool of Life: The Autobiography of a Punjabi Agony Aunt* (2013, with Kailash Puri), *Making Nothing Happen: Five Poets Explore Faith and Spirituality* (2014, with Gavin D'Costa, Mark Pryce, Ruth Shelton and Nicola Slee) and *Sikhism: A Very Short Introduction* (second edition, 2016).

David Parker is a lecturer in the School of Sociology and Social Policy at the University of Nottingham. His wide-ranging research and publications encompass ethnicity and identity (with particular reference to overseas Chinese and mixed-race identities), urban life, the public realm, and social and cultural theory. He is currently researching issues of belonging and community-making in East Birmingham.

Michael J. Thate is a post-doctoral research associate at Princeton University as well as an Alexander von Humboldt Fellow at Tübingen University. His current research revolves around material messianisms during the early twentieth century, measurements of time and the temporal effects of technology. He co-edited *'In Christ' in Paul* (2014) and *Albert Schweitzer in Thought and Action: A Life in Parts* (2016). He is the author of *Remembrance of Things Past? Albert Schweitzer, the Anxiety of Influence, and the Untidy Jesus of Markan Memory* (2013).

Grant Underwood is a professor of history at Brigham Young University. He is the author or co-editor of several prize-winning volumes, including *The Millenarian World of Early Mormonism* (1999) and *The Joseph Smith Papers: Documents, Volumes 1–3* (2013–2014), and is co-author of the forthcoming *Mormonism among Christian Theologies*. He was founding co-director of the American Academy of Religion's Mormon Studies Group, a session of which Douglas Davies participated in at the annual meeting. Underwood likewise participated in Davies' two international Mormon Studies seminars in the UK in the 1990s.

Charles Watkins is Professor of Rural Geography at the University of Nottingham. His principal research interests include rural geography, landscape history, nature conservation, rural land management and the cultural geography of trees and forestry. He has worked on many interdisciplinary projects linking cultural studies with the natural and social sciences. His latest books are *Trees, Woods and Forests* (2014), *Europe's Changing Woods and Forests* (2015) and *Uvedale Price: Decoding the Picturesque* (2012), the first biography of the influential eighteenth-century landscape aesthetician. He is Chair of the Society for Landscape Studies.

Matthew Wood completed his doctorate with Douglas Davies at the University of Nottingham. He was Lecturer in Sociology at Queen's University Belfast, having previously held posts at the University of Cambridge, the University of Roehampton and Richmond, the American International University in London. His research covered issues of power in the New Age Movement, the effects of globalization on Methodism in London and the contribution of Pierre Bourdieu to the sociology of religion. In addition to a wide range of scholarly articles, he published *Possession, Power and the New Age: Ambiguities of Authority in Neoliberal Societies* in 2007. Sadly, Matthew passed away after a long illness before this book was published, in 2015.

Introduction

Transgressing boundaries

*Martha Middlemiss Lé Mon
and Mathew Guest*

This book is, as the reader will quickly note, an eclectic collection of essays covering heaven and earth and most things in-between or, as the title suggests, death, life and laughter. We hope, however, that the worst excesses of diversity leading to lack of clarity have been avoided and that this volume is a coherent whole worthy of the academic it is written to honour. The wide-ranging nature of the contents of this book is nothing more and nothing less than a reflection of the broad and generous nature of Douglas Davies' scholarship. It is also an attempt to contribute to an academic approach which he represents, namely making innovative connections where others do not see them and daring to challenge disciplinary boundaries to further the greater aim of developing the science of the study of religion and theology. Davies has pursued this greater aim for the best part of 45 years now, providing, along the way, nuanced insights into important questions of our time and always having fun while doing so.

In this introductory essay, we would like to accomplish three things. First, we offer a brief account of the life of Douglas Davies, placing his contributions to scholarship within the context of his broader biography. Second, we outline the contents of the present volume, taking each of its essays in turn and connecting these with the contours of Davies' scholarship. Third, we explain how this book came into being. Along the way, we offer some comment on laughter as a lens through which to view the orientation to life and work embodied in our indomitably jocular friend.

Douglas Davies: a life lived at the boundaries

Douglas James Davies was born on 11 February 1947 in Bedlinog, South Wales, the son of Gladys and Llewellyn Davies, a coal miner. Like many of his generation, the path to wider opportunities was presented by the grammar school, in this case the Lewis Grammar School in Pengam. By the age of 18, he had secured an undergraduate place to study at the University of Durham and spent his first year studying zoology, psychology and anthropology. While this combination prefigures a life-long fascination with the biological sciences and reflects an embryonic preference for occupying the spaces across, rather than within, academic disciplines, it was nevertheless in anthropology that Davies eventually took his degree, graduating in 1969.

Maintaining a long-standing ambition to be a member of the clergy, Davies' direction of travel was altered by an unexpected meeting with then Professor of Anthropology Philip Mayer, who instructed him not only to 'do research' but also to do it in Oxford. Following his teacher's advice, and with some guidance from the then Principal of St John's College, Durham, Jim Hickinbotham, but without any notion of a research topic and never having been to Oxford before, Douglas registered for the research BLitt degree at St Peter's College. As an anthropologist, but without a clear research topic, he was initially referred for supervision to Godfrey Lienhardt, author of the famous study of the Dinka in southern Sudan. After it was clear their interests did not coincide, Davies was instead referred to sociologist of religion, Bryan Wilson. It was in an initial conversation with Wilson that the subject of Mormonism arose; Davies had been aware of their established presence in Merthyr Tydfil, located in the next valley to his own village back in Wales. He also knew that a brand-new Mormon church had just been built in this town, a striking development within a context in which secularization was the sociological orthodoxy and the decline and closure of churches was commonplace. Wilson strongly advised him to study the Mormons for his research project, and so it transpired, via serendipity and the confident direction of idiosyncratic academics, that Douglas Davies began researching for his dissertation on the Mormons of Merthyr Tydfil. This signalled his first experience of empirical research, his first academic publication (Davies 1973) and the beginnings of a life-long and prolific academic interest in the Church of Jesus Christ of Latter Day Saints (LDS).

Davies was unusual in occupying both a place at Oxford's Anthropological Institute – attending the lectures of luminaries Rodney Needham and E.E. Evans-Pritchard – and at Wilson's weekly seminar in the sociology of religion, alongside notable young scholars such as Jim Beckford, Peter Jupp and Richard Gombrich. In another example where anthropology and sociology overlapped, Godfrey Lienhardt played a part in examining Davies' BLitt thesis alongside an external examiner from the LSE, David Martin, who, along with Wilson, was responsible for the sociology of religion achieving serious profile from the 1960s onwards. At the level of disciplinary association, Davies refused to confine himself within conventional boundaries, adopting a more pragmatic approach whereby knowledge was embraced insofar as it illuminated religion as a human phenomenon.

Indeed, Douglas Davies' emerging intellectual orientation to the study of religion drew on a wide range of cross-disciplinary sources. This is partially explained with reference to his anthropological training, anthropology always fostering a more theoretically generous culture of scholarship than sociology, especially during the decades following the Second World War, when ideological preoccupations with Marxist and existentialist thought fed a narrow secularism within sociological circles. But Davies' more eclectic leanings were also informed by his personal perspective vis-à-vis Christianity, and, like David Martin, he has spent his academic career also functioning as an active churchman. During much of his time at the University of Nottingham, he was also honorary assistant curate at St Leonard's, Woolaton; a long-standing connection with the St John's Ambulance Service led him to serve as chaplain to the Order of St John both in Nottingham and in Durham at different times. Davies' Christianity was an outworking of his childhood churchgoing, in his case in the Welsh Valleys, in which chapel singing and a low to moderate Anglicanism informed a life-long attachment to liturgy and music. This was nurtured further during his days as an undergraduate in the Cathedral city of Durham, in which students to this day are presented with a vibrant Christian subculture structured around the many churches clustered near its centre and etched into the architectural symbolism of a town with Norman foundations. Living in St John's College also exposed Davies to the vibrant evangelicalism thriving there in the late 1960s.

The study of religion as an academic pursuit has always, for Davies, sat alongside an enthusiastic involvement in the ritual, theological and at times pastoral life of the Church of England. It is highly significant, then, that, following completion of his Oxford BLitt, Davies should choose to return to Durham to train for ordained ministry in the Anglican Church, undertaking a further degree – this time in Theology – as part of the process. The Theology Department at Durham was, at that time, much more closely aligned with the life of the Anglican Church than it is now, and while ministerial formation was undertaken within the affiliated theological college, Cranmer Hall, the university department's curriculum remained firmly structured around scripture, church history and doctrine, most of the academic staff were Anglican clergy and some started lectures with prayers. At the forefront were the twin giants of New Testament scholarship, C.K. Barrett and Charles Cranfield, whose legacy still colours Durham's reputation as a centre for biblical study in the present day.

Douglas Davies was ordained priest in the Church of England in 1976. By this time he had already been appointed lecturer in the Department of Theology at the University of Nottingham, then led by one of Davies' former teachers at Durham, Professor John Heywood-Thomas. A student of Paul Tillich and intrigued by his theology of culture, Heywood-Thomas was keen to expand Nottingham's traditional theology syllabus by appointing a 'lecturer in the phenomenology of religion'. After securing the post, Douglas Davies taught for many years a course in the 'philosophy and phenomenology of religion' alongside Heywood-Thomas, an experience that was highly formative within his emerging scholarship. Davies' intellectual interests gravitated to the legacy of evolutionism for the study of religion and to scholars such as Alfred Schutz, Gerardus Van der Leeuw and Wilhelm Dilthey, all associated with the experience-focused approach known as the phenomenology of religion, appropriated within the discipline of sociology by Peter Berger and Thomas Luckmann. It was Berger and Luckmann's (1967) application of Schutz's phenomenology to the sociology of knowledge that formed the intellectual foundation for what would become Davies' PhD thesis, taken in 1979 at the University of Nottingham and published as his first monograph in 1984.

Meaning and Salvation in Religious Studies is by today's standards a bold and ambitious first book. Relatively short at 164 pages, it is densely written, in some sections highly theoretical, and tackles an apparently inscrutable problem, namely the relationship between the human drive for meaning and the human quest for salvation. This central concern encapsulates several enduring features of Davies' scholarship, not least his unblinking confrontation of 'meta-questions' that at once defy and challenge disciplinary boundaries. The ambition to question the way in which scholarship defines its conceptual parameters lies at the heart of this book, which grapples critically with the troubled waters between traditional theology and the emergent discipline of Religious Studies. The argument arises in part from Davies' unease with the category of 'salvation religions' typically applied to Abrahamic faiths and contrasted with 'primitive religions', a false distinction he attributes to the evolutionist presuppositions of the nineteenth century. Here we see his anthropological instincts for cultural nuance used to question the generalist assumptions of western thought, assumptions often reinforced by Christian theologies driven by a mission agenda. Davies' counter-argument that 'salvation' questions may be found in every culture (1984: 2) may now be criticized for simply exchanging one set of western (liberal Protestant?) assumptions for another, and recent work in the anthropology of 'belief' might be used to challenge the centrality Davies accords to 'meaning' itself. But in its ambition for the big questions, which are grappled with in evocative detail, the book is a refreshingly confident treatise, determinedly unfashionable at a time when the western intelligentsia were cowed in their embrace of postmodernist ideas.

Meaning and Salvation also signalled Davies' ease in drawing upon an eclectic range of academic sources in the service of his argument. The bibliography includes sociology (Robert Bellah, Max Weber, Bryan Wilson), anthropology (Raymond Firth, Claude Lévi-Strauss, Victor Turner), psychology (Philip Rieff, Sigmund Freud), philosophy (J.L. Austin, Paul Ricoeur), theology (Thomas Aquinas, Austin Farrer, Paul Tillich), as well as thinkers who, like Davies himself, appear to resist easy disciplinary placement, such as John Bowker and Hans Mol. While theoretically driven, the book expands and applies its argument via a series of case study chapters which build, in part, on the author's own empirical research. Notable here are Davies' chapters on Mormonism and Sikh religion, his interest in the latter nurtured by a sabbatical leave from Nottingham spent as a visiting lecturer at Punjabi University in northern India. These chapters are also an example of the comparative method in which Davies has shown a continued intellectual interest over the years. His introduction to comparative method in his *Anthropology and Theology* (2002) is a particularly good illustration, pointing not only to an academic justification of comparative method but also of the importance of facing and challenging one's own beliefs, opinions and prejudices as a key element in the scientific endeavour. In *Anthropology and Theology*, he comments that for many the very endeavour of comparative method is 'difficult to think', by which he means that 'a kind of philosophical distress emerges when we try to examine the very classification of reality by means of which we normally think' (2002: 3). Such approaches involve, in other words, a degree of self-knowledge and distance from the self in order to think about the self. A complex, but necessary, process in Davies' book and his continued use of comparative method in his work highlights a clear line throughout his scholarship of a preparedness to take on those questions which are 'difficult to think'.

Davies' period at Nottingham spanned over 20 years, during which he established himself as a popular teacher and respected scholar. He also maintained his persistent tendency to embrace new areas of academic endeavour that defied the confines of traditional disciplinary boundaries. Notable here is 'The Rural Church Project', Davies' first major piece of collaborative research, undertaken alongside the rural policy specialist Michael Winter and geographer Charles Watkins, whose chapter in the present volume marks an especially novel branch in Davies' eclectic network of interests. *Church and Religion in Rural England*, co-authored by Davies, Watkins and Winter, was published in 1991 and drew on an extensive empirical study of church life across several rural Anglican dioceses. Co-funded by the Archbishops' Commission and the Leverhulme Trust, the project also reflects Davies' emerging aptitude for building relationships with non-academic bodies in a quest to explore questions that command intellectual interest while also speaking to the needs of broader publics. Another example would be *Reusing Old Graves* (1995), co-authored with Alistair Shaw, which reported on popular British attitudes concerning death, memorialization and the afterlife. This study was made possible by financial support from a nation-wide range of local authorities and cemetery committees, and broader engagement has been developed more recently through Davies' work with the National Council for Palliative Care.

Reusing Old Graves also marked Davies' growing interest in death studies, which led to his long-standing position on the editorial board of the journal *Mortality* and publication of his influential 1997 volume *Death, Ritual and Belief: The Rhetoric of Funerary Rites*. It was in this book that Davies first developed the notion of 'words against death', an interpretative framework for understanding the human drive for meaning in the face of experiences that highlight the end of life. A second edition was produced in 2002, and *Death, Ritual and Belief* has now been published in Italian as well; his later *A Brief History of Death* (2004) has also achieved global acclaim, now available in translations in Spanish, Czech and Greek, while *The Theology of Death* (2008) places Davies' research into human responses to death in the service of theological questions, again illustrating an enthusiasm for crossing disciplinary boundaries. Davies' work on death, dying and disposal continues to this day via projects involving the National Health Service, the Church of England, secular funeral service providers and central UK government. In this field, he has also in recent years put his interest in interdisciplinary research into practice, founding the Centre for Death and Life Studies at Durham University. This centre, of which he is also director, exists to foster and conduct research into life values, beliefs and practices that relate to living and dying, and it seeks particularly to encourage and facilitate interdisciplinary approaches wherever possible between the humanities, the social and life sciences and medicine.

Davies remained at Nottingham until 1997, after being promoted to senior lecturer and then Professor in the Study of Religion. He then returned to his *alma mata* as Professor in the Study of Religion in the Theology Department at Durham University, also taking on the job of Principal of the College of St Hild and St Bede. Since this transition, and especially after his assumption of a full-time academic post in the department in 2000, Davies' scholarship has been prolific. Perhaps most acclaimed have been his volumes on the LDS, which emerged from a career-long interest in the Mormon tradition and a concerted attempt to learn from and within long-standing relationships with LDS members, leaders and scholars. Davies' gentle, principled and honest engagement with LDS figures and organizations and his determined adoption of a Weberian Verstehen-based approach, foregrounding empathy and an openness to 'the other', has earned him wide-ranging respect within LDS circles (much as his teacher – Bryan Wilson – maintained warm and respectful relations with a variety of religious sects during his career, none of which commanded his personal allegiance). The resulting subtle, mature understanding is strikingly apparent in Davies' *The Mormon Culture of Salvation* (2000), which offered a characteristically interdisciplinary treatment, Davies' introduction stating that 'the arbitrary divisions between academic disciplines often hinder the emergence of the fuller picture' (2000: 7). What Davies calls his 'composite perspective' (2000: 7) permits insights from LDS history and historiography, social theory, anthropology and theology to come together in an original and complex account. Moreover, his willingness to take seriously both theories external to the LDS world and discourses emerging within it engenders a sensitivity to nuance and empirical variation. This is not least apparent in his argument for Mormonism as a variant on the Protestant conversionist sect, driven less by a call for personal repentance and a cleansing from sin via Christ's atoning sacrifice and more by a logic of exclusivity based on its claim to be the true Church, its sacred texts and rites providing the institutional foundation for a true life of faith (Davies 2000: 25–26).

Douglas Davies has written or edited twenty-two books and published over eighty essays and articles during his prolific career. His interests have always ranged far and wide, from the rural church in England to the legacy of Victorian intellectual and educator Frank Byron Jevons, and more latterly the significance of the emotional dimension of religious identities. One of his abiding contributions to scholarship will be his creative engagement in interdisciplinary dialogue, and this is most striking in his prolific scholarship on LDS and the human response to death, including those recent volumes such as *Joseph Smith, Jesus and Satanic Opposition* (2010), in which he has sought to connect his two primary research interests. Drawing from a range of disciplines, Davies has always refused to be positioned within conventional academic boundaries, and while, in this respect, he embodies the eclectic and multifaceted character of the British social scientific study of religion more generally (Catto, 2015), few scholars in this field have developed an interdisciplinary approach in such depth and with such a profundity of cross-disciplinary understanding.

While his academic home has alternated over the years between the three UK universities of Oxford, Nottingham and Durham, Davies' scholarship has been far from merely national in its scope. He has held visiting fellowships at the University of Punjab, the Huntington Library in the USA and at Helsinki University in Finland, as well as regularly collaborating with academics at universities across the world, not least Brigham Young University in the USA and Uppsala University in Sweden. The high esteem in which he is held as a scholar is evidenced in the honorary doctorate granted to Davies by the latter institution in 1998, to which can be added a DLitt from the University of Oxford in 2004, a fellowship of the Academy of Social Sciences in 2009 and of the Learned Society of Wales in 2012.

In addition to his scholarship, Douglas Davies has made significant contributions to the civic life of the country, through pastoral training of the Anglican clergy and as a trustee of the St Martin's Trust, Birmingham. He has also been a life-long supporter of the St John's Ambulance, for which he remains chaplain for the north-east of England. These examples illustrate Davies' active involvement in the institutions of the Church of England alongside academic life, and yet it is important also to mention his consistent unease with connections between academe and religious bodies that make faith commitment a factor in what are ordinarily matters of purely academic judgement. Davies has often invoked the case of a Victorian hero, William Robertson Smith, who was dismissed from his academic post after a heresy trial because his published work on the Old Testament did not endorse the biblical literalism upheld by the Free Church of Scotland, of which he was a minister. Davies has always supported a clear institutional boundary between church and academy: each has its own purpose, best achieved when independent from the other and best achieved when in conversation with one another. And yet his significant contributions to ministerial training – and publications in pastoral theology – reflect an enthusiasm for applying the insights of academic endeavour in the service of the Christian church. Davies explains this bifocality in terms of his approach to teaching the study of religion, which he has never viewed as a Christian endeavour in terms of its goals and purpose; in practical terms, he also never needed the lecture podium to be a pulpit, because as a serving Anglican priest he already had a pulpit from which to speak on Sundays. More profoundly, the disciplinary tensions some of his peers found between theology and religious studies were clearly not tensions for Davies, whose intellectual openness and untroubled Anglicanism seems to have fostered a consistent ease with interdisciplinary conversation over anxious boundary maintenance. It is tempting to speculate that his regular immersion within quotidian parish life relativized the theological questions posed with such urgency in university theology departments; the precise dynamics of the atonement seem of less cosmic importance following a pastoral visit to relatives grieving the recent loss of a loved one.

At both temporary and more long-term academic residences, an important aspect for Davies has always been the support of the social as well as academic aspects of scholarly life. Whether as warden of a hall of residence (Nottingham), member or principal of a college (Oxford and Durham), he has contributed actively to forming and maintaining a collegial spirit and fostering a new generation of academics. His cheerful sociability has been integral to the success he has enjoyed and the respect he has earned, and in this regard it is impossible to separate the man from the scholar. Indeed, his magnanimity has been as instrumental as his learning in inspiring generations of undergraduates, postgraduates and young scholars to pursue the study of religion with confidence and imagination. This is illustrated in the numerous students he has employed over the years as collaborative partners on research projects, never seeing their naiveté or youth as an impediment to involvement or even co-authorship. His natural enthusiasm and passion for intellectual innovation is, at its best, infectious, and colleagues and collaborators have appreciated his indomitable sense of academic possibility; the occasional 'go for it!' and encouraging 'why not?' go a long way within a higher education sector often constrained by disciplinary traditionalism or administrative fatigue. The seminar room is a different place with Douglas Davies in it.

While it is indeed almost futile to try to separate the scholar from the man, it would nevertheless be unjust to leave this brief portrait with the impression that Davies has lived solely as an 'institution man', his energies channelled largely by universities and the Anglican church. This would be to forget his love of cacti (an entire room of his house devoted to his extensive collection), his prowess as a squash player, his enthusiasm for antique shops and his creative, colourful approach to interior decoration. It would also be to forget his love of good food and his passion for wine and port, all of which have coloured numerous social occasions with a welcome touch of flamboyance as memorable as the man himself. It would be to forget his love for his garden, painstakingly tended and enjoyed, visitors offered a tour on which potatoes, succulents and a passing frog are given equal attention to the flowers that happen to be in bloom. It would be to forget his love of singing, whether traditional Welsh hymns, Victorian parlour songs or The Teddy Bear's Picnic, his resonant tenor carried along the corridors of university campuses. Then there is the 'laughter', so important in any appreciation of Davies' life and work that we included the word in the title of this book. Anyone who has worked with or perhaps even encountered Douglas Davies will recognize here a reference to the hearty laughter that observes no boundaries. Many a meeting, meal and conversation has been lightened and brought back to life as a consequence of such involuntary contributions. Ingvild Gilhus, in her study of laughter in the history of religion, captures the significance of rare individuals like Douglas Davies when she refers to 'a conception of laughter where it is seen as a positive contributor to human liberation, spiritual growth and wisdom. Laughter relieves tension, vanquishes rigidity and helps to cultivate a playful attitude toward life. Homo ludens is celebrated as one of the ideals of this century, and laughter has become a ticket to the lost paradise of play' (1997: 109).

This goes some small way towards getting at the heart of Douglas Davies, whose delight in life is impossible to capture in a list of academic accomplishments and institutional appointments. To understand his achievements and influence, it is also necessary to take note of the joy he finds in everyday moments of light and eccentricity, seeing glimpses of beauty and life amongst the mundane and everyday, but seeing them frequently and never failing to be delighted by their presence. Equally enthusiastic about the smell of a fish and chip shop, the elegance of a fuchsia petal and the positivity of a robin, singing in a garden tree: a passion for scholarship has been matched – and undoubtedly enhanced – by a passion for life.

The structure of the volume

The title of this volume does not indicate thematic sections as such, but rather aspects which run through the volume as a whole and are picked up to varying degrees in its different chapters. Neither have we used the different religious movements to which Douglas Davies has devoted particular attention as thematic markers. The book is rather structured following three topics, which represent aspects of the study of religion to which Douglas Davies has contributed throughout his academic career. These are: Cultures of Meaning and Religious Identity; Ritual, Symbolism and Identity; and Disciplinary Identity and the Boundaries of Understanding. The 'identity' refrain reflects a long-established seam that runs through Davies' scholarship, at once elusive and yet rooted in the ever-present process of human meaning-making. Under these three sub-headings, a distinguished collection of Davies' colleagues and students have contributed a range of essays which both engage with Davies' own work and reflect emerging trends within the disciplinary fields to which he has contributed over the years.

Cultures of meaning and religious identity

The theme for the first section, Cultures of Meaning and Religious Identity, is inspired by the title of Davies' PhD thesis, later published as the monograph,

Meaning and Salvation in Religious Studies (1984) and reflects Davies' long-standing interest in issues of meaning and salvation in a variety of religious traditions. In his endeavours in this field, Davies, like many scholars of religion, has attempted to study that which many consider impossible, yet in taking a broad and often interdisciplinary approach, he has been able to make use of insights into human experience generated by researchers with a different focus and thus enrich the science of the study of religion. In his essay 'Death, Sometimes, Has Its Price? How Douglas Davies, Sergio Leone and the Bible Settle Differences', James Crossley follows Davies' passion for interdisciplinary engagement, integrating biblical studies, film studies and elements of the sociology of religion in his application of the work of Douglas Davies to the Italian westerns of Sergio Leone. Taking cinema as a site for the expression and negotiation of human values in the emerging neo-liberal West, Crossley shows how themes of death and money are allowed to inform the presentation of Christianity and Christian symbolism. Demonstrating how biblical hermeneutics operate within the media of popular culture, Crossley's essay ends with a call for biblical studies to be brought more firmly into the humanities and social sciences as a means of capturing the broader cultural significance of Christian themes in the development of western societies. This is a plea which resonates well with Douglas Davies' own endeavours at the crossroads between biblical studies and the social sciences (e.g. Davies 1995), pointing to the illuminating possibilities that emerge when each approaches the other with candour and seriousness.

Seth Kunin's contribution is similarly reflective of the methodological innovation characteristic of Davies' work. In his essay, Kunin applies to the Book of Mormon the structuralist method developed from the work of Claude Lévi-Strauss, which he has applied in other publications to the texts of the Old Testament. Kunin's detailed textual analysis of themes within the Book of Mormon exposes patterns in its handling of identity and exclusion, and this, he argues, can be correlated with the theme of immigration that has been so important in the experience of the American people, although refracted through a shifting encounter with the cultural other during the history of the nation. The theoretical reasoning which he employs at the intersection between structuralist method and social analysis leads him to the innovative suggestion that the Book of Mormon may be seen as the quintessential American Scripture.

In engaging with the Book of Mormon, Kunin's contribution exists in conversation with Davies' work on the LDS, but while he is extending a discussion into variations of the anthropological method, Grant Underwood's essay engages more historical and theological questions. Underwood, an historian and LDS member, revisits the Arian controversy that saw the early Christian church working out its thinking on the doctrine of the Trinity during the fourth century. He uses this controversy as a lens through which to address the distinctive qualities of the Mormon approach to this same idea, deploying the tools of historical comparison to explicate Davies' (2010) observation that while Mormons have rejected traditional understandings of the Trinity, they have nonetheless highlighted the Trinity as a key marker of Christian identity. In so doing the chapter not only contributes to the academic conversation at the heart of much of Davies work on meaning and salvation, but is also an example of comparative method put to work by a scholar prepared to think what is 'difficult to think'.

Ritual, symbolism and identity

In her contribution, psychologist of religion Valerie DeMarinis offers an analysis of how the connections between spiritual, physical and mental well-being can, through ritual, be built upon in the promotion of health. Her examples of the positive role which ritual has played in the lives of two Swedish women following abortions echoes Davies' conviction that many rituals are positive for the individuals who choose to take part in that they 'help create and sustain people's identity in a world that can often be problematic' (Davies 2011: 38). This interdisciplinary field of scholarship, making connections between religion, culture and health, is an area in which DeMarinis and Davies have collaborated in recent years, not least in considerations of the relationship between emotions and religion. In her essay, DeMarinis draws on Davies' integration of anthropological insights into an interdisciplinary orientation to issues of health and human vitality; the emergent discussion places clinical perspectives within a cultural perspective, highlighting the benefits of cross-disciplinary encounter not just for research but also for its application within urgent episodes of human vulnerability.

Christian Karner and David Parker also enter into conversation with Davies' recent work on the connections between emotion, identity and religion as well as addressing questions of ritual responses to unsettled aspects of contemporary urban life. In their analysis of reactions to the introduction of a CCTV surveillance system in a deprived, ethnically and religiously diverse area of inner-city Birmingham, they discuss how residents of the area utilize religious words and practices in responding to the 'given facts' of their social lives. Sensitive to the problems related to the 'essentializing' of culture and religion, Karner and Parker are also keen to highlight the rootedness of local encounters in a variety of discourses that cut across conventionally defined boundaries of self, community and 'other'. In capturing this complexity, they echo Davies' repeated call for an attentiveness to religion that avoids philosophical reductionism and takes seriously its ritualized, embodied expression amidst the material circumstances of local communities.

Another friend and collaborator of many years, Anders Bäckström also explores the topic of ritual in context, but in this case with a focus on the rituals of the majority church in a comparative discussion of Britain and Sweden. In Bäckström's analysis, the comparative method is used to study two churches – the Lutheran Church of Sweden and the Anglican Church of England – which both theologically and sociologically can be seen to be much alike. Here the method is employed as a way of highlighting more subtle differences that might be obscured in a comparison with a more radically different context. Bäckström is interested in what participation in the rites of the church can say about an individual's relationship to public religion in contemporary Europe. In this respect, he is evoking both Davies' substantial scholarship on funerary rites and their joint involvement in pan-European projects concerning religion and social values (Bäckström 2011; Bäckström et al. 2010).

One further piece in this section focuses on death, but this time in terms of symbolism rather than ritual: Charles Watkins' essay on the symbolic importance of trees and more specifically the introduction and reception of the cedar of Lebanon in England. Watkins refers to Davies' writing on the 'evocative symbolism' of trees which can provide both actual and symbolic links with the past and with sacred places. He charts the introduction of the Cedar of Lebanon into England from the seventeenth century onwards and explores how the sacred associations connected with the tree fuelled its reception and use in churchyards. The essay offers a novel engagement with Davies' work on memorialization and burial grounds, but also earns its place in a volume to celebrate the work of Douglas Davies in that it mentions his favourite tree: the Aruncaria or Monkey Puzzle. One of the many projects Douglas Davies has considered undertaking when he retires is a book on this unusual tree, but given his continued output of academic studies on religion, the casual observer would be forgiven for thinking that this volume may never materialize.

Disciplinary identity and the boundaries of understanding

Writing on the differences between the academic systematization of religious belief and what individuals actually experience in their everyday lives, Douglas Davies has commented that 'The "logical approach" of formal education allows educated people to be described as "disciplined" in thought, while academic disciplines are divided into particular "subjects". But ordinary life, religious or otherwise, is not so divided. Life lived is not as life documented' (2002: 20). Some systematization is necessary in the quest to find order and meaning amid the complexity, but it is perhaps this fundamental questioning of the ability of scholarly approaches to adequately represent the disorder of life and belief as lived by ordinary people that has led Davies to stretch and challenge disciplinary boundaries throughout his career. In this respect, his work has prefigured more recent debates about 'everyday' or 'lived' religion (Ammerman 2007; McGuire 2008) and offers innovative strategies for capturing religious identities in a way that deploys, but is not restricted by, inherited theoretical frameworks or disciplinary conventions of method.

One scholar whose career has run parallel to that of Douglas Davies is sociologist of religion James Beckford. In his contribution to this volume, he turns his attention to 'the interface between religion and development' and assesses changes in the perceived relationship between the two over the past few decades. Beckford comments on the proliferation of interdisciplinary studies as well as centres for the study of religion and development and addresses how emerging scholarship may shape overarching theories of the role of religion in the contemporary public sphere. Beckford echoes Davies in highlighting the benefits of cross-disciplinary scholarship and the importance of detailed and contextualized empirical studies as the basis for theory development. Beckford also discusses the complex relationship between religion and power, including religions and the state, maintaining a focus on organizations as the principal object of analysis. David Martin pursues a related conceptual problem, but using a different approach, and evokes Douglas Davies' long-term interest in the relationship between religion and power as both a sociological and a theological problem. It is the relationship between the two which has inspired David Martin's reflections on the notions of power and religion that draw equally on sociological and theological perspectives. Martin explores in particular spiritual power within Christianity, with a special focus on the rise of Pentecostalism in the Global South in recent times.

Also addressing issues of power is Matthew Wood's chapter on the social role of language and what this means for sociological research. Picking up on Davies' thoughts on the difficulties of accruing research data which can be said to be an adequate representation of the lives or thoughts of research subjects or participants, Wood writes that 'it cannot be assumed that how people speak or write in research settings is an absolute, once-for-all representation of how they perceive or interpret themselves and their world'. Wood makes use of Davies' notion of the 'pool of potential orientations' which exist in any one religion or culture and which individuals pick up on and utilize differently, arguing that this is a helpful tool through which to explain how ambiguities can exist in social life without being meaningless. Thus, he argues that language needs to be seen within the framework of its social context and practice. Social research, Wood claims, calls people, including the researcher, to speak and to position themselves. This does not mean that what is said in these contexts is somehow 'false' or untrustworthy, but its contextualized status does call for careful and constant reflection on the part of the researcher.

Hugh Goddard's reflections on the development of Islamic Studies are a comment on the different pathways which new areas of study can take while pushing at the boundaries of understanding and disciplinary tradition. That Islamic Studies should have a natural home within religion and theology departments is a natural extension, for Goddard, of such moves as the introduction of the 'phenomenology of religion' as a subject in the Theology Department at Nottingham University decades ago. Disciplinary boundaries are not just defined in conceptual terms but are negotiated within institutional contexts and shaped by variant cultures of academic hospitality and the vision of influential individuals. This latter aspect also connects Goddard's chapter to Davies' own work, which has often reflected a fascination with visionary individuals who have reshaped the contours of academic scholarship. One of his heroes – and the subject of an intellectual biography written by Davies (1991) – is the Victorian polymath Frank Byron Jevons, and it is Jevons' thought on the nature of education that is the starting point for Mathew Guest's chapter. Guest brings Jevons into conversation with contemporary literary scholar Stefan Collini, building on the work of both in examining the function and status of the twenty-first-century university. The emerging picture is empirically developed with reference to recent research into the lives of Christian undergraduates and highlights how attempts to trace – and police – the boundaries between education, identity formation and religion need to pay close attention to the experiences of students.

Davies' scholarship on method in the study of religion has always been accompanied by a sensitivity to how different forms of human experience challenge academic conventions. The challenge of offering an authentic, 'truthful' account of human phenomena demands reflection on how adequate normative modes of communication really are. Eleanor Nesbitt's contribution to this volume is a comment on this insight. It takes up the embodied nature of research and addresses the issue of interdisciplinarity by leaving the sphere of academic writing to present material in a different medium, in this instance poetry. Nesbitt reflects on the pitfalls and advantages of daring to leave the comfort zone of the template of scholarly prose and then presents us with a number of poems which shed light on issues and emotions that have emerged from her experience of research.

The volume concludes with an essay by Michael Thate, who offers a critical engagement with Douglas Davies' work taken as a whole. Applauding Davies' capacity to produce scholarship that is good to 'think with', Thate takes three central strands – meaning-making, identity and death – and channels his engagement with Davies into a subversive vision for the study of religion. His essay is followed by a select bibliography of Davies' work, stretching across over 40 years in academia – a suitable appendix to Thate's wide-ranging consideration of Davies' scholarship.

How this book came into being

All of the contributors to this volume have worked with Douglas Davies in the capacity of student, colleague, collaborator or a combination of all three. His vast network of academic collaborators, built up over many years and spanning several continents, presented the editors with far more willing and eminently qualified potential contributors than we could possibly accommodate within a single volume. Those featured in this book were selected as those who have worked closest with Douglas, and with an intention to capture something of the professional development of his career and the intellectual contours of his scholarship. It is a great pleasure to be able to include an essay by David Martin, for example, not only for his insightful thoughts on the relationship between theology and the social sciences – an enduring strand within Davies' own work – but also because Martin was external examiner for his postgraduate thesis on the LDS in Wales. Marking Davies' long-standing links with Sweden, we feature contributions from sociologist of religion Anders Bäckström and psychologist of religion Valerie DeMarinis, while his tenure in the Department of Theology at the University of Nottingham is acknowledged in the inclusion of chapters by former colleagues Hugh Goddard and Charles Watkins. In choosing these contributors, we have tried to balance the personal, professional and academic, and the 'List of Contributors' includes brief biographies describing the academic background of each author as well as their professional connection with Douglas.

We are enormously grateful to all of our authors for their dedication, scholarship and patience during the process of putting this volume together. It has been a great pleasure to work with such an eminent range of academics and a joy to share in their enthusiasm for making this book a reality. Thanks also to our colleagues at Ashgate and Routledge, especially Sarah Lloyd for her support, professionalism and belief in the project and David Shervington for assistance in the latter stages of publication. Our endeavours took an unexpected turn when Grant Underwood suggested holding an event celebrating the career of Douglas Davies, which came with the generous offer of hospitality at Brigham Young University's (BYU) London Centre. It was here, in December 2014, that the editors, along with Grant and a group of Douglas' former colleagues, collaborators and students, together with Douglas himself, gathered for two days of papers, discussion and conviviality. We would like to thank all of those present – Anders Bäckström, Jim Beckford, James Crossley, Hugh Goddard, Peter Jupp, Christian Karner, Eleanor Nesbitt, Hannah Rumble and Charles Watkins – for their invaluable contributions and excellent company. Immense gratitude should also be extended to the staff of BYU's London Centre for their warmth and hospitality, and to Grant Underwood for ensuring the event was a fitting tribute to our colleague and friend (with just the right balance of scholarly engagement and excellent catering!). This event also enabled us to announce the existence of this volume to Douglas himself, having been kept in the strictest of secrecy since its inception five years earlier. Douglas was delighted with the occasion and, things now out in the open, agreed to compose a response to the essays to be featured in the forthcoming festschrift. This response is included as our final chapter; we are grateful to Douglas for engaging so thoughtfully with the discussions presented and for taking them one step further as intellectual comment on live debates within the study of religion.

This volume began as a conversation between the editors, who wanted to put together a fitting intellectual tribute to Douglas Davies on the occasion of his imminent retirement. Douglas' remarkable and enduring passion for both research and teaching is reflected in the fact that, at the time of writing and to the delight of his colleagues, this retirement is still yet to happen. So this book is offered more in recognition of his immense contribution to scholarship so far, in the sincere hope that we will continue to have occasion to celebrate for some years to come. To our colleague, fellow scholar and friend, we offer this collection of essays, with our thanks.

References

Ammerman, N. T. (2007) *Everyday Religion: Observing Modern Religious Lives.* New York: Oxford University Press.

Bäckström, A. (Coordinator) (2011) *Welfare and Values in Europe: Transitions related to Religion, Minorities and Gender. National Overviews and Case Study Reports.* Volume 1. Uppsala: Uppsala University.

Bäckström, A. and Davie, G. with Edgardh, N. and Pettersson P. (eds) (2010) *Welfare and Religion in 21st Century Europe: Volume 1. Configuring the Connections.* Farnham: Ashgate.

Berger, P. L. and Luckmann, T. (1967) *The Social Construction of Reality: A Treatise in the Sociology of Knowledge.* New York: Anchor.

Catto, R. (2015) 'Sociology of religion in Great Britain: interdisciplinarity and gradual diversification', in A. Blasi and G. Giordan (eds) *Sociologies of Religion: National Traditions.* Leiden: Brill, pp. 107–131.

Davies, D. J. (1973) 'Aspects of Latter-Day Saint eschatology', in M. Hill (ed.) *A Sociological Yearbook of Religion in Britain.* Volume 6. London: SCM, pp. 122–135.

Davies, D. J. (1984) *Meaning and Salvation in Religious Studies.* Leiden: Brill.

Davies, D. J. (1991) *Frank Byron Jevons, 1858–1936: An Evolutionary Realist.* Lewiston, NY: Edwin Mellen Press.

Davies, D. J. (1995) 'Rebounding vitality: resurrection and spirit in luke-acts', in M. D. Carroll, D. Clines and P. Davies (eds) *The Bible in Human Society.* Sheffield: Sheffield Academic Press, pp. 205–223.

Davies, D. J. (1997) *Death, Ritual and Belief.* London: Cassell.

Davies D. J. (2000) *The Mormon Culture of Salvation: Force, Grace and Glory.* Aldershot: Ashgate.

Davies, D. J. (2002) *Anthropology and Theology.* Oxford: Berg.

Davies, D. J. (2010) *Joseph Smith, Jesus, and Satanic Opposition: Atonement, Evil and the Mormon Vision.* Farnham: Ashgate.

Davies, D. J. (2011) *Emotion, Identity and Religion: Hope, Reciprocity and Otherness.* Oxford: Oxford University Press.

Gilhus, I. S. (1997) *Laughing Gods, Weeping Virgins: Laughter in the History of Religion.* London: Routledge.

McGuire, M. (2008) *Lived Religion: Faith and Practice in Everyday Life.* New York: Oxford University Press.

Part I
Cultures of meaning and religious identity

1 The Book of Mormon

The American Gospel?

Seth D. Kunin

Knowledge at the turn of the twenty-first century

More than twenty years ago I arrived at Nottingham University as a newly minted PhD to work with Douglas Davies in the Department of Theology. At the time the Church of Jesus Christ of Latter Day Saints (LDS) were the main focus of his work, a religious community of which I was aware but had never studied. His enthusiasm led me to begin to think about the Book of Mormon (BoM), utilizing the structuralist methodology that I had developed from my earlier research on the Old Testament.[1] I soon became aware that the BoM seemed to have a consistent structure that was significantly different from either the Old or New Testament. This initial research culminated in a paper for a conference Douglas chaired on Mormon Studies at Nottingham and over the years in additional short pieces, particularly focusing on material from the BoM (Kunin 1996, 2003). This chapter brings together and extends my previous work and more consciously brings it into dialogue with Douglas' work on LDS theology, particularly drawing on his distinction between salvation and exaltation.

Structuralist analyses of texts from the BoM have suggested that the textual material is based on a triadic structure that has associations with both biblical and Christian structure, but is significantly and interestingly different from both. While both the Old Testament and New Testament have a binary structure – in the Old Testament, the two categories are strongly oppositional; and in the New Testament, the categories overlap[2] – the BoM is characterized by three distinct categories with complex relations between the three. This structure is already fully developed in the BoM and is taken up in the ritual and theological developments instituted by Joseph Smith's followers with what appears to be a remarkable degree of consistency. This transformed underlying structure raises questions for structuralist theory. In its traditional form, the theory cannot easily account for the very significant degree of structural transformation, which appears to come like Athena fully formed from the head of Joseph, nor can it account for the speed of transformation and uptake.

Two avenues of explanation suggest themselves: that LDS structure is a strongly emergent[3] phenomenon that was in gestation but unpredictable

from the previous conditions; or that it was a weakly emergent phenomenon, which while being a significant transformation was based on and is
predictable via previous conditions. This second explanation suggests that
it was both a transformation and emerged from a previously existent trans-
formed/ing structure. While theoretically strong emergence is a possibility,
due to its denial of the possibility of proper explanation (as the emergent
properties are by definition unpredictable), it should only be utilized if the
other forms of explanation are not in themselves sufficient to provide an
explanation for the transformation in the system. This chapter focuses on
the second model and suggests that there is a possible weakly emergent
explanation that, while being speculative, in the context of this short discussion provides an avenue for future research.

The argument presented here is divided into two sections; the first and
more completely developed section presents the textual, theological and
social basis for the existence of a particular form of triadic structure. This section brings together the brief discussions of triadic structure that have been
developed in previous publications (Kunin 2003, 2004). It demonstrates that
the same structural form is present in a wide range of forms and contexts
within LDS culture. Most importantly, this section also demonstrates the
role that this structure plays in the development of the LDS understanding
of the person and their social identity. The second section – brief, less developed and more speculative – suggests the basis of an argument that seeks to
contextualize LDS structure within a developing American structure (which
in turn may have its roots in developments within Reformation structure).
The primary source of comparison relies on the developing American model
of the immigrant as the basis of the American person. If this argument is
considered plausible, then it provides a theoretically grounded explanation
for both the consistency and apparent speed of development (and uptake)
of Mormon theology and ideology and suggests that the BoM might be seen
as the quintessential American Scripture.[4]

Textual analysis: 1 and 2 Nephi

The BoM is a fascinating and complex scripture which was written in the
period between 1828 and 1830. Within the LDS community, it is believed
that the text was translated by Joseph Smith from ancient Egyptian sources –
discovered with the help of divine/angelic inspiration.[5] The text includes a
wide range of genres, ranging from narrative history to complex parables.
We provide a structuralist analysis of material from both genres as well
as an analysis of material that emerges from the more broadly theological
aspects of the text. The opening chapters present the origins and early narrative history of the descendants of Lehi, with the remaining sections being
told from the perspective of particular prophets, including Mormon. While
much of the analysis and debate about the BoM concerns the historicity
or lack thereof of the origins and content of the text and the theological

implications of the text, our argument moves in a more literary or anthropological direction.[6] While our argument does situate the text in a particular historical context, the analysis of the LDS material does not depend on this contextualization. The underlying structural argument emerges directly from the textual and other ethnographic material analysed. The argument relating to the contextualization within emergent American culture is a second-order argument, arising from the comparison to two independent structuralist analyses.

The opening sections of the BoM, particularly 1 and 2 Nephi, which present the early history of the Saints, focusing on the emergence from the Land of Jerusalem and culminating in their settlement of the land of Nephi across the sea, are built around a set of interrelated triads. This structural pattern is most clearly found in relation to the sons of Lehi and the land from which and to which they travel. Lehi has six sons, who are sub-divided into three pairs: Laman and Lemuel the two oldest sons, Nephi and Sam the middle two, and Jacob and Joseph. The sons are distinguished by their behaviour within the text, the location in which they were born and the nature of their names.

Thus, Laman and Lemuel, the two oldest sons, are consistently portrayed negatively within the text. They consistently rebel against their father and brother Nephi and are ultimately rejected. Their negative portrayal is found from the opening chapters of 1 Nephi. Thus, for example, in 2.11 they are described as stiffnecked – a description that associates them with the Jews of the biblical text and the society from which the family has come, and which is rejected by God. 1 Nephi 3.28 depicts Laman and Lemuel as smiting their brother Nephi – symbolically associating them with Esau and other rejected biblical figures.

The two middle brothers are depicted positively. Nephi the older of the two is the chosen son; he accepts his father's prophecy and he has prophetic visions. Sam, while not having visions himself, accepts the words of his brother and is structurally associated with him. The nature of their relation, and their opposition to Laman and Lemuel, is emphasized in 1 Nephi 2.16–19. In verse 17, Nephi tells Sam of his visions and his words are accepted. Verse 18 presents a clear opposition between Sam, on the one hand, and Laman and Lemuel, on the other. Sam listens to and accepts Nephi's words and visions, while Laman and Lemuel reject them. This mirrors a similar opposition between Nephi and his two older brothers. In 2.16, Nephi specifically states that he heard and accepted the words of their father Lehi while Laman and Lemuel do not.

In many respects, the BoM text mirrors on the narrative level aspects of biblical texts, particularly those of Genesis. This is particularly evident in the relationship between elder and younger brothers and the rejection of older brothers in favour of their younger sibling (see, for example, texts about Jacob and Esau and Joseph and his brothers). There is, however a significant narrative and structural difference. While in the biblical text

older brothers, exemplified by Esau, are fully rejected and are by definition outside the covenant (representing the nations other than Israel), in
the BoM, Laman and Lemuel are not as completely rejected. Thus, they are
set in opposition (though not complete opposition) to the Jews who are the
epitome of rejected other. They also at times accept their father's words and
do accompany him in his departure from Jerusalem. The relatively weaker
oppositionality is also found in the texts where they smite Nephi, although
this has similarities to the symbolic and actual deaths/sacrifices in the biblical text – the violence is more muted, and the symbolic death (of Nephi) is
not as fully developed.

The final two brothers, Jacob and Joseph, are born in the wilderness – a
location which, although not the final dwelling place, is described as boun-
tiful (1 Nephi, 18.7). While they do not play an active role in either 1 or
2 Nephi, Jacob and Joseph, particularly Jacob, are singled out as markedly
different from their other four brothers. This is particularly developed in
texts describing the settlement of the new land across the sea to which Nephi
has led his father and brothers. In chapter 2.1, Jacob is singled out as Lehi's
'first born in the days of my tribulation'. His is specifically opposed to his
brothers in general (though probably alluding to Laman and Lemuel) in the
final words of the same verse:

> And behold, in thy childhood thou hast suffered much sorrow, because
> of the rudeness of thy brethren.

The following verse again repeats that Jacob is symbolically his first-born
and emphasizes that Jacob knows 'the greatness of God'. The following
verses include further statements about Jacob's quality and vocation.

Joseph, like Jacob, is particularly singled out in chapter 3. Joseph, the
youngest, in a similar way to biblical figures, is the chosen inheritor of the
new land (3.2). He is also particularly associated with biblical Joseph. Like
Jacob, he is portrayed as strongly positive and as the final and permanent
inheritor of the chosen line of descent. The terms used are covenantal and
reminiscent of biblical texts relating to the permanent vocation of Israel.

2 Nephi chapter 5 presents the final narrative section of this book (much
of the remainder of 2 Nephi is interestingly taken up by prophecies of his
brother Jacob). In this chapter, Nephi and his younger brothers separate
themselves from Laman and Lemuel. In verse 2, Laman and Lemuel are
depicted as trying to slay Nephi. Due to this, they remove themselves to
a new part of the land, which they call 'Nephi'. This new land becomes a
place of prosperity and is crowned by the building of a new Temple.

The structural relationships between the three categories exemplified by the six brothers are complex. They can initially be divided into
three distinct categories – Laman and Lemuel (A); Nephi and Sam (B);
and Jacob and Joseph (C). (A) is generally a rejected category, but has
degrees of mediation.[7] Thus, at one end it is specifically associated with

the Jews, through both a range of words utilized to describe the category and their connections with Ishmael and his sons. At the other end, they are associated with Nephi and Sam, through their common familial relations and origins and by their potential inclusion in the chosen community (they are consistently exhorted to behave properly and remain within the communion). (B) is consistently a chosen category, with Nephi, its primary element, being consistent in his belief once he has accepted his father's words and is himself the primary mover within the two books bearing his name. (B) shares a key element with (A), as emphasized in the texts from 2 Nephi chapters 2 and 3, in that the members of both categories were born in Jerusalem, in effect outside the covenant, and enter into it by their rejection and abandonment of Jerusalem. (C) has many similar characteristics to (B). Its members are also consistently chosen [and prophesy in a similar way to (B)]. The key distinction between (C) and (B) is that (C) was born into the covenant, symbolized by the location of their birth, rather than coming to it from a different status. The final relationship between (B) and (C) is developed in chapter 5. (B) and (C) are depicted as one, in contradistinction to (A) which is rejected by being symbolically abandoned – in a similar way to the abandonment of Jerusalem.

The structural relations between these categories can be abstracted from the above analysis. The structural relation between (A) and (B) is one of mediation and possible (though not necessary) transformation. (A) has the potential to become part of (B) but in the narrative ultimately fails to do so. Thus, this relation can be defined as:

$$(A) \; n \; (B)$$

In this relation, (B) is positively valenced and mediation is positive.

The structural relation between (B) and (C) is more complex. The text clearly indicates two distinct categories; nonetheless, both are positively valenced and ultimately defined together. This suggests that there is a positive relation between the categories – that is, while the categories are defined differently, the contents of the categories are ultimately identical. This relation can be defined as:

$$(A) + (C)$$

The direction of movement is from (B) to (C), with (C) providing the final definition.

A key aspect of this structure is that the relation between (C) and (A) is different than the relation between (B) and (A). Whereas (B) has aspects of mediation with (A), (C) does not. The structural relation between (C) and (A) is strongly oppositional. Thus, the structure as a whole can be defined as:

$$(A) \; n \; (B) + (C) - (A)$$

A is repeated in the equation in order to illustrate its differential relation with (C).

In a previous publication (Kunin 2004: 145), I suggested that LDS structure was circular rather than linear – with the (–) relation between (C) and (A) closing the circle. This way of conceiving the structure is helpful as it emphasizes that the structural relation between (C) and (A) is a key part of the structure and a defining characteristic of (C), which is thereby defined as intrinsically different from (A). It also allows for a clear distinction in definition between (B) and (C) in relation to (A): (B) non-intrinsic distinction and (C) intrinsic distinction.

It might be suggested that the Jews in the text provide a potential fourth category which is wholly negative. This argument, however, can be challenged by the origins of Lehi and his first four sons, all of whom come from the Jews and Jerusalem and various texts in which Nephi emphasizes this origin, and by the consistent symbolic association between Laman and Lemuel and the negative aspects of biblical Israel. This symbolic association helps to clarify the dual aspect of (A). In relation to (B), (A) has the potential to be transformed and in effect moves from (A) to (B). In relation to (C), (A) is depicted as the rejected category which can be symbolically associated with the Jews.

Returning to the narrative level, the structural elements are associated with behaviour, location of birth and relationship with the covenant. Thus, (A) is born in Jerusalem (outside the chosen land), generally behaves in a negative way with the possibility of positivity and is born outside the covenant with the possibility of joining the covenant through faith. (B) is born in Jerusalem, behaves positively and enters the covenant by choice through faith. (C) is born in the wilderness, acts positively and is born into the covenant.

Interestingly, the structure also finds an outlet in the names used for the six sons. Both Laman and Lemuel have names which, despite sounding biblical, are not. Nephi's name similarly is not biblical, while Sam's is partially biblical (Sam as opposed to the biblical Samuel). Jacob and Joseph's names are biblical in origin. Thus, (A)'s names are outside the covenant, (B)'s names are potentially within the covenant and (C)'s names are completely within the covenant.

An interesting aspect of this triadic structure is its relationship with both Old Testament and New Testament Christian underlying structural equations. The first half of the BoM structural equation [the n relation between (A) and (B)] is similar to the New Testament equation. Both equations are based on a model of mediation and transformation, with elements potentially moving from one category to the other, usually in the positive rather than negative direction. In both cases, the operative mechanism for the movement is faith. The faith or belief element is explicitly emphasized throughout the BoM as it is in the New Testament.

The final part of the BoM equation [the (–) relation between (C) and (A)] is similar to that found in the Old Testament. In both cases, the model is based on intrinsic elements. In the Israelite case, the intrinsic distinction is between those born into the covenant and those not. In the BoM, it is similarly based on being born into the covenant rather than coming to it by faith.

The nature of the distinctions discussed here is found in the status of the six sons. Laman and Lemuel (A) are born outside of the covenant. Nephi and Sam (B) are also born outside, but come to the covenant through faith. Jacob and Joseph (C) are born within the covenant and they and their descendants are intrinsically part of it.

No doubt, it will already have been noted that geography shares the same underlying structure as the other narrative aspects discussed thus far. Sacred geography can be explored on two levels, one which is more generalized and includes Jerusalem, and a more specific LDS sacred geography that does not. The first form has three main elements. Jerusalem fits into category (A). Although it is rejected, it has mediating aspects as Nephi and his first four sons are born there and, based on faith, abandon it. The wilderness fits into category (B). It is the place of origin of the final two sons, as well as Nephi's prophecies, and is positive in quality. The land across the sea is the final geographic space and fits clearly into category (C). The important aspect at this level is that all elements in category (B) are also found in (C). The second form of geography utilizes the names of the sons to identify its quality. At this level, the wilderness is the initial category, called the land of Laman by Lehi. Within this context, it clearly fits into category (A), as do Laman and Lemuel. The land across the sea contains the final two spaces. The initial space includes all brothers and expresses category (B). The final division (C) is found in the removal of Nephi, Sam, Jacob and Joseph to the final and most sacred space, the land of Nephi. The intrinsic nature of this space is clearly expressed by the building of the Temple. It is important to note that no symbolic element necessarily is used in the same structural category – the meaning or categorization of an element depends on the symbolic context. Thus, in the first structuring of space we start with Jerusalem, which leads to the first form of structuring, while in the second, we start with wilderness, which leads to the second form of structuring. A similar pattern can be noted in relation to people – if we start with the Jews (A), then Laman and Lemuel can be placed either with them or in category (B), whereas if we start with Laman and Lemuel, then they are clearly in category (A).

The allegory of the olive tree

The structures thus far are all developed within the narrative sections of the BoM. In order to demonstrate the pervasive nature of underlying structure, we need to touch on other forms of textual material. The allegory of the olive tree, found in a range of texts in the BoM, while presenting an allegory for the presentation of the salvation history of humanity also develops the same underlying structures.

While there are several versions of this parable, the most detailed version is found in Jacob 5.[8] In a similar way to the material discussed thus far, the text includes three main elements: wild branches, the original branches from the tree and the root of the tree itself. The narrative uses the fruit of the tree to express the quality attached to each of these elements. The geography of the garden, like that discussed above, is also used to express the quality and nature of the different elements.

The original branches of the tree start out attached to the root, and producing good fruit. They become progressively negative, with their fruit described as bad and with their removal and distancing from the root. The text ultimately concludes with them being returned to the root and producing good fruit. A similar process occurs with the wild branches; they are initially negative, but after being grafted on to the root and the best selected from them, they produce good fruit.

The term 'natural' as used in the text is significant. It is used for the first category of branches and is used in relation to the term 'tame'. This is set in relation to the term 'wild' which is consistently used for the second category of branches. The ultimate statement of the text in relation to both sets is found in verse 17: 'And it came to pass that the Lord of the vineyard looked and beheld the tree in which the wild olive branches had been grafted; and it had sprung forth and begun to bear fruit. And he beheld that it was good; and the fruit was like unto the natural fruit'.

The text thus creates three categories analogous to those discussed above. Category (A) includes the wild branches that are not selected for grafting and never attached to the root and never bear good fruit. These branches are not structurally transformed in the text; they remain negative throughout. It is important to note, however, that they had the potential to be transformed, that is to become part of (B), but were not chosen or selected for this transformation. Category (B) includes the wild branches that are selected and grafted to the root. They are not original growths of the root but nonetheless, through the grafting process, become part of them. This category is ultimately the main focus of the text. They undergo a double transformation. Their initial grafting brings them into the house of Israel, but they are still anomalous, damaging the root. The transformation is only complete when they are joined with the original branches and made like onto them. This suggests that the final stage of transformation is moving them from category (B) to category (C); this reflects the (+) structural relation between (B) and (C) discussed above. Category (C) are thus both the natural, tame branches, which, although apparently moving away from the root, and being cut off and distanced, ultimately are intrinsically good and produce good fruit (within the text, these branches are not structurally transformed; at the onset, they produce good fruit, and despite the narrative temporary distancing, they return to their original place and again produce good fruit); and the former wild branches, which, through selection, grafting and transformation, have become part of this category. In the concluding sentence in the verse quoted above, (A) is the fundamental aspect of the text in relation to both (B) and (C), that is, the wild branches produced fruit identical to the natural branches and thus were indistinguishable from them.

The vicissitudes suffered by the natural tame branches are interesting in that they seem to challenge the underlying structure. The important aspect, however, is that these branches are a natural growth from the root, born to it and, even when distanced from the root, are perfectible. The parable, like all texts, works on several levels. On the narrative level, it presents a complex allegory not only of LDS identity but of the history of the 'House of Israel' from its journey to the new world, to its historical experience described in the remaining chapters of the BoM. On the underlying structural level, the text works on establishing and defining the nature of the three categories discussed here.

Davies, in a recent discussion examining the role of Satan in LDS theology, provides an important narrative/theological explanation for the vicissitudes discussed here. Quoting Terryl Givens' work, he argues that '"salvation" for Mormons is not only an "an endless project" . . . but is also "agonistic" in nature, "predicated on a process of ceaseless struggle"' (Davies 2010: 1). This struggle mirrors the struggles in Jesus' life and can be equally seen in the vicissitudes discussed here – just as Jesus, (C) has struggles, so do the tame, natural branches, that is, the Saints in America (C). His discussion also touches on the apparent contradiction indicated here that, within the doctrine of election, 'people could fall from grace (by sin) even though elected or "sealed" up unto eternal life' (Davies, 2010: 181).

If we return briefly to the two versions of the parable found in 1 Nephi, we can see that their abbreviated form highlights the structural level of the Jacob text. The first of the texts, 1 Nephi 10.11–14, focuses on the 'House of Israel', that is, the Saints set in opposition to the term 'gentile'. This text is directly related to the sections relating to category (C) in the Jacob text. These branches in Jacob are clearly defined and their direct and intrinsic association, through being the actual branches of the tree, are emphasized – they shall ultimately be gathered up and returned to the tree and have true knowledge of the Messiah. Interestingly and significantly, the language is similar to that used by the Old Testament for the Jews, who, although having similar historical vicissitudes, are intrinsically chosen through birth, as are the 'House of Israel' in the parables.

The 1 Nephi 15.12–15 text uses the term natural branches, which are grafted in to refer to the gentiles, and relates to category (B) and (C) in the Jacob text. The text is significant as the gentiles who are part of the community (who are grafted onto the tree) become the means through which the knowledge of the Messiah is communicated to the remnants of the House of Israel. Thus, the text includes both category (B) in the grafting process and the ultimate transformation of (B) into (C) with the former gentiles being a key part in redemption.

Conversion and identity

Both the narrative elements and the underlying structure found in these texts have a close relationship with the LDS understanding of conversion and identity. While the conversion process is both ethnographically and theologically more complex than we have time to discuss here, its essential elements have been helpfully analysed by Douglas Davies in terms of salvation and exaltation (Davies 2003: 5, 198). These two terms highlight two stages in the conversion/transformation process. The first term relates to a process analogous to other forms of Christian mission and conversion and is focused on the work of mission among the LDS. It includes rituals that are also similar to those of other Christian communities, that is, baptism and confirmation as sacraments. This level of conversion moves and transforms individuals from the rejected category of gentiles to membership in the Church. It is thus analogous to the move from category (A) to category (B) discussed above.

The second term, exaltation, is unique to the LDS and reflects the identification of category (B) with category (C). This final identification is achieved through the secret Temple rituals, including marriage for eternity and endowment rites. It also includes baptism for the dead (see Davies 2003: 209–211), which importantly provides a key symbolic mechanism for the identification of category (B) with (C). The process of baptism of the dead allows for the conversion of all of an individual's ancestors back to Adam. This process in return implies a transformation in status of the individual himself. Prior to the Temple ritual, the individual was not born into the Church, after the ritual, since all the individual's ancestors were part of the Church, then the individual was in fact, himself, always and intrinsically part of the Church. This practice thus emphasizes the nature of the relationship between categories (B) and (C). The two categories (at least potentially) contain the same content: category (B) reflects the non-intrinsic aspects of salvation, which is conditional, while category (C) reflects the intrinsic nonconditional aspects of exaltation.

Davies' discussion also highlights a similar structure found in relation to sacred place and links back to the division in geography discussed above (2003: 5). LDS practice involves two ritual spaces: the meeting house and Temple. The meeting house, category (B), is used for weekly gatherings and is the place in which congregational, salvific action takes place. The Temple is used only periodically and is the sacred place in which exaltation takes place. Within this context, the world of the gentiles would be categorized as (A). The location and nature of these spaces is significant. The meeting houses are found throughout the world, in both small and large cities and towns; hence, like the above relation between categories (A) and (B), it reflects the possible transformation of both people and places from category (A) to (B).

The Temple (or more precisely Temples) are much more limited in number than the meeting houses (for a detailed discussion of the origin and use of Temples, see Davies 2003: 195ff). As Davies emphasizes, the nature of the Temple/s and its/their location/s moves LDS theology to 'be place-related in both a geographical and architectural sense' (2003: 203). In this respect, the Temple is both narratively and structurally similar to the use of the Temple in the Old Testament and in Jewish structure and thought. A key difference between the Old Testament concept of Temple and that of the LDS is that of multiplicity. While in the Old Testament, there is a clear move to focus all Temple activity in one location, within the LDS community the move is in the opposite direction, from one to many. This difference may relate to the more complex nature of LDS structure. The first half of the structure implies the possibility of transformation, certainly of people, and by implication of places. Such transformation is not possible in Old Testament (OT) structure. With the possibility of transformation, any place can potentially move through the categories and ultimately be in category (C) – thus allowing for the multiplicity of sacred places and the multiplicity of Temples.

The use of Temple to demarcate sacred space is also found in the chapters of the BoM discussed here. A Temple is built in the land of Nephi, the final dwelling place of Nephi and his chosen brothers. This building is unique in the descriptions of the movements of the family to this point; none of the other lands were graced with a Temple. This mirrors our identification of the land of Nephi as being in category (C). The land of Nephi is part of the larger land across the sea, the rest of which is distinguished by not having a Temple. The larger land is structurally positive, but is anomalous, as Laman and Lemuel are also there; it is only with the building of the Temple that the final category is established.

One of the features of both Old Testament Israelite/Rabbinic and New Testament Christian underlying structure is that the understanding of the divine is shaped by the same underlying equation – this is to be expected as the divine is as much a culturally postulated and therefore structured feature as are the other cultural artefacts discussed here. In the Old Testament, God is placed in a strongly oppositional position, mirroring Israelite oppositional structure. Thus, God stands in opposition to the entire created world, both distinct and separate from it. Within New Testament Christian-mediated structure, the understanding of God is doubly mediated – with Jesus standing in a mediating position between man and God and the Holy Spirit in effect mediating between the other two aspects of the divine.

It should be unsurprising therefore that we also find LDS triadic structure in relation to the godhead. This structure is most clearly developed in the esoteric concept of the Adam–God doctrine (Davies 2003: 72ff, 2010: 75–77). This doctrine, which has its roots in the BoM in effect posits both an 'equality' of essence between God and man (Davies 2003: 73) and perhaps structurally of more significance, a continuity between man and God.

> God himself was once as we are now, and is an exalted man and sits enthroned in yonder heavens![9]

This doctrine is shaped by precisely the same structure found in other LDS material. The essence of the doctrine and the structure is found in Davies' distinction between salvation and exaltation. Man (who is an embodied spirit being) potentially but not necessarily moves from the rejected category (A) to the saved category (B) and finally is exalted as co-equal with God. This doctrine emphasizes the feature of directionality and movement that is essential to LDS structure. In each of the areas we examined, the key feature is the potential exaltation of category (A). Just as all humans are potentially exalted, and this is emphasized by both the doctrines relating to mission and baptism of the dead, all spaces can ultimately be transformed into Zion; all humans have the potential to become God. The essence of Mormon underlying structure emphasized by the positive relation between (B) and (C) is the (potential salvific/exalted) structural unity of everything that exists.

An American structure?

Structural consistency is one of the fascinating features of the BoM and other early LDS publications. While it may be seen as either a feature of an authentic revelation or an unexplainable emergent phenomenon, it is worthwhile exploring the possibility that it may have its roots within its American social and cultural context.[10] The conceptualization of immigration is the aspect of American culture that, I would like to suggest, has particularly interesting similarities with LDS structure.

The early part of the nineteenth century was one of increasing immigration into the newly formed United States. While in the period immediately after the American Revolution in the eighteenth century immigration was low, nonetheless, this was a significant period in the development of American policy and conceptualization. A key aspect of this was a very positive approach, with America being seen as 'a haven and an asylum for the oppressed' (Purcell 1995: 19). This concept shares a similar conceptual base to the LDS model of mission (though perhaps less proactive). As the century developed, European immigration was increasingly significant and essential for the expanding country.[11] On a narrative level, the concept of immigration has interesting resonances with the concept of mission found in both the LDS and other Protestant communities.

The structure of immigration as it developed is clearly divided into three categories: immigration, naturalization and citizenship. Although initially the processes relating to immigration were left to the individual states, ultimately they were taken over by the federal government. The process involved a period of naturalization prior to the conferment of citizenship.[12] Although the naturalization period varied initially in relation to the various states and latterly to federal regulation, the structure of the process remained constant.

The first category, immigration or more precisely foreign origin, fits precisely with the characteristics of category (A) discussed here. This category is composed of individuals from outside the United States. Some subsections of these people choose to immigrate to the United States, moving into the second category of naturalization. The aspect of choice is similar to the aspect of conversion by a faith dimension found in the LDS structure.

Naturalization/citizenship shares the same characteristics as category (B). It is composed of individuals who have been transformed by choice from category (A) to (B). The category itself includes a processual element through which this transformation is realized. Thus, the naturalization process is in effect the mediating period between the two categories. This mediation process directly reflects the (n) structural relation between the two categories. The (n) relation implies both transformation and mediation, as it is mediation that allows the movement between the categories. Ultimately, the individuals in category (B) are transformed into citizens, with all rights and privileges, save the ability to be elected as president, reserved for individuals born in the United States. This final difference reflects the slight ambiguity retained in this category, an ambiguity also found in the LDS category (B).

There is an interesting analogy between the LDS and American conceptualizations encapsulated in the term naturalization. The term implies that the American identity is the natural one and that foreigners need to be made natural. The Allegory of the Olive Tree also uses the concept of natural to describe categories (B/C). The wild branches need to be made natural to become part of the system.

The final category (C) is made up of the children (and descendants) of category (B). These individuals, citizens, can be seen as intrinsically American, a quality that they are given by place of birth. This fact is also indicated in that a child of foreign parents (non-citizens) who is born in the United States has the right to US citizenship. Individuals in this category have full rights as citizens and are structurally unambiguous. In this sense, they are structurally identical to Mormons in category (C).

The American process of immigration and the movement to citizenship thus includes the same categories and structural relations as found in the LDS. Like the LDS structure, it can be characterized in the following equation:

$$(A) \; n \; (B) + (C).$$

Given the intrinsic nature of (C), the relation between (C) and (A) would be negative. The interesting difference on the narrative level between the two structures is the role of geography in place of genealogy. Whereas in the LDS system (C) is created by real and symbolic genealogy, in the American model (C) is created by location of birth. Despite this narrative difference, the two structures are identical.

It is important to note in relation to this discussion that this process was not seen as open to all. The initial focus and expectation was on Europe and, given some anti-Catholic bias, on Protestant Europe. Although this broadened out to Catholic Europe, discrimination and bias remained, especially in relation to the significant Irish immigration – though the transformative model presented here embraced both Irish and other Catholic immigrants. Other groups were excluded from the process for much of the period in question. Thus, Chinese labourers could work in the United States but were for much of the nineteenth century not allowed to become naturalized citizens. Africans were brought over as slaves and again for much of the century not included in the model.[13]

Native Americans present the most interesting anomaly (particularly as they feature within the LDS theological system in the opposite way). Although they were indigenous to the Americas, and thus clearly born there, and thus could logically have been included in the final intrinsic half of the equation in which geography of birth was the determining factor, they are clearly excluded. While the reasons for the exclusion are racist, economic and political, they may also be seen as creating a structural problem. The American version of the structure seems to be based on a model of immigration, that is, all those included in it are immigrants and thus move through all the categories. The Native Americans are structurally anomalous as, although they fit into the second part of the equation, they do not have the first transformative aspect.

In this respect, there is a significant difference between the American and LDS uses of the structure. The LDS model, as particularly emphasized in the allegory of the olive tree, has both wild, that is, transformed elements, and natural, tame, that is, untransformed elements. Both are part of the system and necessary to it. And, perhaps ironically, the Native Americans are included as they are seen as being descendants of the original community and thus intrinsically part of the community.

Thus, a broad-brush discussion of immigration/citizenship supports the suggestion that LDS structure is not a strongly emergent phenomenon but arises in relation to its broader cultural context and is an American cultural form rather than separate from it or in opposition to it. In this sense, we suggest the BoM is an American Scripture in at the very least a structural sense.

Conclusions

In this discussion, we present a detailed analysis of key aspects of LDS structure, utilizing both narrative and ritual examples. It demonstrates a consistent structural equation: $(A) \cap (B) + (C)$ [with a negative relation between (C) and (A)]. The structure identified is seen to be significantly different from structures found in both Old Testament/rabbinic $[(A) - (B)]$ and New Testament/Christian $[(A) \cap (B)]$ cultural material, though interestingly in effect bringing the two together into a single complex triadic structure. We suggest that, rather than being an unpredictable emergent phenomenon, this structure may be related to underlying structures developing in the cultural context of the United States. The brief analysis of the structure of

American immigration and citizenship is suggestive in this regard, indicating a potential identity or commonality in underlying structure, with the elements of foreigner (A), naturalization/citizen (B), citizen (C) being structurally identical to gentile (A), convert (B), saint (C). In order to demonstrate this conclusively, a more extensive analysis of American immigration and other cultural forms, religious traditions and ideologies is needed.

Notes

1 The structuralist methodology utilized is built particularly on the work of Lévi-Strauss (1963) and Leach (1996). A very fine recent example of the methodology in practice can be found in Miles-Watson (2009).

2 Old Testament and New Testament structure are compared with BoM structure in Kunin (2004: 233–239).

3 For the purposes of this chapter, we are utilizing two forms of emergence, strong and weak. Strong emergence is that in which the emergent phenomena cannot, by definition, be predicted from the starting conditions. Weak emergence includes the same degree of transformation as found in strong emergence, but suggests that if the starting conditions are understood then the emergent properties are both predictable and developmental or evolutionary.

4 A similar suggestion, based on a different theoretical basis, is made by Viola Sachs who calls the BoM 'the New World scripture' (1992: 21–22).

5 Welch provides a helpful chronology for understanding the LDS view of the translation process (1992: 1–7). See also Terryl Givens' discussion of the discovery and translation of the BoM (2002: 11–42).

6 Both the historical and theological arguments are analysed and critiqued in detail in Givens (2002).

7 In the structuralist analysis presented here, (–) or negative means that the two categories do not overlap, that is, there is no common material in both; (n) or neutral means that the categories overlap to some extent, that is, there is common material in both; (+) or positive means that the two contain the same material, but they are defined differently. Mediation means that the categories both overlap and there is movement in one or both directions.

8 Two abbreviated versions of the parable are found in 1 Nephi 10 and 1 Nephi 15. The chapter 10 version focuses on the status of the 'House of Israel', and the chapter 15 version focuses on that of the gentiles. In chapter 10, the tame, natural branches move from positive to negative to positive, with the root being untransformed. In chapter 15, the natural branches move from negative to positive.

9 This text from the *Teachings of the Prophet Joseph Smith* is quoted in Davies (2003: 73).

10 Davies touches on the roots of LDS thought both in relation to its Masonic background (2003: 17–20) and more importantly, for our purposes, its American Puritan roots. He links the 'born again' type with the American self-identity as well as concepts of expansionism and manifest destiny touched upon in our arguments (Davies 2010: 6, 12).

11 Immigration became increasingly significant in the 1820s with 152,000 immigrants, increasing to 2.6 million in the decade before the Civil War (Purcell 1995: 23).

12 The Naturalization Act of 1790 required a two-year period of naturalization; subsequent Acts, while increasing the time required, were conceptually and structurally identical (Purcell 1995: 20). Although there were differences in attitude between different political groupings (witness the Alien Acts of 1798), the general attitude fits within the structures identified here.

13 The Fourteenth Amendment to the US Constitution (1868) broadened the definition to include all individuals born in the United States (save Native Americans who were born on reservations). The Naturalization Act of 1870 extended the naturalization process to Africans.

References

Davies, D. (2003) *An Introduction to Mormonism*. Cambridge: Cambridge University Press.

Davies, D. (2010) *Joseph Smith, Jesus, and Satanic Opposition*. Farnham: Ashgate.

Givens, T. (2002) *By the Hand of Mormon*. Oxford: Oxford University Press.

Kunin, S. (1996) 'The death/rebirth mytheme in the Book of Mormon', in D. Davies (ed.) *Mormon Identities in Transition*. London: Cassell, pp. 92–203.

Kunin, S. (2003) 'The allegory of the olive tree: a case study for (neo) structuralist analysis', *Religion* 33: 105–125.

Kunin, S. (2004) *We Think What We Eat*. London: T&T Clark.

Leach, E. (1969) *Genesis as Myth*. London: Jonathan Cape.

Lévi-Strauss, C. (1963) *Structural Anthropology*. New York: Basic Books.

Miles-Watson, J. (2009) *Welsh Mythology: A Neo-Structuralist Analysis*. Amherst: Cambria Press.

Purcell, L. E. (1995) *Immigration*. Phoenix: Oryx.

Sachs, V. (ed.) (1992) *L'Imaginaire-Melville: A French Point of View*. Saint-Denis: Presses Universitaires de Vincennes.

Welch, J. (1992) *Reexploring the Book of Mormon*. Salt Lake City: Deseret Book Co.

2 'Death, sometimes, has its price'
How Douglas Davies and Sergio Leone cope with capitalism and change

James G. Crossley

The works of Douglas Davies and Sergio Leone have much in common. Death features strongly as a main theme for both, both reflect on the social function of money, and both interpret social behaviours in light of these interests. It might, therefore, be expected that the sociological and anthropological work of Davies can shed further light on the increasingly investigated work of Leone's films – and, indeed, vice versa. What I will attempt here is a speculative application of some of Davies' work on social behaviour to an understanding of historical *change* while implicitly suggesting that such a reading of Leone's westerns can provide a complementary economic dimension to Davies' analyses.

Leone's westerns consist of *A Fistful of Dollars* (1964; US release 1967), *A Few Dollars More* (1965; US release 1967) and *The Good, the Bad and the Ugly* (1966; US release 1967) – collectively known as the Dollars Trilogy – and *Once Upon a Time in the West* (1968; US release 1969). The Dollars Trilogy largely follows the quest for money and typically focuses on Clint Eastwood's bounty killer character popularly called The Man with No Name, though he is only known by others in the films as Joe (*Fistful*), Manco (*Few*) and Blondie (*Good*). *Once* has another dangerous gun-toting central character in Harmonica, but he gives way to Jill McBain, a non-violent former prostitute and inspiration for the building of the new town of Sweetwater. These westerns were part of a genre dubbed 'Spaghetti westerns' based on their origins in Cinecittà Studios of Rome and having an Italian director. Nevertheless, Leone's version of the western, as Christopher Frayling would famously show, was also a critical commentary on what had come before in America (Frayling 2006 [2001]).

While study of the Leone's westerns has since tended towards identity politics, masculinities and gender, hybridity and cultural distinctiveness (Frayling 2006: x), what I want to do here is to provide another approach to an old question in the study of Leone's westerns: 'why did the "moment" of the Italian westerns appeal so much to children of Marx and Coca Cola in Europe, especially the generation of May 1968?' (Frayling 2006: xv). Frayling labelled this question as one of the 'redhot' debates of the late 1970s, and such critical study of the western was dominated by a more static analysis of ideology inspired by Althusserian Marxism, formalism and structuralism (cf. Wright 1975; Frayling 2006: 39–67), while more precise contextualization of Italian westerns in the political debates of their time has rarely surfaced in scholarly studies (Fisher 2011: 2). I want to revisit such questions in light of my own concerns with historical change and some of Davies' sociological and anthropological insights. In particular, I will focus on how tensions in the critique of capitalism in Leone's westerns were precisely the sorts of critiques soon to be absorbed into the rise of neoliberal capitalism since the 1970s. Whereas much interpretation of Leone's westerns turn to the cultural contexts of Italy and 'the Mediterranean', my concerns will look at why the stories survived and flourished in the context of western capitalism more generally, thereby supplementing Austin Fisher's more detailed presentation of the political and apolitical receptions of the Italian westerns (Fisher 2011: 163–215). I will couple these interests in historical change and survival with the ways in which social (and thus historical) change can be focused on prime social values invested in death, money and those practices deemed religious.

Death, money and studying religion: Davies

Davies notes that anthropological work involves the study of areas of human culture integral to human survival (sex, reproduction, kinship, fertility, marriage etc.) and the ways in which these are related to 'sources of power' and the 'preservation of prime values' (Davies 2004: 263–264). Such sources of power find meaning through a range of ritual and symbolic representations. Conversely, actions against symbolic representations of such sources of power can lead to dangerous blasphemous acts and be seen 'to attack the heart of things that, for many, make life worth living' (Davies 2004: 264). Building on related work on purity and taboo, Davies develops such anthropological concerns with reference to the ways in which monetary behaviour becomes a focal point for the prime social value (the Holy Spirit) in the Acts of the Apostles. Deceit over monetary behaviour, he argues, represents a form of blasphemy. One of the significant things about Davies' analysis of monetary behaviour in Acts, and the value(s) it represents, is that it lays the foundations for a new movement, 'a new type of life, a new focus and locus of a paramount world of meaning' (2004: 266). This is significant because the centrality of monetary value has obvious relevance to an understanding of modern capitalist societies particularly with the dominant neoliberal ideology of the past 40 years.

What I want to do with Davies' insights is to show how the range of key human practices, symbols and rituals are inverted and, to some extent, emptied of their power while simultaneously, and however unintentionally, representing and pointing towards 'a new type of life, a new focus and locus of a paramount world of meaning'. This is where another related area of anthropology to which Davies has made a significant contribution becomes important: death studies (e.g. Davies 1998, 2002, 2005, 2008). One of Davies' theses (2002) involves the ways in which human beings construct 'words against death' as part of the affirmation of life and hope for the future. Death is an intrinsic part of human existence which the human animal can hardly avoid. But, Davies suggests, this can provide the means for individual adaptation and society's survival: 'having encountered and overcome this experience, both the individual and society are transformed and gain a sense of power which motivates ongoing life' (2002: 1). Language, rhetoric, performance, ritual and so on are all important ways in which this transformation is carried out, and Davies uses a wide variety of examples, including those directly relevant here: music and film. In the case of Leone's westerns, I want to show how the overarching theme of controlling death is part of a broader narrative of socio-economic change which was starting to develop in western societies in the 1960s and that understanding this theme is integral to understanding both Leone's grand narrative and the survival and popularity of the films long after their initial releases.

Death is a significant way of understanding transformation in human societies because if the (live) human body can express social values, then illness and death provide some kind of challenge to society (e.g. Davies 2002: 10; 2008: 16, 73, 115). Davies (e.g. 2002: 16–17) also builds on the suggestion of Zygmunt Bauman that institutions hide the reality of death by implying that death is under control and that if this were not the case the full force of the reality of death might be devastating for social life. If Bauman is right, Davies argues, then 'death ritual serves the purpose of removing the dead from the world of the living so as to enable the survivors to give their minds to life-issues as soon as is possible' (2002: 17). What we see with Leone's westerns is what might happen when the full force of the reality of death is unleashed. Indeed, in such films we are in a world where 'death and life inhabit literally the same space' (Campbell 2010: 12) and where life has no value but death, sometimes, does. However, while Leone's films portray a world where institutions cannot control death, once we look at the grand narrative of Leone's vision of the West we see that he too sees that a new symbolic universe has to be created, with death controlled once death has done its destructive duty, wiping out old values and replacing them with the new values of a new type of capitalism. Here we may detect echoes (though in a more depersonalized form) of Davies (e.g. 2002, 2004; cf. 2008) and his idea of 'rebounding vitality' (creatively developing, for instance, Maurice Bloch), in the sense that in controlling threats to the world a new power or vitality helps drive it forward.

Death, money and Christianity: Leone

A theatrical interest in death is common in Italian westerns, and Leone's westerns became especially famous in part for their focus on violence and death. Death certainly played a part in American westerns (e.g. John Ford's), but there is also a clear emphasis on the creation of community, civilization and law and order which would provide protection for the Whites from the outside forces of death (Mitchell 1996: 229; Campbell 2010: 4–5). In contrast, these boundaries are broken down in Leone's westerns and we find a world where borders mean little and no one is immune from the threat of death and violence. Rather than, say, the Whites/Indians and Insider/Outsider dichotomies, the town in *Fistful* is divided between the Rojos and the Baxters – a cramped binary and one in between which Joe can move relatively freely, just as he can between borders (Campbell 2010: 6–7). This lack of significant boundaries means that death cannot be pushed to the wilderness and away from the towns and instead we get an indiscriminate death toll. With these boundaries comprehensively overcome, the theme of death pervades all Leone's westerns, where corpses pile up in towns like San Miguel in *Fistful*, while towns like Agua Caliente in *Few* can so easily become morgues, as the bandit Indio puts it.

This understanding of death in Leone's films enhances the general reading that these films transform the traditional optimistic view of the frontier found in American westerns into a world full of death, greed and decay (cf. Frayling 2006: 130). This shift is made strikingly clear from the beginning of the first of Leone's western, *Fistful*. On Joe's arrival at San Miguel, death and coffins are almost immediately the result. Indeed, we are introduced to one man so outrageously quick on the draw that he can kill several people at once. It is fitting that Joe explains that he has never seen a town as 'dead' as San Miguel and that Silvanito calls it 'a town of cadavers'. The cemetery on the outskirts of San Miguel is a place said to suit Joe. The cemetery not only suits Joe's usual associations with death, but it also suits him for practical reasons as he dupes the factions with two corpses posing as live humans sleeping against graves. Even when Joe escapes from the Rojos, he is forced to seek refuge with the undertaker and hides in a coffin where he watches the destruction of the Baxters through an opening of the lid as the camera gives us the coffin's perspective, a particularly striking example of Lee Mitchell's suggestion that Eastwood's character takes on certain attributes of the dead (Mitchell 1996: 236–237). From the outset, then, we see the focal town with a marked lack of the sort of protection found in the towns of traditional westerns and how death spreads throughout.

The pattern of bounty killer bringing death on arrival is maintained throughout Leone's westerns. In *Few* we are introduced to the aptly named Mortimer and then to Manco, both as successful bounty killers. The opening scenes of *Good* introduce the audience to Tuco, Angel Eyes and Blondie and their ability to kill. In *Once*, a film Leone would describe as a 'dance of death' (Frayling 2005: 31), the entrances of three of the major characters – Frank, Harmonica ('People like that have something inside, something to do with death') and Cheyenne – are likewise surrounded by killing, murder and bullets. After witnessing the escape of Cheyenne, Jill McBain's arrival in Sweetwater is met by the murdered McBains laid out on tables at the house ready for the funerals. At the end of each of the films, death is likewise emphasized, though, as we will see, *Once* does so to put death back in its place away from Sweetwater. After Joe has killed Ramón and his family, the Rojos and Baxters have been wiped out and bodies are cleared away; after Mortimer finally kills Indio, Manco leaves with a wagon full of corpses; and in the final shootout in *Good*, Angel Eyes is shot into a grave, a point reemphasized in his still at the end, as Tuco finds himself stranded on a grave.

The ubiquity of death in town and wilderness is underscored in the handling of the American civil war in *Good*: towns are indiscriminately decimated by the constant firing of canons; on the journey away from the monastery, Blondie and Tuco see dead bodies strewn across the ground; in the concentration camp, the commandant is dying as Angel Eyes takes advantage by torturing prisoners; and the battle over the bridge is described by Blondie as a meaningless waste of life. Throughout, Leone does not take sides between North and South. Indeed, both sides are blurred (morally and visually) making devastation and death all-pervasive and even making the viciousness of bounty killers appear insignificant (cf. Frayling 2006: 128, 172). It is death on this scale that has to be controlled before the next stage of historical development can occur (in *Once*), according to Leone's portrayal of America.

A cursory viewing illuminates the centrality of money as some indicator of the prime social values intersecting with the films. The first two films of the Dollars Trilogy make the goals of the main protagonist clear enough in the title alone (*Fistful of Dollars*, *For a Few Dollars More*), and the ultimate goal in *Good* is $200,000. Wanted posters with reward money run throughout *Few*, and Indio's gang is discussed in terms of its financial value. Whereas Joe in *Fistful* does not like to take money 'unless I've earned it', Angel Eyes in *Good* states that when he is paid he always sees the jobs through (initially $500 from Baker to get a name and kill Stevens) though not without taking money for another job ($1,000 from Stevens to kill Baker). As Frayling (2006: 160) points out, money is more than mere cash in the Dollars Trilogy: it is a prize whereby the characters can exhibit certain values and skills (Mitchell 1996: 237). There is never any serious indication that it will be invested by bounty killers (as Harmonica states in *Once*), and Eastwood's character moves along to chase another prize at the end of each film. Money is, therefore, precisely the sort of thing that will reveal some kind of special social value, namely the expectation of accompanying deceitful or trickster-like behaviour. Yet, as we will see, monetary reward is not, ultimately, the prime motivation for the gunslingers in *Once*. Rather, money is understood differently by the end but remains just as important: its primary association is now with investment and the emerging business class.

Money and death are combined and overlapping themes, as well as occurring at key points in the plots. In *Fistful*, the undertaker makes a healthy profit and the only major profit maker (apart from Joe) who survives. *Few* is effectively framed in terms of money in relation to death.

After the opening credits, we read the following explanation on the screen: 'Where life had no value, death, sometimes, had its price. That is why the bounty killers appeared'. The film ends with Manco carrying the valuable wagon-load of dead bandits and picking up a bag of money en route. In *Good*, Blondie is rescued by the ghost carriage carrying a pile of corpses and an almost dead Bill Carson who holds the secret of the $200,000, though he too has to die for the plot to progress. The secret of the location of the money in a specific cemetery and specific grave is now to be split between Tuco and Blondie and forms the basis for the rest of the film.

As with money and death, Christianity is used relentlessly in Leone's westerns. Such imagery was common enough in American westerns, including holy family imagery of ragged settlers (Frayling 2006: 123–124), an image particularly striking in, and central to the plot of, *Fistful*. Continuing his famous critique of, and dialogue with, visions of the Old West, Leone's imagery is, however, emphatically Catholic and Latin and not the traditional white Protestantism of American westerns.[1] In *Fistful*, there is a rowdy Last Supper scene in the Rojo household after the hostage exchange and replicated in the rundown church-hideout in *Few* amidst all the broken statues and disused crosses. In *Fistful*, the outsider Joe rides into the Mexican border town under a noose as bells, of a distinctly Latin church, ring and a dead man on horse rides away. One of the very few (almost) positive institutions is the Catholic hospital-monastery where Tuco's brother Pablo lives and works, though again decaying statues and crosses are evident.

This 'desacralization' or 'profanation' of the church has long been noted as a central issue in the Dollars Trilogy, though Timothy Campbell (2010: 10–11) sees this as an epitome of Leone's West as a whole. Campbell broadens this 'profanation' out to include the political sphere. To this we might add that the religious symbols and language constructed as having a profane function in marking the transformation to, and intersection with, successful central cultural values – typically involving deceit, cunning and macabre entrepreneurship in the Dollars Trilogy – focus around death and money in the films, in addition to marking the chaotic historical period which will be controlled by the end of *Once*. We can see and hear this in the form of church bells, a common feature throughout the Dollars Trilogy. In *Fistful*, Joe is welcomed by the bell-ringer who says everyone gets rich or dies in this town suited to bounty killers and laughs about death and wealth. Towards the climax of *Fistful*, Joe sets fire to the Rojo house/prison on his escape to the undertaker and the bell rings marking the shift towards Joe's final victory. In *Few*, Groggy's clique marks their arrival at the church hideout by shooting at the church bells, and the scene is followed by a grotesque Last Supper and Indio's sermon. Or, again, in *Once*, bells chime at the murders of Timmy and Harmonica's brother (cf. Frayling 2006: 197–198), though, as we will see, now marking the end of the era of the 'ancient race' of gunslingers. Crosses appear at moments of death. There is the image of a burning cross as the Baxter house gets destroyed in *Fistful*. As Ramón and his men stand waiting for Joe at the end of *Fistful*, a church cross is visible in the middle of the screen and, after the Rojos are shot, the cross is directly above Ramón's head as he awaits his final moments after being fooled by Joe. In *Once*, an image of a crooked cross appears after Harmonica kills two of Frank's men as he ingeniously protects Jill McBain (and her investment). And, of course, the ramshackle crosses of the graveyard (including the grave holding the $200,000) permeate the final scenes of *Good* when Blondie tricks his way to both the money and the killing of Angel Eyes.

The intersection of death, money and Christianity is projected on to the major characters. In *Few*, the opening scene after the statement about death sometimes having its price is a close-up of a Bible. From behind the Bible, we hear Mortimer's voice but he is mistaken for a reverend by a fellow traveller on the train. The Bible lowers and reveals the face of a dangerous man whose first action after forcing the train to make an emergency stop is to look directly at a $1,000 'wanted' poster. The idea of gunslinger-as-preacher is clear elsewhere in the film. Indio gives his sermon from a pulpit in the run-down church/hideout. His 'nice little parable' concerns a carpenter who made a safe disguised as a cabinet for the Bank of El Paso and ending with Indio killing the carpenter after he acquired the secret of the safe.

Christianized titles are often ironically given to major characters in Leone's westerns where deceitful characteristics are vital for survival. In *Good*, 'The Bad' character is a cold-hearted killer called Angel Eyes. Angel Eyes sees Tuco about to be hanged but tells a coach passenger that even someone that filthy has a golden-haired angel looking over him. At that point we see Blondie and the soundtrack turns to choir music, just before he dupes Tuco and leaves him stranded in the wilderness. For this action, the golden-haired angel gains the label 'Judas' which was previously given by Tuco as part of their duplicitous double-act. Indeed when Tuco almost gets his revenge by nearly hanging Blondie, he half-caringly interprets the canon fire as thunder, arguing that even when Judas hanged himself there was a storm too. There is, as might be expected at this point, some irony at play with the label 'Judas' because in the world of Leone's westerns, a lack of loyalty and trust in pursuit of money is standard and embraced by Eastwood's character in the films in the chaotic epoch before *Once*. Harmonica likewise gets the label 'Judas' in his mock-betrayal of Cheyenne (itself designed to trick Frank's men) who still manages to make sure the label sticks despite Harmonica's claims of anachronism ('There were no dollars in them days!').

Resurrection plays a grotesquely transformative role in at least three of Leone's westerns which leads to the ultimate deaths and to the ultimate prize. In *Fistful*, a near-dead Joe escapes in the coffin. When he finishes watching the carnage at the Baxter household through the coffin lid, he shuts it and the screen goes black for a few seconds. The immediately following scene is the beginning of his resurrection in, naturally, a cave. Joe dramatically returns through dynamite smoke and even deadlier as he now appears immortal thanks to his metal vest. In *Good*, Blondie gets brutal treatment from Tuco and the desert sun to the point where he is close to death. But once he gains half of the secret of the $200,000, he is taken to the monastery where, despite Tuco's claims that Blondie is dying, he recovers and coolly takes control of events until he gains the prize. In his first scene in *Once*, Harmonica is shot and left for dead, yet in his next appearance he seems unscathed (jacket aside) and appears as an avenging angel of death (Frayling 2006: 198–199), listing the names of the dead whenever questioned and finally killing Frank. Before chaos is controlled and brought under order, then, the standard understanding of Christianity in the western has been flipped into something grotesque and macabre and, like the values associated with money, will have to be brought in to order by the end of *Once* to mark the next stage of historical development.

Neoliberalism: 'a new type of life, a new focus and locus of a paramount world of meaning'

We can now turn to see the broader cultural resonances of these takes on death, money and Christianity in the context of western capitalism at the 'moment' of the Italian western. The cultural changes simultaneously taking place from the 1960s onwards can now help explain the old question of why these Italian westerns were both durable and successful. The values associated with Leone's protagonists are compatible with, and sometimes critical of, dominant values of that contemporary manifestation of capitalism – neoliberalism – and all the political tensions that fed into its ongoing dominance from the 1970s onwards. Among the relevant features of the rhetoric of neoliberalism are that it advocates individual property rights, promotes the private sector over the public sector, supports deregulation of the market, challenges traditional manifestations of state power, encourages individual responsibility and downplays systemic problems as a cause of individual failure (Crossley 2012: 21–37). In this respect, Leone's amoral entrepreneurial bounty killers in their obsession with private money are a macabre fit, even if an awareness of systemic problems remains present.

Assisted by the rise of the mass media and communications, the instant image and PR has become more prominent than ever before in an age of neoliberalism. We might think of how suited the Dollars Trilogy would become in this world dominated by instant images and pastiche. The cigar-smoking, poncho-wearing image of Eastwood is as instantly recognizable as pop art images of Marilyn, Elvis or even Che, with Eastwood even going to court to protect his Dollars image. As Frayling puts it: 'And so it came to pass that a hero who had started life in Italy as a mixture of James Bond, Che Guevara, Hercules and Judas, had become by the late 1970s a new kind of Hollywood hero as well: the hero as style statement, rather than as crusader. The superhuman hero whose catch-phrases and clothing tell you all you need to know about him' (2006: xiv; cf. 169). This is an example of what David Harvey calls 'the neoliberalism of culture' (2005: 47); indeed he and others (e.g. Harvey 1989; Jameson 1991; Anderson 1998) have shown the links between late capitalism or neoliberalism and postmodernity. In this respect, Leone's playful pilfering of cinema would anticipate that postmodern icon of filmmaking, Quentin Tarantino, himself an admirer of Leone while relentlessly borrowing from his films. As Fisher has shown, such postmodern cinema picks up on 'cool' pop cultural stylistics of the Italian westerns while bringing the Italian westerns into the world of playful referencing drained of their ideological significance and removing the political element of their violence (Fisher 2011: 193–201).

The intellectual origins of neoliberalism and postmodernity come from across the political spectrum, and they were a crucial part of the emerging political contexts in which Leone was making these films. Aside from the obvious economic contribution to the rise of neoliberalism from the political Right and the growing critique of Marxist metanarratives in the rise of postmodernity (if indeed we can separate these two tendencies), leftist challenges to traditional authority in the 1960s were important in ushering in cultural and economic shifts that were taking place. It is also a notable feature of Harvey's acclaimed analyses of postmodernity and neoliberalism (1989, 2005) that he downplays the long-term oppositional significance of the events of 1968 and sees the rhetoric of freedom and rights as one of the factors in the emergence of postmodernism and its connections with contemporary manifestations of capitalism. While Harvey certainly has a point, he probably goes too far in that a number of radical groups and movements emerged or re-emerged after 1968 which meant the Left was no longer dominated by Marxist or Communist parties, even if this fragmentation is nevertheless typical of postmodernity.

Western capitalism has managed to absorb and control the tensions and potential contradictions associated with neoliberalism. Hollywood has since even managed to make an industry of accommodating, transforming and selling criticism of capitalism in its films in order to promote a society of openness (Fisher 2009: 12–13). This tension, or absorption, is crucial to understanding the survival of Leone's westerns. The emergence of these general cultural contexts outlined above, and the intersection of values the films shared with them, helps explain how popular and culturally significant these films became. Nasty businessmen and critiques of early forms of corporate greed are found in the Dollars Trilogy, as they were in other Italian westerns. Most explicitly this critique is in *Once* where Morton is a caricatured capitalist railroad boss. In line with more political Italian westerns and relevant currents in political thought (Fisher 2011: 43–44, 61–62, 72–74, 143), bandits are treated as more complex and ambiguous and products of harsh socio-economic circumstances (e.g. Tuco) who can gain popular support (e.g. in Agua Caliente).

But in Leone's amoral universe radical political critique remains muted. In crucial ways, the tensions in the films reflect tensions present in Leone's political thinking. Leone was writing in a general context where radical Italian politics were amply represented in the traditions of the Italian westerns and Italian cinema more generally (Fisher 2011). Yet Leone described himself as a 'disillusioned socialist'. He was concerned that 'consciousness-raising films' were too parochial and lacked a wider audience and so he felt it was his task to embrace a mass audience without entirely disengaging political issues. Leone was also aware of the tensions between his socialist, anti-fascist upbringing and dreams of wealth distribution, on the one hand, and the incompatibility of owning a villa and being a communist, on the other (Frayling 2000: 305–306). Moreover, Gian Maria Volonté, the Communist Party member who played Ramón and Indio, rejected Leone's westerns as an effective medium for radical politics and would turn down the role of Tuco in *Good* to pursue more overtly political roles (Fisher 2011: 142). Indeed, when Leone did directly tackle the issue of revolution in *Duck, You Sucker!* (1971), it is an attempt to satirize political westerns and revolution, reflecting post-'68 disillusionment (Frayling 2006: 231).[2]

Re-inscribing capitalism

To get a full picture of the role of capitalism in Leone's view of the progress of history, we must now turn in more detail to the grand narrative of Leone's westerns and how it functions as a re-inscribing of the previously critiqued values of capitalism. There are two transformative stages of capitalism in Leone's westerns, both representing what Davies might have referred to as 'a new type of life, a new focus and locus of a paramount world of meaning' in their own right and both of which more precisely resonate with the tensions leading to the emergence of neoliberalism.[3]

The first transformative stage of capitalism is represented by the Dollars Trilogy where chaos and death rule (cf. Mitchell 1996: 228). This is the world of the Eastwood character and Tuco, both of whom acquire a fortune, and a world with which Mortimer must keep pace to gain his revenge. Here the deceitful, untrustworthy and morbidly entrepreneurial latch onto death as a commodity and survive, flourish and form part of the overturning of the old era of feudal capitalism represented by the Rojos and Baxters. Unlike the fixed entities of the warring families, Joe moves freely and sells his services to both sides. As Campbell argues, Joe 'comes to stand in for a technological form linked to that mode of postmodern capitalism in which circulation of bodies, objects, and labor power is key' (2010: 8). San Miguel is wiped out of Rojos and Baxters, and with no market left to exploit (and with bodies being cleared up), Joe and his services move on to another market (cf. Frayling 2006: 130). Recall the words opening *Few*: 'Where life had no value, death, sometimes, had its price. That is why the bounty killers appeared'.

The critique of traditional authority associated with the influence of the late 1960s, resonating with an American counterculture experiencing the impact of the Vietnam War (Fisher 2011: 167–171, 181; cf. Mitchell

1996: 223–226), is a marked feature of the capitalist world of the Dollars Trilogy. The world of the Dollars Trilogy is one where forms of state, government and local authority are undermined and in their place is a form of individualism which can flourish once the rules of the new environment are understood. In Leone's westerns, the corrupt sheriff is not, as Manco points out, 'courageous, loyal and above all honest'. Manco can, without repercussion, take the sheriff's badge, toss it in the direction of passers-by and say that the people need a new sheriff. In *Fistful*, Sherriff John Baxter has no authority over Joe who simply tells Baxter to bury the dead when Baxter unconvincingly says Joe will be strung up. Throughout the Dollars Trilogy, the Eastwood character regularly does as he pleases and bypasses authority almost at will, often without repercussions. There is no concern for law and order here and it is all part of the overall plan of our (anti-)heroes to gain the reward money for criminals (and for Mortimer's revenge). Similarly, Mortimer, who will stop a train when it is in his own interests, may well be comfortable in elite circles due to his reputation, but he has no respect for such figures and institutions and merely uses them to get to Indio. In *Good*, the justice system may well be trying to hang Tuco, but the viewer is hardly encouraged to condemn Tuco. After collecting the reward for Tuco, Blondie, clearly within sight, further humiliates local justice by shooting the hats off various powerless authority figures. There is an uneasy tension involved with the breakdown of this authority. Certainly audiences might be expected to side with Manco when he throws away the sheriff's badge, but equally audiences might agree with the commandant that Angel Eyes deserves to be brought to justice. And it is this breakdown of authority that is another marked feature of an era of uncontrolled death with which the authorities are complicit.

The local authorities are either corrupt or ineffective, but the bigger authorities are utterly destructive and indifferent to suffering. In *Good* the naïve commandant may want to bring Angel Eyes to justice, but it is made clear that this cannot happen. Both sides in the civil war are destructive and this is also why neither side is favoured: the bigger authorities just lead to torture, death and destruction. Moreover, despite moments of compassion from Blondie, both sides are only to be used where possible by the three major characters. Angel Eyes only enlists because he is looking for Bill Carson while Blondie and Tuco need to blow up the bridge for both sides to fight elsewhere – even as they pretend to be collecting the bodies of the wounded or dead.

But this – 'a new type of life, a new focus and locus of a paramount world of meaning' – found within the narrative world of the Dollars Trilogy is replaced by a second – the world of *Once*. *Once* is vital for Leone's narrative of history because it is, as he put it, the story of 'a birth and a death … a cinematic fresco on the birth of America … the end of the Western's golden age and the demise of the Western as a fable' (Frayling 2005: 31). *Once* therefore continues Leone's critique of, and dialogue with, previous westerns, but the critique now incorporates his Dollars Trilogy as part of the 'golden age'. As is often pointed out, the era of the gunslinger is clearly coming to an end. Frank and Cheyenne have to die and come to know that they do not have a role in the world of railroads, business and booming towns (cf. Frayling 2006: 192–216). Even the one survivor from the 'ancient race', Harmonica, has to leave and is last seen taking the dead body of Cheyenne away from Sweetwater. The beginning of the film has two classic western actors (Jack Elam and Woody Strode) killed off, roles initially hoped to be played by Eastwood, Lee van Cleef and Eli Wallach, reprising their roles from *Good* (Frayling 2006: 141). At the end of the film, with Cheyenne dying and Frank and Harmonica fighting to the death, the development of Sweetwater continues relentlessly. The actions of Morton and his extensive vision of the railways indeed illustrate a form of barely controlled capitalism but are also part of the process of historical change as he struggles to come to terms straddling the two periods. But he must die too. The past is purified by the deaths of Morton, Frank and even Cheyenne and points to a bright new future ('it would be nice to see this town grow', as Cheyenne ruefully puts it). The character focus now shifts to the thriving Jill McBain who represents the American future. Money associated with the hired gun has already shifted to protect Jill McBain from the dying embers of the previous form of barely controlled capitalism. The scene was set for Jill McBain's dominance when her late husband had 'paid for in cash' building materials for a town and had bought the place in the desert because of its strategic location. Cheyenne says Harmonica could make his fortune, but Harmonica is not interested (like the 'old man' Mortimer in *Few* who was also out for vengeance) and thus Harmonica (again like Mortimer) has to leave once he gets his revenge because he does not belong to this new world.

Re-inscribing technology

Appreciating this re-inscribing of capitalism helps us to understand the related manifestations of 'a new type of life, a new focus and locus of a paramount world of meaning' throughout the film and in both stages of transformative capitalisms. Perhaps the clearest example of this is in the function of technology (Campbell 2010). The focus on the value of death shows the devastating environmental impact of capitalism and the behaviour of its representatives. Weaponry, as Campbell notes, is the most obvious form of technological devastation, such as Ramón's Gatling in *Fistful* which mows down bodies or indeed the indiscriminate and ubiquitous cannons in *Good*. This devastation is emphatically highlighted at the beginning of *Few* as we get the perspective of the rifle/killer (Campbell 2010: 9–10) who kills a lone rider in the distance with no means of self-defence despite, presumably, being a vicious killer himself. A visually striking contrast with the past is Angel Eyes' introduction in *Good* when the freely moving master of the new weaponry arrives from the wilderness to the peasant household with its outdated and immovable technology (e.g. the boy endlessly circling a well on a mule). Inevitably, Stevens and his eldest son are murdered by the solitary killer who exits the household unscathed.

All Leone's main characters (with the crucial and partial exception of Jill McBain) embrace the new weaponry including the ones closest to being 'good guys' (e.g. the Eastwood character, Mortimer, Harmonica) as much as the obvious 'bad guys' (e.g. Ramón, Indio, Angel Eyes) to the extent that the films come close to being about technologies competing to survive. In *Fistful*, Joe and Ramón argue over the virtues of a .45 and a Winchester respectively, a topic revisited when Joe kills Ramón. In *Few*, Manco puzzles over the oddities of Mortimer's 'contraptions' as they discuss the virtues of weaponry after an exchange of firearm power which fascinates and terrifies the locals. Mortimer, Eastwood's character, and Tuco are all seen expertly fiddling with the mechanics of the weaponry, and the trilogy regularly focuses on the specific sounds of different and competing guns. When he is trying to shoot the rope for his new partner, Shorty, Blondie's rifle (and another camera angle from the perspective of the weapon) even has the wildly anachronistic addition of a telescopic lens (Frayling 2006: 170). But the anachronism only further emphasizes the onslaught of technology and this time in the hands of the closest thing the film has to a hero.

This embrace already suggests that there is a tension in the critique of technology at the heart of Leone's westerns. The destruction all the main characters (good or bad) bring with their weapons is clear and would initially cause controversy and confusion on release. When we first see Mortimer in action in *Few*, he and the musical score reveal an elaborate range of firearms. Calloway repeatedly fires at Mortimer at a distance, but it is clear that the advanced technology helps Mortimer kill him off with one efficient shot. In the following scene, we find out that Manco (as with Tuco) is just as fast and ruthless with his gun as Mortimer is with his contraptions. In all cases, the technology and the human are almost indistinct (Campbell 2010: 7). In *Few*, Manco's very presence in the hotel causes great fear. On arrival at sleepy Agua Caliente, Manco and Mortimer bring to fruition the suggestion that it could become a morgue and give advanced warning with their different sounding guns shooting apples off a tree. And these two characters who are the closest to successful 'good guys' as any in the film are as much part of making Agua Caliente a morgue as Indio's gang.

Yet this dangerous new form of technological change itself becomes absorbed and controlled in the next stage of capitalist development in *Once*. The brutal behaviour and advice of Harmonica and Cheyenne ultimately defend and aid Jill McBain in establishing Sweetwater which is eventually freed of all known gunslingers, including Harmonica and Cheyenne. The absorbing of another death-bringing technological change in Leone's westerns is the railway, a major theme for westerns (e.g. Ford's *Iron Horse*) and is likewise given the distinctive Leone treatment. The dangers of failing to control the railway, with its killer-hiring and aptly named owner Morton, are ever-present in the race-against-time to get the Sweetwater station built. Such dangers would have been known from the Dollars Trilogy. The train ferries destructive troops and criminals in *Good*. The Prophet in *Few* blames the trains for almost all social ills – even for turning Mortimer into a bounty killer – and they continually shake and ruin his house.

Once the railway is in place and the McBains have taken advantage of the situation through control of the water and labour, technology is presented as the next part of capitalist development as *Once* looks forward to an era of economic prosperity. Already at the beginning the railway is no longer the mode of transport for the armies as in *Good* but for different ethnic groups to move from town to town, bringing commerce and, ultimately, introducing Jill McBain to Sweetwater after a significantly lengthy detour which building the new train station will address. All the old, violent characters of the West die off or are removed from the railway, technological developments and the general drive of History. Mortimer, Manco, Harmonica, Cheyenne, even Frank (who eventually realizes he is not a businessman after all) and, to a lesser extent, Tuco are not interested in, contemptuous towards or do not take seriously the development of the railroad.

Death and destruction is once again placed outside and a noticeably more ethnically diverse community is building up in this stage of multicultural capitalist development. In *Once* there are now Native Americans casually getting off the train when Jill McBain initially arrives (Native Americans are effectively absent from the Dollars Trilogy). It is also worth mentioning the distinctive and striking casting of Italians and Hispanics in Leone's westerns rather than the traditional Whites of the Hollywood western. Taking the grand narrative of the Dollars Trilogy and *Once*, Leone's retelling of the 'golden age' of the West portrays how the new technology brought with it the forces of death everywhere, before it is then controlled, and put back in its place through the erection of new towns, new boundaries and the inclusion of a range of ethnicities, as indeed Leone suggested was his aim (Frayling 2005: 31). The building of Sweetwater and its railway effectively marks the new boundaries between town and wilderness with the wilderness as the threat to family; death, brought by bounty killers and the like, is finally conquered and placed outside – or indeed in the past. This also marks the 'birth of America', where capitalist development awaits a future crisis with the advent of powerful transnational corporations, to be tackled in another genre which Leone himself would later embrace – the gangster movie (or, in the case of *The Sopranos*, TV series).

Concluding remarks

Davies' studies of the importance of death, money and associated social values help us understand further the survival and importance of Leone's westerns. The emphases on death, money and Christianity in the films present us with crucial ways of understanding social values turned on their head in terms of the narrative world of the westerns, the cinematic tradition of the western, and in line with broader emerging cultural trends of neoliberalism and post-modernity. Those values involving the importance of an amoral capitalism, untrustworthiness and a certain form of individualism at the expense of traditional forms of authority and community resonate in particular. These values, accompanied by the unleashing of the full forces of death, were emerging as the Vietnam War and antiauthoritarianism were taking hold in American culture. But the amoral capitalism of the Dollars Trilogy is then challenged and eventually replaced in *Once* where the entrepreneurship of the McBains and the new world of the expanding railway and booming towns brings the forces of death and chaos under control and makes the claim for the American future. It may well be significant that the optimistic *Once* was not the immediate success that the Dollars Trilogy was (it was also heavily edited) and it was not until Vietnam was long behind America that it started to develop its reputation as a cinematic classic (with an extended version released in 1984). In turn, this reading of the films ties Davies' socio-anthropological approach to death to broader economic and historical changes and the ways in which recurring themes in human societies can play an important role in marking and identifying human understandings of such transformations.

Notes

1 When we do find white Protestant sensibilities, Tuco is about to be hanged in front of a puritanical crowd, and yet, despite all the depraved things of which he is accused, he remains a sympathetic comedic character.
2 From early on, it was noted that Leone's films celebrate capitalism while simultaneously critiquing it (Frayling 2006: 164), a tension heightened by the moral ambiguity of Eastwood's character. We should not be surprised that in their reception Joe ends up being adored by gangster-capitalist Biff Tannen in *Back to the Future 2* (1989) but that his nemesis, the hero Marty McFly, also identifies himself as Clint Eastwood (complete with poncho) when he goes back in time to the Wild West and fights the earlier Tannen in *Back to the Future 3* (1990). Like a photo and its negative, it is Joe's final fight with Ramón that is either replayed (Tannen) or mimicked (McFly). Or, again, while Leone's westerns may have resonated with social breakdown accompanying Vietnam, the introduction of the individualistic gun-toting, anti-bureaucratic Eastwood character leads almost immediately to being absorbed and transformed in to a high-profile reactionary in *Dirty Harry* (1971) (Fisher 2011: 187–188).
3 For different but complementary political typologies of the world of the Italian western, see Frayling (2006) and Fisher (2011).

References

Anderson, P. (1998) *The Origins of Postmodernity*. London and New York: Verso.
Campbell, T. (2010) 'The corrupting Sea, technology and devalued life in Sergio Leone's Spaghetti Westerns', *California Italian Studies* 1: 1–15.
Crossley, J. G. (2012) *Jesus in an Age of Neoliberalism: Quests, Scholarship and Ideology*. Sheffield and Oakville: Equinox.

Davies, D. J. (1998) 'Popular reactions to the death of Princess Diana', *Expository Times* 109: 173–176.

Davies, D. J. (2002) *Death, Ritual and Belief: The Rhetoric of Funerary Rites.* 2nd edition. London: Continuum.

Davies, D. J. (2004) 'Purity, spirit and reciprocity in the Acts of the Apostles', in L. J. Lawrence and M. I. Aguilar (eds) *Anthropology and Biblical Studies.* Leiden: Deo Publishing, pp. 259–280.

Davies, D. J. (2005) *A Brief History of Death.* Malden: Blackwell.

Davies, D. J. (2008) *The Theology of Death.* London: T&T Clark.

Fisher, A. (2011) *Radical Frontiers in the Spaghetti Western: Politics, Violence and Popular Italian Cinema.* London and New York: I.B. Tauris.

Fisher, M. (2009) *Capitalist Realism: Is There No Alternative?* Winchester: Zero Books.

Frayling, C. (2000) *Sergio Leone: Something to Do with Death.* London: Faber and Faber.

Frayling, C. (2005) *Sergio Leone: Once Upon a Time in Italy.* London: Thames and Hudson.

Frayling, C. (2006) *Spaghetti Westerns: Cowboys and Europeans from Karl May to Sergio Leone.* 3rd edition. London and New York: I.B. Taurus.

Harvey, D. (1989) *The Condition of Postmodernity.* Oxford: Blackwell.

Harvey, D. (2005) *A Brief History of Neoliberalism.* Oxford: Oxford University Press.

Jameson, F. (1991) *Postmodernism, or, The Cultural Logic of Late Capitalism.* London and New York: Duke University Press.

Mitchell, L. C. (1996) *Westerns: Making the Man in Fiction and Film.* Chicago: University of Chicago Press.

Wright, W. (1975) *Sixguns and Society: A Structural Study of the Western.* Berkeley: University of California Press.

3   Mormonism and the fourth-century search for a Christian doctrine of God

Grant Underwood

The Trinity. God as three persons in one being, or as John Donne expressed it, a 'three-personed God' (1982: ii). The devout celebrate it as 'divine mystery'. Unbelievers denigrate it as, to use Thomas Jefferson's words, 'metaphysical insanity'. Twentieth-century Christian historian Cyril Richardson quipped, 'It has been observed that by denying it one may be in danger of losing one's soul, while by trying to understand it one may be in danger of losing one's wits' (1955: 235). In the fourth century, Gregory of Nazianzus offered similar sentiments. Challenging a detractor, he taunted, 'You explain the ingeneracy of the Father and I will give you a biological account of the Son's begetting and the Spirit's proceeding – and let us go mad the pair of us for prying into God's secrets' (St Gregory of Nazianzus 2002: 122). Substantial development of the doctrine of the Trinity took place in the fourth century A.D. in what historically has been called the 'Trinitarian controversy' or 'Arian controversy' but might more accurately be characterized as the 'search for a Christian doctrine of God'.[1] Revisiting that search and highlighting certain of its ideas and debates can help identify important points of convergence and divergence between Mormonism and historical Christianity, an endeavour to which Douglas Davies has long been deeply committed and to which he has made signal contributions. Additionally, Davies' close association with, and commitment to, Anglicanism, with its historic attention to patristic Christianity, inspires my selection of the particular temporal locus for this chapter's comparison with Mormonism. The chapter has as its particular objective to bring Mormon thought into close conversation with the early church fathers on the subject of the Trinity. It is an attempt to explicate what Davies recently called 'the Mormon paradox of not accepting traditional *ideas* of the Trinity whilst accepting the *idea* of the Trinity as a mark of authentic Christian identity' (2010: 61). In the spirit of Davies' deep immersion in the theological viewpoints he explores comparatively (and his unusually profound penetration of Mormonism is a prime example), detailed attention will here be given to the nuances of fourth-century Trinitarian thought, something not always adequately attended to in comparative reflections on Mormon theology.

To understand the fourth-century search for a doctrine of God, one must understand something of contemporary Greek philosophy, for it provided the conceptual and linguistic universe within which the search was carried out. As early as the second century, Clement of Alexandria could write approvingly that philosophy was 'the handmaid of theology' given to the Greeks by God as 'a schoolmaster to bring the Hellenic mind . . . to Christ' (Roberts, Donaldson and Coxe 2007: 305). Key among the perceived strengths of Greek philosophy were its notions of divine transcendence and the corresponding incompatibility of that perfect, unchanging, immaterial realm of Ideas or Forms with the irrationality and unpredictability of an ever-changing physical universe. Philosophical notions of transcendence blended readily with Jewish and Christian monotheism to create a conception of God as an incomparable, immaterial and ultimately incomprehensible Being existing in perfect, solitary self-sufficiency prior to creation (see Stead 2000). All of this was well and good for strict monotheists, but Christians had to explain the place of a divine Christ, whom they also worshiped as God. Is he to be understood as equal to, or something less than, the transcendent God? If he is equal to God, is that not ditheism rather than monotheism? If Christ is a lesser divinity, what attributes does he lack? What role does he play?

From the second century to the fourth century and beyond, church fathers laboured to develop a Hellenistically compatible set of answers to such questions, in part by drawing on the philosophical concept of the *Logos*. The Greek term *logos* can be defined simply as word or speech, but some philosophers expounded its broader meaning as reason or rationality and saw in it the rational order that structures the cosmos. As the ordering principle of existence, the Logos had always been part of God, indeed was Divine Reason itself. When God chose to create the physical universe that his Logos had conceived, he simply externalized the Logos to perform the work of creation. Canonical texts like the Gospel of John, with its opening declaration that 'in the beginning was the *logos* and the *logos* was with God and the *logos* was God' (John 1:1) enabled church fathers to link the philosophical notion of the Logos to the preexistent Son of God by whom originally 'all things were made' and who in time was 'made flesh' as Jesus Christ (John 1:3, 14). Other texts, however, such as the scriptural declaration that he was *monogenes* (the 'Only Begotten Son'), raised questions about whether the Son/Logos was eternal or had a beginning point.

Such was the intellectual context for a dispute that broke out early in the fourth century in Alexandria, Egypt, the nerve centre of Hellenized Christianity (and Judaism). The controversy erupted in the late 310s or early 320s when Arius, one of the city's presbyters, along with a handful of supporters challenged the teaching of Alexander, Alexandria's bishop. Alexander held a view, particularly well developed by his Alexandrian predecessors, that the preexistent Son, as God's Logos, *was* eternal. In contrast, Arius and his associates insisted that the Father alone was eternal and uncreated. Because the Son was 'begotten' at some point, 'there was when he was not'. Arians were, however, 'careful to avoid the saying "There was a *time* when the Son was not", since he was begotten "before time"' (Bettenson 2011: 42n).[2] Moreover, because he was created by God, albeit the first and highest of all creatures and the one empowered to create the universe, he was still a creature and thus substantially and qualitatively different from, and less than, the Father. Arius felt such views were necessary to preserve the incomparability and indivisibility of God. In response, Alexander excommunicated Arius and reportedly sent him and his followers into exile. Far from being cowed into submission, Arius launched a vigorous campaign to persuade other bishops to side with his views. Various local councils were held and issued either strongly anti-Arian or pro-Arian statements, but these did little to quell the agitation.

Finally, in 325, the emperor Constantine convened an empire-wide council in Nicaea near his new capital Constantinople. As it turned out, the council was attended primarily by bishops from the Greek-speaking east, although the bishop of Rome did send a pair of delegates. A variety of items were discussed at the council with the idea of standardizing and unifying Christian practice throughout the empire, but the issue of greatest consequence was the controversy that had erupted in Alexandria. Constantine wanted to resolve it before it became as entrenched and difficult to settle as the contemporaneous Donatist schism in North Africa. Arius did not attend the council both because he was a presbyter and more importantly because he was under censure, but Athanasius, Alexander's secretary and later his successor, did. In time, the combative Athanasius became the iconic, but not the only, opponent of Arius and 'Arianism'. Although a number of bishops attending the council held views similar to Arius, the majority eventually endorsed the Creed of Nicaea as something they could live with:

> We believe in one God the Father all-powerful, Maker of all things both seen and unseen. And in one Lord Jesus Christ, the Son of God, the Only-begotten begotten from the Father, that is from the substance of the Father, God from God, light from light, true God from true God, begotten not made, consubstantial (*homoousion*) with the Father, through whom all things came to be . . . And those who say "there once was when he was not," and "he was begotten he was not," and that he came to be from things that were not, or from another substance (*hypostasis*) or essence (*ousia*), affirming that the Son of God is subject to change or alteration-these the catholic and apostolic church anathematizes.
>
> (Pelikan and Hotchkiss 2003: 159)

Although Arius is not mentioned by name in the creed, opposition to his teaching is clearly discernible in such affirmations as the Son of God is 'from the substance of the Father' and is 'begotten not made, the same substance with the Father'. The concluding anathemas (cursings) against 'those who say', however, made repudiation of Arius' views, including his famous slogan – 'there was when he was not' – most explicit.

As can be seen, the debate at Nicaea centred on ontology (theory of being), on how best to understand the nature of the Son and his metaphysical relationship to the Eternal Father. Arius sought to preserve God's monotheistic uniqueness as the one and only eternal, uncreated Being. Yet the corollary view that Christ was part of the (lesser) created realm, even if the highest of all creation and the one through whom all other creatures were made, seemed to Arius' opponents to diminish Christ's divinity and to make him 'subordinate' to the Father. A century earlier a position known as Monarchianism attempted to keep Father, Son and Holy Spirit equally divine by contending that the Son and the Holy Spirit were merely God (the Father) by other names. Praxeas, a prominent early Monarchian, reportedly taught that at Jesus' birth the Father himself entered the womb of Mary. Such a notion prompted Tertullian, the famous North African theologian, to quip that Praxeas 'crucified the Father'. Thereafter, this version of Monarchianism bore the moniker *Patripassianism* (Father-suffers-ism).[3] It has also been designated 'Modalism' because of its notion that Father, Son and Holy Ghost are merely names for the progressive modes or phases through which the one God interacts with the world. From this perspective, God functioned as Father when he created the world, as Son when he became incarnate, and now as Holy Spirit who superintends and sanctifies the Christian community.

During the fourth century, however, the attempt to solve the paradox of how the Father, Son and Holy Spirit could be equal yet distinct, how they could be a Trinity, revolved around two key words – *homoousios* and *hypostasis*. *Homoousios*, a term employed in the Creed of Nicaea, is a compound of *homo*, which means same or common (in the sense of shared), and *ousia*, which is derived from the Greek verb to be or to exist and means being, essence or nature of a thing (Liddell et al. 1996: 579). As a single word, *homoousios* literally means 'same or shared essence, substance, nature', though it has been commonly translated into English somewhat awkwardly as 'consubstantial'. Precisely how the creedal declaration that the Son was '*homoousion* with the Father' should be understood was far from clear or uniformly agreed upon by fourth-century (and subsequent) disputants. Acceptable positions had to avoid, on the one hand, the Scylla of describing 'same substance or being' in the Monarchian sense that Father and Son were one person, not two, and, on the other hand, the Charybdis of viewing the Father and the Son as two separate divine beings who simply shared a generic class of existence known as divinity.

Hypostasis – *hypo* (under) and *stasis* (standing, state) – is a particularly challenging term because of the multiple meanings it carried in classical Greek, including the real nature of a thing, its essence or substance, and thus was sometimes confused with *ousia*. Indeed, its direct translation into Latin was *substantia*, from which the English substance is derived. The plural form *hypostases* can also be understood as distinct individualities or individual existences and as such came to be the term of choice for the three persons or distinctions within the single God of the Trinity. Although in everyday English 'persons' tends to be understood as 'people', such a construal is problematic because in Trinitarian terms it implies three Gods (tritheism), a concept which was almost universally unacceptable in the fourth century. Instead, most fathers shared a deep commitment to not let God's oneness be compromised by his threeness. Gregory of Nazianzus expressed it well when he wrote, 'So we adore the Father and the Son and the Holy Spirit, dividing their individualities (*hypostases*) but uniting their godhead (divinity); and we neither blend the three into one thing, lest we be sick with [the Monarchian's] disease, nor do we divide them into three alien and unrelated things, lest we share Arius's madness' (*Orations* X.5, as cited in Daley 2006: 100). Gregory of Nyssa in his treatise *On Not Three Gods* emphasized that Father, Son and Holy Spirit are a unity, not a partnership which would imply that the three divine hypostases are 'filled with individual psychological content' (Ayres 2002: 464, 470).

Against this fourth-century background of decades-long debate over the nature and status of the Son, as well as how God is both three and one, we jump to the twenty-first century and to Mormon reflection on these issues. How, for instance, do Latter-day Saints understand the three-yet-one nature of 'the Godhead', as they prefer to designate the Trinity? The short answer is that Latter-day Saints view the Divine Persons as one in every significant way *except* as a single being. A Mormon Apostle expressed it thus: 'We believe these three divine persons constituting a single Godhead are united in purpose, in manner, in testimony, in mission. We believe Them to be filled with the same godly sense of mercy and love, justice and grace, patience, forgiveness, and redemption. I think it is accurate to say we believe They are one in every significant and eternal aspect imaginable except believing Them to be three persons combined in one substance' (Holland 2007: 12). This explanation illustrates *how* Latter-day Saints interpret statements in their own scriptures that sound traditionally Trinitarian such as the affirmation found in Joseph Smith's revelations that the 'Father and the Son, and the Holy Ghost is one God, infinite and eternal, without end' (Smith 2013: 122).[4]

Although LDS theology embraces the unity of the Godhead, it *emphasizes* the threeness of the Trinity. In large part, this is because Mormonism's founder, Joseph Smith, reported a foundational vision in which he saw the Father and the Son as separate, embodied beings. Not surprisingly, when Latter-day Saints discuss the divine Triad, they cite many of the same Bible verses to support their doctrine that the Father, Son and Holy Ghost are three separate beings that Trinitarians use to demonstrate that there are three 'distinctions' (*hypostases*) within the single Deity. Mormons not versed in early Christian theology often miss the fact that patristic discussion of three divine *hypostases* or persons does not refer to three separate *beings*, which is what Latter-day Saints intend when they talk of the three personages of the Godhead. Davies noticed this subtlety when he remarked that LDS Trinitarian expositions 'always hang on the meaning of terms', and he singled out the use of 'personage' as an example (2010: 63). Still, in the earliest centuries, before the extensive discussion of the Trinity as three *hypostases* in one *ousia*, church fathers sometimes viewed the Father and the Son as separate entities. For second-century apologists who assimilated the Platonic idea of the Logos to the Son, 'there seemed to be no way around the fact that this theology made it sound as though there is a first and a second God – in other words, two Gods' (Heine 2013: 44). And Origen's third-century *Dialogue with Heraclides* makes it clear that the idea was not uncommon among ordinary Christians that the Father and the Son were two Gods, though one in power. These examples illustrate that the fine theological distinction between two *persons* and two *beings* (or personages) has sometimes been difficult to make.

In the fourth century, Arians were often charged with perpetuating this notion of ditheism. For this and other perceived similarities, Mormon perspectives on the Trinity are sometimes labelled Arian. That characterization, however, requires some qualification. In the *Thalia*, Arius' one surviving theological treatise, he wrote: 'The substances (*ousiai* [plural]) of the Father, the Son, and the Spirit are divided, distinguished, and separated in nature and they differ from and do not participate in each other . . . their individual realities (*hypostases*) do not mix with each other, and they possess glories of different levels . . . the Word [Christ] is different from and in all points unlike the Father's substance . . . because [the Father] remains without beginning' (translation in Hanson 2005: 14). Arius and Latter-day Saints may share the conclusion that Father, Son and Holy Ghost are three distinct *ousiai*, yet they do so for different reasons. Arians arrived at their understanding in accordance with Greek philosophical principles, while Mormons do so through Joseph Smith's teachings about God.

Smith understood the anthropomorphic theophany he experienced as revealing the actual embodied nature and physically separate character of God the Father and God the Son. He did not interpret his experience as a visual 'accommodation' to the limited comprehensive capacity of finite human beings. Eventually, Smith taught: 'The Father has a [glorified] body of flesh and bones as tangible as man's; the Son also' (Doctrine and Covenants 130: 22). The Mormon prophet's experiences, as well as a tendency towards literalism in scriptural interpretation, led Latter-day Saints to construe 'appearances' passages in the Bible as evidence of God's intrinsic corporeality, and they eschewed what one nineteenth-century Anglican cleric called the 'morbid terror of anthropomorphism' (Henry L. Mansel quoted in Roberts 1903: 85). The Mormon embrace of notions of a corporeal deity harks back to the ancient Israelite views recounted by Jewish scholar Benjamin Sommer: 'The God of the Hebrew Bible has a body. This must be stated at the outset, because so many people, including many scholars, assume otherwise. The evidence for this simple thesis is overwhelming, so much so that asserting the carnal nature of the biblical God should not occasion surprise' (Sommer 2009: 4–5, 1; see also Garr 2003 and Moore 1996). Moreover, in the Mormon case, the idea of a corporeal God reflects a fundamental philosophical materialism. As Douglas Davies has noted, the Mormon doctrine of deity 'is grounded in the belief that anything that exists is matter of some sort. Even "spirit" is matter, albeit of a finer form than the "denser" matter of flesh' (2000: 112).

As to the oneness of the Trinity, for Mormons and Arians alike the divine unity is located in a perfect agreement of will, action and attributes. Athanasius often oversimplified the Arian position to disparage it (just as critics have done with Mormon theology), but he was not entirely wide of the mark when he claimed that Arians taught that 'what the Father wills, the Son wills also, and is not contrary either in what He thinks or in what He judges, but is in all respects concordant [*symphonos*] with Him, declaring doctrines which are the same, and a word consistent and united with the Father's teaching, therefore it is that He and the Father are One' (translation in Newman 1980: 399). A century earlier, in his *Commentary on John*, Origen explained the oneness of the Father and Son in similar terms. The Son's perfect cooperation with the will of the Father made it such that 'the will of the Son has become indistinguishable from the will of the Father, and there are no longer two wills but one. It was because of this one will that the Son said, "I and the Father are one"' (Book 13.228, cited in Beeley 2012: 25). In *Against Celsus*, Origen affirmed that Christians 'worship only one God, the Father and the Son . . . they are two distinct existences [*hypostases*], but one in mental unity, agreement, and identity of will' (8.12, cited in Beeley 2012: 27). Latter-day Saints have a long history of interpreting Christ's prayer in John 17 in a like manner. One of the theological lectures included in early versions of the canonical *Doctrine and Covenants* interpreted the oneness figuratively: 'As the Father and the Son are one, so, in like manner, the Saints are to be one in them, through the love of the Father, the mediation of Jesus Christ, and the gift of the Holy Spirit. They are to be heirs of God and joint-heirs with Jesus Christ' ("Lecture Fifth of Faith" Doctrine and Covenants (1835 ed.): 54). Joseph Smith taught simply that the true meaning of the prayer in John 17 could best be grasped by replacing the word one with agreed: 'I am *agreed* with the Fa[the]r & the Fa[the]r is *agreed* with me & we are agreed as one'. Thus, Christ's petition to the Father that the disciples become one 'as we are one' was metaphorical, not metaphysical. 'Why', continued Smith, if all the disciples 'are to be crammed into one God', he would be 'a wonderful big God – he would be a Giant' (Discourse, 16 June 1844, in Ehat and Cook, eds., 1980: 380; emphasis added).[5] Sarcasm aside, Mormon philosophical materialism made inconceivable any proposition that a physically embodied Son could share the same substance and be *homoousion* with the Father, whom Latter-day Saints also considered to be physically embodied.

Fourth-century Christians shared a number of assumptions about the Eternal God, some of which Mormons accept and others that they do not.

One that divides the two groups is the aforementioned matter of materiality. The idea that God is immaterial was fundamental to patristic theology, grounded as it was in Greek philosophy. It was thought that matter does not, and cannot, exist in eternity, the ontologically unique realm of deity.[6] Moreover, that which is infinite and eternal, by philosophical definition, cannot be seen or perceived by created, finite beings. Christians came to stress that God was only 'visible' through Jesus Christ. Whereas Monarchians interpreted literally such passages such as John 14:9 – 'he that hath seen me, hath seen the Father' – to prove that Jesus *was* the Father, most Christians read the statement in light of Colossians 1:15 that Christ 'is the image of the invisible God'. Cyril of Jerusalem wrote that 'since nobody was able to see the face of the Godhead and live, [the Son] took the face of humanity in order that we might see this and live' (2007: 54–66). This interpretation, however, finds little resonance in Mormonism because of the theological potency of Joseph Smith's visionary account of seeing the Father as well as the Son. Mormons interpret 'he that hath seen me hath seen the Father' to mean that the incarnate Son resembles in appearance the separately embodied Father.

Moreover, Latter-day Saints affirm an even greater resemblance when speaking of the resurrected, glorified Christ. In Christ's exaltation, he is virtually indistinguishable from the Father. Davies has correctly discerned that Christ's 'glorified body serves to reinforce the LDS theological affirmation that his heavenly father also possesses a glorified body' (2009: 173). This is clearly seen in the writing of B. H. Roberts, the great turn-of-the-twentieth-century LDS church leader-theologian, who reasoned from the fact that the exalted Son of God had resurrected flesh to argue that celestial corporeality was not out of the question for the Father either: 'Will that resurrected, immortal, glorified [Christ] ever be distilled into some bodiless, formless essence? Will He become an impersonal, incorporeal, immaterial God, without body, without parts, without passions? . . . [No,] He has a body, tangible, immortal, indestructible, and will so remain embodied throughout the countless ages of eternity . . . so, too, the Father must be a man of immortal tabernacle, glorified and exalted: for as the Son is so also is the Father, a personage of tabernacle, of flesh and of bone as tangible as man's, as tangible as Christ's most glorious, resurrected body' (Roberts 1910: 180).[7] It is important to point out that although Mormons espouse the unusual view that the Father has a celestial body, they do not see God as confined to, or identical with, that body. To be sure, he is understood to possess such bodily properties as locality, but these corporeal characteristics are not thought to compromise his omnipresence. Just as most Christians do not dispute the omnipresence of the glorified, embodied Christ, Mormons view the Father as possessing a divinized, fleshly body yet still being omnipresent and omnipotent.

Latter-day Saints do not, however, embrace the common patristic notions of divine immutability and divine impassibility. In large part, this is so because most Mormons neither interpret biblical texts nor articulate their theology in the concepts or vocabulary of western philosophy. Although it should also be noted that the divine attributes classically ascribed to God are not self-evident in Scripture. As theologian David Brown has remarked, 'Those who dogmatically insist that they are all already there in Scripture seem to express pious hopes rather than claims with a firm basis in reality'. To be sure, 'patristic and medieval accounts of the divine attributes can certainly be defended as legitimate developments beyond Scripture, but what is certain is that this can hardly be justified on grounds of exegetical continuity alone' (Brown 2011: 22). LDS lack of interest in, even aversion towards, philosophical theology reflects an Enlightenment-influenced, general antipathy towards the Christian theological tradition that was strong at the time and in the place of Mormonism's birth. Philosophy was also unattractive to many Latter-day Saints because it had long been a powerful ally in stressing divine transcendence, whereas Mormon theology worked to draw God and humans closer together, even to the point of bridging what historically had been considered the unbridgeable ontological gap between them.

Unconstrained by the regnant philosophical assumptions of the fourth century, Mormonism espouses a dramatically different cosmogony (theory of creation). LDS doctrine posits that at some point prior to creation of the physical universe, during what is called the preexistence, God begot not just Christ but *all* human souls or spirits (the term more commonly used in Mormon discourse), thus making him literally 'the Father of spirits' (Hebrews 12:9). For this reason, Mormonism rejects the two most common Christian theories of the origin of souls – *creationism*, the idea that in an ongoing process of divine creation God tailor-makes a soul for each new human embryo and infuses it into the foetus sometime between conception and birth; and *traducianism* (from the Latin *traducere*, to lead across, transport, transmit), the theory that the soul is transmitted biologically from generation to generation (God created only one soul – Adam's – and from that point forward soul is part of the biological inheritance parents pass on to their children).

Although Platonically influenced ideas of the preexistence of souls were certainly not unknown in the fourth century (Augustine identified several versions), the Mormon theory is distinctive. Several divergences are important to note. First, in the LDS view, souls are not immaterial but are composed of spirit-matter. LDS scripture declares, 'There is no such thing as immaterial[ity]; all spirit is matter, but is more fine or pure' (Doctrine and Covenants, 131:7). Moreover, these material spirits are corporeal, resembling in their refined spirit-matter the embodied Father in whose image they were created. In addition to rejecting a metaphysical substance dualism, Mormonism also renounces *creatio ex nihilo*. Joseph Smith's reflections on the Hebrew *bara* led him to conclude that the word 'does not mean to create out of nothing; it means to organize – the same as a man would organize materials and build a ship. Hence we infer that God had materials to organize the world out of chaos – chaotic matter, which is element, and . . . element had an existence from the time He had' (Fielding Smith 1938: 350–351). Such ideas would have had some resonance with non-Christians in the fourth century who embraced Platonic notions of the creator as *demiurgos* (Craftsman, Artisan), but they had not been acceptable to most Christians since the second-century battle with Gnosticism. Because Mormons imagine that God organized their souls from uncreated primal element, they believe that in some irreducible way part of every human, not just the Son, is co-uncreated (*agennetos*) and co-eternal with the Father. Or, as Davies put it, 'All human beings, therefore, share with Jesus in being of the same substance as the heavenly father, they differ only in degree of development'. This leads him to conclude perceptively that in LDS theology 'there is no need for any discussion of Jesus possessing "two [ontologically distinct] natures" in one person and [thus] renders the normal language of traditional creeds redundant' (Davies 2009: 178). In short, Latter-day Saints not only reject the Arian slogan 'there was when He [the Son] was not', they would also repudiate the formulation: 'there was when *we* were not'.

Perhaps the key distinctive of the Mormon cosmogony is its proposition that human beings are literally God's 'spirit children'.[8] LDS canon proclaims that all people "are begotten sons and daughters unto God" (Doctrine and Covenants 76:24). As a result, Mormons understand *monogenes* (Only Begotten) as only begotten *in the flesh*. Only Christ can claim God as *physical* Sire. In an earlier period of Mormon history, as noted by Davies (2003: 69, 70), the logic of a materially corporeal God led some Latter-day Saints to imagine that Mary was physically impregnated by an embodied Father. Later twentieth-century leaders, while not disavowing the Father's literal paternity of Jesus, preferred not to imply they knew exactly how it occurred. J. Reuben Clark, Jr., member of the church's First Presidency from 1933 to 1961, remarked, 'The Divine Conception I do not understand. But I know it existed and I take it on faith' (1962: 97). Later church president Ezra Taft Benson, while clarifying that Jesus was not 'begotten by the Holy Ghost', could only add that 'the paternity of Jesus Christ is one of the mysteries of godliness' (1983: 2).

Given their distinctive understanding of the origin of souls, Latter-day Saints also interpret the occasional New Testament designation of Christ as *prototokos* (Firstborn) to mean that among the billions of God's begotten 'sons' and 'daughters', Christ was first in terms of birth sequence as well as status. An official doctrinal pronouncement by the LDS church's First Presidency declares: Jesus 'is the firstborn among all the sons of God – the first begotten in the spirit, and the only begotten in the flesh. He is our elder brother, and we, like Him, are in the image of God' (LDS 1909: 78). Jesus may share a 'sibling' relationship to the rest of the Heavenly Father's spirit children, but he is seen as the preeminent Son, qualitatively superior to his 'brothers' and 'sisters' in every way.

Although authoritative Mormon sources do not explain *how* spirits were begotten, over time birth and procreation (or their cognates) became the primary vocabulary for discussing the spirit creation. Early on, as Davies has noted, the inner logic of this language led to contemplation of the existence of a Heavenly Mother (2003: 186). Still sung by Latter-day Saints today are words first published in a hymn in 1845:

> O my Father, thou that dwellest in the high and glorious place; When shall I regain thy presence, and again behold thy face? In thy holy habitation, did my spirit once reside? In my first, primeval childhood was I nurtur'd near thy side? . . . I had learn'd to call thee father through thy spirit from on high, but until the key of knowledge was restor'd, I knew not why. In the heav'ns are parents single? No, the thought makes reason stare. Truth is reason – truth eternal tells me I've a mother there.
>
> (Snow 1845: 1039; see also LDS 1985, #292 and
> Mulvay Derr 1996–1997)

An official 1995 statement issued jointly by the LDS church's First Presidency and Quorum of Twelve Apostles reaffirmed Mormon belief that 'all human beings – male and female -- are created in the image of God. Each is a beloved spirit son or daughter of heavenly *parents*, and, as such, each has a divine nature and destiny' (LDS 1995: 102; emphasis added). These words echo language used at the beginning of the twentieth century in a First Presidency statement on the Origin of Man: 'All men and women are in the similitude of the universal Father *and Mother* and are literally the sons and daughters of Deity' and 'man, as a spirit, was begotten and born of heavenly *parents* and reared to maturity in the eternal mansions of the Father, prior to coming upon the earth in a temporal body' (LDS 1909: 78, 80; emphasis added). The 1995 Proclamation adds: 'Gender is an essential characteristic of individual premortal, mortal, and eternal identity and purpose' (1995: 102). Although the doctrine of a Heavenly Mother has been consistently affirmed in LDS discourse, detailed discussion is restrained by the fact that no authoritative texts explain her role in the process of spirit birth or discuss other aspects of her divine nature and activities (see Paulsen and Pulido 2011). Lacking such knowledge, Latter-day Saints today find themselves in fundamental agreement with what Hilary of Poitiers said about the begetting of the Son. Hilary wrote that although God was willing to accommodate finite human understanding by using examples from human birth, believers should not take such analogies so far, or be so literal, as to include such reproductive details as 'coition, conception, lapse of time, delivery' (cited in Hanson 2005: 506).

Pro-Nicene fathers found intolerable the Arian idea that the Son was created because it seemed to detract from his divinity, making him ontologically inferior and subordinate to the Father. But Arians did not seek to demote, let alone denigrate, the Son. He was the greatest of all creatures. Still, wrote Arius, the Father 'is above [the Son], as being his God' (as translated by John Henry Newman 1980: 458; alternate translation 'for [the Father] as [the Son's] God . . . rules him', Rusch 1980: 32). Arians took at face value Christ's declaration 'My Father is greater than I' (John 14:28). Though he is called 'the Mighty God [Isa 9:6]' he 'in some degree worships the Greater' (Arius, Thalia cited in Hanson 2005: 15). With all of this, Mormons are in agreement, but not for ontological reasons. Rather, it is what Davies calls the LDS 'principle of progressive development in which achievement and advancement relate to a kind of spiritual-cosmic stature. In this the heavenly father has a greater degree of experience than Jesus as the divine son' (2009: 175). In any case, Mormons spill little ink differentiating the relative glory of Son and Father. The important conviction in popular Mormonism is that the Son's oneness with the Father means that he possesses every perfection and attribute appropriate to divinity and, therefore, is fully empowered to redeem and fully worthy of worship.

Still, Davies' observation about 'progressive development' points to another resonance that Mormon theology has with Arian teaching – the concept of the Incarnate Son's *prokope*, a word variously translated as advancement, improvement or progress. By very definition, *prokope* entails change, and any idea of change or mutability on the part of the eternal Son, either before time or in time, was unacceptable to the pro-Nicene fathers. It suggested imperfection and inferiority. As Cyril of Jerusalem expressed it, the Son did not gradually achieve divine perfection either in time or in eternity, but was 'begotten as that which he is now' (Gregg 1985: 85–105). Thus, the Arian notion of Christ's earthly *prokope* to divinity was a major target of anti-Arian polemics. Eusebius of Emesa spoke for many when he repudiated the idea that Son was exalted as a 'reward for his obedience', stating that Christ was 'not somebody who was promoted to being God because of his behavior' (cited in Hanson 2005: 390). Was Christ God by grace or by nature? This was central to the debate between Arian and pro-Nicene fathers. Discerning the Mormon position is not difficult. A canonical gloss on the Prologue of John reads: 'And I, John, saw that [Christ] received not of the fulness at the first, but received grace for grace; And he received not of the fulness at first, but continued from grace to grace, until he received a fulness; And thus he was called the Son of God, because he received not of the fulness at the first' (Doctrine and Covenants 93: 12–14).

Both Arians and Mormons add their own distinctive views to the common Christian emphasis on the soteriological significance of the Son fully assuming the human condition. 'What the Arians are proclaiming is not a demotion of the Son, but a promotion of believers to full and equal status as Sons' (Gregg and Groh 1977: 272). The experiential solidarity between the Saviour and other 'sons of God' leads Latter-day Saints and Arians alike to emphasize such biblical passages as 'we have not an high priest which cannot be touched with the feeling of our infirmities', but rather one who 'himself hath suffered being tempted' and who 'is able to succor them that are tempted' (Hebrews 4:15; 2:18). A similar declaration in the Book of Mormon proclaims, 'he will take upon him their infirmities, that his bowels may be filled with mercy, according to the flesh, that he may know according to the flesh how to succor his people according to their infirmities' (Alma 7:12). Within the overarching Mormon vision of the possibility of eternal progression (*prokope*) for all God's spirit children, Latter-day Saints emphasize their similarity rather than dissimilarity to the Son, deriving a sense of reverential camaraderie with Christ from the realization that a fully human Jesus had to pursue the same path to glory as they do (McConkie 1980: 4–7; LDS 2000a: 10; 2000b: 25). A stanza from a popular Mormon hymn proclaims, 'He marked the path and led the way, And every point defines; To light and life and endless day Where God's full presence shines' (LDS 1985, #195).

What, then, can be said by way of overall observation about the relationship between Mormon thought and the fourth-century search for a Christian doctrine of God? How full or empty the comparative cup is depends on one's vantage point, of course, and on what is being compared. Certainly, there are fundamental differences. Mormonism's dissolution of the great ontological divide between Creator and creature, between eternity and time, between spirit and matter is a major metaphysical gulf that separates Mormons from early church fathers of whatever theological persuasion and makes exploration of their respective views look somewhat like the proverbial comparison of apples and oranges. The Mormon materialist doctrine of deity is a far cry from fourth-century debates over whether Father, Son and Holy Spirit are all incorporeal, immaterial and ingenerate or whether only the Father is. Instead, Latter-day Saints stress that the Father has a heavenly body of glorified flesh and that he procreated the embodied souls of all human beings, endowing them with something of his divine nature and enabling them through his assisting grace to eventually become like him in the distant afterlife. God and humans are essentially, monistically, a single, divine race at different points in their eternal progression. The Mormon doctrine that divinely procreated spirit children share an intrinsic, ontological connection to, and potential to become like, their Heavenly Father, that they are, in the words of one LDS church president, gods 'in embryo', could hardly be more antithetical to the philosophical assumptions of nearly all Hellenized Christians of the fourth century (Taylor 1882: 268).

On the other hand, it is clear even from this brief survey that early Christian fathers held a wide range of views as to the proper understanding of God, and some of these views have considerable resonance with Mormon thought. Assumptions about a single, monolithic interpretation of the Nicene Creed in the fourth century are as misguided as is the presumption that the American 'Founding Fathers' all understood the Declaration of Independence or the US Constitution in the same way. Lewis Ayres (2004), for example, emphasizes fourth-century Trinitarian pluralism and criticizes scholars who continue to write monolithically about 'Nicene theology'. Further study will likely refine perceptions of similarity and difference, but what is clear even now is that both Mormon Christians and fourth-century Christians, each within their own distinctive thought worlds and using their own vocabulary, hammered out positions on many of the same issues, occasionally coming to strikingly similar conclusions. Vibrant interfaith dialogue and robust comparative religious studies of the kind fostered by Douglas Davies bode well for the future of this fascinating cross-cultural conversation. And with the passage of time, it will become ever more apparent that long before there was a Mormon moment, Davies' prescient interest in, and pioneering approach to, the study of Mormonism significantly paved the way for future generations of scholars.

Notes

1 Still one of the most thorough treatments of the entire controversy is R.P.C. Hanson, *The Search for the Christian Doctrine of God: The Arian Controversy, 318–381* (1988), which provides the inspiration for this chapter's title. Subsequent scholarly refinements to the story of that "search" can be found in Ayres (2004) and in Young with Teal (2010).
2 English idiom cannot render this phrase (*en pate hote ouk en*) literally.
3 In the Greek East, it was typically designated Sabellianism, after the "heretic" Sabellius who, a decade after Tertullian critiqued Praxeas, was excommunicated by Pope Callistus for teaching something similar.
4 When Joseph Smith's revelations were first published in 1835 as a collection titled *Doctrine and Covenants of the Church of the Latter Day Saints* (Kirtland, Ohio, 1835), the phrase "is one God" was changed to "are one God" (p. 79). The plural form of the verb has been retained in all subsequent publications of the *Doctrine and Covenants*, which is recognized as scripture by Latter-day Saints. Unless there have been significant wording changes, hereafter all citations will be to the current version of *Doctrine and Covenants*.
5 Although Smith knew little Greek, he reportedly claimed that 'the Greek shews that i[t] shod. be agreed' (Ehat and Cook 1980: 380). The term in the Gospel of John is *heis* and is the standard Greek term for the number one. However, just as in English in certain contexts, "one" *can* signify agreement.
6 A standard treatment of this is Eusebius of Emesa's *De Incorporali et Invisibili Deo* (On the Incorporeal and Invisible God). Theologically, *eternity* is more about a category of existence than never-ending time. Indeed, classical theology distinguishes *time* from the categorically distinct *eternity*, which is viewed as time*less*.
7 Elsewhere, Roberts wrote, 'So long as [Christ's] immortal body of flesh and bones, glorified and everlasting, shall keep His place by the side of the Father, so long will the doctrine that God is an exalted man hold its place against the idle sophistries of the learned world' (188).
8 Augustine was famously undecided about which theory of the soul's origin to embrace, but he was absolutely certain that the soul was immaterial and incorporeal and that it must be ontologically distinguished from its Creator. The soul, wrote Augustine, "comes from God as a thing which he has made, not as being of the same nature as he is, whether as something he has begotten or in any way at all produced from himself." *On Gen*, VII, 2, 3 (Ramsey 2002: 325).

References

Ayres, L. (2002) 'On not three people: the fundamental themes of Gregory of Nyssa's Trinitarian Theology as seen in to Ablabius: on not three Gods', *Modern Theology* 18(4): 445–474.

Ayres, L. (2004) *Nicaea and its Legacy: An Approach to Fourth-Century Trinitarian Theology*. New York: Oxford University Press.

Beeley, C. A. (2012) *The Unity of Christ: Continuity and Conflict in Patristic Tradition*. New Haven: Yale University Press.

Benson, E. T. (1983) *Come unto Christ*. Salt Lake City: Deseret Book.

Bettenson, H. (2011) *Documents of the Christian Church*. 4th edition. Oxford: Oxford University Press.

Brown, D. (2011) *Divine Humanity: Kenosis and the Construction of a Christian Theology*. Waco: Baylor University Press.

The Church of Jesus Christ of Latter-day Saints (LDS) (1835) *Doctrine and Covenants of the Church of the Latter Day Saints*. Kirtland, Ohio: LDS.

LDS (1985) *Hymns of The Church of Jesus Christ of Latter-day Saints*. Salt Lake City: LDS.

LDS (1909) 'The origin of man', *Improvement Era*. November: 75–81.

LDS (1995) 'The family: a proclamation to the world', *Ensign* 25. November: 102.

LDS (2000a) *Doctrines of the Gospel: Teacher Manual*. Salt Lake City: LDS.

LDS (2000b) *The Life and Teachings of Jesus & his Apostles: Course Manual*. 2nd edition. Salt Lake City: LDS.

LDS (2013) *Doctrine and Covenants of the Church of the Latter Day Saints*. Salt Lake City: LDS.

Clark, J. R. Jr. (1962) *Behold the Lamb of God*. Salt Lake City: Deseret Book.

Cyril of Jerusalem [1893] (2007) 'The catechetical lectures, Lecture X', in P. Schaff and H. Wallace (eds) *Nicene and Post-Nicene Fathers*, Series 2 Volume 7. New York: Cosimo, pp. 54–63.

Daley, B. (2006) *Gregory of Nazianzus*. New York: Routledge.

Davies, D. J. (2000) *The Mormon Culture of Salvation: Force, Grace and Glory*. Aldershot: Ashgate.

Davies, D. J. (2003) *Introduction to Mormonism*. Cambridge: Cambridge University Press.

Davies, D. J. (2009) 'Christ in Mormonism', in O. Hammer (ed.) *Alternative Christs*. Cambridge: Cambridge University Press, pp. 170–189.

Davies, D. J. (2010) *Joseph Smith, Jesus, and Satanic Opposition*. Farnham: Ashgate.

Donne, J. [1633] (1982) 'Holy Sonnets, XIV', in W. J. Hill, *The Three-Personed God: The Trinity as a Mystery of Salvation*. Washington, D.C.: Catholic University Press, ii.

Ehat, A. F. and Cook, L. W. (eds) (1980) *Words of Joseph Smith*. Provo, Utah: BYU Religious Studies Center.

Fielding Smith, J. (ed.) (1938) *Teachings of the Prophet Joseph Smith*. Salt Lake City: Deseret News Press.

Garr, W. R. (2003) *In His Own Image and Likeness: Humanity, Divinity, and Monotheism*. Leiden: Brill.

Gregg, R. C. (1985) 'Cyril of Jerusalem and the Arians', in R. C. Gregg *Arianism: Historical and Theological Reassessments*. Philadelphia: Philadelphia Patristic Foundation, pp. 85–105.

Gregg, R. C. and Groh, D. E. (1977) 'The Centrality of Soteriology in Early Arianism', *Anglican Theological Review* 59: 260–278.

Hanson, R. P. C. (2005) *Search for the Christian Doctrine of God: The Arian Controversy 318–381 AD*. Edinburgh: T&T Clark.

Heine, R. E. (2013) *Classical Christian Doctrine*. Grand Rapids: Baker Academic.

Holland, J. R. (2007) 'The only true God and Jesus Christ whom He hath sent', *Ensign* 37(11): 40–42.

Liddell, H. G., Scott, R., Jones, H. S. and McKenzie, R. (1996) *Greek-English Lexicon*. 9th edition. Oxford: Oxford University Press.

McConkie, B. R. (1980) 'The child, the boy, the man few people knew', *New Era*. December: 4–7.

Moore, S. D. (1996) *God's Gym: Divine Male Bodies of the Bible*. New York: Routledge.

Mulvay Derr, J. (1996–1997) 'The significance of "O My Father" in the personal journey of Eliza R. Snow', *BYU Studies* 36: 84–126.

Nazianzus, St Gregory of (2002) *On God and Christ: The Five Theological Orations and Two Letters to Cledonius. Translated into English by F. Williams and L. Wickham*. Crestwood: St Vladimir's Seminary Press.

Newman, John Henry trans. (1891 [1980]) 'Arius to Alexander of Alexandria', in *Nicene and Post-Nicene Fathers*, Series 2 Volume 4. Grand Rapids, Michigan: Eerdmans, p. 458.

Newman, John Henry trans. (1891 [1980]) 'Against the Arians', in *Nicene and Post-Nicene Fathers*, Series 2 Volume 4. Grand Rapids, Michigan: Eerdmans, pp. 303–447.

Paulsen, D. L. and Pulido, M. (2011) '"A mother there": a survey of historical teachings', *BYU Studies* 50: 71–97.

Pelikan, J. and Hotchkiss, V. (eds) (2003) *Creeds and Confessions of Faith in the Christian Tradition*. Volume 1. New Haven: Yale University Press.

Ramsey, B. (ed.) (2002) *The Works of Saint Augustine; A Translation for the 21st Century: On Genesis*. New York: New City Press.

Richardson, C. (1955) 'The Enigma of the Trinity', in R. W. Battenhouse (ed.) *A Companion to the Study of St. Augustine*. New York: Oxford University Press, pp. 243–244.

Roberts, A., Donaldson, J. and Coxe, A. C. (eds) (2007) [1885] *The Writings of the Fathers Down to A.D. 325. Volume II. Fathers of the Second Century*. New York: Cosimo.

Roberts, B. H. (1903) *The Mormon Doctrine of Deity*. Salt Lake City: Deseret News.

Roberts, B. H. (1910) *The Seventy's Course in Theology, Third Year: The Doctrine of Deity*. Salt Lake City: Caxton Press.

Rusch, W. G. (ed.) (1980) *The Trinitarian Controversy*. Minneapolis: Fortress Press.

Smith, J. (2013) *The Joseph Smith Papers: Documents Volume 1: July 1828–June 1831*. Salt Lake City, Utah: The Church Historian's Press.

Snow, E. R. (1845) 'My father in heaven', in J. Taylor (ed.) *Times and Seasons*. Volume 6. Nauvoo, Illinois: John Taylor, p. 1039.

Sommer, B. D. (2009) *The Bodies of God and the World of Ancient Israel*. New York: Cambridge University Press.

Stead, C. (2000) *Doctrine and Philosophy in Early Christianity*. Aldershot: Ashgate.

Taylor, J. (1882) *Journal of Discourses*. Volume 22. London: Latter-day Saints' Book Depot.

Young, F. M. with Teal, A. (2010) *From Nicaea to Chalcedon: A Guide to the Literature and Its Background*. 2nd edition. Grand Rapids: BakerAcademic.

4 Words and deeds against exclusion

Deprivation, activism and religiosity in inner-city Birmingham

Christian Karner and David Parker

Introduction

In 2010 lampposts topped by surveillance cameras appeared in parts of Birmingham, Britain's second largest city. Unannounced, strategically placed at traffic intersections and along main roads, the cameras initially caused bemusement. The camera system, codenamed 'Project Champion', comprised over 200 devices explicitly targeted around two areas of mainly Muslim residence. The objective of the scheme was to 'Create a vehicle movement "net" around two distinct geographical areas within the city of Birmingham [and]) Capture . . . CCTV evidence' (Thames Valley Police 2010: 7). In response, local people soon expressed anger at public meetings in June and July 2010 at being stigmatized for being Muslim, their neighbourhoods portrayed as a seedbed for terrorism plots (Lewis 2010). Following a campaign uniting civil libertarians and concerned local residents, the cameras – part of what turned out to be a surveillance system funded by the UK government's counter-terrorism budget – were covered with bags pending a review in the face of public disquiet. In one local resident's words, 'the blue bags over the cameras look like suspects when they are interned'. In December 2010, the system's removal without having been switched on was sanctioned by the local police force that had spent £3m on its installation, with all the cameras removed by summer 2011.

We open with this example of how a population countered a surveillance system to show how the relationship between religion and power encompasses the interface between local space, the state and technologies of remote monitoring. In an era where communities are distinguished by the style in which they are surveilled (also see Fiske 2000), some religious faith is equated with greater risk of terrorism and becomes the basis for the attempted installation of a centrally held database of all vehicle movements into and out of a locality.

In this chapter, we reflect on our ongoing qualitative research in Alum Rock, one of the two areas in inner-city Birmingham covered by the cameras, to examine the complex local intersections of religiosity, power and inequality. Following an outline of the theoretical context to the argument developed below as well as of our research location and methods, we discuss the following thematic foci emerging from our data: social actors' complex emotional investments in a 'troubled' locality that is simultaneously experienced as 'home'; the local significance of religiosity in fostering resilience in the face of deprivation; and the discursive significance of religion in interpretative frameworks used to make sense of (local) frustrations and perceived social ills. We then conclude by very briefly returning to the implications of the above-mentioned 'Project Champion' and local opposition to it and offer some reflections on how this may feed into the contemporary and interdisciplinary study of urban religiosity.

Theoretical context

In *Death, Ritual and Belief*, Douglas Davies detects in the 'words against death' uttered particularly in the context of funerary rites a 'way people transform the given facts of biological life into values and goals of humanity' (1997: vii). Invoking Maurice Bloch's (1992) theory of 'rebounding violence' and its underlying notion of a 'transcendental order', which echoes conceptualizations of religion as premised on diverse understandings of – and approaches to – a 'superplausible', 'transcendent other', an 'ultimate reality' or 'ultimate moral authority' (Davies 2011: 7, 67, 241), Davies analyses how the end of a biological life is discursively and socially utilized to 'gain a sense of power which motivates ongoing life' (1997: 1). Crucially, however, this is not a one-sided engagement with the discursive (and more or less self-conscious) aspects of religious life, but it reflects Davies' general and often reemphasized appreciation of religions requiring *both* words *and* deeds, language and ideas as much as ritual and embodiment. In a later formulation, Davies (2007: 313) thus emphasizes the value of 'exploring diverse modes of participation in religious ideas' such as the 'complementary topics of embodiment . . . and philosophical enquiry'. Located on a 'knowledge continuum', philosophical enquiry and embodiment imply different degrees of implicated consciousness or lack thereof, which warrant detailed attention in their own right. Elsewhere, we are reminded of how the appeal or efficacy of ritual or embodiment often outweigh those offered by reflection and debate, especially in emotionally charged circumstances:

> [R]eligious responses to life experience regularly address the problematic, troubling, bizarre and contradictory aspects of life, providing an enclosure for, and a mode of response to, them. It is this ability to respond to problematic areas through action that furnishes an extremely powerful adaptive feature of human life. When philosophy fails, ritual may succeed.
>
> (Davies 2002: 15)

In this chapter, we ask whether Davies' insights can be meaningfully extended to another arena, in which religious words and deeds arguably also effect a transformation for those articulating or participating in them: do the residents of a deprived, ethno-religiously diverse inner-city area of Birmingham, in which we have been conducting research for the last seven years, utilize religious words and practices in order to respond to the 'given facts' of their social (rather than biological) life? And if so, which 'values and goals' are being affirmed in the process? Finally, what are the implications of this for the sociological study of religion? In what follows we analyze parts of our data collected in the Alum Rock area of inner-city Birmingham by building on key arguments Davies develops in his recent discussion of *Emotion, Identity and Religion* (2011). These central conceptual threads pertain to the emotional significance of specific localities – or 'home' – and the particular relevance of religion in late modern urban settings; to the importance of 'hope' and often, though not invariably, religiously underpinned resilience in the face of deprivation and suffering; and to the discursive uses of the category 'religion' in people's attempts to explain the divergences of 'realities' from 'ideals', or what Davies terms the 'unsatisfactoriness of life' (2011: 75).

In addition to the theoretical connections we draw in what follows, this chapter also resonates with another aspect of Davies' wide-ranging activities throughout his career. For a number of years Douglas Davies acted as a Trustee for the St. Martin's Trust, a charity supporting the activities of the Anglican Church in Birmingham.[1] Our research, and the resulting discussion presented in this chapter, into religious beliefs, activities and organizations prominent in Alum Rock thus also echoes geographically Davies' philanthropic work beyond the academy, as well as in terms of our shared interest in the public, civil societal manifestations and workings of religiosity. Before exploring these and related issues, however, we turn to an outline of our ongoing research in Saltley, Alum Rock.

Researching Alum Rock

The population of the Alum Rock area east of Birmingham's city centre, and part of the Washwood Heath ward, comprises a South Asian majority (mainly of Pakistani and Bengali descent), a minority of longstanding white English, Irish and Afro-Caribbean working-class residents, more recently arrived Somali refugees and eastern/central European migrants. In terms of the religious categories employed in the 2011 census, 77 per cent of residents of the Washwood Heath ward self-defined as Muslim and 12 per cent as Christian. Applying categories of ethnicity, the 2011 Census recorded 57 per cent of the local population as Pakistani, 6.5 per cent Bangladeshi, 1.9 per cent Indian, 8.7 per cent 'Other Asian', 12.3 per cent as White, 8.7 per cent as Black, 2.8 per cent as Mixed, and 1.8 per cent as belonging to 'other ethnic groups' (Office for National Statistics 2016a). Alum Rock in particular ranks among the most deprived parts of the UK, with local average life expectancy seven years below that in affluent suburbs only a few miles away (Birmingham Public Health Network 2005), and a recent report on wealth distribution in Britain estimating half the local population to be living in breadline poverty (Dorling et al. 2007: 50). More widely, households in the Washwood Heath ward have the lowest income in all of Birmingham, 94 per cent of the ward's population live within the 5 per cent most deprived neighbourhoods in the country, and in April 2013, Job Seekers Allowance claimants in the Washwood Heath ward constituted 11.0 per cent of the working-age population, and in June 2016, out-of-work benefit claimants in the Washwood Heath Ward constituted 6.4 percent of the working-age population (Office for National Statistics 2016b). External media representations have almost invariably depicted Alum Rock in particular as fostering 'parallel lives' (for example, in the context of the widely reported arrests of several local men on terror-related charges in January 2007) and as qualifying as a 'no-go-area' for (white) non-Muslims (e.g. Nazir-Ali 2008; Harrison 2008). Most recently, this has manifested in media headlines pertaining to a 21-year-old man from the area being charged with terrorism offences (Birmingham Mail 2012b) and to 'Guns and gangs fear after man shot in Alum Rock' (Birmingham Mail 2012a).

In this chapter, and extending our previous research (Karner and Parker 2008, 2011; Parker and Karner 2010, 2011), we draw mainly on some 80 extended semi-structured interviews conducted in Alum Rock between 2006 and 2012 with a variety of local residents and entrepreneurs of different ethnic/religious backgrounds, whose homes, businesses or places of worship are (or previously have been) near the main commercial artery, the Alum Rock Road. Our interviewees have also included two local councillors, activists and religious spokespeople (from different strands of Islam and Christian denominations). Focusing on local biographies and the quotidian, our interviews centre on people's experiences of living or working in the area, their responses to media representations of the locality, the significance of religious and ethnic boundaries as well as their everyday negotiation in Alum Rock, interviewees' thoughts on local politics, and their feelings, hopes and visions for the area. Other methods of data collection employed in our research have included ethnographic immersion in various local organizations (e.g. in an inter-faith network, a neighbourhood association, a local football team) and social historical research focused on various cultural representations that have emerged from the locality since the period of initial South Asian migration to, and settlement in, the area in the 1950s and 1960s (see Parker and Karner 2011).

Before turning to three particular themes recurring in our data, it should be stressed that this research was not initially conceived as a study in the sociology of religion. We started this research committed to understanding a locality, its deprivations, identity politics and everyday struggles. As such, we have attempted to avoid the trappings of treating an ethnic or religious group, a priori, as the central or only unit of analysis (see Levitt and Glick Schiller 2007). Seven years of interviews and ethnographic engagement with Alum Rock have shown time and again that while the locality cannot be understood without paying close attention to religious beliefs, practices, boundaries and identity politics, the area cannot be reduced to religiosity – as external, often derogatory representations of the area tend to do – either. This, as we argue below, strengthens the case *for* a 'locality approach' (also see Karner and Parker 2012), capable of researching *across* ethno-religious boundaries, and *against* a community study confined by such boundaries. As such, this analysis runs against the grain of 'congregational' (e.g. Cavendish 2000; Green 2003; Marti 2008) or single ethnic/religious community studies (e.g. Khan 2000; Yukleyen 2009). Instead, we add to an existing body of work, important contributions to which have been made in the US (e.g. Lee 2006), the UK (e.g. Baumann 1996; Dench, Gavron and Young 2006; Knott 2009) and continental Europe alike (e.g. Tufte and Riis 2001), and which take a particular urban locality as a starting point for an investigation of the multiple identity negotiations and intra- as well as inter-group interactions unfolding there.Our particular contribution in this chapter lies in connecting such a 'locality approach' with Davies' recent work on the interfaces of religion and emotion.

At home in a 'troubled locality'

Echoing recent work on *Emotional Geographies* (Davidson, Bondi and Smith 2005), Douglas Davies (2011: 13) has commented on the profound emotional salience and meaning of 'some special place', with locations 'carrying deep religious significance' in countless people's biographies. While this echoes traditional religious studies' concerns with sacred spaces, it also manifests in profane places that, though part of the more mundane realm of the everyday, are no less significant for it. In this latter sphere of the quotidian, the emotional resonance of, and investment in, particular localities shows most clearly with regard to people's experiences of 'home', which Davies relates to 'the mutual commitment of support from familial others in familiar territory', to a shared (Bourdieusian) habitus, and a resultant 'sense of security, of being safe, and of sanctuary' (2011: 250).

In the context of Alum Rock, this raises important questions: (how) do local residents experience a place that suffers multiple deprivations as well as stigmatizing external representations as home? Is the locality, by those who know it as home, perceived as outsiders perceive and portray it? Conversely, and its negative external 'reputational geography' (Parker and Karner 2010) notwithstanding, does Alum Rock evoke positive emotions and enduring attachments among those 'born and bred' there? Our interview data includes ample evidence of a profound mismatch between the monolithic, invariably negative representations of Alum Rock by outsiders, on the one hand, and local residents' profound attachment to – and distinctly more positive, though rarely uncritical portrayal of – the area, on the other. The following extract from an interview with a prominent religious (in this instance Christian) figure in the area is a case in point:

> I'm not saying that it isn't an area with major problems, because it clearly is, and different problems from other parts of this city, but the perception that it's a no-go area, or that it's an unfriendly area, or that you won't be made welcome? If you want to be made welcome round here, you will be made welcome, and the welcome you'll get is a welcome you won't experience in other parts of the city, it's just so, so loving. That's not something from just the Afro-Caribbean community, it's from all communities, right the way across. We've got to remember that Saltley has always been the traditional landing-pad for new communities coming in.

Yet, rather than replacing Alum Rock's external representations as an alleged 'no-go-area' with a similarly reified, over-romanticized counter-image, there is considerable ambivalence in the sentiments and judgements offered by many locals. Rather than reproducing an unrealistically simplistic either-or logic (i.e. either a place offers opportunities *or* hopelessness, is experienced as a source of pride *or* shame), many of our interviewees have painted more nuanced pictures. In those, the locality's many problems and tensions are fully acknowledged, but so are people's deep-seated attachment and felt responsibility to the area, despite the odds:

> I've done youth and community work throughout my childhood there, and I know how many bright people there are, there are quite a few educated young people I've met who've gone off to university, and there are doctors, and people with Masters degrees, and there's actually a lot of potential in Alum Rock that isn't being focused on because of all the negative aspects [. . . To those who criticize Alum Rock . . .] I've said there's community work and youth work that happens in the area, and the people who live in Alum Rock, a lot of them love it, people who live in Alum Rock do love it, they don't like hearing bad about the area, and I've said, 'OK, if there's nothing else you can say about Alum Rock, I'm from Alum Rock, you know me as a person, you've known me for however many years, Alum Rock is part of my history and part of my life, say something bad about me'.
>
> ('Myra', local resident)

Further, there is a significant temporal dimension to some such more nuanced accounts. Articulating a discourse of loss and some nostalgia, several of our research participants have contrasted present-day Alum Rock with the area as they remember it from the 1970s or 1780s. This earlier era, they have argued, was a time of true and 'successful' multiculturalism. One Muslim family, for instance, spoke with affection of the Jewish family from which they bought their business in the 1970s:

When we first took over the Goldbergs told us where they were buying from, and surprisingly enough I don't think that kind of business would happen now because of the religious state of life. But they were 100% Jewish and we were 100% Muslim. The two could gel together like the way we did because there were no barriers put up. Everybody was open-minded.

('Riz', local businessman)

One long-standing local shopkeeper reflected on his experience of the 1970s:

There was a good Irish community, and West Indian, Asian was not that strong then, but it was good integration, there wasn't any tension or problems. There were obviously English people as well. I think everybody felt akin. If you were Irish, if you were West Indian, if you were Asian, you had your problems, but you always felt, "Well, we're all coming from the same background", so at the end of it we know the same feelings, so we've got to get on with each other as well.

('Ahmed')

Such findings strongly resonate with existing arguments about the emotions attached to particular places or memories of those places (e.g. Jones 2005), and with the realization (Parr, Philo and Burns 2005: 90) that being 'placed' involves a 'psychodynamic' that is shared rather than purely individual, structural rather than exclusively personal. Put differently, an understanding of the affective dimensions of space demands – in C. Wright Mills' spirit (1959) – the application of *The Sociological Imagination* capable of structurally contextualizing the biographical and of thereby understanding seemingly 'private troubles', or sentiments, as 'public issues'. Alum Rock, as any locality, confirms that 'neighbourhood[s] (. . .) [are] social formations[s] within which particular structures of feeling are produced' (Appadurai, quoted in Tufte and Riis 2001: 335).

On 'hope' and resilience

Experiencing a 'troubled locality' as a place of rich meaning and enduring emotional importance does not, of course, in itself predict how one responds to local difficulties and deprivations. It is with regard to this second dimension, people's interpretations of local problems and attempts to counter them, that religion assumes particular significance in Alum Rock. There are two strands in Davies' recent work that relate directly to some of our empirical findings pertaining to these very issues.

First, Davies detects a particular power in urban religiosity, which many an influential urban sociologist – both 'classical' (i.e. as in the case of much of the Chicago School of the inter-war period) and contemporary (e.g. Dear 2002) – have tended to overlook:

The mass of humanity now living in cities cannot be aware of the complex emotional lives of those passed daily in the street or even met at work. This is one reason why religious groups are important in urban life, providing space and time for sharing experiences, for evaluating them in moral terms and, often, for fostering positive goals despite the negativities of life . . . Such small-scale communities show the importance of contexts in which individuals may experience shared emotion in ways that are intelligible to others and conduce to a sense of meaning in life.

(Davies 2011: 184)

Without being reducible to such experiences of collective meaning and derived resilience, local religiosity – whether Muslim or Christian – in Alum Rock is indeed able to counteract the potential for urban anomie and fragmentation, as one local Christian minister argues:

We have a role to play here, and we have a role to play for the potential Christian community, but we have equally a role to play for those who aren't of our faith, in a supporting way, and showing that Christians and Muslims can work together . . . We can show a picture here of where very, very strong Christian views as within the Christian church can exist easily alongside other faiths, provided they're sensitive to the differences and respectful of those differences.

(Father 'Robert')

Rather than reflecting a general 'urbanism' that advances an atomization and 'secularization of life' (e.g. Wirth 1938), the institutional and everyday workings of Alum Rock derive much of their impetus and structure from religious organizations and networks (also see Karner and Parker 2008). Asked to comment on the local significance of religiosity, two key actors in two different local Christian congregations offered the following observations:

There's lots and lots of talk about Britain becoming a secular society. Personally I don't think it will ever be possible to understand communities like this one unless it's recognised . . . that religion with a small and big 'r' is a major issue and without understanding that communities like this can't be understood at all, and I think that would go for many comparable communities.

I would say the universal God has a much bigger part to play in everyday life than in other parts of the city . . . I couldn't imagine a Saltley or Washwood Heath without what is now such a diverse religious community, it just wouldn't work.

Significantly, observations such as these also relate, at least in part, to relationships and experiences that cross ethno-religious boundaries.

In currently fashionable terminology, such accounts reflect social capital both of the 'bonding', or intra-group, and of the 'bridging', or inter-group, kinds (Putnam 2000). Or, and without intending to simply invert the area's negative external portrayals with a similarly distorted, romantic counter-image that would overlook tensions and conflicts that certainly are part of the local life-world, Alum Rock also displays what Paul Gilroy (2004) terms 'conviviality': a taken-for-granted pluralism, which accepts or positively embraces diversity as intrinsic to contemporary multicultural living. Religious institutions, networks and initiatives are crucial to channelling and facilitating such conviviality, whether in the form of inter-faith initiatives, a religiously diverse neighbourhood association, or the everyday sharing of sacred space across religious boundaries (as in the case of a women's sewing group meeting in the local Methodist church).

The second strand in Davies' take on religious emotions highly pertinent in this context relates to what he terms the creation of 'hopeful meaningfulness':

> [A] major function of historical religions . . . involve[es] the management of human emotions in the face of life's sorrows and joys . . . [H]ope becomes an inescapable attitude that helps orient people towards their future activity by bringing a sense of significance to their current endeavours.
>
> (2011: 21–22)

Davies places particular emphasis on religious rituals in fostering such resilient hopefulness. While this echoes wider social theoretical insights into the largely unconscious psychological benefits of ritualized action in maintaining social actors' 'ontological security' (Giddens 1984), it is also of obvious empirical relevance to the numerous contemporary contexts, in which our era of 'liquid modernity' (Bauman 2000) has widened inequalities and intensified uncertainties, and to which – in turn – religious faith, networks and practices provide seemingly much-needed antidotes (see Karner and Aldridge 2004). However, our Alum Rock data also suggests that the link between religiosity and resilience in the face of adversity does not always and inevitably rely on rituals providing religious actors with ontological security on a barely noticed, semi-/unconscious level. On the contrary, some local activists cite – in positively self-reflexive manner – religion as the very reason why they are committed to working in and for the area:

> The teachings of Islam stay with a believer 24 hours a day, every step he takes. And that is true of me, that's how I look at it, here, at home, on the street and everywhere. It's not something that when I go to the mosque or I go to Friday prayers, so therefore Islam stays with me for just that half an hour, not when I come out of it.
>
> ('Majid', local resident)

I have fear of God in me, and anyone who holds a position of power and is educated, and can change things and who doesn't and sits back, when he goes up there he will be asked. Being a religious person, that scares the life out of me. I don't want to stand in front of Him and say that I could have done something and didn't, or I made the wrong decision for the community.

('Imran', local resident)

In appropriation of different strands of Davies' work, we may thus describe important aspects of religiously inspired or underpinned social action in Alum Rock as providing *words and deeds against the multiple effects of multiple deprivations*. What is more, such diverse reactions emanate from different points of the above-mentioned 'knowledge-continuum', stretching from self-consciously political actions (i.e. in the form of social activism) to highly ritualized behaviour and, correspondingly, implicating various degrees of consciousness or lack thereof.

Explaining local 'ills': 'religion' vs. 'culture'

Much religious practice is, of course, deeply embedded in people's biographies and daily lives, taken-for-granted and rarely explicitly spoken about. In wider social theoretical terms, religiosity of this kind is part of what Pierre Bourdieu (1977; also see Davies 2011: 275) describes as *doxa*, the 'universe of the undiscussed', or, in a similar vein, what Anthony Giddens (1984) defines as 'practical consciousness' enabling routinized action without yielding itself very easily to translations into, or explanations through, language. Alongside these highly significant though rarely explicitly problematized dimensions of religious life, however, religiosity also assumes – certainly in Alum Rock – distinctive discursive dimensions.

The category of 'religion' thus assumes a common sense-making function in the accounts local residents offer of the social changes that have profoundly affected the area over recent decades. Put slightly differently, *religion* provides recurring interpretative frames in the accounts of many of our research participants. The first form this assumes articulates the earlier mentioned discourse of nostalgic loss, which presents the period of the 1970s and 1980s as a golden era of 'real multiculturalism'; this, it is argued, has since gone into decline, a deterioration attributed to the rise of certain forms of religiosity and religious politics. One female resident dates the emergence of what she termed 'Islamism' to before the events of September 2001, citing the Iranian revolution and the Salman Rushdie affair as significant influences on the religious biographies of some of her relatives:

I watched one nephew of mine . . . he started going to a mosque . . . he was suddenly not even wearing Asian clothes, but the Arabic tunic, so suddenly religion was taking over. There were more religious shops, and what I saw was more and more the British Asians were . . . at first I thought they were immigrants . . . but then I saw more of the British Muslims starting to wear the beard, and the Asian clothes, and the Palestinian scarves.

('Sameena' local resident)

Certainly not all accounts of recent social changes in the area report or focus on alleged local inroads by forms of Islamic radicalism. Other Muslim residents have criticized the recent proliferation of mosques and madrasas of different devotional leanings in the area; this, it has been suggested to us, has produced a counter-productive form of religious fragmentation:

You have this huge mushrooming of religious places of worship, where religious priests have been shipped in from Pakistan because of their knowledge and experience. Once they've arrived here they've seen the potential, and built up their contacts . . . Some religious establishments have become almost like power bases, and if you own that or run that particular mosque, the people that come to your mosque and the activities that you do gives you this power base.

('Abraham', local resident)

I think the worst thing the British government did, or local authorities ever did, is giving permission for so many mosques to open up, and I'm a Muslim saying this. I was talking to an elderly man and he said this to me, 'They destroyed our community with these mosques.' He goes, 'This is not Islam, what have they done to it?' What's happened is that these people are promoting their own brand of Islam. Everybody's got their own brand.

('Bilal', local resident)

The second recurring discursive function religion performs in the narratives of some of our research participants also bemoans the status quo but employs the categories of religious belief and practice very differently. In these accounts the social ills affecting Alum Rock, are attributed to the absence of religiosity or of what is presented as the 'right kind of religiosity':

Now, there's a lot of things happening that bear no resemblance, no correlation whatsoever to the teachings of Islam. Most of these people claim to be Muslims, but the tragedy is, the tragedy that I know, and it's not going to go away . . . is that just by saying that I'm a Muslim and going to the mosque, doesn't make anybody a better Muslim than anybody else. . . . If people knew the basic responsibilities, the very basic responsibilities and teachings [of Islam], honestly Alum Rock and Saltley would be a far better world to live in.

('Abdul', local resident)

Another key observation contained in Davies' *Emotion, Identity and Religion* is highly relevant here, concerning religiously informed responses to the perceived 'unsatisfactoriness of life':

> Experiences of misfortune, disappointment, shame and illness all reflect the many ways in which human identity is felt to be fractured or life circumstances problematic, with a major function of religions then consisting in answering these concerns.
>
> (Davies 2011: 74–75)

In Alum Rock, one recurring manifestation of this is encountered in how some local residents explain the divergences between the ideals they orient their lives towards and the realities they live with. In a prominent discourse in the area, people juxtapose 'religion' and 'culture' as mutually exclusive discursive-interpretative categories: while the former, religion, thereby stands for the ideal of the right(eous) way of living life, 'culture' is blamed for people's shortcomings and the many problems experienced in the area. While religion is positively connoted, culture is used as an interpretative device for explaining what is wrong in Alum Rock. The following accounts exemplify this:

> Most of the Asian councillors – they win the seats on the grounds of family clan, rather than on the grounds of being elected as the right candidate – I mean that if you belong to a certain tribe. These Kashmiri or Pakistani people they have tribal structures, for example there will be a Raja or a Chaudhry, or some other tribe, but if my majority is the Chaudhrys, who are in the majority. Most of the councillors are Chaudhrys.
>
> ('Ihsan', local resident)

> Some of the present, emerging future leaders, movers and shakers, everyone's got hidden agendas, but some of them are roped up in the old schools of thinking, the old clanships unfortunately and those clanships are beginning to play out their negative effects even among people in their 20s, 30s and 40s. So the present councillors, they're all on a clan basis, and because they're on a clan basis they've had to make their compromises and go with the clan mentality to give the skips, facilitate the planning applications and all the rest of it . . . And that's one of the things which has resulted in people moving out and disengaging with change in this area. Potential good, honest, sincere leadership has moved away because of this kind of environment, there is a more sinister side.
>
> ('Zaheer', local resident)

'Zaheer' also spoke of what he saw as an emerging religious 'regeneration and reinvigoration' drawing on Islamic tradition with a specifically Sufi inflection encouraging service to the wider community:

One of the things I've noticed here, and in other areas of the city, is a contribution to society element . . . One of the things is that this whole issue of service to humanity is quite deeply ingrained in Islamic teaching . . . but there's this movement and I think more of it falls within a Sufi domain . . . there's this element of social welfare and of contribution back to humanity . . . and I think in my opinion it has grown for the better, because I think it tends to disseminate tolerant views, and it tends to also facilitate change with patience and compassion.

('Zaheer', local resident)

In other words, 'culture' in the guise of allegiances described as 'tribal' or based on 'clan' is portrayed as the realm of human misunderstanding, misdirection and shortcomings. 'Religion', by contrast, is associated with a divinely sanctioned blueprint for the ideal life. Importantly, this also provides religion with the 'disruptive' potential (also see Smith 1996) to inspire social change and political activism, thus challenging the common conflation of religion with tradition and structural reproduction. Were it not for cultural misunderstandings and constraints, we may paraphrase such discourses, people would be able to live more righteous lives and areas such as Alum Rock would be better off.

In terms of the analysis of such data, this presents somewhat of a conundrum: if or how to attempt to resolve a potential contradiction between the two layers of what Anthony Giddens describes as the 'double hermeneutic' (1984: 284) intrinsic to social analysis; while the first hermeneutical layer relates to social actors' interpretations of, and meanings given to, their lives, the second layer pertains to the analyst's 'second-order' interpretations of insiders' local discourses. Returning to our data reported above, this double hermeneutic includes the potential for a contradiction between emic categories and meanings and our meta-interpretations of those to arise. On the one hand, as we have seen, the distinction between 'culture' and 'religion' is crucial to the interpretative frameworks employed by some local residents in making sense of their local lives and frustrations. On the other hand, and to quote Davies once more, though we know that 'in complex societies religion is often differentiated from other aspects of social life, we reiterate the fact that religion is a difficult entity to define and to separate out from many other aspects of human activity' (2011: 186). This reemphasizes the value of the aforementioned 'locality approach' informing our work, to which we return by way of a conclusion to this discussion and which offers a possible means of 'thinking our way through' such analytical tensions.

Concluding remarks

Alum Rock, with its deprivations and resilience, can only be understood through a serious engagement with the centrality of religious faith and networks in the lives of many of its residents. As we have argued in this chapter, there are several crucial dimensions to the local significance of religiosity. These include its ability to inspire hope in an area that is both 'troubled' and a 'home' with all the associated emotional resonance; to motivate activism in the face of deprivation; and to provide central categories in various interpretative frameworks employed to make sense of local problems or, more generally, of the 'unsatisfactoriness of life' (Davies 2011: 75). Yet, and all this having been said, Alum Rock cannot be reduced to the local importance of religion either, as indeed those external commentators alleging religiously underpinned 'parallel lives' in the locality tend to do. The simultaneous importance of the non-religious in Alum Rock was reflected, for example, in local opposition to the earlier mentioned and enormously controversial 'Project Champion'. This opposition was not led by religious organizations but, feeling targeted as a security risk on the grounds of religious faith, was allied to the secular vocabulary of civil rights violations in the campaign against the cameras.[2]

A more helpful approach to understanding Alum Rock must start with an acknowledgement of the multiple forms of social action and diverse institutions, both religious and non-religious, that shape the area: mosques, madrasas, churches and inter-faith groups; neighbourhood associations and youth clubs; convivial, conflictual as well as ambivalent encounters and relationships in the spheres of business, work, education and quotidian interaction. These local entanglements of the religious, the inter-religious and the non-religious justify and strengthen the case for a 'locality approach', which – rather than pre-defining religious or ethnic groups as *a priori* units of analysis – aims to capture as many kinds of relationships and interactions occurring in (but also transcending) a particular locality. Through such a 'spatially-informed approach to the study of religion in locality', we may indeed hope to 'reconnect' religion with other aspects and dimensions of social and cultural life (Knott 2009: 154, 159). In a similar vein, Tufte and Riis have argued (2001: 332–333) that a localized and distinctly 'multiethnic approach' to our ethno-religiously diverse inner-cities enables us to avoid 'essentializing culture' and to thereby sidestep what Paul Gilroy (2004) describes as 'the problem of ethnic absolutism'. As this discussion has shown, a more nuanced, less reified and distinctly local approach derives important conceptual momentum from Douglas Davies' work on the interfaces of *Emotion, Identity and Religion*. Further, and as part of this theoretical borrowing, a locality approach also furnishes a possible answer to the hermeneutical conundrum mentioned in the previous section: i.e. the seeming contradiction between a local discourse that insists on separating 'culture' from 'religion' and the analytical realization that, in historical terms and indeed in terms of people's everyday practices, this distinction is hard and sometimes impossible to maintain. In examining the many lived entanglements of the religious with the non-religious, a locality approach echoes Davies in appreciating that there is much more to social and religious life than 'philosophical enquiry' (or discourse); a complementary focus on embodiment, ritual, and multi-faceted lived identities is indeed urgently needed.

Notes

1 http://www.charityperformance.com/charity-details.php?id=17885
2 http://spyonbirmingham.blogspot.com

References

Bauman, Z. (2000) *Liquid Modernity*. Cambridge: Polity Press.
Baumann, G. (1996) *Contesting Culture*. Cambridge: Cambridge University Press.
Birmingham Mail (2012a) 'Guns and gangs fear after man shot in Alum Rock'. Available at: http://www.birminghammail.net/news/top-stories/2012/04/20/guns-and-gangs-fear-after-man-shot-in-alum-rock-97319-30802519/ (Accessed 20 April 2012).
Birmingham Mail (2012b) 'Birmingham Man Charged with Terror Offences'. Available at: http://www.birminghammail.net/news/top-stories/2012/05/01/birmingham-man-charged-with-terrorism-offences-97319-30880545/ (Accessed 1 May 2012).
Birmingham Public Health Network (2005) *Birmingham New Ward Health Data: Washwood Heath*. Birmingham: Birmingham Public Health Network.
Bloch, M. (1992) *Prey into Hunter*. Cambridge: Cambridge University Press.
Bourdieu, P. (1977) *Outline of a Theory of Practice*. Cambridge: Cambridge University Press.
Cavendish, J. (2000) 'Church-based community activism: A comparison of black and white Catholic congregations', *Journal for the Scientific Study of Religion* 39(1): 64–77.
Davidson, J., Bondi, L. and Smith, M. (eds) (2005) *Emotional Geographies*. Aldershot: Ashgate.
Davies, D. (1997) *Death, Ritual and Belief*. London: Cassell.
Davies, D. (2002) *Anthropology and Theology*. Oxford: Berg
Davies, D. (2007) 'Mormon history, text, colour, and rites', *Journal of Religious History* 31(3): 305–315.
Davies, D. (2011) *Emotion, Identity and Religion: Hope, Reciprocity, and Otherness*. Oxford: Oxford University Press.
Dear, M. (2002) 'Los Angeles and the Chicago School: invitation to a debate', *City and Community* 1(1): 5–32.
Dench, G., Gavron, K. and Young, M. (2006) *The New East End: Kinship, Race and Conflict*. London: Profile Books.
Dorling, D. et al. (2007) *Poverty, Wealth and Place in Britain: 1968–2005*. Bristol: Policy Press.
Fiske, R. (2000) 'White watch', in S. Cottle (ed.) *Ethnic Minorities and the Media*. Buckingham: Open University Press, pp. 55–66.
Giddens, A. (1984) *The Constitution of Society*. Cambridge: Polity Press.
Gilroy, P. (2004) *After Empire*. London: Routledge.
Green, J. (2003) 'A liberal dynamo: the political activism of the Unitarian-Universalist clergy', *Journal for the Scientific Study of Religion* 42(4): 577–590.
Harrison, D. (1 June 2008) 'Christian preachers face arrest in Birmingham', *Sunday Telegraph*, p. 16.

Jones, O. (2005) 'An ecology of emotion, memory, self and landscape', in J. Davidson, L. Bondi and M. Smith (eds) *Emotional Geographies*. Aldershot: Ashgate, pp. 205–218.

Karner, C. and Aldridge, A. (2004) 'Theorizing religion in a globalizing world', *International Journal of Politics, Culture and Society* 18(1–2): 5–32.

Karner, C. and Parker, D. (2008) 'Religion versus Rubbish: deprivation and social capital in inner city Birmingham', *Social Compass* 55(4): 517–531.

Karner, C. and Parker, D. (2011) 'Conviviality and conflict: pluralism, resilience and hope in inner-city Birmingham', *Journal of Ethnic and Migration Studies* 37(3): 355–372.

Karner, C. and Parker, D. (2012) 'Religious and non-religious practices and the city', *Diskus: The Journal of the British Association for the Study of Religion* 13: 27–48. Available at: http://www.basr.ac.uk/diskus/diskus13/KarnerParker.pdf (Accessed 3 August 2016).

Khan, Z. (2000) 'Muslim presence in Europe: The British dimension – identity, integration and community activism', *Current Sociology* 48(4): 29–43.

Knott, K. (2009) 'From locality to location and back again: A spatial journey in the study of religion', *Religion* 39(2): 154–160.

Lee, J. (2006) 'Constructing race and civility in urban America', *Urban Studies* 43(5–6): 903–917.

Levitt, P. and Schiller, N. G. (2007) 'Conceptualizing simultaneity: a transnational social field perspective on society', in A. Portes and J. DeWind (eds) *Rethinking Migration*. New York and Oxford: Berghahn Books, pp. 181–218.

Lewis, P. (4 June 2010) 'Surveillance cameras spring up in Muslim areas – the targets? terrorists', *The Guardian*. Available at: http://www.guardian.co.uk/uk/2010/jun/04/birmingham-surveillance-cameras-muslim-community (Accessed 4 August 2016).

Marti, G. (2008) 'Fluid ethnicity and ethnic transcendence in multiracial churches', *Journal for the Scientific Study of Religion* 47(1): 11–16.

Mills, C. W. (1959) *The Sociological Imagination*. New York: Oxford University Press.

Nazir-Ali, M. (6 January 2008) 'Extremism has flourished as Britain has lost its faith in a Christian vision', *Sunday Telegraph*, p. 4.

Office for National Statistics (2013) 'Official labour market statistics for the Washwood Heath Ward'. Available at: http://www.nomisweb.co.uk/reports/lmp/ward/1308627825/report.aspx?town=washwood heath.

Office for National Statistics (2016a) 'Neighbourhood statistics for the Washwood Heath Ward on ethnic group'. Available at: http://www.neighbourhoodstatistics.gov.uk (Accessed 4 August 2016).

Office for National Statistics (2016b) 'Official labour market statistics for the Washwood Heath Ward'. Available at: https://www.nomisweb.co.uk/reports/lmp/ward2011/1140857490/report.aspx?town=washwood%20heath (Accessed 4 August 2016).

Parker, D. and Karner, C. (2010) 'Reputational geographies and urban social cohesion', *Ethnic and Racial Studies* 33(8): 1451–1470.

Parker, D. and Karner, C. (2011) 'Remembering the Alum Rock Road: reputational geographies and spatial biographies', *Midland History* 36(2): 292–309.

Parr, H., Philo, C. and Burns, N. (2005) '"Not a display of emotions": emotional geographies in the Scottish highlands', in J. Davidson, L. Bondi and M. Smith (eds) *Emotional Geographies*. Aldershot: Ashgate, pp. 87–102.

'Police Authority "Trust and Confidence" Meeting Backfires'. http://spyon
birmingham.blogspot.co.uk/2010/08/police-authority-trust-and-confidence.html
(Accessed 4 August 2016).

Putnam, R. (2000) *Bowling Alone*. New York: Simon and Schuster.

Smith, C. (ed.) (1996) *Disruptive Religion*. New York: Routledge.

Thames Valley Police (2010) *Project Champion Review*. Available at: http://www.
statewatch.org/news/2010/oct/uk-project-champion-police-report.pdf (Accessed
4 August 2016).

Tufte, T. and Riis, M. (2001) 'Cultural fields, communication and ethnicity:
public libraries and ethnic media supply in a neighbourhood of Copenhagen',
International Communication Gazette 63(4): 331–350.

Wirth, L. (1938) 'Urbanism as a way of life', *American Journal of Sociology* 44(1):
1–24.

Yukleyen, A. (2009) 'Localizing Islam in Europe: religious activism among Turkish
Islamic organizations in the Netherlands', *Journal of Muslim Minority Affairs*
29(3): 291–309.

Part II
Ritual, symbolism and identity

5   Religion and ritual markers between the public and the private
Funerary rites in Sweden

Anders Bäckström

Rites are both private and public[1]

In this chapter, I will consider the place and development of funerary rites in Sweden and also discuss attitudes towards death in late modern society. This will be done in conversation with Douglas Davies' reasoning on *Death, Ritual and Belief* (1997) and his more recent studies on the new spirituality, which is part of what he calls a second wave of secularization in Britain. This is what we in Uppsala have called a new visibility of religion, part of a new social and religious plurality that has created a need for a negotiation of values connected to identity and belief (Bäckström 2014). In relation to earlier studies, primarily those undertaken in Sweden, I will argue that rites and places of quality function both in traditional and new ways as arenas between the private and the public and that rites performed at the end of life bind together the private life of the individual with a collective and regulated public society in a particular manner. In the Nordic countries the majority churches still function as stewards of a collective memory made explicit in relation to death, burials and crises. At the same time, it is possible to see that personally shaped rites are developed within the frameworks of burial services. A growing emphasis on the personal aspects of the rite can be regarded as an adjustment to late modern values focussing on the body and personal identity. This emphasis can also be interpreted as indicating a need for secular institutions to pay greater attention to a religiosity that is increasingly defined as spirituality.

I write this chapter in the context of the research agenda on Religion and Society which is to be found in Europe today and which is present at Uppsala University through the ten-year research programme entitled 'The Impact of Religion: Challenges for Society, Law and Democracy (2008–2018)'.[2] This research focuses on the new visibility of religion in an increasingly diverse society. Growing social and religious diversity has increasingly thrown into question a previously self-evident relationship between the religious and the private and the secular and the public. Casanova (1994) questioned such a one-sided theory of secularization and promoted instead an 'American' idea of civil society as a public arena for religion. There is also, within the research on the visibility of religion, an idea that religion is returning to public discourse as a partner in the renegotiation of future values and therefore could recover its social role. Habermas (2006, 2008), who has, among others, proposed this idea believes, however, that a religiously inspired discourse has to conform to the language of the secular society in order to become recognized as valid. This makes the whole idea of the participation of religion in public debate on its own merits unclear (Beckford 2010). The point is rather that religion never has disappeared from public life in the way that secularization theory predicted (Beckford 2012; Joas 2014). Funeral rites, with their ability to adjust to views of death that are consistent with modern society, are a good example of the capacity of religion to survive in public life. Funeral rites, with their religious content, even if only vaguely expressed, therefore challenge the implicit assumption of much scholarship that a European distinction between the religious and the secular is a necessary consequence of the development of the modern world (Berger, Davie and Fokas 2008: 48).

The role of funeral rites

Funeral rites oscillate between the public and the private. *On the one hand*, one can see that funeral rites are publicly regulated as part of the organization of a particular society concerning the handling of the dead. In fact, nine authorities are involved when an individual dies in Sweden (Möller 2011: 6), and the public management of the burial business has always been delegated to the Church of Sweden. Even after the reform of Church–State relationships in 2000, the Church of Sweden was entrusted with responsibility for the burial enterprise including the care of graveyards (which in Sweden are public parks and well cared for). A special levy to cover the costs of this was introduced in 2000, which all citizens have to pay (regardless of whether they are members of the Church). This role can be regarded as a welfare service which the state has delegated to the Church of Sweden, and it can also be regarded as a prolongation of Church–State relations after the year 2000. This makes the Church of Sweden a manager of a collective memory alongside other institutions in Swedish society.

On the other hand, the World Value Survey (Inglehart 1997) shows that the populations of the Nordic countries are among the most individualized in the world, with a strong emphasis on quality of life and the value of freedom. The development of private life is more important than social coherence. A secular condition, in the words of Charles Taylor (2007), predominates in the Nordic countries. This means that beliefs are strongly deregulated and transferred to the individual. This does not only concern beliefs connected to religions, but also political ideologies (Bjereld and Demker 2011). This is a deregulation which can, paradoxically, be regarded as a welfare service as it contributes to the integrity of the individual. Funerary rites are thus located within the field of tension between collective values, which are legitimated by the welfare state, and individual values that concern personal identities. This makes them particularly interesting to study.

England and Sweden, both similar and dissimilar

When the Swedish situation is analysed and compared to the English one, it is important to remember that during the twentieth century Sweden has developed a much clearer state-oriented welfare system where the Church of Sweden is, through laws passed in 1930 and 1998, regulated through a specially organized legal structure more similar to official institutions than to voluntary organizations (Thidevall 2000). This is indicated by the continued presence of the political parties as decision-making entities within the Church's structure. This is totally unknown in England where decision making within the Anglican Church is built up according to a synodical structure (Welsby 1985). Esping-Andersen (1990) shows, in his ground-breaking study on European welfare regimes, that the English welfare system can be regarded as a liberal voluntary system which can be more easily compared with the United States and New Zealand than with the Nordic countries. Similarities with the Nordic countries can be found within the health care system and in the established natures of the respective Churches with the Queen and King respectively as formal figureheads of the Churches (Middlemiss LéMon 2015). Differences are marked by the fact that the economy of both social care and the Church in England is based more on voluntary work and donations than is the case in Sweden, although we are currently witnessing a deregulation and privatization of public institutions in Sweden which partly mirrors British developments (Olofsson 2013; Hort 2014).

Both countries are today affected by global neo-liberal capitalism, which focuses on consumption and treats consumerism as identity-conferring (Bauman 2007; Martikainen and Gauthier 2013). The neo-liberal development has, however, had a number of varying outcomes depending on different historical backgrounds where the state plays different roles. This is one of the reasons, according to Grace Davie (2012), why the national aspect of the anchorage of religion is more clear in the Nordic countries (and on the continent) while a New Age-inspired, more free-floating spirituality, partly based on economic thinking, is more visible in the English context (Woodhead 2012). This situation is also mirrored when it comes to the place and content of rites where the emphasis in the two countries is slightly different, despite similarities of contexts composed of established Churches alongside private spirituality.

Church ceremony as rite

The tradition of burials and conceptions surrounding death, and life after death, have been investigated in several studies in Sweden, based in Uppsala and Lund. I will refer to some of their findings in order to illustrate the theoretical reasoning above and also link to Douglas Davies' own studies. According to Reimers (1995: 138), rites can be defined as '. . . recurring, culturally transmitted formalised actions which involve a group of people. They have a dramatic, performative character; they are justified by reference to authority and express a symbolic representation of a dimension which in some sense is viewed as supra-individual and timeless, i.e. in some sense transcendent'. By saying that the rite is performative, Reimers means that persons who participate in a rite expect to encounter an immediate effect from it. This effect has to be something that can be experienced.

Given the above definition, it is interesting to ask whether Swedish citizens really use the services offered by the Church of Sweden as rites and what meaning they attach to them. Before reporting the results it is important to remember that about 65 per cent of the population of Sweden are members of the Church of Sweden (according to 2014 figures). They pay an annual fee to the Church which is collected by the tax authorities.[3] It is also important to note that 78 per cent of all burials take place according to a Church of Sweden ritual (2013).

In a study of Church ceremonies (Bäckström 2004), the following question was asked: 'How important do you think it is to have a Church or religious ceremony when one wishes to celebrate a birth, a marriage or a death?' By formulating the question in this way, it was hoped that the ritual character of the services offered by the Church would emerge. In the questionnaire, respondents were able to indicate by means of a seven-point scale whether they considered the ceremony important (5–7) or less important (1–3). The results show that 78 per cent, a clear majority of the population, consider a Church or religious burial service to be important when a close relative dies. Thus, a majority of the population want the rite to take place in a Church or in a religious context. It should be observed that the findings are not based on a direct question, but rather on a combined weighting of results according to a seven-point scale. It is therefore the tendency which is of interest here, not the exact percentage figure.

Personal relationships and Church ceremony

The second question in the study aimed at more directly investigating the significance of Church ceremonies for the individual. The question was as follows: 'Different phenomena and events which are linked to Churches and religious communities have different importance for different people. With the help of the scale, is it possible for you to indicate how important the following things are for you personally?' The possible answers included burial. The respondents once more indicated on a scale from 1 to 7 the Church ceremonies which had great or little significance for them.

The findings largely agree with the data discussed earlier. When the question is posited in terms of the significance of a burial service for the respondents personally, 70 per cent indicate that it is of importance. It is obvious that a burial is looked upon as a fitting form of saying farewell even if not all, and young people in particular, are able to associate burial with experiences of a positive nature.

The meaning of Church burial

The third question concerns the sample population's view of the content of Church burials. The question was as follows: 'Which of the following statements about Church burial corresponds most closely to your own view?' The answers were formulated so as to ascertain the various ways of perceiving the burial service, whether as a civil ceremony, a Church or cultural tradition, or a religious-theological ceremony. The results were as follows (the statement is followed by the percentage of respondents who agreed with the statement): (1) A Church burial is a fitting way of taking leave of the deceased, but the belief which is expressed in this context is not particularly important; 29 per cent. (2) A Church burial is the way in which in Sweden one usually takes leave of the deceased and it is a valuable tradition; 48 per cent. (3) A Church burial implies that the act of taking leave of the deceased is given a Christian form; 9 per cent. (4) A Church burial signifies that one affirms the Christian hope of resurrection and eternal life; 14 per cent.

The results show that 48 per cent consider burial to be a valuable tradition and constitutes the 'normal' way of taking leave of the dead, about one-quarter ascribe a religious/theological meaning to burial with an emphasis on the notion of resurrection and 29 per cent look upon the burial service as a fitting way of saying farewell, which does not necessarily carry any religious overtones. It is looked upon virtually as a civil act. The results, thus, show that about 70 per cent of the Swedish population accept the religious or collective cultural function of the burial ceremony. This implies that a majority of the Swedish adult population look upon burial as a basic rite which should preferably take place within a Church context. It should, however, be noted that these data were collected some 10 years ago. It is therefore possible that the figures are now lower as figures of attendance at Church of Sweden ceremonies have decreased somewhat over the decade. The general picture is, however, the same (Bromander 2011).

Experiences of quality in funeral rites

These quantitative results were followed up in a qualitative study in 2006 in Uppsala, where 20 widows and widowers were interviewed about their experiences of the burial service of a close deceased relative (Wiig-Sandberg 2006). Those interviewed represented a cross-section of Swedes according to belief. One widow was 50 years old and the rest about 70 years or older. The results of the interviews have been sorted into categories and show:

1   that the relatives conceive of the burial service as a manifestation of the will of the departed and that the burial service is therefore informed by the personality of the departed and his/her possible life after death;

2   that the relatives focus on the ability of the funeral service to help them through their grief by emphasizing the importance of the site and the presence of the relatives as supporters in a liminal situation. The clergyperson is also important as leader of the liturgical drama and the person who speaks about the deceased person;

3   that relatives are most likely to experience quality in a burial service when it is anchored both in the present culture of the country and expresses freedom of choice (which is a strong cultural value);

4   that the burial service is perceived as part of a longer process, which starts at the bed of the sick and ends at the funeral (or occasionally at the burial of ashes).

From this perspective, the funeral rites can provide an experience of quality if there is a clear relationship between the values of the producer and the user of a burial ceremony. Wiig-Sandberg (2006: 82) argues that this quality is manifest if there is (a) a balance between the feelings of renewal engendered by the rite and its ability to shape social change; (b) a balance between the feelings of security in tradition and an experienced freedom of choice; and (c) a balance between closeness and distance, i.e. the capacity of the clergy to transfer personal closeness to the deceased with the result that the relatives of the departed can distance themselves and dare to lose control in the liminal situation. In order for a burial ceremony to convey a sense of quality to the individuals involved, there is a need to make the relationship between the values of the Church and the values held by the surrounding society visible in a credible way. This would help avoid what Davies and colleagues (1991: 297) call 'a "dual purpose ritual" where the priest intends one goal and the people another'. This means that the vague beliefs that most Swedes bring to a funeral need to be cared for and related to the ability of the rite to promote strength and change. These results correlate with Davies' thoughts about the capacity of the rite to shape change by confronting existentially difficult feelings and convey hope for the future. The study indicates interesting possibilities with respect to how patterns might compare in different countries.

Growing cremation tradition

One of the particular contributions of Davies' work has been his focus on the increase in cremation as one of the major changes of the twentieth century. In connection to this, he also introduces a discussion of cremation as part of value change in a society where medical institutions have taken over the role of the Church in determining a biological death. He also brings in late modern ideas about cremation as part of a growing private sphere where a secular focus on the body, and on the personality of the departed, results in a retrospective perspective in the rite. The explicit focus on the life and personality of the individual explains the custom in England of scattering ashes in places that are related to the life of the dead person (Davies 1990, 1995, 2005a; Davies and Shaw 1995).

A comparison between Sweden and England shows strong similarities in development, partly attributable to a shared Protestant history. Different welfare systems are, however, made visible by the incorporation of cremation within the Church of Sweden's parish system. The crematoria that were built by voluntary organizations in the nineteenth and early twentieth centuries have gradually been incorporated into the organization of graveyards delegated to the Church by the state. No privately run crematoria exist in Sweden.

The first cremation in Sweden took place in Stockholm in 1887 and was handled by an association called 'Eldbegängelseföreningen'[4] (Enström 1964: 67). In Sweden, as in England, this issue was championed by liberal or radical groups (Davies 1990). At the same time one could observe a hesitant stance towards cremation among representatives of the Church. This hesitation was linked to the notion of the resurrection of the body and the ideal model of the death and resurrection of Jesus Christ. The hesitation of the Church meant a slow start to the development of cremation. In 1929 there were crematoria in only six cities in Sweden. An acceleration in development occurred in the years between the wars with the establishment of 18 new crematoria. During this period the clergy also started to accept the theological statement that it is the soul that passes on after death, hence rendering the treatment of the body after death less important (compare Davies 2008: 136). Financial and hygienic-related reasons also drove the growth in numbers of cremations (Dahlgren and Hermansson 2006: 10). In 1959 the rate in Sweden was 25 per cent, in 1979 about 50 per cent and presently the rate is well over 70 per cent (Dahlgren and Hermansson 2006: 12; Möller 2011: 81). Sweden has thus, together with England, the highest rate of cremation in Europe (Davies 2008: 136).

The legislation for the handling of cremated remains is however more strict in Sweden than in England. It is still compulsory to get permission from the County Council before the scattering of ashes privately over water or land (SFS 1990: 1144). Normally the ashes are placed in an urn and put into a grave (about 50 per cent) or are scattered in a 'garden of remembrance' which is part of the graveyard (about 30 per cent). The result is that a majority of the relatives have a place which can be visited on certain occasions. As Davies (2005: 115) notes, places of memory are important for the well-being of relatives and friends of the departed.

It has, however, become more customary today to ask for permission to scatter ashes in places other than graveyards, although still only 2 per cent of the deceased have their remains scattered privately after permission has been granted from the County Council (Dahlgren and

Hermansson 2006: 28). To summarize the statistics for the present time: Church of Sweden funerals represent 78 per cent of all deaths, funerals conducted by other Churches, denominations or religions are about 7 per cent and civil ceremonies make up about 12 per cent. Finally 3 per cent of deaths receive no ceremony at all. They are cremated directly after death and the staff of the graveyard will scatter the ashes in an anonymous place (Aggedal 2012; Svalfors and Bäckström 2015).

A particular feature of Swedish burials is that the time between death and burial is relatively long. The reason behind this is a combination of, on the one hand, the regulation of working time for the staff of the graveyard but also, on the other hand, difficulty in finding a time and date suitable for all the relatives of the departed. The length of this period can be perceived as an effort to postpone the reality of death as such. The practical and emotional difficulties, which arise as part of this situation (together with increased costs) have resulted in a decision by the Swedish government to reduce the period of time allowed between death and burial to not more than one month. This law was established on 1 May 2012 (Government Bill 2011/12: 51), illustrating the complex relationship between the apparently 'private' handling of the corpse and the regulation of the burial industry by public bodies.

Lund University studies on funeral traditions

The results of the cremation studies discussed above are part of a comprehensive research programme on funeral traditions conducted at the University of Lund (Gustafsson 2003). The programme covers the function of hymns in burial services (Evertsson 2002), growing professionalization of funeral directors (Davidsson Bremborg 2002), symbols used in funerary advertisements (Dahlgren 2000) and the development of 'funeral orations' (griftetal) (Aggedal 2003). In these studies, it can be observed that the tradition of Church funerals is relatively stable; it continues to be the choice of a majority of the population with about the same number of participants taking part in funeral services over time (diminishing slightly in recent years). At the same time changes are taking place, for example, through the growth of cremation and also increased emphasis on personal aspects of the rite. Gustafsson (2006: 90) states that there is an ideal typical understanding that clergy representing a majority Church should have personal relationships with the people living in a local parish. As this is impossible in urban settings the clergy have developed a kind of professionalism in creating relationships through contacts made while planning Church ceremonies. In Sweden nearly all burials are preceded by a so-called 'burial conversation', when the clergy meet the relatives in advance of the ceremony to orient themselves about the deceased and about the wishes of the close relatives. This makes the clergy known to the parishioners and the relationship between the private and the public part of the rite easier to combine.

Discussion

This overview indicates the central role that funerary rites have within the cultures of the two countries discussed. This is true even in a privatized consumerist culture (with a Protestant tradition) where it is what the relative wants that counts. In a Nordic context the rites are so self-evident that the religious content becomes invisible as long as the rites connect to the dominant values of the culture. For the majority, a church funeral service is a natural way to say farewell and the religious qualities are imbedded in the collective frame of the rite. At the same time it becomes increasingly apparent that the content of the ceremony varies according to religious attitudes and expectations. From that perspective cremation could be regarded as a 'de-collectivization' of the rite. The fact that the tradition of cremation is nearly one hundred per cent in urban areas makes it evident that it is possible to find all orientations from belief in resurrection, via belief in the life of the soul after death, to unbelief within the realm of cremation. Therefore, it seems more probable that cremation should be seen as an integrated part of a wider development during the twentieth century, which includes a general shift from beliefs to (spiritual) action. This does not mean that a collective sensibility has vanished; it has, however, altered in content.

Davies (1997: 190) reminds us that death remains an existential fact, despite trends towards rationalization and privatization in western societies. 'We can dispute and debate all sorts of theories about life and eternity, but we cannot deny the very existence of ourselves as bodies' (Davies and Shaw 1995: 105). So the body, which is the arena of meaning, for many individuals, is at the same time the weakest point of all. 'It is no wonder that doctors and funeral directors are likely to be blamed if things go wrong, with treatments or with funerals; they are dealing with bodies that are very heavily invested with personal and private value' (Davies and Shaw 1995: 105). This explains why people more actively seek to develop quality of life through looking for places of quality such as historical sites or sites of natural beauty as well as the gym or spa (Davies 1994). Through these activities the individual can push aside the existential fact of death by focussing on life in the present.

The religious qualities of the rite

This development indicates how unclear the notion of religion has become and that religion appears in different forms in different surroundings at the same time (Beckford 2003). This is emphasized by the fact that religion can not only de defined through its substantive content or its organizational frames. Religion can also essentially be defined through the actions that the individual performs (Hervieu-Léger 2000). In the same way it is possible to state that the rite has become more complex and dependent on the particular situation (Bell 1997). The rites which have framed death can, for some participants, be given a clear content of belief (for example, being eschatological in character) at the same time as the rite does not have any religious connotation at all for others (retrospective in character focussing on the identity of the departed). For all participants, however, the rite confers meaning at a very important time.

It is also difficult to identify which part of a series of rites is the *essential* rite of death. A so-called death rite is in fact a combination of a series of rites starting with the one found at hospitals, or at homes for the care of the elderly where death is biologically determined and the individual is dressed in clothes intended to mark the personality of the departed before the funeral (Bremborg 2002: 85; Row 2010: 25). The burial ceremony is then most often followed by a meal, which also follows a ritual pattern and which, in Davies' words, shows that life is continuing to resist death (Bremborg 2006: 62).

Recent research suggests that about 15 per cent of the Swedish population believe in life after death, and that another 36 per cent claim that there is something after death, but we do not know what; another 25 per cent are unsure and 24 per cent claim that there is nothing – death is the end (Bäckström 2004: 102). The respondents who are uncertain often claim that there is an inner force within the individual or within nature which becomes visible in times of trouble, for example, when someone dies. This becomes even more apparent in relation to catastrophes such as the sinking of the ferry *Estonia* in 1994, the murder of the Swedish foreign minister Anna Lindh in 2002, the Asian tsunami in 2004 or the murders at Utøja in Norway on 22 July 2011. In all these tragedies, the invisible religiosity becomes visible and the Churches cooperate with public institutions, either to help individuals or through the performance of public ceremonies of memorialization. These memorial services are always attended by representatives of the government and the monarchy.[5]

There is within the research on rites a thought that all basic rites of passage, especially death rites, have a capacity to convey social change and an experience of strength in life. This strength helps the individual to manage in a difficult situation and to take the step into everyday life again, but in a new social role. This view is shared by Davies (1997) who has become well known for his phrase 'Words against Death', that is, the power of words, within the context of funeral rites, to bring about a hope beyond death (p. 6). This hope can be part of Christian (religious) belief and can easily be attached to the liturgy of burial services. It can also, however, be linked to a relationship to new generations or to a kind of ecological idea of circulation in nature.

Following Davies' interpretation, the purpose of funeral rites may be understood as to give hope, perhaps especially as they help a grieving person to confront an existential crisis. In this sense, hope as a ritual feature is dominant and conveys a transcendent quality independent of any specific religious content. This line of thinking is in accordance with van Gennep's (1960) view of funerals as rites of passage, their ultimate goal being to reorder the roles within a group after the loss of one of its members (Davies 1986: 41). But Davies wants to add another quality to the rite, borrowed from Maurice Bloch and his theory of 'Rebounding Conquest', which invokes what might be referred to as a transcendental power of the rite. It is in particular the liminal phase of the rite (Turner 1969), which creates the condition in which a shift of roles takes place (Davies 2002: 124). The liminal condition therefore has two functions, partly to indicate a social shift through alteration of roles, partly to instil renewed strength in the mourning individual, not least through the establishment of *communitas*, experienced as a face-to-face encounter with common humanity that underpins these roles. The rites have this transcending capacity as they are oriented towards the sacred and therefore function as an arena of communication between, using Durkheim's (1984) terms, the sacred and the profane.

Davies (2011, 2013) has, however, also cited the rites of the life cycle, and rites related to special occasions during the year, as being part of a cultural normality which fosters an intensification of identity. To be a member of society is to be socialized into one's group and its life-framing narratives. This provides access to events which intensify identity through emotional feelings of hope about future possibilities in life. Some life events hold these qualities more than others. Christmas celebrations are one example of a cultural context which embeds core values in stories and events that are widely shared. By participating in Carol Services, Nativity plays and Christmas shopping, individuals are drawn into the core ideas which evoke within them shared cultural emotions. According to Davies, cultural intensification and self-transcendence belong together (compare Day 2011).

These theoretical arguments have generally been supported by the Swedish studies referred to above. They show that funerary rites are of great importance for the individual whether the rite is described in terms of theology or cultural tradition. These studies also illustrate how the funerary rite helps to link the individual with a collective community and express that connection. This community is experienced in transcendental forms independent of worldview and relation to the respective Church. This shows that the funerary rites are located in a field of tension between transcendence and immanence and that the rites include attributes that are based both on religion and cultural tradition at the same time.

This discussion illustrates the complexity of the relationship between rite and religion and how rites are embedded in emotions related to the core values of a given culture. According to a broad definition of religion, the rite has transcendent qualities independent of its substantive content. In this way the rite becomes a transmitter of tradition at the same time as participants are free to choose their view of life. This might be one reason why the rite has survived, despite changes of values in society from an emphasis on the theological content of the rite to a focus on actions performed and to experiences of quality. This means that actions remain although content changes (Driver 1991).

Conclusion

This overview shows that funerary rites continue to have an important status in Sweden, where a majority are buried or cremated according to a religious rite. We have also seen that the rite has 'transcendent' qualities, i.e. it creates feelings of connections to the supra-individual and timeless (Reimers 1995: 138), which impart to it a capability of adjusting to the values of late modern society with its focus on the person and individual choice. The studies show further that the state has a continued interest in regulating death and burials. The handling of death, especially in connection with disasters, is a political question of high dignity. The long-term investigations after the Estonia disaster in 1994 (still not settled properly) indicate the kind of political unrest that can accompany shared experiences of existential uncertainty. In the same way, new religious traditions in Sweden (especially those signalled by the presence of Islam) have provoked debate about religious customs at the beginning and end of life.

The borders between private and public life in society have become more uncertain as a result of the deregulation of the nation-state and an increased dependence on the global consumption of the market. This means in practice that it is important that the public role of religion is not only analysed in relation to the state or to politics where legislation expresses power. A rapid deregulation of the institutions in Swedish society since the 1990s (including education, social care, health care and the Church) has resulted in the emergence of several public arenas beside the state and the political sphere. This concerns not only organizations in civil society (including faith-based organizations) or family life, assuming public and private roles respectively. It also concerns sites that function as arenas between the public and the private, especially (a) shopping malls as symbols for identity in relation to consumption; (b) sites like parks, historical monuments and tourist destinations (e.g. Cathedrals) which provide the individual with feelings of collective belonging; (c) sites where the treatment of the body dominates, for example hospitals or institutes for healing/therapy where professional assistance is mixed with spiritual belief; (d) sites for personal growth like schools, universities and centres for spiritual development. Every area is connected to the basic idea of quality of life, the dominant issue of western culture.

This development towards institutional pluralism lies behind Douglas Davies' (2009) observation that spirituality is becoming ever more free-floating and has achieved several meanings beyond a religious, a New Age-inspired or a humanistic (or atheistic) outlook. The notion of 'spirituality' is today also to be found as part of the philosophies of education and health/social care and has thus become part of the concerns of the welfare society. That is a spirituality that speaks of a human creativity that fosters reflexive or transcendent awareness in relation to meaning, purpose and ultimate values. If a New Age-oriented spirituality (which centres on the self) was functioning as a critique of institutional authority in the 1960s, the 'new spirituality' could be interpreted as a need to find both language and rites which function in secular and professional surroundings. This need is especially apparent within palliative care where ethical and existential questions are often linked together with a spiritual dimension. In this way spirituality becomes the 'Missing Piece' in care which is directed to the whole person and to their life concerns (Davies 2010). If the responses to the processes of the 1960s were ecumenical and individual, the responses to the processes of the 1990s are cross-traditional, bringing together religious groups, humanist associations and professional secular institutions in order to develop cohesion through negotiation from the bottom up.

This is a new and broader attempt which gives the notion of spirituality a new meaning. This will most likely change the role of funerals as they become part of a broader definition of religion linked to several identity-giving institutions in society. That is why today we see a new need for cooperation between different organizations with the aim of achieving the good society for every citizen (Casanova 2006). As we have seen, the role of religion as spirituality in a broader sense can be viewed as identity giving, quality giving, trust giving or as a developer of inner life. Religion can thus function as both an individual and cultural resource simultaneously (Lövheim 2011). The point is that rapid social change with growing global connections leads to a need to renegotiate relations and values connected to social cohesion, trust and personal identity.

So, it can be argued that funeral rites function as an arena between the private and the public as they socially acknowledge a medically defined death at the same time as they accept the freedom of choice of the individual and the need for 'transcendent' qualities in life. The rite continues to have these qualities as long as there is a connection between the deliverer or administrator and the user of the rite. If this relationship is disconnected, the rite seeks new paths of development, and we see signs of this today. This concerns, for example, rites conducted at homes for the elderly and rites at the locations of accidents, which are focussed on in the mass media, and in this way become publicly accessible. This can also include such traditions as a focus on graves during All Saints Day in November in Sweden, which has become a major marker of the memory of the departed though the lighting of candles (Rehnberg 1965: 250). This tradition has appeared in modern times and can be seen as a kind of resistance to the privatization of death through acknowledging the relationship between cultural and individual memories, illustrated more commonly in the visit to the graveyard (Bailey 1982: 10; Bäckström and Bromander 1995: 125).

All this shows that death rites are a natural part of life in Sweden. The paradoxical situation is that religion, though often expressed privately, becomes part of public life through the ability of the rites to function as an arena of communication which binds the private sphere of the individual together with the collective values of society. Research on rituals indicates that the European distinction between the secular, as the public, and the religious, as the private, does not function when the transcendental character of the rite is taken into account. This transcendental character does not have much to do with the discussion of a return of religion. From a ceremonial perspective, it can be stated that religion never left public life during the twentieth century (Davie 2015). It has, however, become visible again through the need of society to handle social care in a dwindling economy, to handle the risks created by modern technology and identity questions characterized by global uncertainty. This transcendental quality is now renegotiated in an ever more religiously and culturally diverse situation in which institutions develop spirituality as the 'missing piece' in care. This gives religion, through death rites, the possibility of continuing to convey hope, an experience of meaning and social renewal for both individual and society. As long as Church ceremonies continue to relate to a collective sphere, which the rites and symbols represent, they will most probably continue to have a role to play in public life.

Notes

1 I owe gratitude to Douglas Davies for a long-standing cooperation, first around student exchange between our universities which began in the 1980s and later over the issues discussed in this chapter. As a token of this gratitude and for anticipated contributions to Uppsala University, Douglas Davies was awarded the title of honorary doctor by the Faculty of Theology in 1998. He has been senior researcher in the Uppsala-based welfare and religion projects since 2003 (Davies 2005b; Bäckström and Davie 2010; Bäckström 2011).
2 The research programme www.impactofreligion.uu.se includes six themes with 40 researchers from six faculties at Uppsala University. It connects to the British Religion and Society Research Programme financed by AHRC/ESRC 2008–2013 (Woodhead and Catto 2012), to which Douglas Davies contributed a study (Davies 2012).
3 Following the Church–State reforms in 2000, other churches and religious communities are also offered the same service by the state.
4 Cremation society
5 On 26 December 2014, an anniversary was held in the Cathedral of Uppsala in memory of the Tsunami of 2004, when 543 Swedes lost their lives. The Archbishop Antje Jackelén together with the Prime Minister Stefan Lövén spoke in the presence of the royal family (Upsala Nya Tidning 2014).

References

Aggedal, J-O. (2003) *Griftetalet mellan trostolkning och livstydning: en pastoralteologisk studie* [The funeral address between profession of belief and interpretation of life: a pastoral theological study]. Lund: Arcus.

Aggedal, J-O. (2012) Nya riter och seder kring begravning [New rites and practices around burials], *Svensk kyrkotidning* 10: 192–194.

Bailey, E. (1982) *A Kind of Christianity: The Implicit Religion of an English Parish*. Bristol: Winterbourne Rectory.

Bauman, Z. (2007) *Consuming Life*. Cambridge: Polity Press.

Beckford, J. A. (2003) *Social Theory and Religion*. Cambridge: Cambridge University Press.

Beckford, J. A. (2010) 'The return of public religion? A critical assessment of a popular claim', *Nordic Journal of Religion and Society* 23(2): 121–136.

Beckford, J. A. (2012) 'Public religions and the postsecular: critical reflections', *Journal for the Scientific Study of Religion* 51(1): 1–19.

Bell, C. (1997) *Ritual: Perspectives and Dimensions*. New York: Oxford University Press.

Berger, P., Davie, G. and Fokas, E. (2008) *Religious America, Secular Europe? A Theme and Variations*. Aldershot: Ashgate.

Bjereld, U. and Demker, M. (2011) *Den nödvändiga politiken: makt och motstånd i en individualiserad tid* [The necessary politics: power and opposition in an individualised era]. Stockholm: Hjalmarsson & Högberg.

Bremborg, A. D. (2002) *Yrke: Begravningsentreprenör. Om utanförskap, döda kroppar, riter och professionalisering* [Profession: Funeral director. On exclusion, dead bodies, rites and professionalization]. Lund: Lund Studies in Sociology of Religion, 2.

Bremborg, A. D. (2006) 'Mat och minnen. En studie av samlingar efter begravning' [Food and memories. A study of receptions following funerals], in C. Dahlgren and G. Gustafsson (eds) *Kring begravningar i nutid. Tre studier* [On contemporary burials. Three studies]. Lund: Lund Studies in Sociology of Religion, 6: 57–84.

Bromander, J. (2011) *Svenska kyrkans medlemmar* [The members of the Church of Sweden]. Stockholm: Verbum.

Bäckström, A. and Bromander, J. (1995) *Kyrkobyggnaden och det offentliga rummet. En undersökning av kyrkobyggnadens roll i det svenska samhället* [Church buildings and public space. A study of the role of the church building in Swedish society]. Uppsala: Svenska kyrkans utredningar, 5.

Bäckström, A., Edgardh Beckman, N. and Pettersson, P. (2004) *Religious Change in Northern Europe: The Case of Sweden*. Stockholm: Verbum.

Bäckström, A. and Davie, G., with Edgardh, N. and Pettersson, P. (eds) (2010) *Welfare and Religion in the 21st Century Europe: Volume 1. Configuring the Connections*. Farnham: Ashgate.

Bäckström, A. (ed.) (2011) *Welfare and Values in Europe. Transitions related to Religion. Minorities and Gender. National Overviews and Case Study Reports. Volume 1. Northern Europe: Sweden, Norway, Finland, England*. Uppsala: Acta Universitatis Upsaliensis. Studies in Religion & Society, 4.

Bäckström, A. (2014) 'Religion in the Nordic countries: between private and public', *Journal of Contemporary Religion* 29(1): 61–74.

Casanova, J. (1994) *Public Religions in the Modern World*. Chicago: University of Chicago Press.

Casanova, J. (2006) 'Rethinking secularization: a global comparative perspective', *The Hedgehog Review* 8(1–2): 7–22.

Dahlgren, C. (2000) *När döden skiljer oss åt . . . Anonymitet och individualisering i dödsannonser: 1945–1999* [When death parts us . . . Anonymity and individualisation in announcements of deaths: 1945–1999]. Stockholm: Databoksförlaget AB.

Dahlgren, C. and Hermansson, J. (2006) '"Här skall mina aska vila". Nya platser och riter för gravsättning av aska på andra platser än begravningsplats' [My ashes shall rest here. New places and rituals for the internment of ashes at places other than burial grounds], in C. Dahlgren and G. Gustafsson (eds) *Kring begravningar i nutid. Tre studier* (On contemporary burials. Three studies). Lund: Lund Studies in Sociology of Religion, 6: 7–56.

Davie, G. (2012) 'A response to Linda Woodhead', in A. Row and P. Pettersson (eds) *Consolidating Research on Religion: Moving the Agenda Forward*. Uppsala: Acta Universitatis Upsaliensis. Studies in Religion & Society, 8: 25–30.

Davie, G. (2015) *Religion in Britain: A Persistent Paradox*. Chichester: Wiley Blackwell.

Davies, D. J. (1986) *Studies in Pastoral Theology and Social Anthropology*. Institute for the Study of Worship and Religious Architecture: University of Birmingham.

Davies, D. J. (1990) *Cremation Today and Tomorrow*. Nottingham: Alcuin/Grow Books.

Davies, D. J. (1994) *Quality Places for Quality Time*. Internal Publication: Department of Theology, Nottingham University.

Davies, D. J. (1995) *British Crematoria in Public Profile*. Maidstone, Kent: The Cremation Society of Great Britain.

Davies, D. J. (1997, 2nd edition 2002) *Death, Ritual and Belief: The Rhetoric of Funerary Rites*. London: Cassell.

Davies, D. J. (2002) *Anthropology and Theology*. Oxford: Berg.

Davies, D. J. (2005a) *A Brief History of Death*. Oxford: Blackwell Publishing.

Davies, D. J. (2005b) 'Welfare, Spirituality, and the Quality of Life and Place', in Bäckström, A. (ed.) *Welfare and Religion. A Publication to Mark the Fifth Anniversary of the Uppsala Institute for Diaconal and Social Studies*. Publications of the Uppsala Institute for Diaconal and Social Studies 10: 88–94.

Davies, D. J. (2008) *The Theology of Death*. London: T & T Clark.

Davies, D. J. (20th November 2009) 'Spirituality, cultural wisdom and salvation', Lecture given at the Royal College of Psychiatrists; Spirituality and Psychiatry Special Interest Group.

Davies, D. J. (14th October 2010) 'The missing piece: meeting people's spiritual needs in end of life care', Lecture given at Dying Matters conference. London.

Davies, D. J. (2011) *Emotion, Identity and Religion: Hope, Reciprocity, and Otherness*. Oxford: Oxford University Press.

Davies, D. J. (2012) 'Changing British ritualization', in Woodhead, L. and Catto, R. (eds) *Religion and Change in Modern Britain*. London: Routledge, pp. 203–218.

Davies, D. J. (2013) 'Thriving through myth', in C. Cook (ed.) *Spirituality, Theology and Mental Health: Multidisciplinary Perspectives*. London: SCM Press, pp. 160–177.

Davies, D., Watkins, C. and Winter, M. (1991) *Church and Religion in Rural England*. Edinburgh: T & T Clark.

Davies, D. and Shaw, A. (1995) *Reusing Old Graves: A Report on Popular British Attitudes*. London: Shaw & Sons Limited.

Day, A. (2011) *Believing in Belonging: Belief and Social Identity in the Modern World*. Oxford: Oxford University Press.

Driver, T. F. (1991) *The Magic of Ritual: Our Need for Liberating Rites that Transform Our Lives & Our Communities*. San Francisco: HarperCollins Publishers.

Durkheim, E. (1984) *The Division of Labour in Society*. New York: Macmillan.

Enström, B. (1964) *Kyrkan och eldbegängelserörelsen i Sverige 1882–1962* [The church and the cremation movement in Sweden 1882–1962]. Lund: Gleerups förlag.

Esping-Andersen, G. (1990) *The Three Worlds of Welfare Capitalism*. Cambridge: Polity Press.

Evertsson, A. J. (2002) *'Gå vi till paradis med sång'. Psalmers funktion i begravningsgudstjänster* ['We go to paradise singing'. The role of hymns in funeral services]. Lund: Arcus förlag.

Van Gennep, A. (1960) *The Rites of Passage*. Chicago: University of Chicago Press.

Government Bill (2011/12) '51 concerning burial questions'. Available at: https://data.riksdagen.se/fil/30C40FC4-352D-427D-A8F7-2A097E0F78BE

Gustafsson, G. (2003) *När det sociala kapitalet växlas in. Om begravningar och deltagande i begravningar* [When social capital is cashed in. On burials and participation in funeral services]. Lund: Lund Studies in the Sociology of Religion.

Gustafsson, G. (2006) 'Kände prästen den döda? Känner sorgehusen prästen? Om personliga relationer vid begravningar' [Did the priest know the deceased? Do the mourners know the priest? On personal relationships at funerals], in C. Dahlgren and G. Gustafsson (eds) *Kring begravningar i nutid. Tre studier* [On contemporary burials. Three studies]. Lund: Lund Studies in Sociology of Religion, 6: 85–132.

Habermas, J. (2006) 'Religion in the public sphere', *European Journal of Philosophy* 14(1): 1–15.

Habermas, J. (2008) 'Notes on a post-secular society', *Signandsight.com*. Available at: http://www.signandsight.com/features/1714.html (Accessed on 20 February 2013).

Hervieu-Léger, D. (2000) *Religion as a Chain of Memory*. Cambridge: Polity Press.

Hort, S. E. O. (2014) *Social Policy, Welfare State, and Civil Society in Sweden. Volume II. The Lost World of Social Democracy 1988–2015*. Lund: Arkiv förlag.

Inglehart, R. (1997) *Modernization and Postmodernization: Cultural, Economic, and Political Change in 43 Societies*. Princeton: Princeton University Press.

Joas, H. (2014) *Faith as an Option. Possible Futures for Christianity*. Stanford: Stanford University Press.

Lövheim, M. (2011) 'Ungas religiositet: tidigare forskning och nya frågor' [Young people's religiosity: Previous research and new questions], in M. Lövheim and J. Bromander (eds) *Religion som resurs? Existentiella frågor och värderingar i unga svenskars liv* [Religion as a Resource? Existential questions and values in the lives of young Swedes]. Skellefteå: Artos förlag, pp. 77–106.

Martikainen, T. and Gauthier, F. (2013) *Religion in a Neo-Liberal Age: Political Economy and Modes of Governance*. Farnham: Ashgate.

Middlemiss Lé Mon (2015) *Frivilligarbete inom och för kyrkan: En lösning på de problem som kyrka och samhälle står inför?* [Voluntary work in and for the church: A solution to the problems faced by church and society?]. Stockholm: Forum.

Möller, L. (2011) *Hej då! Begravningsboken* [Goodbye! The burials book]. Malmö: Arena.

Olofsson, J. (2013) 'Välfärdspolitiska vägval' [Crossroads in welfare politics], in H. Swärd, P. G. Edebalk and E. Wadensjö (eds) *Vägar till välfärd – idéer, inspiratörer, kontroverser, perspektiv* [Roads to welfare – ideas, inspirers, controversies, perspectives]. Stockholm: Liber, pp. 284–299.

Rehnberg, M. (1965) *Ljusen på gravarna och andra ljusseder. Nya traditioner under 1900-talet* [Candles on graves and other practices. New traditions during the 1900s]. Stockholm: Nordiska museets handlingar, 61.

Reimers, E. (1995) *Dopet som kult och kultur. Bilder av dopet i dopsamtal och föräldraintervjuer* [Baptism as cult and culture. Pictures of baptism in conversations preceding baptism and interviews with parents]. Stockholm: Verbum.

Row, A. (2010) *A Good Death: A Qualitative Exploration of Staff's Attitudes towards Death in a Residential Care Home in Sweden.* Masters dissertation in the Sociology of Religion, Uppsala University.

Svalfors, U. and Bäckström, A. (2015) *Trossamfundens sociala insatser – en preliminär undersökning* [The social initiatives of religious organisations – a preliminary investigation]. Stockholm: Socialdepartementets skriftserie.

Svensk författningssamling, SFS (Swedish Statuary Book) (1990) '1144 (the burial law)'. Available at: https://www.riksdagen.se/sv/dokument-lagar/?doktyp=sfs&q =Begravningslagen

Taylor, C. (2007) *A Secular Age.* Cambridge and London: Belknap Press.

Thidevall, S. (2000) *Kampen om folkkyrkan. Ett folkligt reformprograms öden 1928–1932* [The Theology of the Folk Church. The Struggle over National Identity: The Fate of a Folk Church Reform Programme 1928–1930]. Stockholm: Verbum.

Turner, V. (1969) *The Ritual Process: Structure and Anti-Structure.* London: Routledge & Kegan Paul.

Upsala Nya Tidning (27 December 2014) Minnesgudstjänst i domkyrkan. [Memorial Service in the Cathedral].

Welsby, P. (1985) *How the Church of England Works.* London: CIO Publishing.

Wiig-Sandberg, U. (2006) *Den nödvändiga riten? Om upplevelser av kvalitet i begravningsgudstjänsten* [The Essential Rite? On Experiences of quality in the funeral service]. Uppsala: Diakonivetenskapliga institutets skriftserie, 13.

Woodhead, L. (2012). 'Religion: from state to market: some reflections', in A. Row and P. Pettersson (eds) *Consolidating Research on Religion: Moving the Agenda Forward.* Uppsala: Acta Universitatis Upsaliensis. Studies in Religion & Society, 8: 15–24.

Woodhead, L. and Catto, R. (eds) (2012) *Religion and Change in Modern Britain.* London: Routledge.

6 Facing existential meaning challenges through a post-secular clinical model

Swedish case illustrations following abortion

Valerie DeMarinis

Sweden has been characterized as one of the most secular countries and cultural contexts in the world, as interpreted primarily through secularization theory (Heelas, Scott and Morris 1996; Heelas and Woodhead 2005). With the change in 2000, when the Church of Sweden ceased to be the state church and the weakening hold in other contexts, as well as the move to an ever-more individualized way of approaching existential meaning and worldview questions as noted both in Sweden and other secularized cultures, the meaning of secularization has needed to be more carefully examined (Pettersson 2002; Heelas, Scott and Morris 1996; Heelas and Woodhead 2005). Those working with more psychological and psychosocial perspectives – such as Bauman (2000) and DeMarinis (2003, 2008), in the Swedish context – have focused on the challenges of understanding secularization in the lived experiences of individuals, as well as the need for so-called 'secular' societies, not least those hosting large numbers of refugees with traditional religious backgrounds, to develop more sophisticated understandings of their contexts, where a variety of religious and secular worldviews coexist.

Attempts to understand the emergence or re-emergence of religiosity, spirituality and novel modes of existential meaning-making have led to a debate on how best to understand the concepts of 'secular' society and 'post-secular' critical reflection (Habermas 2008; Casanova 2013, 2014). The use of 'post-secular' as a working framework for analysis (Baker and Beaumont 2011) signals the emergence of a different perspective. From a psychological perspective, the term 'post-secular' may capture more accurately than 'secular' the actual psychosocial needs related to existential meaning among those living in 'secularized' contexts. From a psychological perspective, existential meaning needs are human needs, which may take many forms in a given cultural context. These concern both ultimate needs regarding questions such as the nature of life, death, morality, as well as needs arising from these as they impact decision making amidst the challenges of daily life (DeMarinis et al. 2011). From this perspective, existential needs exist just as much for members of the majority population who may be consciously or otherwise experimenting with different beliefs, rites and myths, as those in religious and/or ethnic minority groups who may be struggling with how to live out their traditional faith in the midst of the surrounding – more secular – culture.

This chapter focuses on psychology, particularly clinical psychology of religion, within the increasingly post-secularized Swedish cultural context. It needs to be understood against the backdrop of the two 'populations' of existential meaning-seekers noted above – the ethnic majority population and the religious minority population. Two case illustrations will be used, drawn from actual clinical work. Though very different, the factor in common for the women in these cases is the experience of having undergone an abortion and the existential meaning challenges this experience has triggered over time.

The quotations below are from the experiences of these two women, with whom I have consulted in psychotherapeutic contexts in Sweden over the past decade.

> It was as though a wall of silence surrounded me. But not a calm silence. I could not find anyone to talk about this with. I know I made the best decision to have an abortion in that time of my life, but there were many emotions around this. It was a difficult decision for me. I needed some way and place to grieve. I still do. Some way of marking that this . . . [was happening]. But I did not know what to do. I became depressed and a bit withdrawn. I am an agnostic, so religion is not involved, but I still find it hard to have not marked this in some way. This is a difficult thing to talk about in Sweden and all the politics around it from Europe, the US and changing laws. But there is an atmosphere of dread or maybe fear in talking about this in an open way in Sweden. With all the religious and right-wing movements against abortion, it is really frightening. I am here, finally, as I need some kind of closure on this, I never had any kind of service or in any way did anything after the abortion.
>
> (Anna)[1]

> The abortion for me was something very difficult. If circumstances were different and not so desperate I would not have chosen this. I am religious [Muslim] and this is not approved of, but the situation was really desperate. I have kept this to myself. My husband was very ill and traumatised as we waited for news about asylum. I have not talked about this before. It helps to talk here but still hard to deal with. I am from another country, very different, but I appreciate being here in Sweden where this was possible. But I have much guilt and feel that I cannot be forgiven, or don't know how to help to forgive myself or at least live with this in a different way. I need some way to deal with this, I need to contain all these memories and thoughts and feelings and guilt if I am ever to live life again.
>
> (Zara)

As is evident in their words, it is clear that a number of things have happened or not happened to bring these women to the point of asking for a psychotherapeutic consultation. One factor is especially clear: their experience is framed by global concerns, not least in the form of religious and right-wing political groups aiming to restrict access to abortion. This global reality affects them personally on several levels, including how they engage in meaning-making in general and existential meaning-making in particular.

Understanding their experiences on both global and local levels is necessary for psychotherapeutic work that is informed by just such a multilevel analysis. This need for a multilevel framework for understanding experience is not new to clinical models. However, in order for this to be done in a responsible way, these models need to include an understanding of existential meaning and its functions for individuals, groups and societies, as well as incorporating cultural analysis. However, there is a marked absence of existential meaning-making and cultural analysis from the vast majority of clinical models.

In my attempt to create a model for the clinical psychology of religion, the work of anthropologist of religion, Douglas Davies, has proved invaluable. The breadth and depth of his theoretical and empirical work as well as his well-reasoned and clear multidisciplinary approach provide a very rich resource for psychologists of religion in general and are especially enlightening as well as inspiring for those working in the clinical psychology of religion. He manages to create a perspective for understanding complex phenomena whereby the interactions among individual components as well as between these components and the larger structure can be understood. As Davies notes, 'Today, albeit through transformed routes, these issues of experience are more important than ever given the political and social weight carried by religious conviction, especially when allied with political agendas and religious apologetics' (2013: 1). Davies' words point to the importance of understanding critical events in the lives of individuals in a wider as well as deeper perspective. For those working in clinical fields, sources of information informing clinical practice need to be broadened to include political as well as anthropological dimensions of a client's life, dimensions that impact how a particular decision and its consequences are understood and interpreted. Likewise, clinical assessment needs to incorporate an understanding that matters concerning existential meaning – both beliefs and practices – are not reducible to a single unit of information, but constitute a multilevel source of information that may well include conflicting elements that need to be explored. Moreover, these elements may not be conscious to the client but manifest in unexpected somatic or psychological symptoms. The orientation in this chapter is linked to four important aspects of Davies' interdisciplinary contributions to the clinical psychology of religion. First, in a number of different studies, Davies has emphasized the importance of including a larger, historical cultural analysis (2013, 2012, 2011) and a more focused social anthropological analysis of a given situation (2012, 2002a), thereby ensuring that the understanding of place and context is part of the sociological and psychosocial research processes. Second, Davies has greatly contributed to a deepened understanding of the human need for ritualization, and the particular rituals preserved or reinvented, both socially and individually, to meet the conditions of spiritual survival and significance within changing contexts (2012, 2011, 2006, 2005, 2002b). Third, Davies has illuminated the changing and maintaining patterns of religious/spiritual institutions and the importance of understanding the difference in levels of analysis between sociological investigations of institutional change and anthropological investigations of how individuals and groups experience their interactions with such institutions (2012, 2011). Fourth, Davies has incorporated a sophisticated understanding of both the complexity of and the necessity for understanding the dynamic and life-long interactions among experience, emotion and embodiment in terms of how meaning is made, especially existential meaning (2013, 2012, 2011, 2006, 2005, 2002b).

These four areas of Davies' work and the post-secular backdrop are necessary in order to understand this chapter's model for understanding meaning-making and existential meaning-making in psychotherapeutic mental health contexts. The model is of special importance when working with clients who are, as individuals, struggling with personal, existential experiences that need to be understood in cultural, global and political perspectives. Though this is the case, to a greater or lesser extent in much of mental health work, these levels of analysis and awareness are often implicit at best. However, when dealing with certain topics at certain times there is a need to make these levels explicit. It is here argued that this is a need for many women who have undergone an abortion and who are experiencing mental health concerns. In fact, this is the case not only for women as in many instances the men involved in the process may also experience such concerns. However, this chapter focuses upon the experiences of two women I have met with through psychotherapeutic consultations in Sweden. Though the actual number of consultations I have had with women who have experienced abortions is much larger, these two illustrations are chosen as they represent very different approaches to meaning-making and very different worldview orientations in Sweden today (DeMarinis 2003, 2008), each drawn from majority and minority cultures, respectively. I argue that understanding this range, and getting to the core of the foundational phenomena common across this range, is important for those involved in mental health care who are working with women and families that are experiencing psychological distress and struggling with post-abortion concerns.

Brief background and presentation of the model

The following model was originally developed for my research with an Afro-Brazilian group in Salvador, Brazil (DeMarinis 2011). In that context, all the different levels of analysis were necessary for accurate clinical assessment and treatment planning due to sociopolitical and public health concerns related to this group who were discriminated against within this social context (see also Seligman 2005).

The application of the model in Sweden has been generally within the context of consultations with asylum-seeking groups and individuals, whose lives are framed by global and sociopolitical factors. Yet even in work with those who have been granted asylum in forced migration cases, the need for a complex analysis and assessment framework has been necessary. This is especially the case where families have been split and family reunion issues are unresolved and/or where both 'survivor' guilt (for being the one who has left and now has asylum) and grief issues for those left behind are dominant causes of depression and anxiety as well as post-traumatic symptomology. However, the majority of mental health contexts in Sweden appear ill-prepared in addressing meaning-making concerns, especially when experiences touch the existential dimension of meaning for the individual involved (DeMarinis 2013; DeMarinis et al. 2011).

Before proceeding to the presentation of the model itself and its application in the case illustrations, a word about clinical models may be useful. In mental health contexts, a clinical model provides both an orientation to mental health as well as an operating system for identifying problems, resources, treatment strategies and other types of intervention. Clinical models are tools for use in clinical contexts. However, clinical models are also cultural products. They reflect both the evidence-based science available concerning disease and distress, as well as interactions with the particular cultural context in terms of the cultural constructions of illness (Kleinman 1992; DeMarinis et al. 2009). This means that clinical models of this type also need to be considered as cultural artefacts. The role of culture in the formation of such models is not always consciously acknowledged. This fact is best illustrated in the long-term debate taking place about the importance of cultural information and analysis in mental health diagnoses and in treatment planning (see DeMarinis et al. 2011). An acknowledgement of the importance of gathering cultural information, including existential meaning information, for all patients is in line with the understanding of culture in the latest edition of the *Diagnostic and Statistical Manual of Mental Disorders* (DSM-5) (American Psychiatric Association 2013).

Model of levels of analysis for psychotherapeutic work in relation to meaning-making analysis

This clinical model (see Figure 6.1) identifies the areas of information needed to gain a thorough impression of the situation for the individual who is presenting signs of distress and accompanying symptoms. Depending on the situation it may not be necessary to gather information at all of the levels involved. However, information related to the meaning-making section is essential in

- Global analysis (past and current situation)
- Culture and subculture analysis
- Sociopolitical analysis
- Gender analysis
- Analysis of public mental health
- Analysis of group(s) mental health
- Analysis of individual's and family's mental and somatic health concerns

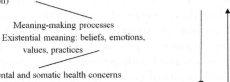

Meaning-making processes
Existential meaning: beliefs, emotions, values, practices

Figure 6.1 An adaption of the clinical model developed by DeMarinis (2011). Used with permission.

each case. The model has seven information levels and a separate information section for meaning-making processes. The meaning-making section is central to the model so a brief description of this comes first. In different branches of psychology as well as other fields, interest in meaning-making is receiving much attention, both in relation to human development and coping patterns. The experience of meaning in life is understood as an important aspect of psychological development (Baumeister 1991). A person's meaning-making processes and resulting 'system', developed in their social and cultural contexts, provide a way of making sense of the world. Often this happens without conscious knowledge, the product of personal experiences and the surrounding culture (Baumeister 1991). Depending upon the embeddedness of the system and its nurture over time, it can be a source of strength in times of adversity. However, depending on the nature of the system and the kind of trauma or adversity encountered, the processes involved may not be able to function and the system itself may be compromised. Intense stress may result, and this may lead an individual to achieve a greater awareness of the meaning system and its dysfunction (Park 2005, 2010; Silberman 2005). When there are discrepancies between the appraised situation and the beliefs inherent in the meaning system, feelings of both loss of control and loss of predictability can lead to intense stress. In such cases a need for change in and to the meaning system is inevitable if healthy functioning is to resume. Evaluation of the situation and reappraisal strategies (Lazarus and Folkman 1984) distinguish between: primary appraisal of a stressful event and the determination of its harm or threat challenge level; and secondary appraisal of the event in terms of evaluating one's abilities and resources to handle the resulting situation. Mikulincer and Florian (1996) distinguish reappraisal strategies from reorganization strategies. In reorganization strategies, the end result is the acceptance of the new reality and its incorporation into mental structures.

Depending on the type of stress experienced and the way it is interpreted by the individual, the challenge to her/his meaning system will vary. When the challenge goes to the core of ultimate life questions *for that person*, the existential meaning dimension is activated (DeMarinis 2011). This dimension, it can be argued, exists in every person's meaning system. However, not all experiences of stress generate questions for or challenges to this dimension. From a mental health perspective, the existential meaning dimension is operative in the here and now and in the living of daily life situations. However, as with the meaning system in general, the existential dimension is lived often at an unreflective level until confronted by some experience that challenges it. When this happens, however, there is a need to address beliefs, emotions, values, and practices (special rites, ceremonies, activities that mark an event) that form a part of this existential meaning dimension (DeMarinis, 1994, 1996, 2011). Building on prior research in dealing with psychotherapeutic processes following challenges to the existential meaning dimension (DeMarinis 2011, 2013), the involvement of a practice to mark an event or circumstance positively contributes to the reappraisal or reorganization strategies for moving forward towards more functional meaning-making.

The seven levels of analysis in the model are interactive. A change at one level can bring about changes at one or more of the other levels. A brief presentation of information contained at each level is presented in Chart 6.1.

Chart 6.1 Meaning-making components and levels of analysis

Meaning-making components

The meaning-making components in the model are relevant for and related to each of the levels below. How meaning is made around issues related to healthcare can be more or less complex depending on the topic in focus. Often this type of information is implicit and is always generated within a specific cultural context. Changes at any of the levels included in the model can influence how meaning is made around a healthcare concern. Meaning-making takes place at many levels. Often it is not a source of conscious thought. However, when healthcare concerns or experiences raise questions about how meaning is made in relation to important life questions, the existential level of meaning is engaged, very often through an uncomfortable sensation of cognitive or another form of dissonance or disruption. The four components are: beliefs (cognitive formulations and associations), emotions (generated emotions: positive, negative, mixed), values (prioritizing of principles for how life should be lived and how life is understood), and practices (symbolic actions and activities done in relation to marking, containing and/or finding a way to define or redefine meaning in relation to an event or experience). All individuals go through meaning-making processes, however the components of such can be very varied and are informed by social and cultural contexts. Existential meaning components and expressions are also a part of every individual's way of making meaning. However, the content of these can vary greatly among individuals and also over time within the same individual.

Level: Global analysis (past and present)

Attention to changing patterns, classifications of mental health problems. New diagnoses. Global concerns related to large-scale trauma. Refugee situations. This level also includes changes in legal classifications of procedures in relation to health care issues and treatments. Changes in country-specific policies in relation to health care issues.

(Continued)

Chart 6.1 (Continued)

Level: Culture and sub-culture analysis

Country-specific cultural codes and practices in general and specifically in relation to health care and mental health issues. Cultural understandings of health and illness. Attention to sub-culture and minority group access to healthcare.

Level: Sociopolitical analysis

Dominant social and political patterns/positions in a given cultural context/country relating to healthcare and welfare policies and practices. While the focus here is on the specific cultural context, this is also influenced by global trends, changing patterns in sociopolitical discourse around particular medical and/or healthcare issues at the international level.

Level: Gender analysis

Issues and concerns related to cultural constructions of illness and health in relation to male and female specific conditions. This level also relates to larger societal issues in relation to healthcare situations or conditions that are associated with moral judgements.

Level: Analysis of public mental health

Population level analysis of epidemiological trends in relation to mental health risks. How public mental health is approached and the types of promotion, prevention and intervention programmes available.

Level: Analysis of group's mental health

Attention to particular minority groups or other identified sub-groups that are in particular risk situations for developing mental health problems due to social circumstances, lack of healthcare services, lack of access to healthcare services, or discriminatory practices.

Level: Analysis of individual's and family's mental health

The individual is in focus here, in terms of the particular mental healthcare concerns presented, and in relation to the immediate context of his/her particular circumstances. Here it is important to form a comprehensive understanding of the biopsychosocial aspects of the condition, illness or presenting symptoms as well as genetic or other relevant information. Family information and family involvement also needs to be included. Potential medical, psychosocial, meaning-making resources need to be identified. The individual's interpretation and perception of the condition, illness or symptoms needs to be accessed and used as a basis for building a common understanding of the situation.

Brief illustration of the model applied in a post-secular Swedish context

The way in which this model can be used is primarily dependent on the needs and situation of the individual experiencing distress as well as the framework through which mental healthcare and consultation is given. This model allows for a glocalization framework to be applied in psychotherapeutic contexts. As glocalization seeks to identify and link issues of globalization with local considerations, application in mental health contexts is certainly needed. This kind of application follows analyses of the implications of globalization, both positive and negative, in terms of interactions with local welfare concerns (Hong and Song 2010). Thinking in this way, complex and interactive levels of analysis might be anticipated, especially when examining issues of large-scale forced migration and natural disasters. Moreover, the meaning-making processes of individuals can be profoundly affected by events and changes taking place across different levels in the model. How these events and changes interact with meaning-making processes in general and with questions related to existential meaning in particular needs to be investigated.

The following is a brief illustration of an application of the model in the secularized Swedish cultural context for two women with mental health concerns related to experiences of abortion. Naturally, space and issues of confidentiality do not permit a full analysis. Rather, this is a brief illustration of why it is important to generate these levels of information, and how they may influence the therapeutic process.

Referring back to the words of Anna and Zara at the beginning of the chapter, and many other women I have encountered who have experienced an abortion and who are struggling with unresolved emotional and existential issues related to that experience, there are several important observations that can be made. Firstly, it is clear that there is a strong awareness of the Swedish cultural context in which they are living and how it differs from many other parts of Europe and the rest of the world in terms of the legal status of abortion and access to safe abortion procedures. The changing global political climate surrounding abortion is a background factor that enters into the meaning systems of both Anna and Zara, although in different ways. This political climate of ongoing debate is inescapable as Heino et al. (2013) note, so that even in countries where the right to abortion is guaranteed by law, the efforts undertaken by certain – often religious – groups, to limit access to abortion have kept a sense of controversy alive. For Anna, an ethnic Swede who is active politically in matters relating to women's healthcare and gender concerns, the current discourse around abortion rights is a contributing factor to her experience of distress. For Zara, a person who has been given asylum in Sweden, there is a deep appreciation of being in a country where abortion is legal and available to those in need. For both Anna and Zara, Sweden represents a legal and literal 'safe space' for women in relation to abortion. However, this genuine safe space is also experienced by both women as a space in which it is difficult to be able to speak about abortion and one's experience of it. As Anna notes, 'But there is an atmosphere of dread or maybe fear in talking about this in an open way in Sweden'.

Anna's experience of an atmosphere of dread and fear in talking openly about abortion in Sweden is influenced by the larger European and international discourses around the morality of abortion, different abortion laws and the narrowing of access to legal abortion. Yet, the cultural context of her experience is specific. Within Sweden, classified as one of the most secular nations in the world (Pettersson 2002), science and rationality provide a canopy of meaning in the public sphere under which healthcare – as well as all other public institutions – functions (DeMarinis 2011). The canopy is clearly not one of a dominating religious tradition. Though there is religious tolerance and to a great extent freedom of religious expression and practice, the majority culture is not dominated by a religious tradition, though its Lutheran heritage does shape, to some degree, cultural values and orientations. Privatized religious or other expressions of existential meaning are more common than church-based traditions among the majority population. In addition to the scientific and rational orientation that characterizes public institutions, questions related to religious or existential beliefs and practices are not standard form in healthcare delivery and in fact are largely absent. This is so not out of a lack of respect per se, but is based to a large extent on norms of practice inherited from a time when other social institutions functioned alongside healthcare to provide such resources (DeMarinis et al. 2010). In a tragically ironic way, this very respect for the privacy and integrity of the individual, expressed by not drawing attention to this level of meaning, now can be seen as problematic and in certain cases even contributing to an iatrogenic consequence worsening the situation for the patient or client.

Evidence of the need for including this kind of information in healthcare, and specifically in the area of abortion care in Sweden, can be found in the multidisciplinary and in many respects ground-breaking study by Liljas Stålhandske et al. (2011, 2012). How this is to be done in this cultural context for this and all other areas of healthcare is a question for current and future research.[2] In a country otherwise considered a leader in public health standards, one can argue that the absence of attention to meaning-making analysis, especially existential meaning, and the related lack of training and tools for implementing this, is a growing public mental health concern (DeMarinis 2008; DeMarinis et al. 2011).

It is in relation to these global as well as culture-specific contexts that the experiences of Anna and Zara need to be situated. The meaning-making processes of Anna and Zara, especially in relation to existential meaning in their lives, are in many respects very different. Anna is an ethnic Swede, a member of the majority culture, agnostic and with a humanistic existential meaning system. Zara came to Sweden as a refugee, her existential meaning system is shaped primarily by her being a religious Muslim, actively participating in the rituals and activities of her local mosque.

However, one thing they have in common is that, prior to seeking therapeutic help for episodes of depression, disturbed sleep, and other mental health concerns, their past experiences of abortion had not been resolved within their existing frameworks of meaning. Applying a mental health analysis using the model above, it becomes clear that meaning-making processes are involved, and that the existential meaning dimension has been confronted and confounded to different degrees in the sub-areas of beliefs, values, emotions and practices. This confronting and confounding of the existential meaning dimension for each of the women touches each of the four aspects emerging from Davies' work that were noted earlier. First, there is a need for cultural analysis in relation to each of the sub-areas of beliefs, values, emotions and practices. In these two case illustrations it is clear that the contents in these sub-areas are dynamic, and that there is a clear interaction with global and local changes. Second, for both women the experience of abortion has become part of a ritualized memory. In order to come to terms with this memory, new ritual experiences are needed, especially for achieving a deeper sense of closure. Third, although Anna and Zara have very different existential meaning frameworks, they both need to reexamine how to find resources from religious or other institutions of existential significance. Fourth, for both Anna and Zara there are complex and changing interactions among their experiences, emotions and the ways in which their symptoms of distress and depression, as well as of hope, are embodied.

Limited space does not permit a thorough analysis of these sub-areas for Anna and Zara; however, the one sub-area that can be explored in more detail is that of practices, crucial for both Anna and Zara in restoring their ability to function in their daily-life routines. The centrality of practice, always involving embodied activity, is supported by findings in the science of cognition (see, for example, Gibbs 2005). Bodily cognition and bodily practices are both deserving of attention here, echoing Davies' own emphases on ritualization and embodiment.

The words of both Anna and Zara point clearly to this need for embodied practice as well. Anna notes: 'I am here, finally, as I need some kind of closure on this, I never had any kind of service or in any way did anything after the abortion'. Zara notes: 'I need some way to deal with this, I need to contain all these memories and thoughts and feelings and guilt if I am ever to live life again'.

One of my roles in the mental health consultation process for both Anna and Zara was to work with each of them to find a way to mark, to contain, to symbolize and express a way of making meaning in relation to their experiences of abortion and its aftermath. One of the end products of these consultations for both Anna and Zara was a ritualized expression that was built from how meaning was made, and from how the existential meaning dimension was made operative in their lives. For Anna this involved a ceremony out in nature, near to her summer cottage, a place of importance and safety for her. As part of the ceremony, Anna buried an object that through the consultation process had served as a symbol of her aborted foetus. Specially invited friends and family members were involved in different parts of the ceremony. For Zara this involved the design of a ritual performed in cooperation with a religious leader who, during the course of the consultation, Zara had met and trusted and was the person she wanted and needed alongside her as she conducted this ritual of symbolic burial of her aborted foetus. Zara burned and then buried the ashes of the symbol at a designated place on the land attached to the religious institution to which the religious leader was connected.

In this way both Anna and Zara formulated a ritualized action and created a ritualized safe space to which they could return both physically and also in their imagination. While both Anna and Zara continued in therapy, for each of them this ritualized action helped in the processes of creating new memories, integrating different levels of meaning-making beginning with the existential dimension. This ritualized experience eventually became a sustainable tool for each of them, an integrating means for dealing with difficult and unresolved issues. Years later I had the experience of meeting each of them again. The impact of including this type of attention to practical meaning-making in the therapeutic process is best expressed in their own words. Anna noted: 'Without that ceremony I am not sure if I ever could have found a long-term way of remembering all that happened then and yet having limits around it. I can recall and feel emotions, often times very sad, but not get lost in them as before'. Zara noted: 'Thinking back now, having the chance to be heard and respected and to find someone from my own religion who could help me in that very concrete way, at the same time as I was gaining other kinds of understanding around these and other issues was really remarkable. I know that planning and experiencing that 20 minute period changed my life, or to be even more truthful helped me regain my life. So simple yet so profound. I still struggle and will always do so, but there is hope there, and that is the difference. The hope comes through'.

Concluding note

Working with difficult clinical cases such as those of Anna and Zara is a daily process for those in clinical psychology of religion and other mental health fields. In the vast majority of mental health training programs in secular contexts such as Sweden and Norway, neither cultural nor existential meaning analysis is included (DeMarinis et al. 2011). In other contexts, the possible inclusion of this analysis is often based on inadequate models that confuse one particular expression of existential meaning for all possible expressions. This is also very problematic, and both the absence or the inadequacy of an approach that incorporates consideration of existential meaning can lead to unintended consequences that impede the healing process for suffering individuals. This chapter has attempted to frame work in mental health contexts within a larger perspective. The work of Douglas Davies has contributed to the creation of this larger perspective, and points to the importance of a clearly defined multidisciplinary perspective in the study of religion, including traditionally defined religiosity as well as other expressions included in an existential meaning framework. Mental health workers are not trained to see clinical models as cultural as well as scientific artefacts. The clinical model offered here places mental health within a larger political, cultural and meaning-making perspective.

Notes

1 The quotes and references used in this chapter are taken from clinical contexts following ethical research guidelines. Naturally, all identifying information has been removed and pseudonyms are used.
2 Attention to such research questions is a focus of the 'Well-being and Health' research theme of Uppsala University's nationally funded, inter-disciplinary research programme 'Impact of Religion on Society, Law and Democracy' (www.impactofreligion.uu.se).

References

Baker, C. and Beaumont, J. (2011) *Postsecular Cities: Space, Theory and Practice.* London: Continuum.

Bauman, Z. (2000) *Liquid Modernity.* London: Polity Press.

Baumeister, R. (1991) *Meaning in Life.* New York: Guilford.

Casanova, J. (2013) 'Exploring the postsecular: three meanings of "the secular" and their possible transcendence', in C. Calhoun, E. Mendieta and J. Van Antwerpen (eds) *Habermas and Religion.* Cambridge: Polity Press, pp. 27–48.

Casanova, J. (2014) 'Secularisation, religion, and multicultural citizenship', in W. Weisse, A. K. Amirpur and A. Kors (eds) *Religions and Dialogue: International Approaches.* Münster: Waxmann, pp. 21–32.

Davies, D. (2002a) *Anthropology and Theology.* Oxford: Berg.

Davies, D. (2002b) *Death, Ritual and Belief.* London: Continuum.

Davies, D. (2005) 'Death, grief and mourning reconsidered', *Thanatological Studies* 1: 27–36.

Davies, D. (2006) 'Forms of disposal', in G. Foley (ed.) *Death and Religion in a Changing World.* London: ME Sharpe, pp. 228–245.

Davies, D. (2011) *Emotion, Identity and Religion: Hope, Reciprocity, and Otherness.* Oxford: Oxford University Press.

Davies, D. (2013) 'Introduction', in D. Davies with N. Warne (eds) *Emotions and Religious Dynamics.* Aldershot: Ashgate, pp. 1–8.

Davies, D. with Park, C. W. (eds) (2012) *Emotion, Identity and Death: Morality across Disciplines.* Aldershot: Ashgate.

DeMarinis, V. (1994) 'Psychological function and consequences of religious ritual experience', in O. Wikström (ed.) *Rit, symbol och verklighet: Sex studier om ritens function.* Tro och Tanke 1994: 6, Uppsala: Svenska kyrkans forskningsråd, pp. 6–15.

DeMarinis, V. (1996) 'A psychotherapeutic exploration of religious ritual as mediator of memory and meaning', in M. B. Aune and V. DeMarinis (eds) *Religious and Social Ritual: Interdisciplinary Explorations.* Albany: State University of New York, pp. 246–258.

DeMarinis, V. (2003) *Pastoral Care, Existential Health and Existential Epidemiology: A Swedish Postmodern Case Study.* Stockholm: Verbum.

DeMarinis, V. (2008) 'The impact of post-modernization on existential health in Sweden: psychology of religion's function in existential public health analysis', *Archive for the Psychology of Religion* 30: 57–74.

DeMarinis, V. (2011) Den kliniska religionspsykologins utmaningar – att förstå candomblé i Brasilien. ['Challenges for clinical psychology of religion-understanding Candomblé in Brazil'], V. DeMarinis, O Wikström och Ö Cetrez (eds) *Inspiration till religionspsykologi.* Stockholm: Natur och Kultur, pp. 13–26.

DeMarinis, V. (2013) 'Forced migration and meaning-making', in D. Davies and N. Warne (eds) *Emotions and Religious Dynamics*. Aldershot: Ashgate, pp. 109–120.

DeMarinis V., Scheffel-Birath C. and Hansagi H. (2009) 'Cultural analysis as a perspective for gender-informed alcohol treatment research in a Swedish context', *Alcohol and Alcoholism* 44(6): 615–619.

DeMarinis, V., Ulland, D. and Karlsen, K. E. (2011) 'Philosophy's role for guiding theory and practice in clinical contexts grounded in a cultural psychiatry focus: a case study illustration from Southern Norway', *World Cultural Psychiatry Research Review* 6(1): 75–83.

Gibbs, R. (2005) *Embodiment and Cognitive Science*. Cambridge: Cambridge University Press.

Habermas, J. (2008) 'Notes on a post-secular society', *New Perspectives Quarterly* 25(4): 17–29.

Heelas, P. and Woodhead, L. (2005) *The Spiritual Revolution: Why Religion is Giving Way to Spirituality*. Cambridge, MA: Blackwell.

Heelas, P., Lash, S. and Morris, P. (eds) (1996) *Detraditionalization. Critical Reflections on Authority and Identity*. Cambridge, MA: Blackwell.

Heino, A., Gissler, M., Apter, D. and Fiala, C. (2013) 'Conscientious objection and induced abortion in Europe', *The European Journal of Contraception and Reproductive Health Care* 18: 231–233.

Hong, P. Y. P. and Song, I. H. (2010) 'Glocalization of social work practice: global and local responses to globalization', *International Social Work* 53(5): 656–670.

Kleinman, A. (1992). 'Local worlds of suffering: an interpersonal focus for ethnographies of illness experience', *Qualitative Health Research* 2: 127–134.

Lazarus, R. and Folkman, S. (1984) *Stress, Appraisal, and Coping*. New York: Springer.

Liljas Stålhandske, M., Ekstrand, M. and Tydén, T. (2011) 'Women's existential experiences within Swedish abortion care'. *Journal of Psychosomatic Obstetrics & Gynecology* 32(1): 35–41.

Liljas Stålhandske, M, Makenzius, M., Tydén, T. and Larsson, M. (2012) 'Existential experiences and needs related to induced abortion in a group of Swedish women: a quantitative investigation', *Journal of Psychosomatic Obstetrics & Gynecology* 33(2): 53–61.

Mikulincer, M. and Florian, V. (1996) 'Coping and adaptation to trauma and loss', in M. Zeidner and N. Endler (eds) *Handbook of Coping*. New York: Wiley, pp. 554–574.

Park, C. L. (2005) 'Religion as a meaning-making framework in coping with life stress', *Journal of Social Issues* 61(4): 707–729.

Park, C. L. (2010) 'Making sense of the meaning literature', *Psychological Bulletin* 136(2): 257–301.

Pettersson, T. (2002) 'Individual values and global governance', *Comparative Sociology* 1(3–4): 127–135.

Seligman, R. (2005) 'From affliction to affirmation: narrative transformation and the therapeutics of candomblé mediumship', *Transcultural Psychiatry* 42(2): 272–294.

Silberman, I. (2005) 'Religion as a meaning system: implications for the new millennium', *Journal of Social Issues* 61(4): 641–663.

7 The cedar of Lebanon in England
The introduction and reception of a sacred tree

Charles Watkins

Introduction

Douglas Davies (1988: 33–34) argued in his paper on 'evocative symbolism' that trees had a practical symbolism that derived 'both literally and metaphorically' from their being living entities 'spanning many generations'. He saw trees as 'historical markers' which could provide actual or mythical links with the past and could 'make ideas more realistic and dynamic in the present' and stressed the 'evocative symbolic response of humans to trees'. Trees are frequently worshipped as gods and held to be sacred. On a recent visit to Hayachine Shrine, which combines Buddhist and Shinto traditions, in the mountains of Iwate Prefecture, Japan, I was shown several *Sugi* trees (*Cryptomeria japonica*) which were worshipped, as they are at many shrines, and there were also rare examples of a weeping *Katsura* tree (*Cercidiphyllum japonicum*) whose leaves were dried and used to prepare incense for the Buddhist festival of Bon. Sir James Frazer (1922: 1–2) opens *The Golden Bough* with an analysis of the landscape around the shores of Lake Nemi in the Alban Hills to the south of Rome where 'stood the sacred grove and sanctuary of Diana Nemorensis'. In this wood grew a tree from which no branch might be broken except by a 'runaway slave' who if he succeeded had the right to fight the 'priest in single combat, and if he slew him he reigned in his stead with the title of King of the Wood (*Rex Nemorensis*)'.

Trees are also of crucial significance in the Norse myths including the creation of humankind. Snorri Sturluson (1179–1241), the rich Icelandic landowner and lawyer, describes how 'Bor's sons were walking by the sea-shore and came upon two logs. They picked them up and shaped them into human beings. The first gave them breath and life, the second understanding and motion, the third form, speech, hearing and sight. They gave them clothes and names' (Page 1990: 59). When the logs became human 'The sun shone from the south on the stones of earth; then the ground was grown with green shoots' (Kristjansson 1998: 41). He also tells of the 'the Yggdrasill, tree of fate, upon which the welfare of the universe seems to depend' which is usually identified as an ash tree (Turville-Petre 1964: 277). And, of course, one of the most significant trees in the Christian Bible is the tree of knowledge of good and evil in the Garden of Eden, the home of Adam and Eve in *Genesis*. Many trees were held to be sacred in Anglo-Saxon England, and this was a worry for early Christian bishops who were anxious about the worship of trees and other numinous places (Hooke 2010; Walsham 2012). There was particular concern about certain species of trees, such as elders and large single oaks and sacred woods. In the sixteenth century, the resurgence of Catholicism created a 'new geography of the sacred' which showed itself, for example, in the great excitement in the discovery of the image of a crucifix in an ash tree which blew down on the estate of Sir Thomas Stradling in Glamorganshire in 1559 (Walsham 2012: 217–218).

In this chapter, using the example of the cedar of Lebanon (*Cedrus libani*), I examine the extent to which introduced and exotic trees became sacred in England. This tree's frequent occurrence in the Bible meant that it had long sacred associations, but following its introduction in the sixteenth century, it came to develop a patina of symbolic association, and its 'cultural and historical precedents' helped it to become increasingly aligned with memorialization (Davies 1988: 33).

From the seventeenth century onwards, the movement of tree species around the world increased rapidly and dramatically. The enormous growth in world trade allowed many new species to be imported to Europe to be tested for their susceptibility to frost and their marketability as potential ornamental or timber trees. By 1550 it is estimated that there were 36 hardy and woody exotic species cultivated in England: 'by 1600, 103 species; by 1700, 239 species; by 1800, 733 species; and by 1900, 1911 species' Jarvis (1979: 157). John Claudius Loudon (1854, vol. I: 54) thought that in the seventeenth century the 'taste for foreign plants' was 'confined to a few, and these not the richest persons in the community; but generally medical men, clergymen, persons holding small situations under government, or tradesmen'. In the following century, however, 'the taste for planting foreign trees extended itself among the wealthy landed proprietors'.

Some of the most enthusiastic planters of new varieties of trees were clergymen. Henry Compton, Bishop of London from 1675 until his death in 1713, had 'a great Genius for Botanism' and had the enthusiasm and opportunity to start collecting trees on a very extensive scale at the Bishop of London's summer residence Fulham Palace, which included a fine garden and parkland. Earlier bishops, such as Edmund Grindal (1558–1570), who is thought to have planted a *Quercus ilex* which still survives, had already started to collect and plant trees and shrubs at Fulham. In his role as Bishop of London, Compton was also head of the church in the American colonies. He was conscientious in looking after clergy in the colonies and was able to appoint some who had a keen interest in botany. In addition, he was happy to share his knowledge and enthusiasm and showed 'great Civilities to, and had an Esteem for, all those who were anything curious in this sort of Study'. John Ray in his *Historia Plantarum* in 1686 listed 15 rare trees and shrubs, many from America in Compton's Fulham Palace garden including the tree angelica and the tulip tree. Compton died in his eighties and there 'were few days in the year, before the latter part of his life, but he was actually in his Garden' ordering the planting and care of his trees and plants (Coleby 2004; Morris 1991; Ray 1686; Loudon 1838; Watkins 2014).

Enthusiastic botanists such as Samuel Reynardson (who lived at Cedar House, Hillingdon, from 1678 until his death in 1721) and Dr Robert Uvedale (1642–1722) of Enfield had large collections of exotic trees. Reynardson 'kept them for the most part confined to pots and tubs, preserving them in greenhouses in winter, never attempting to naturalise them to our climate'. Douglas Chambers (1993: 3) has argued that the widespread availability of popular translations of classical authorities in the eighteenth century helped to encourage the planting and nurturing of trees. Virgil's *Georgics* which had become very popular through Dryden's 1697 translation 'provided both a model for silviculture and an encouragement to the sort of botanical experimentation already taking place'. The influence of the publication of John Evelyn's *Sylva* in 1664, and its successive editions in 1670, 1679 and 1706 in extolling the introduction of new trees, should not be underestimated. Some later authors such as Loudon considered that Evelyn (1670–1706) was 'more anxious to promote the planting of valuable indigenous trees, than to introduce foreign ones' but he 'had a voracious interest in new species, chiefly trees. Throughout his library any reference to the introduction of new species is marked or annotated' (Loudon 1854, vol. I: 41; Chambers 1993: 36, 45; Hartley 2010).

Another crucially important source of knowledge about trees was provided by the Bible with its many references and allusions to the growing and felling of trees. Some trees started to acquire sacred associations because of their biblical connections, and perhaps the most telling example is the cedar of Lebanon. For over 400 years, enthusiastic botanists, tree planters and scholars have compared biblical descriptions of cedars with accounts by contemporary travellers of the trees growing in Lebanon. In this chapter, I first examine the ways in which the cedar of Lebanon became understood through these travellers' accounts and then go on to show how the sacred attributes of the tree encouraged the planting and establishment of cedars in England. Finally I show how the tree became associated with sacred spaces, such as churchyards, and how drawings and photographs of the tree were used to symbolize sacred landscapes.

Early written descriptions of the cedar of Lebanon

The cedar was associated with some of the most dramatic stories in the Bible. Nebuchadnezzar, the powerful young king of Babylon (605–562 BC), celebrated his victories against the Phoenicians and attack on Jerusalem by an inscription at Wadi Brisa in present-day Lebanon. Russell Meiggs (1982: 82) noted that the text 'is accompanied by a relief, now very badly worn, of the king killing a lion' and that a second relief shows 'the king cutting down a tree'. Nebuchadnezzar's death was celebrated by the prophet Isaiah (14: 7–8): 'the whole world has rest and is at peace . . . The pines themselves and the cedars of Lebanon exult over you. Since you have been laid low, they say, no man comes to fell us'. The identification and naming of the cedar of Lebanon as with many trees has a complicated history. Its frequent identification in the Bible combined with the occurrence of ancient cedars actually growing on Mount Lebanon gave it strong symbolic veracity: the biblical references indicated that the tree existed in ancient times; the survival of old trees growing on the slopes of Mount Lebanon demonstrated that this was the species mentioned.

Travellers to Syria[1] visited Mount Lebanon and wondered whether the very trees they saw were the same as those described by biblical prophets. Loudon (1854: 2409) noted that 'almost every modern traveller who has visited Syria has ascended Mount Lebanon, and recorded his visit'. He quotes the French naturalist Pierre Belon (1517–1564) who published an account of his travels through the Near East (1546–1549) in 1553. Belon, like most travellers, was guided to the cedars on Mount Lebanon by the Maronite monks from the monastery of the Virgin Mary. Loudon noted that at this period 'paying a visit to the cedars of Mount Lebanon seems to have been considered a type of pilgrimage'. This caused problems for the trees as visitors 'took away some of the wood of the trees, to make crosses and tabernacles'. The damage was so great that 'the patriarch of the Maronites, fearing that the trees would be destroyed, threatened excommunication to all those that would injure the cedars' and 'exhorted all Christians to preserve trees so celebrated' in the Bible. It was reported that 'the Maronites were only allowed to cut even the branches of these trees once a year: and that was, on the eve of the Transfiguration of our Saviour' which is in August and 'a suitable period for visiting the mountain'. At this festival the 'Maronites and pilgrims' climbed the mountain and 'passing the night in the wood' drank 'wine made from grapes grown on the mountain, and lighted their fires with branches cut from the cedars. They passed the night in dancing a kind of Pyrrhic dance, and in singing and regaling' and on the next day 'the patriarch celebrated high mass on an altar built under one of the largest and oldest cedars'. John Gerard (1597: 1171) describes the '*Cedrus Libani* . . . the great Cedar tree of Libanus' as 'huge and mightie' and as having branches 'so orderly placed by degrees, as that a man may climb up by them to the very top as by a ladder'. He provides a woodcut illustration of the foliage and cones and notes that the 'Cedar trees grow upon the snowie mountains, as in Syria on mount Libanus, on which there remain some even to this day . . . planted as it is thought by Salomon himself' (see Figure 7.1).

One of the earliest first-hand English descriptions of the cedars was provided by Henry Maundrell, a Church of England clergyman and chaplain to the Levant Company's factory at Aleppo in his *A journey from Aleppo to Jerusalem: at Easter, AD 1697*. Maundrell travelled to the cedars on 9 May 1697 and found the 'noble trees' growing 'amongst the snow, near the

Figure 7.1 Cedrus Libani. Woodcut, from John Gerard, *The Herball or Generall Historie of Plantes* (London, 1597).

highest part of Lebanon'. He thought the trees 'remarkable as well for their own age and largeness, as for the frequent allusions made to them in the Word of God'. He found only 16 'very old trees, of a prodigious bulk' but there were 'numerous' younger trees. He measured 'one of the largest, and found it 12 yards 6 in. in girt, and yet sound; and 37 yards in the spread of its boughs' (Maundrell 1749: 142). About 40 years later, the trees were visited by Richard Pococke (1704–1765), Bishop of Ossory, in his *A Description of the East* (Vol. 2, 1745) in which he described his travels from 1737 to 1740. 'From the Convent of St. Sergius (Latin Carmelite Friars), there is a gentle ascent, for about an hour, to a large plain between the highest parts of the Mount Lebanon.' The 'famous cedars of Lebanon . . . form a grove about a mile in circumference, which consists of some large cedars that are near to one another, a great number of small cedars, and some young pines. The great cedars, at some distance, look like very large spreading oaks; the bodies of the trees are short, dividing at bottom into three or four limbs, some of which, growing up together for about 10 ft., appear like those Gothic columns which seem to be composed of several pillars'. He reported on the quality of the wood noting that it 'does not differ from white deal in appearance, nor does it seem to be harder'. He also notes, 200 years after Pierre Belon's account, that 'Christians of several denominations near this place come here to celebrate the festival of the Transfiguration, and have built altars against several of the large trees, where they administer the sacrament' (Pococke 1745: 105).

If we turn to early editions of John Evelyn's *Sylva*, some considerable uncertainty as to what constitutes a cedar is apparent. In the 1670 edition, he uses the reported small number of surviving cedars on Mount Lebanon as evidence for a general call for his readers to plant trees and manage them carefully. He notes that the 'Cedar in Judea was first planted by Solomon, who doubtless try'd many rare *Experiments* of this nature, and none more *Kingly* than that of *Planting* to *Posterity*' (Evelyn 1670: 116). He then refers to travellers' descriptions which indicate that only a few of these biblical trees survive and argues that this is 'a pregnant *Example* of what *Time*, and *Neglect* will bring to *ruine*, if due, and continual care be not taken to propagate *Timber*' (1670: 116). This clear link between cedars and Lebanon becomes blurred, however, when he considers the quality of cedar wood. He notes that the cedar 'grows in all extreams: In the moist *Barbados*, the hot *Bermudas*, the cold *New-England*; even where the Snow lies as (I am assur'd) almost half the year' (Evelyn 1670: 120–121). And although he hopes fancifully that the use of timber by merchants in London in their shops might 'preserve the whole *City* as if it stood amongst . . . the prospects of *Mount Libanus*', it is clear that he is using the term 'cedar' for many different timbers and indeed considers some juniper wood as '*sweet as Cedar* whereof it is accounted a *spurious* kind' (Evelyn 1670: 130).

But in the third edition of his book of 1679, he mentions that he has obtained seeds from Mount Lebanon and he is therefore able to describe at first-hand what the cones looked like (Evelyn 1679: 125). He reports that he has 'received Cones and Seeds of those few remaining Trees' from 'on the Mountains of Libanus', and as they grew there, he questions 'Why then should they not thrive in Old England ?' and argues 'I know not, save for want of Industry and Trial'. He describes the form of the trees from travellers' accounts noting that the cedars are 'of the greatest Antiquity' and are 'indeed majestical' and their 'sturdy Arms . . . grow in Time so weighty, as often to bend the very Stem, and main Shaft'. The most remarkable thing to him was 'the Structure of the Cones and Seeds Receptacles, tack'd and ranged between the Branch-leaves, in such order, as nothing appears more curious and artificial, and, at a little Distance, exceedingly beautiful'. His enthusiasm for the tree is clear in his precise description of the cones, which he handled himself: 'These Cones have the Bases rounder, shorter, or rather thicker, and with blunter Points, the whole circum-zoned, as it were, with pretty broad thick Scales, which adhere together in exact Series to the very Top and Summit, where they are somewhat smaller.' But he also reports continued uncertainty about the status of the tree: 'Botanists are not fully agreed to what Species many noble and stately Trees, passing under the Names of Cedar, are to be reckoned' (Evelyn 1679: 135, 139).

Planting cedars of Lebanon in England

It is not known who first planted and successfully established a cedar of Lebanon in England, but there have been many contenders for the honour.

It is quite possible that John Evelyn was the person and Loudon argues that 'It is extremely improbable that a man so fond of trees as Evelyn, and so anxious to introduce new and valuable sorts into his native country, should have suffered "cones and seeds" of such a tree in his possession, without trying to raise young plants from them; particularly as he was a man of leisure, residing in the country, and fond of trying experiments'. As further evidence he notes that 'Evelyn had doubtless planted some cedars at Sayes court because in a letter to the Royal Society detailing the effects of a bad winter dated April 16 1684 he states "As for exotics, my cedars, I think, are dead"' (Loudon 1854: 2412–2414). Another strong contender is the oriental scholar Edward Pococke (1604–1691) who visited Syria in 1638/1639 while chaplain to the Levant Company. It is reported that 'Several noble trees planted from seeds that Pococke brought back from the east commemorated him long after his death'. These included a 'great plane tree' which 'was at the end of the twentieth century in "Pococke's garden" at Christ Church, and a large fig tree known as the "arbor Pocockiana" which was still "producing fruit in the garden of the Hebrew professor in 1911"'. Edward Pococke was appointed rector of Childrey in Hampshire by Christ Church College in 1642 and 'according to unbroken tradition' a tree there 'which is still healthy and producing viable seed, was planted by Edward Pococke on the rectory lawn in 1646'. If so, this would be the oldest cedar of Lebanon in England, and 'one of the few to survive the harsh winter of 1740, which destroyed most of the other cedar trees growing in Britain' (Toomer 2004).[2]

By the mid-eighteenth century, the fashion for planting cedars of Lebanon was well established among the aristocracy. When Linnaeus' pupil Pehr Kalm visited the Duke of Argyll in May 1747 at Whitton on Hounslow Heath, he found him to be particularly interested in 'Dendrologie' and noted that 'there was a collection of all kinds of trees, which grow in different parts of the world, and can stand the climate of England out in the open air, summer and winter'. He pointed out that the Duke had 'planted very many of these trees with his own hand' and that 'there was here a very large number of Cedars of Lebanon' (Murdoch 2004; Symes et al. 1986). The pleasures of planting were celebrated by George Sinclair, head gardener at the Duke of Bedford's Woburn Abbey, who thought that the 'interest arising from the adoption of foreign trees into domestic scenery' was 'not confined to their picturesque effects', but reminded all 'of the climes whence they come' and the 'scenes with which they were associated'. In exploring 'a well-selected arboretum', the 'eternal snows of the Himalaya', the 'savannahs of the Missouri . . . untrodden forests of Patagonia . . . vallies of Lebanon, pass in review before us: we seem to wander in other climes, to converse with other nations' (Sinclair 1832: 129). Cedars were planted with enthusiasm by both Capability Brown, as at his first major commission at Croome Park, Worcestershire in the 1750s and by his picturesque critic Uvedale Price at Foxley, Herefordshire (Brown 2011; Watkins and Cowell 2012).

One of the most influential writers on trees at the end of the eighteenth century was the Reverend William Gilpin, vicar of Boldre in the New Forest, who published his *Remarks on Forest Scenery* in 1791. Gilpin was well known as a schoolmaster and wrote extensively on picturesque scenery. Gilpin argued that the cedar of Lebanon was preeminent among all evergreens not only because of its own 'dignity' but also 'on account of the respectable mention, which is everywhere made of it in scripture'. He emphasizes that 'Solomon spake of trees from the cedar of Lebanon, to the hyssop that springeth out of the wall: that is from the greatest to the least' (Gilpin 1791: 73). He considered that 'The eastern writers are indeed the principal sources, from which we are to obtain the true character of the cedar; as it is an eastern tree . . . It is generally employed by the prophets to express strength, power, and longevity. The strength of the cedar is used as an emblem to express the power even of Jehovah'. Gilpin (1791: 74–76) argued that two of the principal characteristics of the cedar, the 'multiplicity and length of its branches and its dense canopy of leaves are identified: "His boughs are multiplied, as Ezekiel says, and his branches become long; which David calls spreading abroad"'. He thought that Ezekiel identified 'with great beauty, and aptness' the 'shadowing shroud' as 'no tree in the forest is more remarkable than the cedar, for it's close-woven, leafy canopy'. Gilpin considered that it was the 'mantling foliage' of the cedar which is its 'greatest beauty; which arises from the horizontal growth' of branches which 'forms a kind of sweeping, irregular penthouse'. Moreover, when to this 'idea of beauty' is added 'that of strength' from 'the piramidal form of the stem, and the robustness of the limbs, the tree is complete in all it's beauty, and majesty' (Gilpin 1791: 76).

But Gilpin did not have much optimism for the successful establishment of large numbers of trees in England. In the British climate, he argued, 'we cannot expect to see the cedar in such perfection. The forest of Lebanon is perhaps the only part of the world, where it's growth is perfect'. He thought that young trees were 'often with us a vigorous thriving plant' but that in its 'maturer age, the beauty of the cedar is generally gone, it becomes shrivelled, deformed, and stunted'. There were exceptions however, including the famous tree at Hillingdon, near Uxbridge which when he saw it in 1776 'was about one hundred and eighteen years of age: and being then completely clump-headed, it was a very noble and picturesque tree'. This cedar tree at Hillingdon near Uxbridge had become one of the most famous in England, clearly visible from the main road. It had been planted by Samuel Reynardson who lived there from 1678 to 1721. Gilpin thought it the 'best specimen' of a cedar 'I ever saw in England' and measured it: the 'perpendicular height of it was fifty three feet; it's horizontal expanse ninety six; and it's girth fifteen and a half'. This 'noble cedar' was blown down in 'the high winds about the beginning of the year 1790' and its trunk was five feet in diameter. John Claudius Loudon noted that Sir Joseph Banks had a table made from its timber (Gilpin 1791: 77–78; Bolton et al. 1971: 62; Loudon 1854, vol. IV: 2417).

In the eighteenth and nineteenth centuries, stories circulated about the origin of some of the largest cedars. Loudon wondered, for example, whether 'Supposing Evelyn to have raised plants from his cone, the great cedar at Enfield may have been given by him to Dr Uvedale', as Evelyn's *Sylva* was written in 1664 and Dr Uvedale lived there (1665–1670) and the alternative story that the Enfield Cedar 'had been brought by one of the doctor's pupils from Mount Lebanon rests solely on tradition'. Dr Uvedale was 'famous for his curious gardens and choice collection of exotics. The Cedar, which is now perhaps the largest in the kingdom, was put in the ground by him, a plant brought direct from Mount Libanus'. It became so well known and liked that when it was threatened with felling in the early nineteenth century 'the contemplation of its loss excited so much regret and discontent among several of the most respectable inhabitants in the place' that the owner 'was obliged to relinquish the barbarous design, even after the trench was dug around it, the saw-pit prepared, and the axe almost lifted up for its destruction' (Strutt 1830: 104).

Other famous old cedars were drawn and described by the artist Jacob George Strutt (1784–1867) who produced a set of etchings: *'Sylva Britannica'*, *or*, *Portraits of Forest Trees Distinguished for their Antiquity* in 1822. His wife Elizabeth was a prolific author of devotional works and travel guides. Strutt thought that owing to its origin in 'elevated situations in the Levant' the cedar 'is so hardy, that it can easily adapt itself to any climate. It has not been cultivated in England till of late years; although its quick growth, and its capability of thriving in a meagre soil, render it peculiarly desirable for those bleak and barren situations which have hitherto been principally devoted to the fir'. He noted that 'The frequent and solemn allusions to the Cedar of Holy Writ, seem to give it something of a sacred character' which was reinforced by 'knowledge of the esteem in which it was held by the ancients'. Some individual trees, such as the great cedar of Hammersmith when 'in the full prime of its summer foliage, waving its rich green arms to the gentle breezes, and hiding the small birds innumerable in its boughs', afforded 'a fine exemplification of the sublime description of the Prophet Ezekiel, in his comparison of the glory of Assyria, in her "most high and palmy state"'. Others were growing less well, including those in the apothecaries' garden at Chelsea, apparently planted in 1683, whose branches have 'of late years altogether drooped and languished' owing to the 'pestiferous vapour of the numerous gas-works by which it is surrounded' (Strutt 1830: 103, 106, 108–109) (see Figure 7.2).

It was soon realized that timber produced by the cedar of Lebanon in England was not of a particularly high quality. Loudon (1854: 2417) summarized its commercial value: 'The wood of the cedar is of a reddish white, light and spongy, easily worked, but very apt to shrink and warp, and by no means durable'. Authors found it difficult to equate the quality of the wood grown in France and England with the qualities described by classical authors and in the Bible. Loudon noted that the table Sir Joseph Banks

Figure 7.2 Jacob George Strutt. 'Cedar at Hammersmith House' *Sylva Britannica* (London, 1830). Facing page 106. Private Collection.

had made from the Hillingdon cedar 'was soft, without scent (except that of common deal), and possessed little variety of veining'. Moreover cedar wood 'burns quickly, throwing out many sparks, though but little heat in comparison with that of the oak or the beech; though the flame of the cedar wood is more lively and brilliant, on account of the resin it contains'. Earlier Walter Nicol (1803: 50–51) had noted that 'This celebrated tree is found in the highest perfection in the bleakest and most mountainous sites of the East; but whether it shall be found so on the mountains of Britain, remains to be known'. He compared it unfavourably to the European Larch, which was one of the most profitable timber trees in this period: 'It is much slower in growth, and also less docile than the Larch; nor need we ever expect to see it become so great and acquisition to the nation'. But he agreed with many other authors that as 'an ornamental plant, it ought to be admitted in all extensive designs' pointing out airily that of 'its mighty stature, of the durability of its timber; of its property, in resisting worms; . . . with a hundred more of its *properties*, famed and celebrated for ages, might volumes be filled'. John Elwes and Augustine Henry, writing in 1908, confirmed the low value of cedar wood in Britain: 'Its value in commerce is, however, low, because neither the supply nor the demand is regular; and the cost of removing and sawing up large cedar trees is so great, that I was offered a tree containing 300 cubic feet for nothing if I could get it away' (p. 467).

But the leading foresters and tree enthusiasts all tended to agree that the cedar of Lebanon was one of the most attractive trees to plant. Loudon enthused that 'As an ornamental object, the cedar is one of the most magnificent of trees; uniting the grand with the picturesque, in a manner not equalled by any tree in Britain, either indigenous or introduced' (1854: 2418). He argued that the tree should be given plenty of space to spread its branches: 'On a lawn, where the soil is good, the situation sheltered, and the space ample, it forms a gigantic pyramid, and confers dignity on the park and mansion to which it belongs; and it makes an avenue of unrivalled grandeur, if the trees are so far apart as to allow their branches to expand on every side'. However, if it was 'planted in masses', it would be 'like any other species of the pine and fir tribe, drawn up with a straight naked trunk' and in this case it 'scarcely differs in appearance from the larch, except in being evergreen'. If large numbers were to be planted and 'a distance of 50ft. or 60ft. allowed between each tree' then 'nothing in the way of sylvan majesty can be more sublime than such a forest of living pyramids'. Other Victorian commentators agreed: Augustus Mongredien (1870: 60) thought it to be 'of unrivalled majesty and grandeur when old, and beautiful even in the earlier stages of its growth'; William Ablett (1880: 35) noted that the 'elegant grandeur of the cedar was often used as a type and illustration by the Hebrew prophets, to express the beautiful steadfastness and comely aspects of the spiritual condition of the righteous, which earthly storms, though they might shake, could not remove', while the laconic J. Blenkarn (1859: 72) noted that the 'beauty of this tree is so well known and acknowledged, that any comment here is unnecessary'. The status of the cedar as an ornamental tree by the early twentieth century was almost unrivalled, and W. J. Bean, curator at the Royal Botanic Gardens at Kew, thought that 'Irrespective of its sacred and historical associations, no tree ever introduced to our islands has added more for the charm of gardens than the cedar of Lebanon. Its thick, stately trunk and noble crown of wide-spreading, horizontal branches give to it an air of distinction no other tree at present can rival'. However, the impact of industrial and domestic pollution and the intensity and frequency of smog meant that he was concerned that trees in the suburbs of London were 'becoming fewer and less vigorous' and thought that 'until there is a revolution in the methods of consuming coal in the metropolis, the gaps will never be filled' (Bean 1950: 394).

By the Victorian period, cedars of Lebanon had become a key emblem of country house gardens and parks. At Elvaston Castle, an extraordinarily diverse and intricately designed formal pinetum was established by William Barron for the Earl of Harrington (Glendinning 1849). The pinetum was planted exclusively with evergreens from 1835 around what had formerly been the central drive, the eastern side with pines and the west with firs and spruces. The northern and southern ends of the avenues were planted with cedars of Lebanon and deodars. Other avenues were planted with yews and *Araucarias*. Barron devised a successful tree-transplanting machine and in November 1831 moved 43-foot-tall and 48-foot-diameter cedar of Lebanon into the gardens at Elvaston which had grown by the 1870s from having a trunk of 2 feet in circumference to one of 10 feet (Elliott, Watkins and Daniels 2011: 171–172). John Ruskin celebrated trees for their 'unerring uprightness' like temple pillars and 'mighty resistances of rigid arm and limb to the storms of ages' and he felt they deserved 'boundless affection and admiration from us' serving as 'a nearly perfect test of our being in right temper of mind and way of life' and no one 'can be far wrong in either who loves the trees enough and everyone is assuredly wrong in both, who does not love them'. And it was to Ruskin that the English Arboricultural Society, founded in 1881, later to become the Royal Forestry Society, turned for ideas for a suitable motto in 1887. One of his suggestions was '*Saturabuntur ligna campi et cedri Libani quas plantavil*' (The trees of the Lord are satisfied – the cedars of Lebanon which He hath planted) (Ruskin 1907: 79–81; Ruskin 1887: 156–157).

The cedar in sacred spaces

In the nineteenth century, the cedar of Lebanon became associated with sacred spaces such as churchyards and cemeteries. John Claudius Loudon wrote his influential treatise *On the laying out, planting, and managing of cemeteries; and on the improvement of churchyards* in 1843. Key issues for him were that cemeteries should be open to the sun and that trees should not be closely planted. He stressed that 'too many trees and shrubs impede the free circulation of the air and the drying effect of the sun, and therefore they ought to be introduced in moderation'. Another important consideration was that burial grounds should be visually clearly identifiable places of contemplation and hence that 'Every mode of introducing trees and shrubs which is identical with that practised in planting parks and pleasure grounds is to be avoided, as tending to confound the character and expression of scenes which are, or ought to be, essentially distinct'. In general, evergreen trees with dark foliage were recommended as 'the variety produced by deciduous and flowering trees is not favourable to the expression either of solemnity or grandeur'. Moreover, coniferous tree had the practical advantage of producing 'much less litter than that of broad-leaved trees' (Loudon 1843: 20). One of the principal trees he recommended in his design for a cemetery at Cambridge was the cedar of Lebanon which he thought should be 'planted along the walks at regular distances'. He also recommended the cedar for country churchyards but recognized that, as with many other conifers, its habit of surface rooting could cause problems. Indeed, he thought that if it were not for this 'the cedar of Lebanon would be one of the most fitting of all trees for a churchyard, from the sombre hue of its foliage, and its grand and yet picturesque form; from the horizontal lines of its spreading branches contrasting strongly with the perpendicular lines of a Gothic church; and above all, from the associations connected with it, on account of its frequent mentions in Holy Writ'. To get over this problem, he recommended that in all new churchyards 'two or three spots (each about 30 ft. in diameter) were set apart, not to be broken up by interments, and each planted with a cedar of Lebanon'. In addition, he felt that in many old churchyards across the country 'a spot sufficiently large for at least one cedar might easily be spared; and the clergyman or the churchwardens who should plant a cedar on such a spot, and fence it sufficiently while young, would confer a grand and appropriate ornament on the church, and would deserve the gratitude of the parishioners'[3] (Loudon 1843: 89).

The publication of Loudon's book was part of a general move to improve burial conditions in the nineteenth century. One of the most famous examples of a new cemetery was at Abney Park, Stoke Newington in North London. This was laid out in 1840 with the help of the leading nurseryman George Loddiges and an immense collection of trees and shrubs was planted (Joyce 1994; Solman and Douglas 1995). George Collison, one of its promoters, published a guidebook which extolled the beauty of the existing well established trees on the site which young plantations in other new cemeteries did not have. And while he likened the welcome recurrence and beauties of the new foliage of deciduous trees to the 'strong probabilities and the opening glories of a physical resurrection!' he also admired the old cedars of Lebanon (Collison 1840: 297). The most famous of these trees were those surrounding the former residence of the famous Congregationalist hymnologist Isaac Watts (1674–1748). In about 1712 the prominent dissenting Whig Sir Thomas Abney invited Watts to stay with him 'for what was initially a week's stay' but 'Watts was to spend the rest of his life in considerable comfort with the Abneys' at their various homes, and from 1733 he stayed 'with Lady Abney and her two surviving daughters' who 'represented for him the ideal dissenting household' at Abney Park (Rivers 2004). By the nineteenth century, it was repeatedly claimed that some of the older trees at Abney had been planted by Watts and his friends especially 'the magnificent cedar of Lebanon', therefore providing a direct link with Watts and the past. The 'health and vigour' of the cedar which was 'surprising when its age is considered' was celebrated, and when some of the old and decaying trees and underwood had been removed in converting the site for scientific reasons, to allow 'the free circulation of air', it was claimed that this had benefited the cedar. A story was told that a mower's scythe had been suspended in the trunk of the cedar and having been forgotten about had become surrounded by wood covering the blade except for a small portion of the iron heel (Collison 1840: 205–207). As Isaac Watts had spent much of his life enjoying the grounds, park and trees at Abney House and had written some of his famous works there, the old trees were strongly associated, especially in the minds of dissenters, with his hymns. For promoters like Collison, these specific religious associations were merely part of the general appeal of the contemplation of trees at Abney and 'there needed to be no reminder of the pleasure gained from the contemplation of trees which were "remarkable either for size or longevity" and offered "quiet eloquent" testimony to the 'passage of the ages with their numerous and rich pagan and Christian associations' (Collison 1840: 305–307).

As well as being planted to make particular places more sacred, representations of the trees were used by artists to characterize historical religious paintings, and representations of the tree were used to illustrate sacred books. John Martin used the characteristic form of the cedar in several of his paintings including his very popular mezzotint 'The Fall of Man' which was published in 1831 in which Adam and Eve are depicted having eaten of the tree of knowledge. A contemporary critic, quoting Milton, thought that this was 'a perfect picture of landscape beauty – "clear spring, and shady grove . . ." the dark thick foliage of the foreground . . . melts away into the distance, where a lake sleeps in all the quiet of paradise . . . bounded by woods and mountains, and above and beyond all rises the "verdrous wall" in the sublime grandeur of Alpine scenery' (Campbell 1992: 126). Line-engraved copies of this mezzotint were very popular in the Victorian period and frequently used as illustrations to sacred works such as *The Home Preacher or Church in the House* (1868–1869) and as the frontispiece to *The Imperial Family Bible* (1844) (Campbell 1992: 126). Loudon noted how the 'great artist' Martin had 'introduced the flat head of the aged cedar into his imaginary view of the Garden of Eden' and had also used them in another famous mezzotint, 'The Fall of Babylon' (1831), where he shows them growing in the 'terraces of the gardens of Babylon'. Cedars also appear in his 'The Plains of Heaven' which formed part of his 'Last Judgement' triptych (*c.* 1845–1853) which 'effectively

Figure 7.3 John Martin, *The Fall of Man* Genesis 3:6; Eve offering Adam an apple from the Tree of Knowledge in the Garden of Eden, covering herself with branch; lush landscape with river and waterfall spread out beyond; proof with some lettering; from a series of prints illustrating the Bible. 1831 © The Trustees of the British Museum.

tapped into vernacular Christian culture' (Loudon 1854: 2423; Morden 2010; Myrone and Austen 2012: 182) (see Figure 7.3).

With the increasing popularity of landscape photography, yet more possibilities opened up for the celebration of the cedar of Lebanon, photographs of the cedars actually growing in Lebanon began to be used as illustrations for books, including the Bible. One of the most important landscape photographers was Francis Frith (1822–1898), who turned his early amateur enthusiasm in photography into a profitable business. Frith was a Quaker who had published an influential tract *A Reasonable Faith: Short Religious Essays for the Times* in 1844. He made his reputation with the photographs he took on journeys to the Near East including Palestine and Syria in the 1850s 'where he took pioneering photographs of the landscape and of monuments, often under dangerous and difficult conditions' (Sackett 2004). Photographs sold by the company included general views of the cedar groves and photographs of individual trees. One of the images was used to illustrate *The Holy Bible . . . Illustrated with Photographs by [Francis] Frith* published by William Mackenzie, 1862–1863 (see Figure 7.4).

The increase of visitors and photographers brought about increasing interest in the fate of the cedars of Lebanon. One concern was that the heavy grazing by sheep and goats meant that there was hardly any natural regeneration of the cedars. Elwes and Henry (1908: 454) reported that a 'detailed

Figure 7.4 Francis Frith. Cedars of Lebanon (615), *c.* 1860. © V&A Images E.208:1888–1994.

survey of the basin where the cedars grow' at the head of the Kedisha valley at 6,000 ft. had been made by two Royal Navy surveyors with Sir Joseph Hooker in 1860. Hooker 'believed that the wood used by Solomon and by Nebuchadnezzar in buildings was the Lebanon cedar' (Elwes and Henry 1908: 454, fn 2). The age of the cedars was estimated by making ring counts from a branch of an old tree. The youngest trees were about 100 years old and the oldest 2,500 years old. They noted that one small grove appears 'as a black speck in the great area of the corie and its moraines, which contain no other arboreous vegetation, nor any vegetation nor any shrubs but a few small barberry and rose bushes'. The 'most remarkable and significant fact connected with their size, and consequently with the age of the grove, is that there is no tree of less than 18 inches girth, and that no young trees, seedlings, or even bushes of a second year's growth were found' (454). They noted that S. R. Oliver wrote in the *Gardeners' Chronicle* xii 204 (1879) that 'for want of proper protection against the goats and thoughtless tourists, the present grove is dwindling away, and another generation will exclaim against our supineness in thus allowing a relic of the past to die out prematurely' (454). In addition, Dr A. E. Day wrote in November 1903 that a grove he had visited 'suffers much from being cut' and he noticed that 'Local people obtain from it roof-beams and wood for fuel . . . I have failed to find a single large

CEDAR ON MOUNT LEBANON

PLATE 127.

Figure 7.5 Cornelius Van Alen Van Dyck, 'Cedar on Mount Lebanon' Plate 127 in Elwes, John Henry and Henry, Augustine *The trees of Great Britain and Ireland*, Volume III (Edinburgh, 1908).

tree . . . which has not been cut off, with the result that several branches have taken the place of the principal stem' (454). Elwes and Henry (1908: 457) provide a remarkable photograph taken by Cornelius Van Alen Van Dyck (1818–1895), the American doctor and Protestant missionary and translator, showing a splendidly isolated cedar sheltering sheep and goats, in a scene which temptingly takes us back to Old Testament times (see Figure 7.5).

While the cedar of Lebanon was increasingly threatened in its homeland, in England and many other countries it had become a very fashionable ornamental tree. While it was not a commercially important tree, like other exotic conifers such as the European larch and Norway spruce, it had become a common specimen tree in large gardens and parks. But more than this, there was an explicit and overt attempt to establish the tree as sacred through planting in churchyards and cemeteries. This sacredness showed itself also through its use by the painter John Martin in his enormously popular biblical scenes. The strength of the biblical connections was reinforced by the popularity of photographs of cedars of Lebanon, such as those by Francis Frith, in the later nineteenth century. Here photographs of ancient cedars, which were interpreted as direct, living, connections with Old Testament characters, were used both to ground and place the Bible in the landscape.

Notes

1 During the period of the Ottoman Empire, modern Lebanon was usually classed as part of Syria.
2 http://www.treecouncil.org.uk/community-action/green-monuments/ancient-trees
   It seems Edward Pococke was not related to Richard Pococke. Sir Thomas Hanmer (1612–1678), MP for Flint, has been 'credited with being the first English author to mention the cedar of Lebanon, predicting its future importance' (Martin 2004).
3 He also recommended Douglas Davies' favourite tree, the *Araucaria* – 'A very singular tree, of slow growth, and, as it is certain of attracting general attention, when planted in a cemetery, it ought to be surrounded by a wire fence for 5 or 6 years to protect it from accidental injury' (Loudon 1843: 97).

References

Ablett, W. (1880) *English Trees and Tree Planting*. London: Smith, Elder.
Bean, W. J. (1950) *Trees and Shrubs Hardy in the British Isles*. 7th edition. Volume 1. London: J. Murray.
(1862) *The Holy Bible . . . Illustrated with Photographs by [Francis] Frith*. Glasgow: W. Mackenzie.
Blenkarn, J. (1859) *British Timber Trees*. London: Routledge.
Bolton, D. K., King, H. P. F., Wyld, G. and Yaxley, D. C. (1971) 'Middlesex', in *Victoria County History*. Volume 4. London: VCH.
Brown, J. (2011) *The Omnipotent Magician Lancelot 'Capability' Brown 1716–1783*. London: Chatto & Windus.
Butlin, R. A. (2004) 'Maundrell, Henry (*bap.* 1665, *d.* 1701)', *Oxford Dictionary of National Biography*. Oxford University Press. Available at: http://www. oxforddnb.com/view/article/18378 (Accessed 15 August 2016).

Campbell, M. J. (1992) *John Martin Visionary Printmaker*. New York: Campbell Fine Art.

Chambers, D. (1993) *Planters of the English Landscape Garden*. London: Paul Mellon Centre for Studies in British Art.

Coleby, A. M. (2004) 'Compton, Henry (1631/2–1713)', *Oxford Dictionary of National Biography*. Oxford University Press. Available at: http://www.oxforddnb.com/view/article/6032 (Accessed 15 August 2016).

Collison, G. (1840) *Cemetery Interment: Containing A Concise History of the Modes of Interment . . . Descriptions of . . . English Metropolitan and Provincial Cemeteries, and more particularly of the Abney Park Cemetery, at Stoke Newington, with a Descriptive Catalogue of its Plants and Arboretum*. London: Longman, Orme, Brown, Green, and Longmans, pp. 196–201.

Davies, D. (1988) 'The evocative symbolism of trees', in D. Cosgrove and S. Daniels (eds) *The Iconography of Landscape*. Cambridge: Cambridge University Press, pp. 32–41.

Elliott, P., Watkins, C. and Daniels, S. (2011) *The British Arboretum*. London: Pickering and Chatto.

Elwes, J. H. and Henry, A. (1908) *The Trees of Great Britain and Ireland*. Volume 3. Edinburgh: Privately Printed.

Evelyn, John (1670) *Sylva*, London.

Evelyn, John (1679) *Sylva*, London.

Evelyn, John (1706) *Sylva*, London.

Frazer, J. (1922) *The Golden Bough: A Study in Magic and Religion*. London: Macmillan.

Gerard, J. (1597) *The Herball of Generall Historie of Plantes*. London.

Gilpin, W. (1791) *Remarks on Forest Scenery and Other Woodland Views*. Volume 1. London: R. Blamire, Strand.

Glendinning, R. (1849) 'Elvaston castle the seat of the Earl of Harrington', *Gardeners' Chronicle* 49: 773, 789.

Hartley, B. (2010) 'Exploring and communicating knowledge of trees in the early royal society'. *Notes and Records of the Royal Society* 64: 229–250.

Hooke, D. (2010) *Trees in Anglo-Saxon England*. Woodbridge, Suffolk: Boydell & Brewer.

Jarvis, P. J. (1979) 'Plant introductions to England and their role in horticultural and silvicultural innovation, 1500–1900', in H. S. A. Fox and R. A. Butlin (eds) *Change in the Countryside: Essays on Rural England 1500–1900*. London: Institute of British Geographers, 10: 145–164.

Joyce, P. (1994) *A Guide to Abney Park Cemetery*. London: Abney Park Cemetery Trust.

Kristjansson, J. (1988) *Eddas and Sagas: Iceland's Medieval Literature*. P. Foote (tr) Reykjavik: Hid fslenka bokmenntafelag.

Loudon, J. C. (1838) *Arboretum et Fruticetum Britannicum in 8 Vols*. London: Longman, Orme, Brown, Green, and Longmans.

Loudon, J. C. (1843) *On the Laying Out, Planting, and Managing of Cemeteries; and on the Improvement of Churchyards*. London: Longman, Orme, Brown, Green, and Longmans.

Loudon, J. C. (1854) *Arboretum et Fruticetum Britannicum in 8 Vols*. London: Henry G. Bohn.

Martin, J. (2004) 'Hanmer, Sir Thomas, second baronet (1612–1678)', *Oxford Dictionary of National Biography*. Oxford University Press. Available at: http://www.oxforddnb.com/view/article/38539 (Accessed 15 August 2016).

Maundrell, H. (1749) *A Journey from Aleppo to Jerusalem: At Easter, AD 1697.* 7th edition. London: S. Powell, p. 142.

Meiggs, R. (1982) *Trees and Timber in the Ancient Mediterranean World.* Oxford: Clarendon.

Mongredien, A. (1870) *Trees and Shrubs for English Plantations.* London: John Murray.

Morden, B. C. (2010) *John Martin Apocalypse Now!* Newcastle: Northumbria University Press.

Morris, S. (1991) 'Legacy of a bishop: the trees and shrubs of Fulham Palace Gardens introduced 1675–1713', in *Garden History,* 19: 47–59.

Murdoch, A. (2004) 'Campbell, Archibald, third duke of Argyll (1682–1761)', *Oxford Dictionary of National Biography.* Oxford University Press. Available at: http://www.oxforddnb.com/view/article/4477 (Accessed 15 August 2016).

Myrone, M. and Austen, A. (2012) 'Catalogue' in M. Myrone (ed.) *John Martin: Apocalypse.* London: Tate Publishing, pp. 61–213.

Nicol, W. (1803) *The Practical Planter.* London: C. Wittingham.

Page, R. I. (1990) *Norse Myths.* London: British Museum Press.

Pococke, R. (1745) *A Description of the East.* Volume II. London: W. Bowyer.

Ray, J. (1686) *Historia Plantarum.* London: Clark.

Rivers, I. (2004) 'Watts, Isaac (1674–1748)', *Oxford Dictionary of National Biography.* Oxford: Oxford University Press. Available at: http://www.oxforddnb.com/view/article/28888 (Accessed 15 August 2016).

Ruskin, J. (1860) 'Modern Painters vol. 5', quoted in *Selections from the Writings of John Ruskin.* London: Blackfriars, 1907, pp. 79–81.

Ruskin, J. to John Davidson (24 February 1887) *Transactions of the English Arboricultural Society,* pp. 156–157.

Sackett, T. R. (2004) 'Frith, Francis (1822–1898)', Oxford Dictionary of National Biography, Oxford University Press. Available at: http://www.oxforddnb.com/view/article/37434 (Accessed 15 August 2016).

Sinclair, G. (1832) *Useful and Ornamental Planting.* London: Baldwin and Cradock, Paternoster-row.

Solman, D. and Douglas, G. (1995) Straker, J. (ed.) *Loddiges of Hackney.* London: Hackney Society.

Strutt, J. G. (1830) *Sylva Britannica; or, Portraits of Forest Trees, Distinguished for Their Antiquity, Magnitude, or Beauty: Drawn From Nature.* London: Published by the Author.

Symes, M., Hodges, A. and Harvey, J. (1986) 'The plantings at Whitton', in *Garden History,* 14: 138–172; quotation from Kalm's account of his visit to England on his way to America in 1748, translated by J. Lucas (1892), 31–32.

Toomer, G. J. (2004) 'Pococke, Edward (1604–1691)', *Oxford Dictionary of National Biography.* Oxford: Oxford University Press. Available at: http://www.oxforddnb.com/view/article/22430 (Accessed 15 August 2016).

Turville-Petre, E. O. G. (1964) *Myth and Religion of the North.* London: Weidenfeld and Nicolson.

Walsham, A. (2012) *The Reformation of the Landscape.* Oxford: Oxford University Press.

Watkins, C. (2014) *Trees, Woods and Forests.* London: Reaktion.

Watkins, C. and Cowell, B. (2012) *Uvedale Price 1747–1829. Decoding the Picturesque.* Woodbridge: Boydell.

Part III

Disciplinary identity and the boundaries of understanding

8 Hope and creativity

The shifting nexus between religion and development

James A. Beckford

Introduction

A gloomy room in the basement of All Souls College, Oxford, may not have seemed an auspicious setting for my first meetings with Douglas Davies in the late 1960s when we were regular participants in Bryan Wilson's weekly seminar in the sociology of religion. But that was where I first glimpsed the distinctive approach that Douglas was starting to develop towards a study of religion drawing on social anthropology, sociology and theology. His fieldwork among Mormons in South Wales was clearly not narrowly angled towards conventional questions about rituals or social status or doctrinal beliefs. Instead, he seemed to be aiming at a more 'synoptic' study which combined all these questions – and many more – in a broad appreciation of what being a Mormon in Wales might mean at the individual and collective levels. This broad approach runs like a thread through the wealth of research that he has subsequently conducted at the points where anthropologists, sociologists and theologians have their most productive conversations.

Few scholars can match the skill with which Douglas Davies combines anthropological, sociological and theological insights into subjects as varied as Mormonism, Sikhism, cremation, local churches, rural churches, emotion, inner speech, and the families of Anglican bishops – in addition to extensive scholarship on purely theological questions. It would be unwise for me, therefore, to try to emulate his achievements. Instead, I would like to offer, in Douglas Davies' honour, some reflections on changing fashions in a field of research – religion and development – which has anthropological, sociological and theological dimensions and which is complementary to some of his wide-ranging interests.

Indeed, Douglas may be one of very few scholars who could recognize the source of the following quotation:

> When the practical man uses the results of pure science for some practical end, he is taking them on faith and uses them in the further faith that the end he aims at can be realised, and shall by him be realised, if not

in one way, then in another. The missionary, then, who uses the results of the science of religion, who seeks to benefit by an applied science of religion, is but following in the footsteps of the practical man, and using business methods toward the end he is going to realise.

The quotation is from the introductory chapter of *An Introduction to the Study of Comparative Religion*, written by Frank Byron Jevons and first published in 1908 on the basis of 'The Hartford-Lamson Lectures on the Religions of the World' that he had delivered at Hartford Theological Seminary. Jevons was a Victorian polymath who served not only as professor of philosophy at the University of Durham but also as principal of Bishop Hatfield's Hall for 25 years and warden and vice-chancellor of the university between 1910 and 1912. It was Douglas who stumbled across a cache of Jevons' papers in Hatfield College and who subsequently wrote *Frank Byron Jevons, 1858–1936 An Evolutionary Realist* (Davies 1991). The thrust of Jevons' argument in 1908 was that Christian missionaries needed to be skilled in applying 'scientific' understanding of religion to the task of improving the lives of their charges. And the notion that 'human beings engage practically with their ideas' in ways in which 'the emotion of hope and the capacity for creativity combine' (Davies 2008: 14) runs like a *Leitmotiv* through Douglas' work. Hence the title of this chapter.

My aim is to take stock of the changes that have taken place mainly since the 1960s in research on the nexus of relations between religions and development. These changes form part of the wider processes which have helped to raise the public profile of religions in many parts of the world. But my argument is that this is not simply a case of the 'resurgence' of religions: it also has to do with paradoxical aspects of rationalization in late modernity. As I am not competent to comment on theological dimensions of the intersection between religions and development, I simply exhort Douglas to turn his own creative mind towards them.

There is nothing to be gained here from trying to impose would-be definitive conceptualizations of 'religion' and 'development' since my intention is merely to survey general tendencies in the ways in which these terms have been used. For my purposes, then, broad characterizations are more useful than narrow definitions. Thus, it seems to me that usages of 'religion' frequently evoke sets of ideas, values, emotions, forms of organization, social relationships and collective activities that are associated with conceptions of the divine, the transcendent or the ultimate significance of 'the felt whole'. 'Development' is even more problematic in some ways, but for my purposes the term refers to discourses, policies, strategies and practices aimed at sustainable improvement of the material well-being, health, education and life chances of people living in conditions of significant deprivation relative to standards of living in countries with high levels of gross domestic product.

Prefigurations

Long before the term 'development' entered scholarly discourse, questions about relations between economic life and religions had arisen in various contexts. For example, Ibn Khaldun's *Muqaddimah* (1967), written in the fourteenth century CE, traced the contribution that religion made to reinforcing social solidarity and economic advantage. Several centuries later, Adam Smith (1776) identified connections between religion, market competition and prosperity. Subsequently, Numa Denis Fustel de Coulanges (1864) worked out the intricate relations between the religions practised in ancient Greek and Roman cities and the legal status of property, with all its implications for economic activity. But the best known and most contentious contributions to these debates are Max Weber's (1965) interpretation of the ironic affinities between ideas deriving from early Protestantism and the spirit of modern rational capitalism and R.H. Tawney's (1964) claim that Weber had exaggerated the independent impact of Protestantism on the development of capitalism.

However, it was only when social scientists began in the late 1950s to equate development with processes of modernization and the condition of modernity that the positive and negative contributions of religion came in for more searching examination. Echoing the debates instigated by Max Weber (1948, 1965) and other economic historians about the religious underpinnings and implications of capitalism, analysts of modernity examined religion's intersections with several aspects of development. It is a common error to claim that modernization theory simply marginalized or even ignored religion. In fact, it accommodated religion in ways that tended to 'domesticate' it (Beckford 1983). Three forms of this domestication call for comment here.

(i) Leading the way were Talcott Parsons' theoretical ideas about the transition from traditional to modern forms of society and culture with its attendant changes in values and norms. The clear expectation was that modern ways of living would become institutionally differentiated, less communally guided and more individualist in orientation, thereby fostering instrumental and entrepreneurial attitudes towards work and material well-being. Parsons also expected that the values and virtues of hard work, personal discipline, trust and deferred gratification that had emerged from mainstream Protestantism would become 'generalized' through modern societies to the point where they would infuse all the increasingly differentiated spheres of life. And, while Parsons characterized the outcome of this process of value generalization as 'institutionalized individualism', he maintained that its roots lay in Christianity – even though he did not believe that organized forms of Christianity would necessarily thrive in modernity.

An interesting corollary of Parsons' reasoning was the expectation that the process of value generalization would help marginal groups to achieve inclusion in mainstream culture and institutions. For example, it was argued that participation in ascetic Holiness 'sects' would equip members of 'lower class groups' with values and norms that might overcome their exclusion from 'the dominant, institutionalized values of the larger [American] society' (Johnson 1961: 309). The conclusion was that 'The positive emphasis on self-application, consistency, and achievement, are the principal Holiness themes that directly converge with dominant American values' (Johnson 1961: 316). A similar line of reasoning later emerged in studies of the functions that 'adaptive' cults might play in re-socializing their recruits into the American social system (Robbins, Anthony and Curtis 1975).

(ii) A second debate about the nexus of modernity, religion and development revolved around the question of whether societies in which Protestant forms of Christianity had never been central could nevertheless follow the route to the kind of institutionalized individualism that was supposedly a prerequisite of capitalist development. Speculation centred first on the possibility that Asian societies might already have, or might generate, their own version of the Protestant Ethic. Robert Bellah (1963), S.H. Alatas (1963), Clifford Geertz (1963, 1968) and S.N. Eisenstadt (1968) were among the early contributors to the debate, but Stanley Tambiah (1973) thought that it was time to go beyond Weber because his ideas had been exhausted. Nevertheless, a second round of arguments was inspired by the eventual success of capitalist enterprise in East Asia, South East Asia, Sub-Saharan Africa and Latin America (Alatas 2002; Berger 2010).

Recently, however, the global spread of Pentecostalisms has added a new dimension to old debates about the Protestant Ethic, suggesting that, as David Martin put it, 'the great capitals of the Pentecostal world' such as São Paulo and Buenos Aires show evidence of a:

> vigorous Protestant work ethic, domestic discipline and willingness to look to the longer term rather than immediate gratification. At the same time, the religious ethic is, in an important way, expressed in churches that are themselves economic enterprises rather than in economic enterprises governed by a religious ethic.
>
> (Martin 2011: 79)

The observation that churches could be economic enterprises in themselves is unexceptional if it merely means that their survival partly depends on acquiring economic resources and that their members may incidentally become more prosperous as a result of living in accordance with their religious principles. This is certainly the case with the various 'Quaker enterprises' that flourished in the religiously acceptable confectionery sector of British and American business from early in the nineteenth century (Corley 1972; Windsor 1980; Jeremy 1998). Rural and urban communities in the United States of Old Order Amish (Kraybill and Nolt 1995;

O'Neil 1997), Hutterites (Hostetler 1974), Anabaptists and Mennonites (Redekop, Krahn and Steiner 1994) have also achieved varying degrees of economic success and independence for their members – as have Muslim orders such as the Mourides of Senegal (O'Brien 1977) and some of the millennial movements of Melanesia (Wilson 1973: 466–467). Although participation in religious communities and organizations seems to place constraints on their members' potential to acquire material assets, there is also extensive evidence in support of the idea that economic development is positively correlated with certain religious beliefs, values and practices. Debate continues, however, over the direction of causation between religion and development (de Jong 2011).

Douglas Davies has made two important contributions to these debates. The first concerns the distinctiveness of Mormon theology and practice in relation to economic security and well-being. He has highlighted the need to make some adjustments to Max Weber's notion of the Protestant Ethic in order to understand Mormonism's emphasis on the *communal* benefits of hard work and especially 'a this-worldly commitment to productive farming and community development' (Davies 2003: 160). The theological reasons for the Latter Day Saints' preference for a communal over an individualist ethic are explained as follows:

> Like its Protestant cousin, the Mormon ethic relates salvation to action in the world but does so with a sense of certainty rather than uncertainty . . . The Mormon ethic is typified by a dissonance between a firm belief that endowments can guarantee exaltation but uncertainty as to whether one is properly fulfilling one's vows and obligations to the highest degree.
>
> (Davies 2003: 161)

In effect, Davies argues that Mormonism 'deconstructed' the notion of predestination that prevailed in Protestantism and replaced it with a more causal notion of reciprocity between God's eternal principles of justice and the expectation that human, communal action in the world could also be just. As a result, 'What people earned and deserved was precisely what they received: accordingly, they were to work at their religion in a very practical way' (Davies 2003: 160).

Douglas Davies' (1984) second contribution to debates about the Protestant ethic is more speculative but no less intriguing. It epitomizes his creative melding of anthropological, sociological and theological perspectives. When the charismatic renewal was still relatively new in a wide variety of British churches, he characterized the 'charismatic ethic' as a corollary of post-industrialism and the shift in the UK's cities from employment mainly centred on manufacturing to employment in service industries. This shift again required an adjustment to Max Weber's view of the Protestant ethic:

If Max Weber's Protestant ethic was grounded in worldly activism under the influence of predestination and the inscrutability of the divine will in a pragmatically and rationally organised world of a mechanistic type, then the contemporary charismatic ethic is rooted in a personal fulfilment in supporting relationships in their life within a potentially alienating and atomising world of partial personal relations within the service industries . . . Personal authenticity replaces certainty of an elected status in the eternal decrees of God. Tongues and fruitful group relationships replace economic success as a sign of the divine approval.

(Davies 1984: 143–144)

There are distant, but unacknowledged, echoes of this ambitious hypothesis in some of the anthropological and sociological research on charismatic movements in Africa and Latin America that will be considered later in this chapter.

To return to David Martin's argument that the continuing search for economic wealth is an enterprise close to the primary objectives of certain religious organizations, this implies a further departure from the Weberian legacy. It suggests that religions may generate wealth as a direct consequence of the corporate activities of religious organizations – not as an incidental or ironic by-product of their members' disciplined or ascetic lifestyle. Indeed, some religious organizations have become major economic enterprises either through the production and distribution of strictly religious services and materials and/or through the conduct of businesses with no clear religious associations. Examples include the Japanese lay Buddhist movement of Soka Gakkai[1] (Waterhouse 2002), the Unification Church founded in South Korea by Sun Myung Moon (Introvigne 2000), the Universal Church of the Kingdom of God which originated in Brazil but has spread across much of Sub-Saharan Africa and Western Europe (Freston 2001) and the movement for education and civic reform founded by Fethullah Gülen in Turkey. All of them own extensive properties and profit-seeking businesses that range from the media to educational institutions and heavy industry. Similar claims have been made about businesses engaged in 'selling spirituality' (Carrette and King 2005. See also Matsunaga 2000 for the particular case of Japan). In short, the Weberian and the Parsonian ideas that certain religious values have an affinity with the motivation and diligence required to be successful in business are now complemented by the much more intriguing idea that some religious organizations now act as businesses in their own right. If this is the case, the question arises of how far the corporate power and wealth of such organizations might benefit not only their members but also the wider communities in which they operate. The answer has a direct bearing on ideas about the relations between religion and development and is not unrelated to Douglas Davies' interests in spiritual capital

(Davies and Guest 2007) and his involvement in the Welfare and Values in Europe project (Middlemiss Lé Mon 2011).

(iii) Not only do the Protestant Ethic thesis and theories of modernization share a primary focus on affinities between religion and the conditions favouring capitalist development but they also give rise to a secondary interest in Protestantism's potential for generating the kind of civil society on which democratic politics depends. This is another aspect of development, but instead of focusing on economics it examines the positive and negative contributions that religions can make to social order and civility. The *locus classicus* is David Little's (1969) historical-cum-sociological investigation of Calvinistic Puritanism's contributions towards the emerging legal order, economic institutions and authority structures of seventeenth-century England. Development, in this context, means much more than economic growth. It denotes the consolidation of civil society, civic governance and ideas of civility as well as the rule of law and the more directly political structures of legislatures, parties and elections.

A closely related argument concerns Protestantism's possible role as a catalyst for the formation of the voluntary associations, community organizations and affinity groups that compose much of civil society. The theological and ideological inspirations for this role are explored in Michael Walzer's influential book *The Revolution of the Saints* (1966). It argues that Calvinistic Puritanism failed to establish the kind of totalistic repression that its zealots sought in mid-seventeenth-century England, although the experiments in self-government that they enforced did eventually produce effects on what Michel Foucault called 'governmentality'.[2] Puritanism ironically prepared the way for capitalist entrepreneurialism and liberalism, according to Walzer, only in so far as it instilled self-discipline and self-control. Calvinist doctrines were broadly incompatible with capitalism or liberalism. More important in the long term, in Walzer's view, was the transformation of the voluntary principle that underlay the self-government of Puritan congregations. Coupled with the Arminian notions of Christian perfection that Methodism helped to disseminate on a large scale in the nineteenth century, voluntarism came to thrive in many areas of private and public life. Case studies have illuminated such developments as the religious impetus for voluntary associations of all kinds (Yeo 1976), the contribution of Primitive Methodist chapels in County Durham towards the cultivation of the skills required by leaders of trade union and political activities (Moore 1974) and Wesleyan Methodism's broader role in promoting liberal notions of civic and political life in nineteenth century Britain (Semmel 1974).

The bridge between these formative investigations of the civic and political implications of variants on the Protestant Ethic and current interests in development is David Martin's (2011) discussion of the importance of the voluntary principle as a distinctive religious mode of insertion in social life. He locates the origins of voluntarism in Christian traditions – he even refers to the early Church as a 'transnational voluntary association' – of which Pentecostalism is the most recent manifestation. Its success owes much to its differentiation from states, the entrepreneurialism of its leaders and its capacity to thrive in open markets for religious allegiance. Martin regards the social forms of Pentecostalism as 'an extension of the "free church" principle, represented in England and the United States by denominations like the Baptists and Methodists' (2011: 80) and which represents 'a venture in the autonomous creation of social capital' (2011: 78). The fact that Pentecostalism often flourishes against the background of failed states or failed programmes of state-funded welfare and economic development only strengthens Martin's claim that voluntary associations – like denominations – are best placed to fill the gap between states and individuals.

In sum, theories of modernization in the vein of Max Weber and his successors have had a direct bearing on questions about religion and development. This gives the lie to the widespread postulate that social scientists subscribed unthinkingly to crude versions of secularization theory. In fact, it has become a trope of writings on religion and development to posit a sharp break between, on the one hand, the taken-for-granted views about the inevitability of secularization that allegedly dominated social sciences until recently and, on the other, the post-2000 'discovery' that religion was not only alive and well in many parts of the world but also experiencing revival and resurgence. But the truth is that this trope works only by ignoring the best and most subtle interpretations of secularization which stress its contingent conditions, its fluctuations and its dialectical relation with sacralization (Dobbelaere 2002; Demerath 2007; Martin 2011).

Religion and development: new directions

The term 'development' has a long history of being closely associated with attempts to improve the conditions of life for groups of people experiencing poverty and other forms of deprivation, and its meaning has undergone extensive revision since the late 1940s. This was when methodical elaboration of the category of 'development' as a distinctive set of ideas, values and practices began to gather momentum in response to the perceived need for reconstruction of European societies following the Second World War. Initially, the focus was firmly on economic growth and the material infrastructure of utilities, food production and manufacturing, but the scope of discourses about development gradually widened to include concern with a much broader range of human needs and cultural capacities. Nevertheless, although the leaders of some mainstream churches and religious organizations had been influential catalysts in the post-war development of

European institutions of peace, political integration and reconstruction, the link between religions and enlarged notions of development received relatively little attention. Instead, public awareness tended to focus on either the humanitarian and charitable work of organizations such as Christian Reconstruction in Europe – the precursor of today's Christian Aid – or the emergence of Christian Democracy as a political tendency towards European union (Fogarty 1957; Gehler and Kaiser 2004). Even scholars in the emerging field of development studies tended to ignore its religious dimension until Charles K. Wilber and Kenneth P. Jameson assembled a special issue of *World Development* in 1980 containing fourteen articles on religion and development. Alongside case studies of various developing countries, many contributors suggested that the 'limits to growth' arguments needed to take account of the positive and negative contributions that religious values and organizations could make to growth in both economic and non-economic senses of the term. In particular, Denis Goulet (1980: 488), the deceased doyen of American development ethics, concluded his discussion of narrow-mindedness among secular *and* religious specialists with

> A growing chorus of voices, in rich and poor countries alike, proclaim that full human development is not possible without regard for essential religious values . . . And conversely, it is to be hoped, the resiliency of critically tested religious value systems will invite development experts to enrich their own diagnoses and prescriptions for action. Both categories of one-eyed giants may perhaps come to acknowledge that they need each other if they are, jointly, to gain a wisdom to match modern sciences.

But it was not until the mid-1990s that research, policy making and professional practice among a growing number of development specialists began to embody Goulet's sentiments. But this embodiment has taken at least two different forms which partially overlap each other.[3] I shall separate them for purely analytical purposes.

(a) One of the most interesting and positive responses to Goulet's call for mutual support between religious values and development expertise has taken place at a conceptual level. That is, explicit calls have been made for an *integral* approach to questions of religion and development. This amounts to a departure from conceptualizations of religion and development as categorically separate phenomena. The aim of the integral approach is to show that religion contains some of the keys to successful development and that, conversely, development is only likely to be successful and sustainable to the extent that it is informed by religious worldviews and practices.

One of the interesting aspects of the integral approach is its tendency to conceptualize religion in highly inclusive and possibly homogenizing terms. This is particularly notable in the work of Gerrie ter Haar and Stephen Ellis who are among the leading authorities on the relationship of mutual implication between religion and development in Sub-Saharan Africa. They stipulate that

> religion refers to the belief in the existence of an invisible world, distinct but not separate from the visible one, that is home to spiritual beings with effective powers over the material world.
>
> (Ellis and ter Haar 2004: 14)

In other words, religion is understood to be such an integral part of life that it informs people's material as well as moral and spiritual activities. It follows, then, that religion and development are, by this definition, part of an holistic response to the world. Moreover, ter Haar and Ellis (2006: 354) regard the Christian religion – especially its millenarian beliefs – as 'the historical point of departure for the modern concept of development'. Their view is that religious ideas are relevant to such diverse aspects of development as conflict prevention and peace building, governance, health and education and that an integral vision of development would necessarily take the spiritual dimension of life into account by empowering people in the developing world 'to employ their religious resources as part of a development strategy' (ter Haar 2011: 5). Indeed, they advocate that European development policy should respond positively to the central position that religion occupies in the lives of the people whom development projects are designed to help even if this means that some European governments may have to rethink their principled separation of religion from the state.

If religion is defined less in terms of beliefs and more in terms of identities, emotions and practices embodied in religious traditions (Davies 2011), then another way of envisaging the relation between religion and development is to consider how religions can serve as resources for responding to changing circumstances. This approach – promulgated most explicitly by Deneulin with Bano (2009) – renders the integral perspective more dynamic whilst also acknowledging that 'religion is not always a force for good in the world but can be destructive' (Deneulin with Bano 2009: 68). There can also be tensions and conflicts between religious traditions as well as between them and secular traditions. In short, the integral approach seeks to avoid the trap of an instrumentalist attitude towards the possible utility of religion in development practice. Instead, it regards development as intrinsic to religious traditions – not just an 'add on' to secular projects.

Inevitably, however, the strategy of defining religion in the kind of inclusive terms favoured by the integral approach runs the risk of homogenizing – or flattening out – the differences between religions as different as Christianity, Islam and Buddhism. While this strategy may recommend itself as ecumenical and likely to generate productive dialogue between religions, it may also be unrealistic when it comes to the undeniable tension, rivalry, jealousy and conflict that can complicate and obstruct the engagement of religious organizations in development projects. Research needs to examine carefully not only the things that religions share in common but also the things that make each of them distinctive and possibly incompatible with the others. Development practitioners have to deal with religions as their followers enact and represent them – not as representations of their lowest common denominators. It makes no sense, therefore, to reduce the vibrant movements of 'engaged' or 'compassionate' Buddhism (King 2009) which contribute towards development in East and South East Asia to the beliefs in spirits that are widespread in Sub-Saharan African countries. Equally, the various Islamic movements – such as Muslim Aid or Islamic Relief – that contribute towards development and humanitarian aid in majority Muslim countries especially at times of extreme hardship and disruption can only be properly understood in terms of their own distinctive inspirations and commitments (Benthall and Bellion-Jourdan 2009).

(b) A second embodiment of Goulet's vision of integrated relations between religion and development occurs in the growing chorus of calls for a *'bottom up'* approach that highlights the importance of local activities and experiences. This involves a deliberate strategy of favouring methods of study, policies and professional practices which start from the vantage point of people in developing countries other than elites or experts. Grassroots movements among lay members of the Catholic Church in the latter half of the twentieth century in numerous countries of Central and South America (Lehmann 1990) as well as South East Asia and Poland (Philpott 2004) were among the first demonstrations of a particular religion's capacity to confront problems associated with systemic poverty, discrimination and injustice 'from the bottom up'. But in recent years the focus has shifted towards cases from Africa. For example, Graveling's research in a village in southern Ghana indicated that:

> If development agencies want to be genuinely actor-oriented, seriously taking on board what people say and think, when they engage with religion they must do so in a way that is meaningful and relevant to the everyday reality of people's lives. As well as working to form partnerships with organized religious bodies and institutions they must be aware of the fluidity, eclecticism, diversity and multiplicity that are concealed by the institutional landscapes.
>
> (Graveling 2010: 214)

Indeed, controversy surrounds the question of whether discussions of the potential for democratization in Africa have ever taken indigenous African religions properly into account (Mutua 2002). Research tends to privilege mainstream churches, formal Muslim organizations,

Pentecostal movements and faith-based NGOs. This is all the more reason, then, to examine religion and development from the bottom up.

A major component of the approach to religion and development from the grassroots is the argument that empowering women is often the key to the effective translation of development policies into day-to-day practices that promote social justice, education and wellbeing (Tomalin 2007). Even in cultures and societies where men are the traditional gatekeepers of political power, research has documented the capacity of women to drive through changes that challenge prejudice, discrimination, ignorance and violence (Schulz 2010). Admittedly, there is opposition in some quarters to the very idea that religion could have liberating effects for women. And controversy is rife in relation to claims and counterclaims that religion, by definition, is integral to women's oppression in private and public life. There is also lively debate about the charge that some Western feminist notions of empowerment draw unhelpfully on liberal individualist assumptions that negate the integrity of some non-Western faith traditions.

The contributions made by Evangelical, Pentecostal, neo-Pentecostal or Charismatic churches to development in African countries have been extensively recognized (Gifford 2004; Olowu 2011), although the focus is more often on their leaders – echoing a prominent theme in early studies of Pentecostalism in Latin America (Lalive d'Epinay 1969). Nevertheless, studies of commodity consumption among grassroots Pentecostalists in Ghana (Meyer 1998), the economic implications of Pentecostalism in different national contexts (Woodberry 2008), the practical day-to-day advantages of belonging to Pentecostal groups in Guatemala City in the 1960s (Roberts 1968) and for Pentecostal micro-entrepreneurs in the same city more recently (Gooren 2011), as well as the material attractions of the Watch Tower movement in South Central Africa in the immediate post-colonial period (Cross 1977) have all confirmed that grassroots members of conservative Christian groups may derive economic benefits from their participation. Henri Gooren (2011: 156) is nevertheless right to warn against the inference that a direct relation must therefore exist between religion and economic development:

> Church membership did not so much create the conditions for entrepreneurship, but confirmed and supported the required circumstances and skills that made entrepreneurship possible. The main influences of church membership were access to social networks, to new skills and new knowledge, to charity and counselling, and to a church-supported system of ethics that made them more reliable entrepreneurs in the eyes of their customers and suppliers.

Further reservations about uncritical assertions of a causal link between the grassroots members of religious groups and economic prosperity draw attention to the possibility that excessive and repeated demands for cash donations create insecurity and hardship. Thus, Linda van de Kamp's (2010) research among members of the Universal Church of the Kingdom of God in Mozambique found that some members had gone bankrupt as a result of giving too much money to the church and that their donations ('sacrifices') sometimes benefited church leaders rather than being invested in programmes of social welfare or economic development. In turn, this pattern of behaviour placed strains on traditional relations of reciprocal sharing between kin. The stark conclusion is that 'Pentecostals obstructed development and progress' (van de Kamp 2010: 166) by destroying the traditional bases of social order and by promoting a neo-liberal agenda of individual autonomy in market conditions.

Similarly, in relation to development in a broader context, Paul Gifford (2008: 227) has expressed important reservations about the claim that the leaders of evangelical churches in Africa necessarily challenge traditional patterns of patrimonialism. Churches that began as 'egalitarian spiritual brotherhoods', he argues, have generated many pretentious titles for their increasingly powerful leaders and have become 'businesses'. In addition, they have been used for instrumental purposes by political leaders and have served, in some cases, to entrench popular fears of witchcraft and the occult by melding them with Christian doctrines of evil – instead of extirpating them. Gifford (2004: 171) is also sceptical about claims that the ideas of demonology and deliverance deployed in African Pentecostal churches have actually managed to produce a reordering of the distribution of power relations in their host countries. In short, researchers have not yet delivered unequivocal evidence of these churches' purported achievements in transforming the material lives of their grassroots members, according to Gifford.

Other directions

The growing influence of 'integral' and 'bottom up' approaches is not the only significant sign of change in the relationship between religions and development. Other approaches have been adopted which are, in some respects, at odds with Goulet's vision. Indeed, it is ironic that the calls to take religious values more seriously in themselves have been issued at precisely the same time as some of the world's most formal and instrumentally rational organizations have appeared to heed them. The profile of international and national agencies involved in promoting and facilitating the adoption of religious values in the field of development has risen sharply in the new millennium. This conjunction of the integral with the instrumental – and the elite with the grassroots – deserves closer examination than it has so far received from development scholars (but see Clarke 2007).

Contrary to popular and scholarly claims that religion is resurgent in the public sphere of many countries in the global South, a more balanced assessment of the situation is that:

> The . . . recent irruption of religion into public space, notably through Pentecostal churches and Islamist movements, does not . . . represent a revival of religion so much as a change in the nature of the relation of religion to the state and to politics.
>
> (Ellis 2010: 35)

This assessment also chimes well with my own argument that evidence of a religious resurgence in Western European countries is weak (Beckford 2010a, 2010b). Admittedly, the salience of religion in various public spheres has increased in the past decade but this owes much less to any increase in the vitality of religions than to contextual factors such as increased media interest in violent religious extremism, legal and constitutional disputes about boundaries between the secular and the religious, controversies surrounding faith schools, and the place of faith-based organizations in social welfare policies and programmes. Agencies of the state have taken a leading role in many of these issues either through legislation or through policies promoting partnerships with religious and faith-based organizations.

When it comes to developing societies in the global South, there is also a long history of sometimes hostile and sometimes productive relations between government agencies and missionaries, aid workers and relief agencies representing the world's major religious traditions and interfaith organizations (Clarke 2007). The best known include Christian Aid, Catholic Relief Services, Caritas International, CAFOD (Catholic Overseas Development Agency), Islamic Relief, the Red Crescent, World Jewish Relief, Hindu Aid, SEWA International, and Khalsa Aid.

It is not clear how far government agencies in the global South have also encouraged partnerships with religious groups, but there can be little doubt that the role of ostensibly secular organizations in fostering the involvement of religions in development has expanded significantly since the 1980s. In addition, organizations such as the World Bank, the International Monetary Fund, the Inter-American Development Bank, the Aga Khan Development Network, the World Health Organization and the UN Family Planning Agency have also played roles with varying degrees of importance as donors or co-ordinators of resources for development. The World Bank is particularly interesting because it had no history of co-operation with religions until its former President, James Wolfensohn, instigated discussions with the former Archbishop of Canterbury, George Carey, that led to the launch of the World Faiths Development Dialogue in 2000 and its own Development Dialogue on Values and Ethics (Tyndale 2006; Marshall 2011). The research that the World Bank commissioned gave rise to a particularly influential three-volume series of studies entitled *Voices of the Poor*

(World Bank 2000, 2001, 2002) – as well as to strong opposition from some quarters within the bank (Marshall 2011). Also in 2000 the UN announced the eight Millennium Development Goals (MDGs) that were to be achieved by 2015; leaders of numerous faith communities associated themselves with these goals, although many religious organizations had been delivering the kind of local services that are called for by the MDGs long before 2000 (Tyndale 2011).

In addition, non-governmental organizations (NGOs) with accreditation to the UN have proliferated in the field of religion and development in recent decades. They play specific roles in consultancy, policy formation and advocacy, but some have more direct engagement in the delivery of services aimed at development. Many, but not all, of them have formal links to faith communities; and a growing number can be accurately designated as 'faith-based NGOs' because they derive their principal inspiration, guidance and support from faith traditions. Prominent examples include World Vision and Christian Aid. Even more numerous, however, are the 'faith-based organizations' (FBOs) with development-related objectives but without accreditation to the UN. Many of them are grassroots organizations that operate through local or regional networks using local resources or resources channelled down to them by higher-level agencies. Some of them work in partnership with government agencies and are active in national and international networks; many of them are unparalleled in their capacity to reach the poorest and most marginal populations.

In some cases, FBOs are more experienced than state agencies in delivering social welfare, health care, education and poverty reduction programmes, but relations with the state can be difficult, especially during periods of political instability. Tanzania is a clear example of a country where a policy of nationalization in the days following independence worked against the interest of long-established FBOs but where subsequent economic and political problems created opportunities for FBOs to regain positions of influence (Mallya 2010). But issues concerning the political accountability of FBOs that deliver services on behalf of the Tanzanian state can still be troublesome, and questions remain about the balance of long-term benefits sustained by the FBOs and by the state. Moreover, research conducted by David Skinner (2010) in The Gambia, Ghana and Sierra Leone highlighted the difficulties for these three states of working with Muslim NGOs that lack co-ordination at a national level, compete intensely among themselves for resources, and are suspicious of the motives of politicians.

Another aspect of the institutionalization of concern with religions and development is the growth of specialist centres for academic research and policy analysis – including entire programmes of research – some of which are sponsored or financed by government agencies and private foundations. Examples include the Knowledge Centre Religion and Development in The Netherlands, the Religion and Development research programme funded by the British government's Department for International Development between 2005 and 2010 at the University of Birmingham, the University of Bath's research theme on Wellbeing and Human Development, and the Religion and Global Development programme hosted by the Berkley Centre for Religion, Peace and World Affairs at Georgetown University in the United States. In keeping with the orientation of development studies in general, multidisciplinary and interdisciplinary approaches are prevalent in these research centres and programmes.

Conclusion

In taking stock of the changes that have occurred in social scientific thinking about the intersections between religions and development in recent decades, I have underlined the significance of three particular approaches. One of them proposes an 'integral' perspective that seeks to do more than treat religion as merely an 'optional extra' or 'add on' to economic and political development. The second advocates a 'grassroots' or 'bottom up' approach that gives prominence to the contributions that religions can make to development at local level in the day-to-day lives of people working to combat oppression and poverty. But the third approach is in some degree of tension with the other two because it focuses on the fact that development strategies and practices are heavily conditioned by the power – political and economic – exerted by formal organizations subject to rational and instrumental criteria of efficiency and accountability. Some of them are agencies of the state; some are profit seeking businesses; and others are NGOs and FBOs. This is not to say that religious actors and organizations cannot also be instrumental and rational: it is merely to insist that the integral and grassroots approaches cannot afford to ignore the broader context of political and economic power in which they have to operate.

Notes

1 An article in the *Japan Times Online* in May 2011 estimated the value of the movement's assets at 500 billion Yen or about £4 billion at 2012 exchange rates. http://www.japantimes.co.jp/text/nn20081202i1.html
2 'The associations of the brethren were voluntary indeed, but they gave rise to a collectivist discipline marked above all by a tense mutual "watchfulness". Puritan individualism never led to a respect for privacy . . . [M]agistracy is a far better description of the saints' true vocation than is either capitalist acquisition or bourgeois freedom' (Walzer 1966: 301, 307).
3 For a different reading of developments since 1980, see Deneulin and Rakodi 2011.

References

Alatas, S. H. (1963) 'The Weber thesis and South East Asia', *Archives de Sociologie des Religions* 15: 21–35.
Alatas, S. F. (2002) 'Religion, values and capitalism in Asia', in C. J. Wan-ling Wee (ed.) *Local Cultures and the 'New Asia': The State, Culture, and Capitalism in Southeast Asia*. Singapore: The Institute of Southeast Asian Studies, pp. 107–128.

Beckford, J. A. (1983) 'The restoration of "power" to the sociology of religion', *Sociological Analysis* 44(1): 11–31.

Beckford, J. A. (2010a) 'The return of public religion? A critical assessment of a popular claim', *Nordic Journal of Religion and Society* 23(2): 121–136.

Beckford, J. A. (2010b) 'The uses of religion in public institutions: the case of prisons', in A. Molendijk, J. Beaumont and C. Jedan (eds) *Exploring the Postsecular: The Religious, the Political and the Urban*. Leiden: Brill, pp. 381–401.

Bellah, R. N. (1963) 'Reflections on the Protestant Ethic analogy in Asia', *Journal of Social Issues* 19(1): 52–61.

Benthall, J. and Bellion-Jourdan, J. (2009) *The Charitable Crescent: Politics of Aid in the Muslim World*. London: I.B. Tauris.

Berger, P. L. (2010) 'Max Weber is alive and well, and living in Guatemala: the Protestant Ethic today', *The Review of Faith & International Affairs* 8(5): 3–9.

Carrette, J. and King, R. (2005) *$elling Spirituality: The Silent Takeover of Religion*. London: Routledge.

Clarke, G. (2007) 'Agents of transformation? Donors, faith-based organisations and international development', *Third World Quarterly* 28(1): 77–96.

Corley, T. A. B. (1972) *Quaker Enterprise in Biscuits: Huntley and Palmers of Reading, 1822–1972*. London: Hutchinson.

Cross, S. (1977) 'Social history and millennial movements: the Watch Tower in South Central Africa', *Social Compass* 24(1): 83–95.

Davies, D. J. (1984) 'The charismatic ethic and the spirit of post-industrialism', in D. Martin and P. Mullen (eds) *Strange Gifts*. Oxford: Blackwell, pp. 137–150.

Davies, D. J. (1991) *Frank Byron Jevons, 1858–1936: An Evolutionary Realist*. Lewiston, NY: Edwin Mellen Press.

Davies, D. J. (2003) *An Introduction to Mormonism*. Cambridge: Cambridge University Press.

Davies, D. J. (2008) 'Cultural intensification: a theory for religion', in A. Day (ed.) *Religion and the Individual*. Aldershot: Ashgate, pp. 7–18.

Davies, D. J. (2011) *Emotion, Identity, and Religion: Hope, Reciprocity, and Otherness*. Oxford: Oxford University Press.

Davies, D. J. and Guest, M. (2007) *Bishops, Wives and Children: Spiritual Capital across the Generations*. Aldershot: Ashgate.

de Jong, E. (2011) 'Religious values and economic growth. A review and assessment of recent studies', in G. ter Haar (ed.) *Religion and Development: Ways of Transforming the World*. London: Hurst, pp. 111–140.

Demerath, N. J. III (2007) 'Secularization and sacralization deconstructed and reconstructed', in J. A. Beckford and N. J. Demerath III (eds) *The SAGE Handbook of the Sociology of Religion*. London: Sage, pp. 57–81.

Deneulin, S. with Bano, M. (2009) *Religion and Development: Rewriting the Secular Script*. London: Zed Books.

Deneulin, S. and Rakodi, C. (2011) 'Revisiting religion: development studies thirty years on', *World Development* 39(1): 45–54.

Dobbelaere, K. (2002) *Secularization: An Analysis at Three Levels*. Brussels: P.I.E.-Peter Lang.

Eisenstadt, S. N. (ed.) (1968) *The Protestant Ethic and Modernization: A Comparative View*. New York: Basic Books.

Ellis, S. (2010) 'Development and invisible worlds', in B. Bompani and M. Frahm-Arp (eds) *Development and Politics from Below: Exploring Religious Spaces in the African State*. Basingstoke: Palgrave Macmillan, pp. 23–39.

Ellis, S. and ter Haar, G. (2004) *Worlds of Power: Religious Thought and Political Practice in Africa*. Oxford: Oxford University Press.

Fogarty, M. (1957) *Christian Democracy in Western Europe, 1820–1953*. South Bend, IN: University of Notre Dame Press.

Freston, P. (2001) 'The transnationalisation of Brazilian Pentecostalism: The Universal Church of the Kingdom of God', in A. Corten and R. Marshall-Fratani (eds) *Between Babel and Pentecost*. Bloomington, IN: University of Indiana Press, pp. 196–216.

Fustel de Coulanges, N. D. (1864) *La cité antique: étude sur le culte, le droit, les institutions de la Grèce et de Rome*. Paris: Hachette.

Geertz, C. (1963) *Peddlers and Princes*. Chicago: University of Chicago Press.

Geertz, C. (1968) *Islam Observed*. Chicago: University of Chicago Press.

Gehler, M. and Kaiser, W. (eds) (2004) *Christian Democracy in Europe since 1945*. London: Routledge.

Gifford, P. (2004) *Ghana's New Christianity: Pentecostalism in a Globalising African Economy*. London: Hurst.

Gifford, P. (2008) 'Evangelical Christianity and democracy in Africa: a response', in T. O. Ranger (ed.) *Evangelical Christianity and Democracy in Africa*. Oxford: Oxford University Press, pp. 225–230.

Gooren, H. (2011) 'Religion and development revisited: some lessons from Guatemalan micro-entrepreneurs', in G. ter Haar (ed.) *Religion and Development: Ways of Transforming the World*. London: Hurst, pp. 141–157.

Goulet, D. (1980) 'Development experts: the one-eyed giants', *World Development* 8(7/8): 481–489.

Graveling, E. (2010) 'Marshalling the powers: the challenge of everyday religion for development', in B. Bompani and M. Frahm-Arp (eds) *Development and Politics from Below: Exploring Religious Spaces in the African State*. Basingstoke: Palgrave Macmillan, pp. 197–217.

Hostetler, J. A. (1974) *Hutterite Society*. Baltimore: The Johns Hopkins University Press.

Ibn Khaldun (1967) *The Muqaddimah: An Introduction to History*. Abridged and edited by N. J. Dawood; translated from the Arabic by Franz Rosenthal. London: Routledge and Kegan Paul.

Introvigne, M. (2000) *The Unification Church*. Turin: Signature Books.

Jeremy, D. J. (ed.) (1998) *Religion, Business, and Wealth in Modern Britain*. London: Routledge.

Jevons, F. B. (1908) *An Introduction to the Study of Comparative Religion*. New York: Macmillan.

Johnson, B. (1961) 'Do sects socialize in dominant values?', *Social Forces* 39: 309–316.

King, S. B. (2009) *Socially Engaged Buddhism*. Honolulu: University of Hawaii Press.

Kraybill, D. B. and Nolt, S. M. (1995) *Amish Enterprise: From Plows to Profits*. Baltimore: The Johns Hopkins Press.

Lalive d'Epinay, C. (1969) *Haven of the Masses*. London: Lutterworth Press.

Lehmann, D. (1990) *Democracy and Development in Latin America: Economics, Politics and Religion in the Post-War Period*. Cambridge: Polity Press.

Little, D. (1969) *Religion, Order, and Law: A Study in Pre-Revolutionary England*. New York: Harper & Row.

Mallya, E. T. (2010) 'Faith-based organizations, the state and politics in Tanzania', in B. Bompani and M. Frahm-Arp (eds) *Development and Politics from Below: Exploring Religious Spaces in the African State*. Basingstoke: Palgrave Macmillan, pp. 131–151.

Marshall, K. (2011) 'Development and faith institutions', in G. ter Haar (ed.) *Religion and Development: Ways of Transforming the World*. London: Hurst, pp. 27–56.

Martin, D. (2011) *The Future of Christianity: Reflections on Violence and Democracy, Religion and Secularization*. Farnham: Ashgate.

Matsunaga, L. (2000) 'Spiritual companies, corporate religions: Japanese companies and Japanese new religious movements at home and abroad', in P. B. Clarke (ed.) *Japanese New Religions in Global Perspective*. Richmond: Curzon Press, pp. 35–73.

Meyer, B. (1998) 'Commodities and the power of prayer: pentecostalist attitudes towards consumption in contemporary Ghana', *Development and Change* 29(4): 751–776.

Middlemiss Lé Mon, M. (2011) 'Darlington case study report', in A. Bäckström (ed.) *Welfare and Values in Europe: Transitions Related to Religion Minorities and Gender. Volume 1. National Overviews and Case Study Reports*. Uppsala: Uppsala Universitet, pp. 249–284.

Moore, R. (1974) *Pitmen, Preachers and Politics*. Cambridge: Cambridge University Press.

Mutua, M. (2002) 'Returning to my roots: African "religions" and the state', in L. Gearon (ed.), *Human Rights & Religion: A Reader*. Brighton: Sussex Academic Press, pp. 226–242.

O'Brien, D. C. (1977) 'A versatile charisma: the Mouride Brotherhood 1967–1975', *Archives Européennes de Sociologie* 18(1): 84–106.

Olowu, D. (2011) 'Faith-based organisations and development: An African indigenous organisation in perspective', in G. ter Haar (ed.) *Religion and Development: Ways of Transforming the World*. London: Hurst, pp. 55–80.

O'Neil, D. J. (1997) 'Explaining the Amish', *International Journal of Social Economics* 24(10): 1132–1139.

Philpott, D. (2004) 'The Catholic wave', *Journal of Democracy* 15(2): 32–46.

Redekop, C., Krahn, V. A. and Steiner, S. (eds) (1994) *Anabaptist/Mennonite Faith and Economics*. Lanham, MD: University Press of America.

Robbins, T., Anthony, D. and Curtis, T. (1975) 'Youth culture religious movements: evaluating the integrative hypothesis', *Sociological Quarterly* 16(1): 48–64.

Roberts, B. R. (1968) 'Protestant groups and coping with urban life in Guatemala City', *American Journal of Sociology* 73(6): 753–767.

Schulz, D. E. (2010) 'Remaking society from within: extraversion and the social forms of female Muslim activism in Urban Mali', in B. Bompani and M. Frahm-Arp (eds) *Development and Politics from Below*. Basingstoke: Palgrave Macmillan, pp. 74–98.

Semmel, B. (1974) *The Methodist Revolution*. London: Heinemann.

Skinner, D. E (2010) 'Da'wa and politics in West Africa: Muslim Jama'at and non-governmental organizations in Ghana, Sierre Leone and the Gambia', in B. Bompani and M. Frahm-Arp (eds) *Development and Politics from Below: Exploring Religious Spaces in the African State*. Basingstoke: Palgrave Macmillan, pp. 99–130.

Smith, A. (1776) *An Inquiry into the Nature and Causes of the Wealth of Nations*. London: printed for W. Strahan and T. Cadell.

Tambiah, S. (1973) 'Buddhism and this-worldly activity', *Modern Asian Studies* 7(1): 1–20.

Tawney, R. H. (1964 [1926]) *Religion and the Rise of Capitalism*. Harmondsworth: Penguin Books.

ter Haar, G. (ed.) (2011) *Religion and Development: Ways of Transforming the World*. London: Hurst.

ter Haar, G. and Ellis, S. (2006) 'The role of religion in development: towards a new relationship between the European Union and Africa', *European Journal of Development Research* 18(3): 351–367.

Tomalin, E. (2007) 'Gender studies approaches to the relationships between religion and development'. Working Paper 8. Birmingham: Religions and Development Programme.

Tyndale, W. (2006) *Visions of Development: Faith-Based Initiatives*. Aldershot: Ashgate.

Tyndale, W. (2011) 'Religions and the millennium development goals', in G. ter Haar (ed.) *Religion and Development: Ways of Transforming the World*. London: Hurst, pp. 207–229.

van de Kamp, L. (2010) 'Burying life: pentecostal religion and development in Urban Mozambique', in B. Bompani and M. Frahm-Arp (eds) *Development and Politics from Below*. Basingstoke: Palgrave Macmillan, pp. 152–174.

Walzer, M. (1966) *The Revolution of the Saints: A Study in the Origins of Radical Politics*. London: Weidenfeld & Nicolson.

Waterhouse, H. (2002) 'Soka Gakka Buddhism as a global religious movement', in J. Wolffe (ed.) *Global Religious Movements in Regional Context*. Aldershot: Ashgate, pp. 109–155.

Weber, M. (1948 [1906]) 'The Protestant sects and the spirit of capitalism', in H. H. Gerth and C. W. Mills (eds) *From Max Weber*. London: Routledge, pp. 302–322.

Weber, M. (1965 [1904]) *The Protestant Ethic and the Spirit of Capitalism*. London: Unwin University Books.

Wilber, C. K. and Jameson, K. P. (1980) 'Religious values and social limits to development', *World Development* 8(6): 467–479.

Wilson, B. R. (1973) *Magic and the Millennium*. London: Heinemann.

Windsor, D. B. (1980) *The Quaker Enterprise: Friends in Business*. London: Muller.

Woodberry, R. D. (2008) 'Pentecostalism and economic development', in J. B. Imber (ed.) *Markets, Morals, and Religion*. New Brunswick, NJ: Transaction Publishers, pp. 157–177.

World Bank (2000) *Voices of the Poor: Can Anyone Hear Us?* Washington, DC: The World Bank.

World Bank (2001) *Crying Out for Change*. Washington, DC: The World Bank.

World Bank (2002) *Voices of the Poor: From Many Lands*. Washington, DC: The World Bank.

Yeo, S. (1976) *Religion and Voluntary Organisations in Crisis*. London: Croom Helm.

9 Theology, social science and the 'power' of religion and of the spirit

David Martin

In the course of a remarkably productive life, Douglas Davies has worked at the interface between sociology and anthropology, and theology and religious studies. He has also been interested in specifically theological notions like grace, humility and power in his recent book on religion and the emotions (Davies 2011). So I feel I have warrant for an exploration of the notion of power, including the power of the spirit, as that straddles the territory of theology and sociology, and also for introducing considerations that bear on Christian ideas like grace, humility, obedience to God rather than man, the distinction between God and Caesar, and the importance of sincerity or 'the inward man' rather than outward conformity to ritual and rule. I am addressing the issue of whether religion is powerful in its own right rather than as a 'presenting symptom' or epiphenomenon of social solidarity as understood in the Durkheimian tradition or of an alienated image of human hopes thrown up by class society in the Marxist tradition. I focus in particular on the kind of epiphenomenalism associated with Durkheim.

Of course, to cover the territory of religion and power comprehensively would require an encyclopaedia, not an essay, but one can begin by asking a characteristically sociological question as to whether religion has any power *at all*, prior to examining later some particular kinds of power, specifically in Christianity. After all, the focus of the work of Douglas Davies is almost entirely within the Christian orbit.

Epiphenomenalism: only a modern phenomenon?

My starting point is provided by Steve Bruce. Bruce (2011) argues that insofar as religion is a powerful factor in the modern age, the effective motive force behind it is nationalism. In his view, religion is a social epiphenomenon of the mobilization of the nation for cultural defence, especially when under external attack. Thus religion in Poland is powerful because it has served as a focus for the cultural defence of the nation against external oppression.

However, there is no reason to think it applies only to modernity, whether that is defined from the period of the industrial revolution on or pushed back to the 'early modernity' of the sixteenth and seventeenth centuries. It is a general truth about religion and the obverse of the theory of social differentiation about the declining number of areas of social life under religious aegis. If religion fulfils several functions, it flourishes, for example, in the United States where it is central to voluntary associations operating between the individual and the state. If it loses those functions to other agencies, it is weakened. However, external threats to the nation and its culture can be resisted either by recourse to language or religion, or both. Alternatively, religion can be associated with the rising curve of national confidence and expansion against the generalized global other.

For example, if the vitality of Polish Catholicism is due to the travails of the Polish nation, one might suggest that Victorian Christianity was, among other things, an expression of British nationalism against a generalized global other. Evangelicalism gave religious sanction to Britain's imperial expansion. Yet, along with other forms of Christian mission, it also criticized it, and historians now mostly agree that political and religious expansion proceeded independently (Etherington 2008). In the same way, the trajectory of American confidence and expanding geo-political power proceeds *pari passu* with the expansive vitality and global influence of its religious institutions. As in Victorian Britain, religious bodies both support and criticize the exercise of that power. The social reality of religion is not straightforwardly epiphenomenal.

In the case of Steve Bruce we are dealing with an inference arrived at on positivist grounds by the scrutiny of evidence and of comparative statistics. I mean that Bruce arrives at an epiphenomenal understanding by comparing countries where religion has been seriously weakened, say the Czech Republic and Estonia, with others where it appears to remain vital, say Poland and Romania, and concludes that religion in the two latter cases is sustained by its role as a carrier of national identity. Bruce does not *begin* from a position of principled epiphenomenalism. Indeed, he regards the *theoretical* considerations whereby religion is understood as epiphenomenal, whether on Durkheimian, Marxist or other grounds, as obscuring more than they illuminate. Yet the type of analysis in which Bruce engages happens to be thoroughly Durkheimian in a mode absolutely central to sociology and to the sociology of religion. It follows that the sociology of religion as currently practised is an enquiry into situations where the outward vesture of Society (with a capital 'S') is provided by religion, and situations where some *other* ideational form provides the 'covering note' of the Social. Sociology also examines the conditions under which religion challenges the dominant form of society and the conditions under which some other ideational form acts as a carrier for that challenge.

Not just an epiphenomenon now or then

In all the cases cited so far religion does other things besides providing a 'covering note' for the nation and for nationalism. We have already mentioned the extent to which Christian missions criticized imperial expansion in the nineteenth century as well as proceeding alongside it. But we ought also to notice the role of the Evangelical beliefs in atonement and in eschatology in relation to social and economic theory in the first half of the nineteenth century as analysed by Boyd Hilton. Hilton goes on to discuss the role of expiation in relation to the campaign to abolish the slave trade, and the role of a theology of the Incarnation in relation to social amelioration in the latter half of the nineteenth century (Hilton 1988). In a parallel way social reform in the United States (and the reforming discipline of sociology) drew directly on the Social Gospel. In the Civil Rights Movement the specifically Christian and more broadly Judaic themes of prophecy, exodus, liberation, non-violence and self-sacrifice, provided the primary sign language for the mobilization of a subordinate people. The cultural defence of the Polish nation drew on a fundamental repertoire of Christian themes, like martyrdom, including the martyrdom of individuals alongside the collective martyrdom of the nation. The cross served as a 'sign' of innocent suffering at the hands of the state, for example the workers killed at Gdansk and the martyrdom of Father Jerzy Popielusko, murdered in 1984 by the secret police for his activity as chaplain to the Solidarity movement. As we shall see from the examples I now take from earlier times, the same dialectic of collusion with power, of critique (or prophecy), and of a selective appropriation of the repertoire of Christian signs, occurs throughout Christian history.

Let us go back to the initial centuries of the last half millennium. Just as it seems plausible to see religion as *in part* providing the outward vesture of high Victorian nationalism and imperialism, so it might seem plausible to regard religion as coming to provide the outward vesture of absolute monarchy in the persons of Henry the Eighth, Philip the Second, and later Louis the Fourteenth. Religion was commandeered by the state, in Protestant and Catholic Europe alike, as the state was dramatized and focussed in the person of the monarch. It was therefore implicated in the dynastic power politics of the time, and it provided many of the captions under which wars were fought for a *variety* of disparate reasons. The peace of Westphalia, when it was finally agreed upon in 1648, after years of negotiation, simply formalized that situation to provide a very momentary respite from endemic violence. Religion was *partly* subsumed by the political authority operative in a given territory. I say in part because even in Russia there were many independent expressions of the religious spirit, and, moreover, expressions that appealed to the people. The so-called Westphalian 'solution' was reinforced when enlightened autocrats like Joseph the Second, Frederick the Great and Peter the Great, treated the church as a department of state (Cavanaugh 2009).

That evolution can be restated as follows. Religion has been epiphenomenal in the sense used by Steve Bruce in his analysis of its role in cultural defence – or expansion – for at least the last half millennium. If one were to put that argument in its most sweeping form, the religion of the Italian Renaissance city states was but the outward show of their nascent self-consciousness. Venice, 'the lion city', may seem, to all appearances, a creation of 'the' religious impulse, replete with sublime art, like Titian and Tintoretto, and ornamented by magnificent music, like the Monteverdi Vespers of 1612, but all that is but the gorgeous vesture of power and money. Taking this to its logical conclusion, it would follow that the rhetorical ploy that loads all the blame for violence and repression onto religion is misplaced, and we should rather reserve our righteous indignation for constellations of power and wealth. Believers would not be able to appeal to Chartres for confirmation nor could unbelievers cite the crusades by way of disconfirmation. No doubt the apotheosis of James the First on the ceiling of the Banqueting Hall in Whitehall is impressive but we can neither discover in it a moving expression of 'the' religious spirit nor can we condemn religion for its glorification of monarchical absolutism.

But, as has already been suggested in relation to the mobilization of subordinate nations in America and Europe, such a strong version of epiphenomenalism is too sweeping. Suppose we now adopt a more nuanced view by taking our examples from both the Counter-Reformation and the Reformation. In deploying these examples, I distinguish between those themes in the biblical repertoire that code generic attachments to land and people, and authority, and those that code more specifically Christian themes, such as poverty and the role of Christ's poor, humility, grace, reconciliation, incautious generosity, including non-violence, and the equality of all humankind before God and his judgement. Some themes may appear on both sides of the divide, though differently inflected. They are not confined to either the generic attachments, like land and people, or to the specifically Christian, like non-violent self-sacrifice. In the examples I offer below self-sacrifice figures both in personal and collective immolation for the sake of the nation, as in 1914–1918, and in non-violent personal martyrdoms, as when people offered themselves as substitutes for others en route to Nazi death camps.

Examples: Caravaggio, Luther and Bach

My first example is provided by Caravaggio during the Counter-Reformation in the early seventeenth century. In many ways Caravaggio was dependent on powerful patrons, political and ecclesiastical, but he was also influenced by the piety of Carlo Borommeo in Milan, which laid its emphasis on the Evangelical status of the poor (Graham-Dixon 2009). The art of Caravaggio was simultaneously an artefact of power relations in Milan, Rome, Naples and Malta, and focussed on a theme derived directly from the repertoire of primitive Christianity. To borrow terminology from elsewhere, Caravaggio was *Homo Duplex*, and the two aspects were fused together.

My second example is from the Protestant north of Europe in the time of the Reformation. We may suppose there were dual motives impelling the Reformation forward, both religious and political. In one way the Reformation depended for effective power and for survival, on potentates with an interest in securing total control in their dominions and the expropriation of the wealth of the church. Yet there were specifically religious motivations powering the Reformation, such as the expropriation of the Scriptures by a clerical caste, the sale of salvation to shore up the rapacious desire of the papacy for secular power and glory, as well as a protest against legalism in favour of inward trust and faith in the mercy and grace of God. Luther challenged both pope and emperor in the name of Christianity's foundation documents. He demanded a return 'to the sources', and thereby became, at the onset of early modernity and *still* today, the prototypical man of conscience. At the same time he allied himself with protecting political powers, and was hostile both to the radical peasant movements and the Jews. (The persecutions and expulsions of the Jews precisely illustrate the fusion of 'spiritual' and political motives. We find fragments from totally different contexts in the Gospels, like the clash with the Pharisees and the Johannine passion narrative, reused, among many other religio-political reasons, to fuel resentment at the roles assigned to Jews, especially by indigent monarchs; Rubin 1991.)

Like Caravaggio, Luther was *Homo Duplex* and the Reformation and Counter-Reformation were 'powered' by a fusion of secular and religious motives. Without the secular motives neither movement could have survived. In my conclusion I shall return to this intimate fusion of motifs in the context of my starting point: the role of religion in contemporary nationalism, as exemplified in the Polish resistance to Soviet domination.

What applies to Luther applies equally to Bach two centuries later. Today Bach is celebrated as the fountain head of modern classical music and the paradigmatic instance of inspiration in the service of faith (Wolff 2000). His music for Passiontide, for example, 'composes' in the most sublime manner the sufferings of the Saviour in the work of Redemption. But he was also a state functionary for various minor potentates and he regularly composed music to celebrate the secular authorities, which he then transposed to celebrate the glory of the Saviour. The minor polities of Germany were the *sine qua non* of his activity. Like Caravaggio and Luther, Bach was *Homo Duplex*.

And the radical reformation

The same applies to the Radical Reformation, now often celebrated as the true religious Reformation at the expense of the Magisterial Reformation associated with Luther and Calvin. The Radical Reformation drew on communist and anarchist themes from the original deposit of faith that acquired renewed resonance in our own modernity. The Radical Reformers have been celebrated as forerunners of modern revolution just as Luther has been celebrated as the prototypical man of conscience. But if we take the best known instance of the Radical Reformation seizing power in Münster, it did so at the instigation of a large sector of the powerful bourgeoisie of that city. What followed was a disastrous experiment in anarcho-communism under the heady charismatic leadership of John of Leyden. This was soon crushed with great violence, and the Radical Reformation morphed into the 'historic peace churches', operating outside the main congeries of power and therefore able to implement the injunctions of the Gospel with regard to peace and simplicity of life. At the same time, however, Quaker Philadelphia did not entirely escape the characteristic dilemmas of power.

And the High Middle Ages

From the historical evidence just surveyed one might be inclined to argue that *the* crucial secularization of religion and its simultaneous reduction to an epiphenomenon occurred between 1517 and 1648. But I am arguing that secularization in the sense of a fusion of political and religious elements is endemic. We can go back to the High Middle Ages to ask whether the Christian religion had an autonomous existence when the papacy was a fully independent international power and the monasteries an arm of that power. If one wanted a date it might be 1302, when Boniface the Eighth made the strongest claims for papal supremacy over temporal rulers in the bull *Unam Sanctam*. This bull extended the teaching of Pope Gelasius nearly a millennium earlier on the independence of the spiritual realm and the distinction between the Two Swords, temporal and spiritual.

How then might one characterize the period say from 1150 to 1350 from the point of view of the fusion of a power base with religious motifs? At the centre of the international system of power was the conflict and the collusion of Pope and Emperor, and any number of related conflicts involving the various kings and lords of medieval Christendom. As for the Papacy it was a power base *much like the others* apart from its international standing, the special power of excommunication, and its relation to the monasteries.

The status of this power base, later to morph into the broader idea of the autonomy of a spiritual realm so central to western developments, was coded in different ways, depending on local balances of power and the aspirations of rulers. At the autonomous monastery of Cluny, the balance favoured the Pope, but at Speyer it favoured the emperor, while at Cefalù and Monreale in Sicily, it favoured the Norman kings, translating the Christian theme of the journey to Jerusalem in terms of Norman aspirations to dominate the Mediterranean (Borsook 1990). Yet just as iconography coded the generic themes of power and territory, it also coded the specifically Christian themes of the equality of all before God in the universal Dance of Death and the Last Judgement so often depicted on the tympani over the main entrance to churches, for example at Vézelay. (Luther later objected that this kind of representation actually misrepresented the primitive Gospel because it made Christ the fearsome Judge and shifted the operation of grace to his mother.

Perhaps the late medieval devotion to the suffering of the Mother in relation to the suffering of the Son, expressed in the Pietà and in the Stabat Mater, brought both figures together in unison as emblems of saving grace).

The monasteries were also examples both of generic principles relating to power and wealth and of the specific emphases of the Gospels. On the one hand they represented the dominical injunction to poverty, while on the other hand they were land holders disposing of enormous wealth. They were avowed apostles of peace and yet they used their wealth to finance the crusades. They raised themselves above local borders and jurisdictions, but often did so in the interests of a papal power that deployed spiritual disciplines, like excommunication, to secure the obedience of temporal rulers. Machiavelli was later to note how the papacy conformed to the secular dynamic of power, for example in the machinations of rival families to secure the papal throne, and, from the viewpoint of the Prince and his necessary machinations, to decry the 'uselessness' of the specifically Christian virtues of the monk, like poverty and humility.

Is contemporary Pentecostalism also Epiphenomenal?

We now fast forward to the present and pose the same set of questions in the context of the rapid expansion of Pentecostalism in the two-thirds world, with some sidelong glances at Mormonism, especially given the studies of the Mormon faith carried out by Douglas Davies (Davies 2000). Of course, in the case of Pentecostalism we are not dealing with a backward past in relation to *real* modernity but a backward present in relation to 'real' modernity. According to the epiphenomenalist account, Pentecostalism does not represent the power of religion acting on our contemporary world but rather acts as a transition to a situation where religion ceases to be powerful. It is not an epiphenomenon of nationalism according to the Durkheimian understanding, but of the social protest of the damned of the earth *temporarily* 'veiled' in religious form, and therefore conforming to the Marxist version of epiphenomenalism such as you find in Eric Hobsbawm's *Primitive Rebels* (Hobsbawm 1965).

Nor does Marxism provide the only approach whereby religion lacks *genuine* power, where power is understood as an active and initiating force for positive change. There is also a liberal approach whereby Pentecostalism can be discussed under the rubric of Fundamentalism and Fundamentalism can be comprehensively discussed as *re*-action, not action. Secularizing forces represent the *active* agents for positive change, while Fundamentalism, Pentecostalism included, re-acts. In practice, of course, change of all kinds proceeds by sequences of actions and reactions, whereby secular forces react as well as act and religious influences likewise. The underlying model defining religion as *re*-acting and *re*-sponding, rather than initiating, is a normative one based on a philosophy of history as progress in a 'positive' non-religious direction.

The link with Fundamentalism and re-action is polemical and it depends on defining religion as irrational delusion and therefore capable only of stifling real agency or, in another version, promoting the wrong kind of agency. It is weak to do good, but strong to commit evil. So Pentecostalism is subjected to leading questions: Is it positive? Is it prone to divert energies that should be deployed to support the standard development narrative, or structural change, or even armed rebellion? Is it corrupt, reactionary, exploitative and authoritarian?

All these leading questions and loaded terms imply that the narratives of Pentecostals themselves are more suspect than most. The disjunction between the social scientific accounts and Pentecostal narratives is exceptionally severe, and it has been supplemented until quite recently by an assumption in anthropology that Pentecostalism counts as an 'inauthentic' intrusion on the functional unities of pre-modern societies. Yet nowadays anthropologists increasingly seek to make sense of Pentecostal practices and discourses, including a literally ecstatic rapture and rupture, rather than subsuming Pentecost in generalized notions like anomie or 'reactions' to modernity. For some contemporary anthropologists Pentecostals cannot be dismissed as somnambulists impelled by forces they simply cannot understand. As for the Pentecostal narrative it casts its faith as liberating through the agency of the Holy Spirit. It stimulates participation, opposes corruption, and brings believers a better life in every sense of better, certainly when compared with patchily successful schemes of social development all too often expropriated by local elites.

There is a further approach often closely related to the older anthropological attitude whereby Pentecostalism intrudes on the functional unities of indigenous culture defined as *ipso facto* authentic. Virtue inheres in being *in situ* and vice inheres in arriving from elsewhere. This approach goes back to the link between religion and the legitimation of American culture, and understands the global expansion of Pentecostalism as an instance of American cultural imperialism, sometimes postulating a further link to neo-liberalism beyond the obvious shared interest in unregulated markets, religious in the one case, and commercial in the other. In short, Pentecostalism is an American export, to be condemned or rated positively depending on whether you are well or ill disposed to American culture. In this context the power of Pentecostalism is illegitimately borrowed from the power of American culture, and is therefore a second order instance of malign agency. It has scant power in its own right but by reflecting the real power of American cultural imperialism it exhibits the wrong kind of power.

Mormonism can easily share the same condemnation, and Mormon missionaries set themselves up for adverse comment because they wear good suits, look like American business people, and adopt strategies designed to promote their product. Yet Mormonism is historically a very distinctive case. On the one hand it has been bracketed by Harold Bloom, along with Pentecostalism, as quintessentially American in its emphasis on this world and on an aspiration for the good and the goods together (Bloom 1992). But Mormonism has also sought to create another territorial America based on a new world narrative and located independently in Utah (Hardy 2010). To that extent it is a protest movement drawing people from several cultures to create an alternative America, and then exporting that alternative to the rest of the world.

Here Mormonism may be seriously different from Pentecostalism. Pentecostalism represents first of all an extension of the competitive American religious market, separated form political power and territory; it is not part of the vesture of the body politic. It also presents a fusion of African-American, Hispanic and poor white revivalism pre-adapted to cross any number of cultural species barriers. In its appeal to the Spirit it not only fuses African-American and white revivalism but also fuses with animated worlds all over the globe. Without losing its recognizable character it takes on the local colour and becomes indigenous with remarkable speed.

The social sources of Pentecost and its spiritual repertoire

But to whom does it appeal? Being a transnational movement across boundaries it is more pre-adapted to particular excluded sectors than to territorial groups, though it can take off in excluded minority groups, whether in the Andes or among European gypsies. So, as already suggested, it is very unlike the fusions of territory and power characterizing our earlier European examples. Yet it is a mobilization of relatively excluded and deprived sectors and therefore a fusion of impulses to power, and aspirations to empowerment, with a religious repertoire derived from primitive Christianity. It has a double character in the same way as Victorian Evangelicalism, the Magisterial and the Radical Reformation, and the world of the High Middle Ages, had a dual character. That means it makes sense for Ruth Marshall as both anthropologist and political scientist to write about *Political Spiritualities* in the context of Nigeria (Marshall 2010). In Nigeria and Ghana, and indeed all over the world, for example in Brazil, Pentecostals contend for social and political power.

What then of the spiritual element in this complicated fusion of motifs from the original Christian repertoire and aspirations to empowerment? To recapitulate, we have on the one hand a social movement, Pentecostalism, powered as was the Civil Rights Movement, by the sense of the indignity of exclusion. I use the word 'indignity' because it serves to underline the moral element in its motivation: people suffer indignity and a sense of not being valued. That immediately fuses with the validation of self provided by the experience of salvation, and with a faith that one is of infinite value in the sight of God, notwithstanding the injurious contempt of the secular world. That knowledge of worth draws directly on the specifically Christian repertoire, where Jesus says that even the death of a sparrow is known to God, and adds 'are you not of more worth than many sparrows?' There are many other direct references 'to the sources': to the overturning of the present order of precedence by God, to the way the labourers in the vineyard, last and first alike, receive equal treatment from a gracious God, to the overflow of good things 'pressed down and running over' granted to those who invest their 'talents' in faith and hope, to the healing of the body and to the restoration of the mind by the exorcism of those demons 'that assault and hurt the soul'. Then there is the Pentecostal gift of power to speak confidently through the inspiration of the spirit in a way that crosses all the secular boundaries of place and class.

Among the prime Pentecostal gifts is the power of narrative and the ability to tell a story of displacement and replacement, and about how you have come through tribulation to triumph. Pentecostalism is oral story telling on a New Testament model of a perilous passage between powers of darkness and of the attraction of the light whereby those who keep faith pass from victim to victor, and from slavery to liberty. Pentecostals witness to an empowerment through a power higher than themselves which restores their sense of agency. They are no longer circumscribed by circumstance but enabled to confront circumstance in a protective convoy of others like themselves en route to better things. This is a variant of the most basic of narratives common to politics and religion alike, and though many terrible things may happen on account of it, nothing good can happen without it. The Pentecostal believer is as much *Homo Duplex* as Caravaggio or Bach through a fusion of the sources of social power and the sign language of religion.

The status of aspiration and inspiration

That brings us finally to the question of what we are to make of the autonomous character of the very ideas of inspiration and aspiration as they relate to the fundamental notion of breath or Spirit? In our everyday language we have no qualms about characterizing the music of Bach or the art of Caravaggio as inspired. In a similar way we are not embarrassed to refer to the power of aspiration and hope when it comes to motivation to achieve. We also refer to moral motivations, such as the urge to reverse a sense of indignity and to fight against corruption, and we talk about the power of truth, including its power 'to make us free' as the Gospel promises.

These attributions are made way beyond the enclaves of the church. Václav Havel attributed the fall of communism not only to economic failure but to a failure to tell the truth, and commentators at large spoke of the resilience of the human *spirit* under privations. Adam Smith wrote a theory of the moral sentiments to complement the *Wealth of Nations*. The appeals of John Ruskin in favour of a just estimate of 'wealth' rather than 'illth' were based on a proper sense of what was due, inspired by the words Jesus gives to the landlord in the parable of the early and late workers who earn the same pay: 'I will give unto this last even as unto thee' (Matthew 20:14).[1]

Such sentiments were central to British motivations to political and social reform (Wheeler 2006).

Of course, in the pursuit of our proper calling as sociologists we are bound by protocols of evidence, including metrics, by logic, and by systematic comparison, but we are at the same time only able to make sense of the situations that make sense of Pentecostals on account of the moral saturation of language. We share a universe of language and of signs with our subject matter and we take our cues about what constitutes a problem from other language users and from pre-understandings embedded in language. We take the narratives of our 'respondents' seriously even if the analytic understandings we eventually deploy are somewhat different. We recognize a social territory with objective characteristics *and* we learn and conventionally employ the grammar and the nuances of a language attributing power to spirit, with or without a capital letter. At the very least we need to apply the adage that if things are defined as real they are real in their consequences. People are *moved* by the spirit in every sense of the word move. Our first obligation is to listen and to understand the terms and the narratives in which people understand themselves and their situation. We construct our narratives from the materials provided by their narratives.

The narratives of those we encounter 'in the field' in order to make sociological sense, combine what we conventionally label social forces, circumstances, and processes, with the sign language of religion just as the narratives of sociology combine the elucidation of 'objective' factors with an interpretation of the logic of the situation and an understanding of words and signs. In that latter enterprise it is quite appropriate to refer to our proper intellectual vocation as 'Geisteswissenschaft' (Hodges 1944).

It may be that those who make the long trek to the megacity find the objective conditions of urban chaos and disintegration morally and psychologically intolerable; it may be that marginal ethnicities, like the gypsies or the Maya wish to reverse negative stereotypes and rope themselves together in a modern transnational association; it may be that members of a buried intelligentsia, more interested in effective technology than humanistic cultivation, seize the opportunity to run their own religious show, training on the job; it may be that women desire an arena of expression and prophecy, and a trustworthy and non-violent partner who will come back into the family and shoulder shared responsibility; it may be that the new middle classes of Brazil or West Africa struggle with a rationalized environment and need to be emotionally sustained in an environment where executives may cry. People on the edge of catastrophe, but with just enough autonomy to re-view where they stand, envisage a way through to betterment. They have more to gain by rupture than continuity. They band together to create their own environment, and they protect it with firm boundaries against the incursions of chaos. Such people are predisposed to seek an 'empowerment from on high' that they cannot summon up from their own depleted resources. For them, Pentecostalism initiates a change for the better, including some hope of access to God, the material goods and the moral good. That combination draws strong support form the Hebrew Scriptures, for example Joel.

The generic and the specifically Christian repertoire

In summary I have been arguing that religion works along with other social energies, not only in the period of modern nationalism where it is partly co-opted for the purposes and sign language of cultural defence but throughout its history. In the United States, versions of Christianity, though separated from the state by a wall of partition, have for a couple of centuries provided the symbolic vesture of a Christian nation, as well as creating very successful multistranded associations standing between the individual and the state in a way scarcely paralleled anywhere else. Christianity has performed 'social' services in much earlier times for very different social formations in city states and feudal kingdoms.

The key arguments put forward above distinguish between those parts of the Biblical repertoire that are easily co-opted for the benefit of the dominant classes and institutions, like Solomonic kingship or the Promised Land of Israel, or the duty of obedience, and those that are secreted in the radical substratum of the New Testament. These time-bombs secreted in the New Testament are humility, poverty, chastity, peacefulness, incautious generosity and a large charity, forgiveness, reconciliation and apology, sincerity in the sense of the primacy of the inward inclination of the heart over external conformity, the distinction between God and Caesar, the reversal of power in favour of the poor, and the invitation to all and sundry to enter the kingdom prepared for them.

However, when Christianity is pitch-forked into power by Constantine, and continuously thereafter, these radical virtues can generate paradoxical consequences, as when the peace and poverty embraced by monasticism are transmuted into wealth, and moreover wealth sometimes used to finance violence. In addition, some elements in the Christian repertoire, not initially at the disposal of the imperatives of power, are partly taken over by those imperatives, for example when the 'sacrament' of penance is used to excommunicate recalcitrant rulers and bring them to heel, or when the phrase 'Compel them to come in' (Luke 14:23) in the parable about everyone being invited to the divine banquet, is used to enforce doctrinal conformity.

Grace is a mixed case, since it can refer both to the gratuitous character of God's mercy, or the graciousness of earthly potentates. Service is also a mixed case since it can refer to self-giving for the good of others and to the duty owed to superiors. The Trinity provides many opportunities for political interpretation, some of them supporting the primacy of the Father (the Father of the nation, the Holy Father) and others emphasizing the exaltation of the Son raised with 'all that are in him' to *equality* with the Father, and yet others espousing the freedom of the Spirit to break out on everyone alike, male and female, bond and free. Charisma lights on whom it will without authorization through the 'usual channels'. The idea has been adapted and exploited almost as the founding idea of modern culture, infusing it with a religiose aura in a secular form.

Motifs in the Hebrew Scriptures (the Old Testament), and in the New Testament, shift backwards and forwards between universal spiritual and allegorical meanings, and material and localized meanings. The contrast between enslavement in Egypt and liberation to set out to a promised land, and the parallel contrast between 'this our exile' and a joyous re-entry into the holy city of Jerusalem, engender multiple translations, whether we think of the return of exiles from Babylon, or the events celebrated on Palm Sunday, or the moment when modern Jews fought their way to the Wailing Wall. These translations encompass our spiritual journeys, our pilgrimages to places that promise renewal, and contemporary liberation movements seeking a better future in a restored national territory.

The English Pilgrims seeking a promised land in America understood it as a 'City set on a hill', according to New Testament phraseology, and they moved constantly between the allegorical and the territorial meanings. The case of Poland, discussed earlier, brings all the various meanings together, including ideas of collective suffering and individual martyrdom modelled on the passion of Christ. During the two world wars the model provided by the Passion was adopted by people at large to apply to the sufferings of Passchendaele through the use of the New Testament phrase 'Greater love hath no man than this that he lay down his life for his friends', and the battlefields of Flanders are marked by hundreds of thousands of crosses. Of course, there is a crucial difference between redemptive non-violent suffering on behalf of others, including enemies, and death in battle against the enemy, but the transfer makes emotional sense, assisted by the language of 'the warfare of the cross'. The spiritual and universal reference to mental fight and spiritual warfare is partly, but not wholly, commandeered by the sufferings of physical warfare. One says 'not wholly', because the *rhetoric* of pacifism to the effect that war never changes anything is now an accepted trope of contemporary comment.

In the modern period parts of the Christian (and Jewish) repertoire have been partly separated from their religious origin, notably injunctions to follow conscience (or God) rather than man, as explicitly embraced in the early chapters of the Acts of the Apostles and the need to value spontaneity and sincerity above ritual and external moral conformity recommended by Jesus in his teaching on the primacy of the heart (Seligman 2000). Charisma lights on whom it will regardless of settled authorization through the 'usual channels'. Like the embrace of sincerity, the universal availability of charisma is not without very serious problems, but it has become the founding idea of contemporary culture as well as a leading motif of Pentecostalism (Seligman et al. 2008). One can either regard such translations as a form of secularization, or as the somewhat alarming adoption of the distinctive 'notes' of Christianity, no doubt assisted by elements in the nexus of Pietism and Romanticism, to the point where they are so taken for granted their point of origination is lost to view.

Note

1 The passage is quoted by Ruskin in his *Unto this Last and Other Essays on Political Economy* (1912: 118).

References

Bloom, H. (1992) *The American Religion: The Emergence of a Post-Christian Nation*. New York: Simon and Schuster.

Borsook, E. (1990) *Messages in Mosaic: The Royal Programmes of Norman Sicily 1130–1187*. Oxford: Oxford University Press.

Bruce, S. (2011) *Secularization: In Defence of an Unfashionable Theory*. Oxford: Oxford University Press.

Cavanaugh, W. J. (2009) *The Myth of Religious Violence: Secular Ideology and the Roots of Modern Conflict*. Oxford: Oxford University Press.

Davies, D. J. (2000) *The Mormon Culture of Salvation*. Aldershot: Ashgate.

Davies, D. J. (2011) *Emotion, Identity, and Religion: Hope, Reciprocity and Otherness*. Oxford: Oxford University Press.

Etherington, N. (ed.) (2008) *Missions and Empire*. Oxford: Oxford University Press.

Graham-Dixon, A. (2009) *Caravaggio: A Life Sacred and Profane*. London: Allen Lane.

Hardy, G. (2010) *Understanding the Book of Mormon: A Reader's Guide*. Oxford: Oxford University Press.

Hilton, B. (1988) *The Age of Atonement: The Influence of Evangelicalism on Social and Economic thought 1795–1865*. Oxford: Oxford University Press.

Hobsbawm, E. (1965) *Primitive Rebels: Studies in Archaic Forms of Social Movement in the 19th and 20th Centuries*. New York: Norton.

Hodges, H. A. (1944) *The Philosophy of Wilhem Dilthey*. London: Routledge.

Marshall, R. (2010) *Political Spiritualities: The Pentecostal Revolution in Nigeria*. Chicago: Chicago University Press.

Rubin, M. (1991) *Corpus Christi: The Eucharist in Late Medieval Culture*. Cambridge: Cambridge University Press.

Ruskin, J. (1912) *Unto this Last and Other Essays on Political Economy*. London: Ward Lock.

Seligman, A. B. (2000) *Modernity's Wager: Authority, the Self, and Transcendence*. Princeton and Oxford: Princeton University Press.

Seligman, A. B., Weller, R. P., Puett, M. J. and Bennett, S. (2008) *Ritual and its Consequences: An Essay on the Limits of Sincerity*. Oxford: Oxford University Press.

Wheeler, M. (2006) *Ruskin's God*. Cambridge: Cambridge University Press.

Wolff, C. (2000) *Johann Sebastian Bach: The Learned Musician*. Oxford: Oxford University Press.

10 Called to speak

Language, meaning and the status of research data

Matthew Wood

A personal introduction

Sociologists and social anthropologists build their understandings of the social world primarily upon data that takes the form of language, yet the nature and status of that language is infrequently considered. Research methods such as interviews, focus groups, textual study, participant observation and surveys generate data that is primarily linguistic, in the form of what research subjects say or write.[1] Even quantitative data is linguistic in that it is generated through research subjects responding to written or spoken questions by selecting the answer that best fits them. New methods have developed that are oriented towards non-linguistic data – such as in the study of images, music, material objects and the built environment – but these tend to be interpreted through a consideration of how people talk about them. While this is a correct approach, since it guards against the sort of de-contextualized analysis prevalent in some areas of cultural studies,[2] it leaves us with the fact that sociological data is linguistic.[3] A more promising route out of this reliance upon linguistic data is a thorough study of bodily gestures and of the positions and interactions between bodies more generally.[4] Even so, much interpretation of uses of the body is shaped through the linguistic accounts of those observed or who are present in the same situation, or the accounts of those who are teaching others how to act appropriately. Given the intractability of having to rely primarily upon linguistic data, it is essential to consider the role that language plays for those we study. It certainly cannot be assumed that how people speak or write in research settings is an absolute, once-for-all representation of how they perceive or interpret themselves and their world. Language is far more particular than that – it needs to be seen in terms of social context and practice. While ethnographers, by generating or recording linguistic data *in situ*, are well placed to recognize the contextualized nature of language, the danger of not recognizing that is sharper when other research methods are used (especially without extensive prior contact with research subjects). This is because methods such as interviews take place in an artificial social setting which may mistakenly suggest that research subjects' words are detached, abstract and thus somehow more objective (and true). These considerations require that sociologists reflexively consider the social role of language with the aim of enabling a better understanding of the status of research data and hence the use they make of it.

In a volume celebrating the life and work of Douglas Davies, I am drawn to this topic by Davies' early writing on meaning, specifically his book *Meaning and Salvation in Religious Studies* (1984), which raises issues relating to language and which was my introduction to many of the sociologists and social anthropologists this chapter refers to.[5] In critically engaging with some of Davies' thoughts – which, in this case, is truly the sincerest way to acknowledge my intellectual debt to him – I practise one of the most important elements that I took from his pedagogy, namely to privilege argument in itself. That is, to pursue argument for its own sake, rather than as a mere means to advance understanding of the topic in question – precisely because this, paradoxically, is the best way to advance understanding. In his undergraduate seminars, for example, Douglas would frequently initiate a game by adopting a contentious position and calling on students to argue against him, thereby encouraging debate and disagreement for their own sake and, in the process, revealing important issues about the topic at hand. Whether the roots of this pedagogical technique lie in his upbringing in the laudably argumentative culture of Wales (no doubt resulting, in part, from its contested denominational religious scene) or in his later experiences in English universities – or, more likely, a mixture of these and other influences (including his proficiency at squash, which might be described as a game in which two players have an argument with a ball) – I cannot say, but can certainly attest to its effectiveness in fostering enthusiasm for scholarly pursuits.

Phenomenologically speaking? Language, meaning and power

The subject of this chapter is the social role of language and its consequences for the status of sociological research data. As Weinberg explains, there is a 'fundamental place that language and linguistic interaction occupy in social science methodology and hence the importance of analysing language and linguistic interaction to fully grasp those methods' (2006: 6). In particular, I focus upon the role of speech in social life – writing is a related but somewhat specific and separate issue that there is not space to address here, but which has received small but significant attention in sociological studies of literacy. While discourse and conversation analyses enquire into the details of writing or speech in order to reveal crucial things about what is written or said, this is somewhat different from raising the sociological question about the nature and status of language *per se*. Within the sociological study of religion, this issue has been more forthcoming in recent years, as in the work of Bender (2003), Engelke and Tomlinson (2006), Keane (1997), Robbins (2001) and Wuthnow (2011), particularly by drawing upon the social-oriented philosophies of language of J. L. Austin, Mikhail Bakhtin and John Searle, and the sociological studies of Pierre Bourdieu. In order to address what people are doing when they speak, I take up a number of themes from various writers. It is easy to provide answers to this issue, such as that consciously or unconsciously people may be doing things (language as instrumental), reflecting upon things (language as reflexive or expressive), asserting their status (language as power) or repeating deep cognitive or cultural patterns (language as structure). Sociological theories of language have been founded upon each of those answers and each has a degree of merit.[6] None of these, however, quite gets at what speech is, even if it is fulfilling one (or more) or those functions. For speech is *demanded* in that it is an elicited and solicited response, whether or not that response is immediate or takes place after a considerable length of time.[7] Indeed, given that speech is a basic and intrinsic aspect of being human, social life in general may be seen as a *call to speak*. Simultaneously, it is a *call to listen*. These considerations point us towards the interactional nature of speaking/listening, and so my enquiry proceeds first from phenomenologically based accounts.

The starting point of the account of the social world given by phenomenologists and (deriving from them) the sociologists of knowledge is the *individual's* apprehension of reality. Alfred Schutz, his pupil and colleague Thomas Luckmann and the latter's co-author Peter Berger each addressed the individual's subjective experience of life – that is, the individual's internal consciousness. In this, they continued the approach of the founder of phenomenology, Edmund Husserl. But if Schutz was a phenomenologist attempting to appreciate sociology in his analysis, then Berger and Luckmann were sociologists trying to integrate phenomenology. As such, there are differences: Berger and Luckmann's (1967: 37) starting point was the 'reality of everyday life' as 'intersubjective', rather than Schutz's (1972: 217) 'stream of consciousness of the solitary Ego'. Nevertheless, all address the construction of the social world by paying particular attention to language.

Berger and Luckmann (1967) explore the social construction of reality through the concepts of objectivation, roles and internalization. Objectivation is the process whereby things, in particular social institutions, acquire objective reality to individuals (Berger and Luckmann 1967: 76–77). Roles exist on the basis of this objectivation, since 'Institutions are embodied in individual experience by means of roles' (Berger and Luckmann 1967: 91). But it is with the internalization of such roles that Berger and Luckmann are most concerned as sociologists, since this is what makes individuals 'member[s] of society' (1967: 149) – and it is here that language enters their analysis. Language crystallises and stabilises individuals' senses of subjectivity by integrating their different zones of everyday life into *meaningful* wholes (Berger and Luckmann 1967: 53–55). Language is thus the formative element of reality-construction, as Schutz (1973: 264, 349–350) had proposed; 'The most important vehicle of reality-maintenance is conversation' (Berger and Luckmann 1967: 172). However, the construction of social reality through language in this framework needs closer examination, because the postulation that those sharing a 'common language' in which 'all who employ this same language are reality-maintaining others' (Berger and Luckmann 1967: 173) begs the question of whose reality is maintained and how it has been achieved in the first place. These are central socio-logical issues that Berger and Luckmann's phenemologically based account struggles to acknowledge and address, despite their attention to legitima-tion. Specifically, despite focusing upon intersubjectivity, the positing of the individual *qua* individual within that enables them to offer only a weak view of what is involved in social relations, which downplays relations of power between people and how these are founded upon different positions in social structure and take place in specific social contexts.

From the perspectives of social phenomenology and the sociology of knowledge, then, the social world acquires meaning through language use. This analysis was paralleled by work within social anthropology at around the same time, notably by Clifford Geertz (1966). Davies (1984: 2–5) explains that from the 1960s the concept of meaning became a unify-ing paradigm in social studies, as reflected in his own work, which draws extensively, but not uncritically, upon Berger and Luckmann: 'man [*sic*] is a meaning maker and utilizes religious processes for the construction of ulti-mately secure spheres of certainty' (Davies 1984: 15). This approach raises the issue of the extent to which a focus on meaning is a plausible method for sociological analysis in general and for interpreting the role of language and speech in particular.

It was particularly within the sociological study of religion that criti-cisms of this approach were developed. Asad's (1993) celebrated riposte to Geertz, which argues that religion is not necessarily concerned with meaning-construction but may have more to do with disciplinary power relations, can be compared to Beckford's (1983) criticism of the sociology of knowledge for treating power under the rubric of meaning. This sec-ondary consideration of power – as 'the background "noise" of the social system' – means that Berger and Luckmann's analysis is 'abstract and dis-embodied': it 'encourage[s] us to think of religion as primarily a matter of knowledge susceptible to understanding in the same way as other cogni-tive products – *in particular, language*' (Beckford 1983: 12–13; emphasis added). Nevertheless, such criticisms do not necessarily entail that meaning (or language) itself is of secondary importance: as Tomlinson and Engelke (2006: 3–5) explain, meaning and power are two parts of the same whole, since specific meanings are legitimized through social authorities. This leads them to enquire into the limits of meaning; that is, to see meaning as a process that can involve moments of failure (Tomlinson and Engelke 2006: 23–26; see also Bender 2003: 5). This offers an alternative way of avoiding what Davies (1984: 96) calls the 'nihilistic' view of Needham (1972), who rejects the methodological focus on meaning as a result of the conceptual instability of language.

Working from a phenomenological perspective, Davies proposes that the 'uniqueness and intransigent creativity of the self', especially in embodied and affective terms, provides the basis for a 'personal level of meaning', if not for meaning at the level of interpersonal relations (1984: 93–95). Yet, as already discussed, the phenomenological perspective leaves little room for a sociological account of power – in this case, the manner in which personal meaning relates to structural position, the trajectory through which that position has been reached, and the role of others in being privy in some way to what we consider our 'innermost' experiences (not least in the representations, and therefore anticipation of *potential* responses, of these others within our thoughts). Furthermore, there remains the issue of how sociological analysis of the 'personal level' would be carried out given that research data principally takes a linguistic form – there being, as Ludwig Wittgenstein explained, no such thing as a private language. While Davies is certainly correct in warning against equating social life with language use and in drawing attention to the 'personal level' (even if this must always be interpreted in relation to the interpersonal), Needham's conclusions can be avoided instead by adopting the approach to meaning developed by Tomlinson and Engelke, since this recognizes that social life is able to proceed despite the inherent instability and ambiguity of meaning (and language), and that power relations may depend upon this fact. Insofar as the linguistic elements of culture are concerned, then, any understanding of their relationship to social power must take the issue of meaning into account. The baby of meaning should not be thrown out with the phenomenological bathwater.

The social role of language

Davies in fact provides an important notion that extends and deepens a perspective on meaning and language: the 'pool of potential orientations', which accounts for the way in which any religion contains a 'source [that] provides a ready supply of differently emphasized doctrines which can be selectively utilized as occasion demands', including in the future (Davies 1984: 135). This notion may be extended to culture in general and to the non-doctrinal elements of culture in particular: it enables a way of considering how cultural elements (doctrines, words, gestures, and so on) are open to different interpretations by different people in the same setting, and over time, without such ambiguity necessarily collapsing into meaninglessness. By examining the ways in which Sikhism has changed over time, Davies (1984: 124–36) shows that differences in interpretations must be related to different social, cultural and political conditions (rather than being the wholly unpredictable result of any free exercise of choice by individuals), and that culture itself structures and limits its possible range of interpretations.[8] Since varying conditions (in the form of structural positions and individual trajectories) exist within a group at any given moment in time, the notion of a 'pool of potential orientations' is useful in accounting for instances of ambiguity over meaning, since different people may be orientated towards the same cultural elements differently, and for contestations over the authority to pronounce upon correct or appropriate orientations. Coleman, for example, examines the 'double talk' of a charismatic church leader in Sweden, who is able to meaningfully address both charismatic Christians and secular Swedes despite their different interpretations of his speeches (Coleman 2006: 49–50). This perspective therefore rests upon recognition of the diversity that exists among speakers and listeners in any given social context. In establishing the 'ethnography of speaking', Hymes proposed that people speak as part of a 'speech community' that is itself internally differentiated, being an 'organization of diversity' (Hymes 1974: 433) (it might also be added that they frequently speak as part of a series of related speech communities). But recognition of this diversity only makes sociological sense when we enquire into the dimension of power that exists in such a community, not simply in terms of the structure of social positions and trajectories, but also in terms of the 'linguistic market' itself in which certain ways of speaking are more legitimate than others (Bourdieu 1992: 43–65).

The 'pool of potential orientations' present in culture means that social life, being grounded in culture, is itself potentially relatively unstable and contestable – and becomes more so with greater social differentiation. Given this, the use of language – particularly in the form of speech – is necessary for positing one's social position in relation to others, even though this opens up possibilities for further ambiguity. This leads us back to the comments at the start of this section: social life may be seen as a call to speak in that the spoken (or written or gestural) positioning of those to whom we are socially related requires our positioning in turn.[9] Thus, it is not simply that speaking is the means by which people socially position themselves, or do so in relation to others (as Bourdieu argues), but that speaking is the means by which people are *required* to socially position themselves in relation to others doing so – this involves both *elicitation*, in which such positioning is provoked, and *solicitation*, in which it is requested (though the distinction between the two is no doubt blurred in practice). This is true even in societies that do not operate with a 'modern linguistic ideology', that is, with a cultural representation of the nature of speech that links meaning, interaction and truth (Robbins 2001). In such societies, speech may not be seen by others or by the speaker as trustworthy or as revealing of the speaker's subjective intentions, but nevertheless no doubt is an attempt to claim a position rather than being random; indeed, as Robbins' own examples from the Urapmin of Papua New Guinea show, dissimulation in speech is itself a form of positioning which has social meaning. This means that there is a need to take interactions more seriously than Bourdieu proposes. Bourdieu (1992: 64–65) is quite right to argue against a pure interactionist perspective on the basis that it cannot grasp the structural distribution of what he calls forms of capital and the history that underlies this. Similarly, Pascale argues for an epistemological shift towards the study of language as 'systems of representation' in which 'language use is never fully realized in localized contexts' (2010: 161–62). Yet, the (structured) nature of contestations among social actors requires that we pay attention to interactional practices in addition to situating these in broader fields of power (see Mouzelis 2008). Ethnography is an especially useful method for doing this, as demonstrated by the studies of speaking in Bauman and Sherzer (1974) and Engelke and Tomlinson (2006). These demonstrate how social life is an ongoing series in which people are called to speak and, in turn, call on their listeners to speak, and so on – what Weinberg calls 'the sequence of talk' (2006: 6). The social positioning that speaking involves may be more usefully understood as the way in which people *invest* themselves, since it implies some sort of commitment (although not necessarily a conscious one) to a position that is not cost-free.[10]

However, it is important to recognize that such positioning or investment is not primarily achieved through speech (or other uses of language), rather than through the deployment of various capitals. Speech is only one of these and not the most important. Thus, contrary to Berger and Luckmann, social reality is not built upon language, even if language is an essential medium for its construction. As Marx and Engels note in *The German Ideology* (written in 1845), 'The production of ideas, of conceptions, of consciousness, is at first directly interwoven with the material activity and the material intercourse of men, the language of real life.' (1949: 13–14) Similarly, Giddens views language as a 'medium of practical social activity' (1977: 20). But where language does play a specific role is in articulating or demonstrating social positioning (or the attempt at such positioning). In this sense, language acts as a banner that, once hoisted, is a focus for reaction by others. This 'linguistic banner' *proclaims* the holder's recognized place in social relationships or *claims* for recognition of a new place. Language therefore has significant symbolic importance which explains why it is the object of struggle, as Bourdieu (1992) recognized. As one of the media of power relations, language may not be dismissed as epiphenomenal: it comes to have relative efficacy in its own right, such that incompetent use of language may contribute to the loss of social position or competent use may contribute to the attainment of social position against other claimants (as may be seen in job interviews in which similar candidates compete for a post).

It is from a view of the potential 'force' of an 'utterance' to 'break' from a 'prior context' that Butler argues for the ability of performed language to be insurrectionary (1997: 145). This challenges what Butler describes as Bourdieu's 'epiphenomenal' approach to language: 'In Bourdieu's account of performative speech acts, the subject who utters the performative is positioned on a map of social power in a fairly fixed way, and this performative will or will not work depending on whether the subject who performs the utterance is already authorized to make it work by the position of social power she or he occupies.' (Butler 1997: 156–57) Discrepant performative utterances, however, should not be viewed as having force in their own right, but as requiring a receptive context, even if the match between the two is unusual or surprising to most participants. It is this that may allow one 'to speak with authority, *without* being authorized to speak' (Butler 1997: 157). This points to the multiplicity of contexts that potentially exist in a given social setting, including contexts that are new, are in the process of becoming formed, or have been hidden. Recognition of such multiplicity enables Butler's salient remarks about language use to be given a firmer sociological basis.

Spirit possession provides a good illustration of the understanding of speech that has been developed in this section. As Lewis' (2003) comparative study shows, communication by a possessing spirit claims a new social position for the possessed, but only once other social factors have been fulfilled – without these, the authenticity of possession will be denied. The discourse of channellers in contemporary Euro-American societies, for example, may be seen as an attempt to position themselves in close relation to the authority of science as recognized by their well-educated, lower-middle-class audiences (see Wood 2007).[11] My participant observation in channelling workshops among a religious network in the English East Midlands, for example, revealed that the syntax of channelled discourses was characterized by a high degree of pedantry. By this is meant a fussy use of language that repeats phrases, combined with careful, slow and deliberate speech (and gestures). One channeller repeatedly used the phrase 'such that is' to provide precision about what she said. Such pedantry of speech marked out the scientific rendition of the social world prevalent in the network, as was evident from people's views and explanations of such phenomena as diverse as healing therapies and extraterrestrials. Similarly, Schlemmer and Jenkins (1993: 384–385) explain how Schlemmer's channelled discourses (which were well known in this network) had increased their use of the word 'of' tenfold since she began to channel, because it refers to '"that of" the essence of you', which may be seen as akin to the scientific attempt to reveal the essences of things, and Miller (1990: 166) notes how channelled speech is 'peppered with repetitive phrases like "that which is termed" and "indeed"'.[12]

Such idiosyncrasies should not be seen as mere phrases that those making long speeches require in order to cover up gaps (like the use of 'er' or 'um' in everyday conversations), since silences are an important feature of channelled speech (and themselves present the speech as the product of careful deliberation, rather than a rambling stream of consciousness). Rather, channellers' attempts at conveying precise meanings acted to position their activities and discourses as rational along the same lines as scientific or scholarly discourse, and thereby to claim a similar status as these – as also seen by the fact that specific details, such as percentages and dates, were provided in their discourses.[13] However, the *lower*-middle-class position of channellers (and their audiences) is revealed by the manner in which this claim was made through an extreme pedantry, which indicates an uneasiness with the precision required by scientific rationality. As Bourdieu writes, 'hyper-correction is inscribed in the logic of pretension which leads the petits bourgeois to attempt to appropriate prematurely, at the cost of constant tension, the properties of those who are dominant.' (1992: 83) In other words, the language of channellers and the way in which it was received by their audiences revealed their lack of a dominant social position that would provide them with easy mastery of a form of language that has dominance in the linguistic market.

Research data and the social role of language

It is now possible to consider how an understanding of the social role of language can be used to offer a more fruitful understanding of research data. For a start, it is clear that people's speech must be considered within its interactional context (although that context may be stretched over time and space, rather than being immediate and face-to-face). Sermons, for example, may be responses to conflict that have been voiced within congregations, acting as opportunities for preachers to position themselves within conflicts or outside of them. But it is also clear that by being called to speak within an interactional context, people do so on the basis of their structural position (and the trajectory by which that has been reached), and in relation to the positions and trajectories of their anticipated listeners. Thus, preachers are able to use sermons to position themselves in relation to conflicts precisely because they occupy a certain religious position and its associated capitals (as well as inherited personal capitals that have enabled them to attain this position in the first place). Therefore, whether apprehended by the sociologist as written or spoken, a sermon cannot be understood unless it is situated within both these contexts (interactional and structural), rather than being analysed as a statement *in itself* of the preacher's position or views. Of course, a sermon may reveal the preacher's position or views, but it can do so only by being analysed in relation to those two contexts, in other words relationally.[14]

Furthermore, given that interaction is an ongoing process, rather than an isolated event, people's speech needs to be understood in terms of the interactions that have occurred before – at least, those which are most pertinent – and thus the ways in which speech has been interpreted by interlocutors in the past. What are relevant here, then, are the actual orientations that have developed in relation to a cultural phenomenon's 'pool of potential orientations'. Analysis of a sermon, for example, may need to take into account how a preacher's previous sermons have been received and interpreted; preachers' apprehensions that their previous sermons have been seen as meaningless or have led to erroneous interpretations (or, indeed, that they have been successful) may well affect their preaching at the present time. Of course, the research agenda proposed here is by no means easy to achieve, nor necessarily always feasible, but that should not prevent it being striven towards. The onus lies upon sociologists to reflect upon the limitations and gaps in their research, and to construe their arguments accordingly.

This approach towards research data becomes even more tricky when it has been generated not through the 'natural settings' characteristic of ethnographic research, but in other ways such as interviews, focus groups and surveys. For here the researcher plays a much more prominent role in calling research subjects to speak – in other words, the interactional context through which those subjects position themselves is one dominated by the researcher. All sorts of consequences arise from this: for example, research subjects may speak about issues that they have never spoken about before, or even thought about in detail (indeed, it is common for interviewees to say that this is the case); and they may feel uncomfortable with or intimidated by the researcher's educational capital and position. Consequently, the nature of the interaction between researchers and their interlocutors in these settings must be taken into account when the generated data is analysed.

While issues pertaining to research reflexivity in general are now readily acknowledged and addressed by sociologists, they have tended to stress either the manner in which researchers' personal positions and trajectories affect what they choose to study or, in reaction to that, the researcher's academic positions and trajectories. Bourdieu and Wacquant (1992: 72), for example, consider the former as narcissistic and insist instead upon the latter as more fruitful for reflecting upon the research process, whereas Mauthner and Doucet (2003) attempt a more balanced approach by disentangling these different forms of reflexivity and discussing how together they can form part of the research process, in terms of data generation, data analysis and writing up (see also Wood and Atlglas 2010). While these debates are extremely valuable, they tend not to consider the nature of the effects of the interactions between researchers and those they are researching. Yet, as this chapter demonstrates, this should feature as a key form of research reflexivity. While it is certainly true that such reflexive comments are habitually to be found in written ethnographies (though much less so in publications based upon other research methods, such as interviews and, in particular, surveys), these are rarely considered systematically. One exception is Blackman (2007), who discusses his interactions in fieldwork settings in order to reveal more about them. That, of course, is the point about such reflexivity: its aim is to produce more and better sociological knowledge about what has been studied.

An example of reflexivity regarding interactions can be taken from my research into London Methodism.[15] What is significant here is not so much the fact that I was a British-born white man doing research in congregations that had high proportions of African Caribbean and black African female Methodists who were born overseas, which might question the possibility of my having empathy with them – that is, to see or experience the world as they see or experience it. Reflection on that issue is of limited usefulness for furthering understanding of the research setting, since such a view would reduce those Methodists to a singular position and set of experiences, whereas there were significant differences among them, and furthermore it would limit research to those researchers deemed to have certain social characteristics, thus undermining the humanistic basis of social science in which the ability to conduct research into a topic should not be denied on such grounds. Instead, what is significant was the manner in which people interacted with me as a result of their apprehensions of my social position. For instance, on a number of occasions such Methodists asked if I had thought about becoming a minister – even though they knew that I was not a Methodist. What this helped to reveal to me, in conjunction with other data from fieldwork and interviews, was that their sense of what a Methodist minister, at least in Britain, should be was that of a well-educated, white, British-born man. Our interactions, then, elicited this positioning on their behalf. Knowing this helped to explain some of what went on in these churches in terms of the power relations between laity and ministers (see Wood 2010).

In sum, social research involves calling people to speak (and, concomitantly, calling the researcher to speak) and thus demanding that they position themselves within that interactional context, albeit on the basis of their position and trajectory in a structural context. This does not mean that what people say in these situations is 'false' or untrustworthy; their speech reveals things about them, but only when these contexts have been taken into consideration.

Conclusions

Since language is the medium through which sociological research is carried out from beginning to end, it is necessary to consider the status of research data insofar as it is linguistic. This can only be done by considering the role that language plays in social life in general, since data generated through research is not essentially different in kind. In this chapter, I have argued that language, and in particular speech, is central to how people proclaim or claim social positions in interactional contexts through which, by elicitation and solicitation, they are called to speak. In doing so, they draw upon what Douglas Davies calls the 'pool of potential orientations' that is present in culture, with the result that ambiguities abound within social life without necessarily collapsing into meaninglessness. This view of language furthers sociological reflexivity towards the generation of research data, in a manner that aids rather than undermines analysis. Although it has not been possible to explore the consequences of this in detail for different sorts of research methods, these no doubt vary considerably since different methods call research participants to speak in diverse ways.[16] In fact, by conducting research sociologists are called to reflect upon their practice, or craft, at every stage. And that, as Douglas Davies might say, is what is *vital*.

Notes

1 It is important to note that research data should be seen as 'generated' rather than 'collected' since it is *produced* through the research process rather than simply pre-existing this process and then being more or less accessible to collection. This perspective is essential for the arguments that follow in this chapter. It might be thought that data from participant observation provides an exception to this, but that is erroneous for two reasons: firstly, data here consists of the field notes that the participant observer produces, rather than the totality of the things that were done and said in the research setting (see Emerson, Fretz and Shaw 1995); secondly, the presence of the participant observer necessarily impacts (in however small a way) upon what occurs in the research setting. A related issue is that what social researchers do with the data they generate is also primarily linguistic – it is themed, coded, analysed and written-up through the medium of language (pictures and ethnographic films offer a non-linguistic presentation of data, but these are framed by a written or spoken commentary).

2 For example, Hebdige's (1979) study of the meanings of material objects in youth subcultures such as punk, which was strongly influenced by the semiotic analysis of Barthes (1973 [1957]).

3 In this chapter, the term 'sociological' is used to refer to the method of both sociology and social anthropology.

4 See Mauss' (1979 [1934]) classic essay and, more recently, Tyson, Peacock and Patterson (1988).

5 This chapter draws upon some discussions in Wood (1999).

6 For example, respectively: Malinowski (1948) on 'primitive' and on 'developed' peoples; Bourdieu (1992); Lévi-Strauss (1966).

7 In a similar vein, Jenkins (1999: 202–204) views functionalist explanations of gossip as inadequate since they do not explain the 'compulsion' to speak and the way in which this is distributed across the social group – as such, the creation of in-group solidarity may be seen as a symptom rather than a function of gossip.

8 As recognized by Lévi-Strauss' (1966) concept of *bricolage*. More contentiously, Bloch (1989) argues that in religious settings the scope of meanings conveyed by language may be significantly reduced – see also Bernstein (1973) on language across social classes.

9 This may even take the form that Davies (2006) calls 'inner speech'.

10 Bourdieu (1992: 179–180) discusses investment in social fields, but does not in general consider how an investment relates not just to a field in general but to a particular position within that field – though see his discussions of positional disinvestment and reinvestment in *Distinction* (Bourdieu 1984).

11 As Irvine (1982) explains, possession must be analysed in terms of its social context, particularly its audience's motives and interests, and the historical trajectory of the possessed.

12 Jenkins (1996) was also known for popularizing the notion of 'hundredth monkeying', which was developed from scientific studies of primates' behaviour.

13 The art displayed by these channellers was also pedantic: pictures of the Ascended Masters, whom they channelled, were clear and simple with black lines used to outline different parts of each picture, and thus reminiscent of illustrations found in scientific and scholarly texts.

14 The 'call and response' that characterizes some African American sermons provides a nice example of preachers' direct interactions with congregations; in terms of the interactional context of the written word, Ryan (2008) discusses how African Americans' novels about slavery are best understood in terms of a dialogue with white-authored versions of slavery.

15 This research was funded by the Southlands Methodist Centre, through the School of Sociology and Social Policy, University of Surrey, Roehampton.

16 See the chapters in Part I of Drew, Raymond and Weinberg (2006).

References

Asad, T. (1993) 'The construction of religion as an anthropological category' in *Genealogies of Religion*. Baltimore: John Hopkins University Press.

Barthes, R. (1973) *Mythologies*. St Albans: Paladin.

Bauman, R. and Sherzer, J. (eds) (1974) *Explorations in the Ethnography of Speaking*. Cambridge: Cambridge University Press.

Beckford, J. A. (1983) 'The restoration of "power" to the sociology of religion', *Sociological Analysis* 44(1): 11–32.

Bender, C. (2003) *Heaven's Kitchen: Living Religion at God's Love We Deliver*. Chicago: University of Chicago Press.

Berger, P. and Luckmann, T. (1967) *The Social Construction of Reality: A Treatise in the Sociology of Knowledge*. London: Penguin.

Bernstein, B. (1973) *Class, Codes and Control*. St Albans: Paladin.

Blackman, S. J. (2007) '"Hidden ethnography": crossing emotional borders in qualitative accounts of young people's lives', *Sociology* 41(4): 699–716.

Bloch, M. (1989) 'Symbols, song, dance and features of articulation: is religion an extreme form of traditional authority?', *Ritual, History and Power*. London: Athlone Press.

Bourdieu, P. (1984) *Distinction: A Social Critique of the Judgement of Taste*. London: Routledge.

Bourdieu, P. (1992) *Language and Symbolic Power*. Cambridge: Polity.

Bourdieu, P. and Wacquant, L. J. D. (1992) *An Invitation to Reflexive Sociology*. Cambridge: Polity.

Butler, J. (1997) *Excitable Speech: A Politics of the Performative*. London: Routledge.

Coleman, S. (2006) 'When silence isn't golden: charismatic speech and the limits of literalism', in M. Engelke and M. Tomlinson (eds) (2006) *The Limits of Meaning: Case Studies in the Anthropology of Christianity*. Oxford: Berghahn.

Davies, D. J. (1984) *Meaning and Salvation in Religious Studies*. Leiden: Brill.

Davies, D. J. (2006) 'Inner speech and religious tradition' in J. A. Beckford and J. Walliss (eds) *Theorising Religion: Classical and Contemporary Debates*. Aldershot: Ashgate.

Drew, P., Raymond, G. and Weinberg, D. (eds) (2006) *Talk and Interaction in Social Research Methods*. London: Sage.

Emerson, R. M., Fretz, R. I. and Shaw, L. L. (1995) *Writing Ethnographic Fieldnotes*. Chicago: University of Chicago Press.

Engelke, M. and Tomlinson, M. (eds) (2006) *The Limits of Meaning: Case Studies in the Anthropology of Christianity*. Oxford: Berghahn.

Geertz, C. (1966) 'Religion as a cultural system', in M. Banton (ed.) *Anthropological Approaches to the Study of Religion*. London: Tavistock.

Giddens, A. (1977) *New Rules of Sociological Method*. London: Hutchinson.

Hebdige, D. (1979) *Subculture: The Meaning of Style*. London: Methuen, 1979.

Hymes, D. (1974) 'Ways of speaking', in R. Bauman and J. Sherzer (eds) *Explorations in the Ethnography of Speaking*. Cambridge: Cambridge University Press.

Irvine, J. T. (1982) 'The creation of identity in spirit mediumship and possession' in David Parkin (ed.) *Semantic Anthropology*. London: Academic Press.

Jenkins, P. (1996) *Hundredth Monkeying! Information Pack*. Unpublished manuscript.

Jenkins, T. (1999) *Religion in English Everyday Life: An Ethnographic Approach*. Oxford: Berghahn.

Keane, W. (1997) 'Religious language', *Annual Review of Anthropology* 26: 47–71.

Lévi-Strauss, C. (1966) *The Savage Mind*. Oxford: Oxford University Press.

Lewis, I. M. (2003) *Ecstatic Religion: A Study of Shamanism and Spirit Possession*. 3rd edition. London: Routledge.

Malinowski, B. (1948) 'The problem of meaning in primitive languages', *Magic, Science and Religion and Other Essays*. Glencoe: The Free Press.

Marx, K. and Engels, F. (1949) *The German Ideology*. London: Lawrence and Wishart.

Mauss, M. (1979) 'Body techniques', *Sociology and Psychology: Essays*. London: Routledge and Kegan Paul.

Mauthner, N. S. and Doucet, A. (2003) 'Reflexive accounts and accounts of reflexivity in qualitative data analysis', *Sociology* 37(3): 413–431.

Miller, E. (1990) *A Crash Course on the New Age Movement*. Eastbourne: Monarch.

Mouzelis, N. (2008) *Modern and Postmodern Social Theorizing*. Cambridge: Cambridge University Press.

Needham, R. (1972) *Belief, Language and Experience*. Oxford: Blackwell.

Pascale, C. (2010) 'Epistemology and the politics of knowledge', *The Sociological Review* 58/s: 154–165.

Robbins, J. (2001) 'God is nothing but talk: modernity, language, and prayer in a Papua New Guinea Society', *American Anthropologist* 103(4): 901–912.

Ryan, T. A. (2008) *Calls and Responses: The American Novel of Slavery Since Gone with the Wind*. Baton Rouge: Louisiana State University Press.

Schlemmer, P. V. and Jenkins, P. (1993) *The Only Planet of Choice: Essential Briefings from Deep Space*. Bath: Gateway Books.

Schutz, A. (1972) *The Phenomenology of the Social World*. London: Heinemann Educational Books.

Schutz, A. (1973) *Collected Papers, Volume 1: The Problem of Social Reality*. The Hague: Martinus Nijhoff.

Tomlinson, M. and Engelke, M. (2006) 'Meaning, Anthropology, Christianity', in M. Engelke and M. Tomlinson (eds) *The Limits of Meaning: Case Studies in the Anthropology of Christianity*. Oxford: Berghahn.

Tyson, R. W. Jr., Peacock, J. L. and Patterson, D. W. (eds) (1988) *Diversities of Gifts: Field Studies in Southern Religion*. Urbana: University of Illinois Press.

Weinberg, D. (2006) 'The language of social science: a brief introduction', in P. Drew, G. Raymond and D. Weinberg (eds) *Talk and Interaction in Social Research Methods*. London: Sage.

Wood, M. (1999) *Spirit Possession in a Contemporary British Religious Network: A Critique of New Age Movement Studies through the Sociology of Power*. PhD Thesis, University of Nottingham.

Wood, M. (2007) *Possession, Power and the New Age: Ambiguities of Authority in Neoliberal Societies*. Aldershot: Ashgate.

Wood, M. (2010) 'Carrying religion into a secularising Europe: Montserratian Migrants' experiences of global processes in British Methodism', *Anthropological Journal of European Cultures* 19(1): 9–23.

Wood, M. and Atlglas, V. (2010) 'Reflexivity, scientificity and the sociology of religion: Pierre Bourdieu in debate', *Nordic Journal of Religion and Society* 23(1): 9–26.

Wuthnow, R. J. (2011) 'Taking talk seriously: religious discourse as social practice', *Journal for the Scientific Study of Religion* 50(1): 1–21.

11 Where does Islamic Studies fit?

Hugh Goddard

Back in 1984, the Department of Theology in the University of Nottingham, under the leadership of Professor John Heywood Thomas, was the first in the United Kingdom to appoint a lecturer on Islam, entitled Lecturer in Islamic Theology. This was a response to the increasing religious diversity of the United Kingdom and reflection on the implications of this by different Christian churches, and particularly the British Council of Churches (BCC) under the leadership of (Methodist minister) Kenneth Cracknell, the Executive Secretary of the BCC's Committee for Relations with People of Other Faiths (Cracknell 1996). It was also an acknowledgement of the fact that within this diversity the largest numerical presence was that of Muslims, so, given that it was impractical for a small department to try and teach all the religious traditions of the world, the obvious one to begin with was the Islamic Tradition.

I had the privilege of being appointed to this lectureship, with my background as one of the first PhD students of the Centre for the Study of Islam and Christian-Muslim Relations in the Selly Oak Colleges of the University of Birmingham being a significant factor in this decision, pointing as it did to my interest in both Islam and Christian attitudes towards it. Once appointed to the department, an important question quickly arose, namely where does Islamic Studies best fit within the curriculum of a department of theology?

This was not a completely new question, as the department at an earlier stage of its development had provided teaching about the Buddhist tradition, which had been capably taught by Trevor Ling (1968). The establishment of the lectureship in Islamic Theology raised the question about the teaching of other religious traditions again, however, and the initial answer was in the form of optional courses, designed to recruit not only students from within the department but also from other departments in both the faculty of arts and the faculty of social sciences. This led to the creation of a pair of what were initially called 'Faculty Courses', first of all 'Introduction to Islam' and then, following the Iranian Revolution in 1979 and the growing interest in current developments within the Islamic World, 'Introduction to Modern Islamic Thought'.

Each of these courses attracted a wide range of students from different departments, with particular interest, not surprisingly, from History, given the importance of the Islamic World as Europe's nearest neighbour over many centuries, and Hispanic Studies, where the interaction of Jew, Christian and Muslim in medieval Iberia was a focus of particular interest for students with interests in that period (Goddard 2000b; Menocal 2002).

This arrangement left one obvious problem, however, namely that as an option it was perfectly possible for students of theology not to select either of the courses on Islam, with the result that Islamic Studies might have appeared rather peripheral to the main concerns of the department. Students, on this basis, could graduate without any experience of or expertise in Islam at all; and particularly for those who chose to enter one of the most popular destinations for the graduates of the department – the teaching profession – this became an increasing disadvantage.

Discussions began, therefore, about how best to integrate the study of Islam into the theology degree through incorporating at least some teaching about the Islamic Tradition into the core of the degree. Various possibilities were considered for this, including a historical route, through the inclusion of some teaching about the importance of the two great medieval Islamic philosophers Ibn Sina (Avicenna) and Ibn Rushd (Averroes) for the growth of medieval Christian Scholasticism, which formed such a crucial element of the background to the Reformation, in the core course 'History of Religious Thought in the West'; a more theological route, the inclusion of some material about Islamic teaching about Creation and Salvation in the final-year core course on those two themes in Biblical and Systematic Theology; or a route which focused more on providing some input about Islam within the core course which concentrated most specifically on religion in general – PPR, or The Philosophy and Phenomenology of Religion. It was this last route which was in the end adopted, and so the still relatively inexperienced Lecturer in Islamic Theology found himself teaching within a core course, alongside his head of department, Professor John Heywood Thomas, who dealt with the philosophy, and his colleague Dr Douglas Davies, who handled the phenomenology.

Now PPR was not a course title which was completely original to Nottingham, as it drew to a considerable extent on the ideas of another Welshman, Professsor H.D. Lewis of King's College London who – in the course of his teaching and writing in the field of Philosophy of Religion, for example, in his Teach Yourself volume on that topic published in 1965 – had included a considerable body of material on what would best be described as Phenomenology (Lewis 1965). Nottingham had developed the concept in its own way, however, in the capable hands of its two main lecturers, and the inclusion of some teaching about Islam was thus a further part of this evolutionary process. Which aspects of Islam were to be included, however?

Given the interests of colleagues teaching on the course, it should not be a complete surprise if, alongside discussion of some significant scholars of religion who had a particular interest in Islam, such as Wilfred Cantwell Smith (1978), the themes which found themselves included within the PPR syllabus included such things as 'Religious experience in Islam', 'Mysticism', 'Evil in Islam', and particularly 'Resurrection and the Afterlife in Islam', which outlined Qur'anic teaching about death, the afterlife and judgement, the different ways in which these teachings had been understood in the later Muslim community, and the relationship between Islamic teachings on these topics and earlier Jewish and Christian opinions. Students were intrigued, on the one hand, to learn about how a twentieth-century Indian Muslim thinker such as Muhammad Iqbal reinterpreted some of the terms and language used in the Qur'an for the modern era and, on the other hand, to see some of the remarkable similarities between the language of the Qur'an and the Book of Revelation at the end of the New Testament. Some of the students taking the course, including those who did so as part of their training for the ministry through the Bachelor of Theology degree which the department taught jointly with St John's College Nottingham and Lincoln Theological College, found themselves having, for the first time, to think quite hard about another religious tradition, and although for some this was quite challenging, for the vast majority it was a perfectly acceptable evolution within the whole concept and ethos of PPR.

Teaching about Islam also came to be included in some of the courses which the department undertook off-campus, for example, for RAF chaplains at their headquarters at Amport in Hampshire. One of these occasions provided what was, for me, a particularly memorable example of student feedback when, at the end of a series of lectures on Jesus which had included 'Jesus in the New Testament', 'Jesus in early Christian thought', 'Jesus in modern Christian thought' and 'Jesus in the Qur'an', a particularly forthright participant commented that he saw no earthly reason for the inclusion of the last of these topics, since it was of no relevance whatsoever to the work of an RAF chaplain. Fellow members of the department rallied round magnificently in the defence of their beleaguered colleague, pointing among other things to the increasing religious diversity which was likely to affect the RAF as well as the rest of British society, and the relevance of the topic to wider global affairs. The latter of these was very aptly illustrated when a few months later the First Gulf War broke out and the same RAF chaplain found himself not only ministering to RAF crews in Bahrain but also taking the lead in discussions with local authorities about the provision of facilities for the religious needs of the Christians among them. I was very pleased some time later to receive a slightly chastened note, the gist of which was 'thank-you so much for helping me not to make a complete fool of myself'.

This evolution of the PPR course to incorporate a measure of teaching about different aspects of Islam coincided with Douglas Davies' very significant contributions to the nine volumes of *Themes in Religious Studies*, edited by John Bowker and Jean Holm and published by Cassell in 1994, and aimed very much at both a general readership and teachers of religious education in particular. Douglas contributed the chapters on Christianity, and also the general introductions to six of them. These volumes were extremely innovatory in seeking to provide informative studies of the views of different religious traditions on major themes by insiders to the traditions, which was not always achievable at that stage in the case of Islam, and the reissuing three years later of Davies' chapters from the different volumes of the series in a single volume, *Themes and Issues in Christianity*, with Clare Drury (1997), was hugely helpful for teachers of religious education who at that time were not finding it easy to find good material which presented Christianity from a more phenomenological perspective.

Where Nottingham had led, in terms of appointing a lecturer to teach Islam in the context of a Department of Theology, others soon followed, and fittingly enough given that Islam is now almost certainly the religious faith of between 20 per cent and 25 per cent of the human beings on the face of planet earth, the vast majority of Departments of Theology and/or Religious Studies in the United Kingdom now include a Lecturer on Islam within their body of staff. This includes the Faculty of Theology in Oxford, where Douglas undertook his postgraduate studies, which has now had two lecturers on Islam, and which has also, like Nottingham, recently changed its title to the Faculty of Theology and Religion. Durham, along with Exeter, is one of the few which, as yet, does not have its own 'in-house' lecturer in Islamic Studies, but as we shall see later there are particular reasons for this.

Patterns change in higher education, however, and the shift during the 1990s, at the government's instigation, to semesterization and modularization resulted, among other things, in the demise of larger, year-long, team-taught courses in favour of smaller, shorter and individually taught modules, such as 'Introduction to the Study of Religion' and 'Philosophy of Religion'. As part of this process in Nottingham 'The Islamic Tradition' was also established as a self-standing introductory module, and made it into the core of the Nottingham undergraduate degree, following on from 'Introduction to the Study of Religion', and it was generally appreciated by students, particularly because of the opportunity to gain an overview of an entire tradition in a relatively short amount of time (Christopher 1972).

World events involving different aspects of Islam continued to unfold, both globally and in the United Kingdom, and the events of 11 September 2001 were, of course, a particularly dramatic example of this. That day is one of which I, probably like so many other people, have a very clear memory of where I was when I heard the news, with the departmental secretary, Mary Elmer, coming round after her lunch break and knocking on the doors of all of us who were in the department to tell us the breaking news that she had heard over lunch, and myself then rushing over to the café in Nottingham University's Trent Building to get the live news feed (since it was not possible at that stage to get this on our personal computers), arriving just in time to see the first of the twin towers collapse. All that followed on from that event, in terms of wars in Afghanistan and Iraq, and incidents of violence in different western countries, including the United Kingdom, have combined to present Islamicists with particular challenges, making the teaching of Islam in educational institutions, at any level, probably one of the most demanding subject areas in which to be involved. Difficult questions were raised with reference to the teaching of Islam, and these questions have not necessarily yet been fully answered or resolved.

In the immediate aftermath of '9/11', as it came to be called even in those parts of the world where the traditional expression of the calendar would have described it as '11/9', the Department of Theology in the University of Nottingham underwent subject review by the Quality Assurance Agency. Just a month after the events in New York and Washington DC, Islamicists could probably have been rather more gainfully employed, but there was not a lot of choice in the matter. When, in 2003, the United Kingdom decided to join the United States in an invasion of Iraq, on the basis of what proved later to be some highly tendentious 'evidence', and on the basis of wilful and quite deliberate ignoring by the government of the country's leading academic experts on Iraq, the widespread ignorance of the Middle East region within the British public was only too painfully revealed. Many scholars with an interest in the Islamic World, therefore, as well as in Islam specifically as a religion, sought to do what they could to improve the general level of understanding of the Middle East in particular, and in the context of the University of Nottingham this gave rise, in collaboration with colleagues in a number of different departments, to the establishment of a new interdisciplinary Institute for Middle Eastern Studies, with a jointly taught module 'Understanding the Middle East: Contemporary Challenges and Historical Background' as one of its main activities, with myself as convener.

In each of the years that it ran, this module attracted in the region of 120 students from across the whole university, and did much to provide a wide range of students with a better understanding of at least some of the many different dimensions of a complex region of the world, geographical, archaeological, historical, political, social, architectural, environmental, economic, cultural and religious.

When, on 7 July 2005, four bombs were set off in London, three on the underground and one on a bus, leading to 52 deaths and over 700 injuries, and it turned out that the bombs had been set off by young British Muslims, three from a Pakistani background and living in Leeds and the fourth a convert to Islam from a Jamaican background, living in Aylesbury, further questions were bound to be raised in connection with the teaching of Islam in the United Kingdom. Discussions quickly began to take place, involving different departments of government, including the Home Office and the Department for Education, Britain's Muslim communities, universities, and many others. These discussions did not always shed much light with respect to Islam.

In the context of universities in particular, questions were raised about the content and methods of teaching about Islam, as well as about how the authorities dealt with the issue of Muslim students who might be succumbing to some kind of process of 'radicalization' on university campuses, perhaps through the activities of student Islamic societies. For teachers of Islam in particular accusations were made that somehow a kind of sanitized version of Islam was being presented, covering up the aspects of Islamic teaching which had caused these four young men to carry out their acts of violence, and thus somehow dissimulating and misrepresenting Islam. These were serious charges, which needed to be answered.

Discussions therefore quickly began among academic teachers of Islam concerning these and other questions, and in the course of less than a year three significant reports summarizing some of these discussions appeared. The first heralded from the Al-Maktoum Institute in Dundee, and appeared under the names of Professors Abd al-Fattah El-Awaisi and Malory Nye, though much of the research on which the report's conclusions were based was done by Dr Steven Sutcliffe, now of the University of Edinburgh. The report's title 'Time for Change: the Future of the Study of Islam and Muslims in Universities and Colleges in Multicultural Britain' summarized its main themes well, arguing as it did that teaching in the United Kingdom about Islam needed to be recalibrated, moving away at least to some extent from the traditional study of the classical religious texts of Islam towards the study of Muslims as people (El-Awaisi and Nye 2006). In this respect, of course, the report reflected a wider debate about the teaching of religion in general and indeed Christianity in particular: should these things too be taught on the basis of their texts, or rather on the basis of the practices of their living adherents (Goddard 2000a)?

The Al-Maktoum report appeared in October 2006. Three months later, also from Scotland, a second report appeared, this time from a meeting at the University of Edinburgh on 4 December, entitled 'Islam on Campus: Teaching Islamic Studies at Higher Education Institutions in the UK' (Sulaiman and Shihadeh 2007). This report was the summary of a day of discussions among established academics in the field of Islamic Studies, from the universities of London (SOAS), Manchester, Durham, Leeds, Exeter, St Andrews, Wales (Lampeter), Birmingham, Oxford and Lancaster, as well as Edinburgh, the Markfield Institute of Higher Education, the Institute of Ismaili Studies and the Institute of Islamic Political Thought, the last two based in London, and argued that while the teaching of Islam in British universities should not be complacent, it was certainly not responsible for instances of extremism among students. It was also from this meeting that the idea first came of seeking to establish a British Association for Islamic Studies, in order to facilitate further discussion of these issues and serve as a representative body for all those involved in teaching the subject.

A further four months later, in April 2007, a more official report then appeared, prepared by Dr Ataullah Siddiqui of the Markfield Institute of Higher Education for the Minister of State for Lifelong Learning, Further and Higher Education, Bill Rammell MP, who, as the minister responsible for universities, had taken the lead in asking questions about the role of these institutions in connection with the growth of Islamic extremism (Siddiqui 2007). This report, entitled 'Islam at universities in England: meeting the needs and investing in the future', argued forcefully that there was certainly an urgent need to promote a better understanding of different aspects of Islam in Britain, a task in which universities could play a vital part, but that there was also a need for additional resources to make this possible, and there also needed to be serious thinking about the practical and spiritual needs of Muslim students, both home and international, on campuses and elsewhere.

Two months later, and in his last week as prime minister before leaving Downing Street, Tony Blair then acted on some of the recommendations of the Siddiqui report by declaring that Islamic Studies was to be a strategic subject for UK higher education and providing £1 million in its support. The Higher Education Funding Council for England was given the lead responsibility for working out what this would mean in practice, and following a number of workshops and conferences, the main result of the decision was the establishment of the Islamic Studies Network,[1] to provide a forum for discussion of the issues connected with Islamic Studies and support for various projects designed to reflect on teaching about different aspects of Islam.

Much good work was done by the Network, under its co-ordinator Dr Lisa Bernasek, with the establishment of subject groups for the teaching of Islam in Philosophical and Religious Studies; Languages, Linguistics and Area Studies; Sociology, Anthropology and Politics; Law; Business, Management, Accountancy and Finance; and History. A very useful website was established, a very informative journal, *Perspectives*, was published, in order to facilitate critical reflection on issues connected with the teaching of Islam in particular; and, perhaps most importantly, the resources provided for the establishment of the Network made possible a major stride towards the establishment of a real Islamic Studies community within the United Kingdom's higher education system, bringing together those based in the established centres of Middle Eastern and Islamic Studies in the universities of Oxford, Cambridge, London, Durham, Manchester, Exeter, Birmingham and Edinburgh and those who were delightfully called the 'lone rangers', those who found themselves leading potentially rather isolated lives as the sole Islamicists in particular institutions, such as myself in the Department of Theology in the University of Nottingham.

Similar discussions to those which were taking place in the United Kingdom were also taking place in other European countries, and not surprisingly the outcomes of these deliberations very much reflected, firstly, the different traditions of higher education in individual countries, particularly with reference to teaching about Theology and Religion, and, secondly, the different composition of the Muslim communities present in different countries. Thus, in Germany, with its tradition of confessional faculties of Protestant and Roman Catholic Theology, issues connected with Islam were addressed by the establishment of parallel chairs of Islamic Theology, often in some kind of association with local Turkish communities (German

Council of Sciences and Humanities 2010). In the Netherlands, with its greater tradition of diversity in institutions of higher education, consideration was given to the establishment of an Islamic university in Rotterdam. Other European countries pursued the issues within the parameters of their particular traditions and institutions, as also happened in the United States, where one consequence of 9/11 was a dramatic upsurge in interest in Islam and a resulting dramatic increase in the provision of teaching about the tradition within the American university system (Kurzman and Ernst 2012).

Common to all these discussions was some fairly fundamental reflection about the nature and purpose of Islamic Studies. Should the core of the subject continue to be the Arabic language and the classical religious texts of the tradition, with its inevitable concentration on the geographical region of the Middle East, or should there be some evolution towards a more anthropological and contemporary emphasis, of the kind illustrated so effectively by some of the work of a nineteenth-century figure such as William Robertson Smith, seeking to illuminate some of the Biblical texts of the Old Testament through the study of contemporary nomadic Arab societies in what is now Saudi Arabia? Robertson Smith is of course a figure on whom Douglas has himself written, in a 1995 article comparing Smith's views on Evolution with those of his hero Frank Byron Jevons (Davies 1995).

This newer approach might also shift the focus of Islamic Studies away from the Middle East towards the wider Islamic World, taking account, for example, of the fact that there are today as many Muslims in one country, Indonesia, as there are in the whole of the Arab World, and also of the fact that, from the point-of-view of the United Kingdom in particular, the majority of its Muslim citizens have an ancestral connection not with the Middle East but with South Asia, today's nations of Pakistan, India and Bangladesh, which together make up the legacy of what was British India.

Is there a place, therefore, for a new paradigm of Islamic Studies in higher education in the United Kingdom, and if so where would it best fit? Is it really best for it to continue to be associated, as it is for example in Edinburgh, on the basis of its traditionally close association with the study of the Arabic language, in departments or schools of Languages? Only around one in five of the world's Muslims is an Arabic speaker, even if a larger proportion makes use of Arabic for religious purposes such as the recitation of the Qur'an. Is it really essential for Islamic Studies to continue to be associated so closely with Area Studies, particularly the study of the Middle East, since as current events so tragically demonstrate not everything that happens in the Middle East is necessarily connected to Islam, and equally Islam is not exclusively bound to the Middle East (Bennett 2013; Donnan 2002; Ernst and Martin 2010; Hughes 2007; Rippin 2007, 2008; Shepard 2014). As has been recently argued very persuasively by Sami Zubaida, there is more to the Middle East than Islam, and more to Islam than the Middle East (Zubaida 2011).

The Arabic language and the Middle East are both important, but given that Islam is fundamentally not a language, nor a geographical area, but rather a religious tradition, my suggestion is that, in higher education, Islamic Studies fits best within the context of Religious Studies. Religious Studies has the sensitivity to the different dimensions of religion, so ably outlined in his various classic works by Ninian Smart (Smart 1969, 1996). Religious Studies is sensitive to the different approaches to the study of religion which may be adopted by insiders and outsiders. Religious Studies is crucially aware of the importance and significance of studying texts, communities and people in order to gain a proper understanding of a religious tradition. And Religious Studies is sensitive to the different ways in which religious traditions function, on a global level, in majority and minority contexts. Religious Studies, I suggest, is therefore the place where Islamic Studies fits best, and the new British Association for Islamic Studies[2] is an attempt to represent this view of Islam as essentially and primarily a religious tradition through the establishment of a learned society which is specifically oriented towards promoting it (Capps 1995; Hinnells 2005; King 1990; Braun and McCutcheon 2000).

A difficult question which remains, however, and which is likely to continue to be discussed as long as there are human beings on the face of the planet, is the relationship between Theology and Religious Studies because, on an institutional level, the two sub-disciplines are often linked and in the minds of some students of Theology it has an integral connection with *Christian* theology. This view leaves no place for Islamic Studies. Other views of theology, however, such as that articulated by David Burrell, allow space for other traditions of theology, Jewish and Islamic in particular, and on this basis there is clearly room for the serious study of the Islamic tradition, rather than its a priori dismissal, as commended by some twentieth-century Christian theologians (Bond, Kunin and Murphy 2003; Brown 1989; Burrell 2011; Ford 1999; Lindbeck 1984).

How good it would be, therefore, if at some stage in the future space could be made available in Douglas' alma mater and current academic home, the Department of Theology in the University of Durham, having, like the University of Oxford, recently renamed itself the Department of Theology and Religion, for the teaching of Islamic Studies. The reason for this not having happened yet, as in the University of Exeter, is the existence within the university of one of the United Kingdom's long-established centres of Islamic and Middle Eastern Studies, even if now divided between the School of Modern Languages and Cultures and the School of Government and International Affairs. There is surely space, however, for an approach whose primary emphasis is on Islam as a religious tradition, as distinct from a language or a political system. Where Nottingham led, may Durham follow.

Notes

1 See http://www.islamicstudiesnetwork.ac.uk/islamicstudiesnetwork/home
2 See www.brais.ac.uk

References

Bennett, C. (ed.) (2013) *The Bloomsbury Companion to Islamic Studies*. London: Bloomsbury.

Bond, H. K., Kunin, S. D. and Murphy, F. A. (eds) (2003) *A Companion to Religious Studies and Theology*. Edinburgh: Edinburgh University Press.

Bowker, J. and Holm, J. (eds) (1994) *Themes in Religious Studies* (9 vols.). London: Cassell.

Braun, W. and McCutcheon, R. T. (eds) (2000) *Guide to the Study of Religion*. London: Continuum.

Brown, D. (1989) *Invitation to Theology*. Oxford: Blackwell.

Burrell, D. (2011) *Towards a Jewish-Christian-Muslim Theology*. Chichester: Wiley-Blackwell.

Capps, W. H. (1995) *Religious Studies: The Making of a Discipline*. Minneapolis: Fortress Press.

Christopher, J. B. (1972) *The Islamic Tradition*. New York: Harper and Row.

Cracknell, K. (1996) *Towards a New Relationship: Christians and People of Other Faith*. London: Epworth Press.

Davies, D. J. (1995) 'William Robertson Smith and Frank Byron Jevons: faith and evolution', in Johnstone, W. (ed.) *William Robertson Smith: Essays in Reassessment*. Sheffield: Sheffield Academic Press, pp. 311–319.

Davies, D. J. and Drury, C. (1997) *Themes in Christianity*. London: Cassell.

Donnan, H. (ed.) (2002) *Interpreting Islam*. London: Sage.

El-Awaisi, A. and Nye, M. (2006) *Time for Change: Report on the Future of the Study of Islam and Muslims in Universities and Colleges in Multicultural Britain*. Dundee: Al-Maktoum Institute Academic Press.

Ernst, C. W. and Martin, R. C. (eds) (2010) *Rethinking Islamic Studies: From Orientalism to Cosmopolitanism*. Columbia, SC: University of South Carolina Press.

Ford, D. (1999) *Theology: A Very Short Introduction*. Oxford: Oxford University Press.

German Council of Sciences and Humanities (2010) *Recommendations on the Advancement of Theologies and Sciences concerned with Religions at German Universities*. Berlin: German Council of Sciences and Humanities.

Goddard, H. (2000a) 'Christian-Muslim relations: a look backwards and a look forwards', *Islam and Christian-Muslim Relations* 11(2): 195–212.

Goddard, H. (2000b) *A History of Christian-Muslim Relations*. Edinburgh: Edinburgh University Press.

Hinnells, J. R. (ed.) (2005) *The Routledge Companion to the Study of Religion*. London: Routledge.

Hughes, A. W. (2007) *Situating Islam: the Past and Future of an Academic Discipline*. London: Equinox.

King, U. (ed.) (1990) *Turning Points in Religious Studies: Essays in Honour of Geoffrey Parrinder*. Edinburgh: T&T Clark.

Kurzman, C. and Ernst, C. W. (2012) 'Islamic studies in U.S. universities', *Review of Middle East Studies*: 46(1): 24–46.

Lewis, H. D. (1965) *Philosophy of Religion*. London: Teach Yourself Books.

Lindbeck, G. A. (1984) *The Nature of Doctrine: Religion and Theology in a Postliberal Age*. Philadelphia: Westminster Press.

Ling, T. O. (1968) *A History of Religion, East and West*. London: Macmillan.

Menocal, M. R. (2002) *The Ornament of the World: How Muslims, Jews and Christians Created a Culture of Tolerance in Medieval Spain*. Boston: Little Brown.

Rippin, A. (ed.) (2007) *Defining Islam: a Reader*. London: Equinox.

Rippin, A. (ed.) (2008) *The Islamic World*. London: Routledge.

Shepard, W. E. (2014) *Introducing Islam*. 2nd edition. London: Routledge.

Siddiqui, A. (2007) *Islam at Universities in England: Meeting the Needs and Investing in the Future (Report Submitted to Bill Rammell MP, Minister of State for Lifelong Learning, Further and Higher Education, 10 April 2007)*. Available at: http://dera.ioe.ac.uk/6500/1/Updated%20Dr%20Siddiqui%20Report.pdf.

Smart, N. (1969) *The Religious Experience of Mankind*. London: Collins.

Smart, N. (1996) *Dimensions of the Sacred: An Anatomy of the World's Beliefs*. London: Harper Collins.

Smith, W. C. (1978) *The Meaning and End of Religion*. London: S.P.C.K.

Sulaiman, Y. and Shihadeh, A. (2007) *Islam on Campus: Teaching Islamic Studies at Higher Education Institutions in the UK* (report of a conference held at the University of Edinburgh, 4 December 2006). Available at: https://www.esrc.ac.uk/.../4f0334e6-483e-437c-8d1c-ef2d5a0c5e36.

Zubaida, S. (2011) *Beyond Islam: A New Understanding of the Middle East*. London: I.B. Tauris.

12 From Jevons to Collini (via Douglas Davies)

Reflections on higher education and religious identity[1]

Mathew Guest

During my time as an undergraduate student in theology at the University of Nottingham during the mid-1990s, Douglas Davies taught the anthropology of religion. In one of his especially interdisciplinary lectures, he addressed the work of Frank Byron Jevons (1858–1936), a Victorian polymath whose life and work had fascinated Davies so much that he wrote his intellectual biography after being granted access to Jevons' unpublished papers, housed at their shared *alma mata*, the University of Durham. Jevons was a classicist and philosopher, a pioneer in the embryonic study of religion, a lay Anglican and a speaker and writer on a variety of other subjects, including education. His strongly held convictions about the proper character of a good education are inspiring in their principled idealism and serve as a valuable point of reference in considering reforms to education in schools and universities in the present day. In considering Jevons' time and work, we are alerted to the cultural changes that have transformed common assumptions about the purpose and delivery of educational processes over the last century; while Durham is a place steeped in tradition, its university is a radically different kind of institution from the one overseen by Jevons as its one-time vice chancellor at the beginning of the twentieth century. But reflection on Jevons' perspective on the role of education as a social good also highlights the moral imperatives that have informed critical voices in his time and our own. His fiercely held and widely voiced views on education are, to a degree, echoed among critics of educational reform within twenty-first-century Britain. In this sense, Jevons epitomizes an enduring disposition, generated among university academics as a critical perspective on the very processes their institutions have come to embody.

This chapter considers current debates about the changing nature of university education within the UK context. It begins with Jevons, then brings his work into conversation with one of the most influential and insightful critics of recent higher education reform, Stefan Collini. My argument is that in highlighting their shared, underlying moral imperatives, we are presented with a useful lens through which to consider common assumptions about the capacity of universities to transform the identities of their students. Much debate about the state of higher education rests on assumptions about this matter, and yet empirical evidence is rarely used to connect the impassioned rhetoric with the experiences of students themselves. The second part of my argument calls for a greater dialogue between the critical voices exemplified by Jevons and Collini and a sociology of higher education that takes seriously empirical realities on the ground, including institutional structures and social interaction among staff and students. By way of illustration, the final part of the chapter takes students of faith – in this case Christian students in particular – as a case study, drawing on recent research into how the experience of universities shapes their moral and religious perspectives. Consideration of this segment of the student population highlights the complex ways in which universities have an impact upon the lives of their students and offers insights into how religious identities are constituted within higher education. However, I begin with Jevons, because his convictions about education – even though published a century ago – actually serve as a useful way into these contemporary debates. In this respect, I also pay tribute to Douglas Davies, who has long sustained a passion for bringing the Victorian age and our present one into fruitful conversation.

Visions of education in two ages

Frank Byron Jevons had been a school master before, in 1882, being appointed as a tutor in classics at the University of Durham, where he stayed for the rest of his academic career. His perspective on education, I have learnt from many lively conversations over the years, inspired and continues to inspire Douglas Davies and informs his own university teaching. Jevons believed in the liberating power of education, holding it to be a major force for social progress and equality for all, including marginalized segments of society such as women and the working classes. Jevons also taught courses for the Workers' Educational Association (WEA), aimed at sharing the knowledge nurtured within university contexts with members of the local community. Indeed, Jevons was inclined to see the WEA initiatives as superior to school and university education because they were founded on the principle that no examinations would be held. This, for Jevons, allowed the WEA to embody the true value of education, which was about human flourishing, rather than passing exams, or indeed, the acquisition of qualifications as an instrumental means to economic betterment. As Davies puts it, describing Jevons' viewpoint, 'Prizes and degrees cause a man to work for his own ends while the unselfish desire for education worked out in a group is nobler and conduces to the good of many' (1991: 119). This gets to the heart of Jevons' attitude, which rests on the importance of co-operation, both as a central characteristic of good education and a desirable value to encourage within society as a whole. Indeed, Jevons associates competition – the opposite of co-operation – not just with the fostering of self-centred acquisitiveness but also with humankind's propensity for conflict and war. Jevons' perspective on education is part of a much broader worldview, and in this sense his confidence mirrors the Victorian propensity for grand narrative so typical of the scholarship of his time. Jevons was an idealist, as Davies acknowledges, and his idealism is embedded within a coherent vision of the 'good society', arguably as compelling as it is ambitious.

While very much a product of his era, in other respects Jevons embodies an enduring set of concerns for which we can find ready analogies in the twenty-first century. Davies cites one of Jevons' impassioned speeches on the proper character of education:

> If each man is an end in himself – an end as valuable and as precious as any other man – then an education which fits him merely to be a means is no complete education, no true education. Serve one another we must; and our education must enable us to do service. But it is no part of the function of education to make us useful instruments whereby the millionaire may increase his millions. We too have a right to the education which shall enable us to taste the higher joys of life.
>
> (Quoted in Davies 1991: 131)

Jevons believed knowledge within the right kind of education could free the mind from external authority and foster wisdom. What is anathema to him is the reduction of education to a process of conferring skills for the sole purpose of future employment. Faced with the poor working classes of County Durham around the turn of the twentieth century, he does not view education as something to be debased to their circumstances (reduced to an elementary provision) nor accommodated to their industrial occupations (translated into practical skills). Rather, he wants to take higher learning beyond the preserve of the university and into their lives as a universally edifying good. In a striking parallel, his dismay at an instrumentalization of education is poignantly echoed in critiques of higher education reforms that have emerged in recent years. Increasing student numbers and cuts in public funding have emerged in the United Kingdom alongside policy reforms which increasingly conceive the value of universities in economic terms (Browne 2010). Serving first and foremost the need to enable students to contribute to the economy, universities have also adopted the organizational characteristics of private businesses. They now function, according to some critics, as purveyors of an educational product, their students the consumers (Sabri 2011), echoing the logics of a neo-liberal economics that celebrates diversification via unfettered competition and the fetishization of individual choice. With increasing pressures on today's universities to justify their degree programmes on the basis of 'transferable skills' and 'employability', one can see why academic commentators might find common voice with Jevons in their efforts to resist the commercialization of university life.

One of the most scathing critics of such innovations is the Cambridge Professor of Intellectual History and English Literature Stefan Collini, whose book *What Are Universities For?* (2012) is a collection of essays on this subject. Collini's essays are subtle and perceptive, witty and humorous, and his concerns about how universities have become less and less unlike other – especially commercial – organizations within British society over the course of the last couple of decades, are echoed among academics across the sector. In fact, Collini's work is but one example of the abundance of litera-ture produced over the past few years by academics and other commentators who find in the contemporary university an all-absorbing bureaucracy and slavish kowtowing to the business world as efficiency and cost-effectiveness encroach ever more on the hallowed freedoms of scholarship (e.g. Brown 2013; Giroux 2014; McGettigan 2013; Murphy 2015). As Collini puts it with characteristically acerbic wit,

> One of the supposed benefits of treating universities as though they were businesses is that their efficiency can then be measured and improved. It's well known that universities used to be full of idle, port-swilling dons and equally idle, unemployable students, but now they are lean and mean and geared to meeting national needs through increased pro-ductivity. One thing that needs saying in the face of this self-deluded and self-important twaddle is that in several important ways universi-ties are now *less* efficient than they were twenty years ago before the commercial analogy started to be applied in earnest. After all, two of the most important sources of efficiency in intellectual activity are vol-untary cooperation and individual autonomy. But these are precisely the kinds of things for which a bureaucratic system leaves little room.
>
> (2012: 134)

In some important ways, Collini's concerns echo those of Jevons voiced a century earlier. Although he does not cite him nor show any signs of being aware of his work, he does engage with similar concerns raised by John Henry Newman in the mid-nineteenth century, highlighting the his-torical lineage of this modern debate (Collini 2012: 39–60). Indeed, Jevons and Collini share common clusters of ideals, each constituting a normative vision that is in some important respects reflective of the other. Here, cul-tural and intellectual context is important. Jevons' thinking is shaped by a late Victorian socialism coloured by his experience as an educator in the industrial north of England. Collini embodies the disillusioned perspective of a Cambridge don who views his age as one in which higher education has morphed from public good into consumer product, via depleted fund-ing, increased bureaucracy and increasingly centralized systems of oversight and accountability. The thinking of both arises out of elite British universi-ties and assumes an understanding of education shaped by the disciplines of the humanities, foregrounding the expansion of critical thinking and the irreducible value of knowledge as a human good. This understanding is pitched over and against encroaching forces governed by a logic that is utilitarian, informed by the concerns of industry and private business and the reduction of the individual to the status of self-interested agent. While operating within very different circumstances, both Jevons and Collini emerge within a scholarly tradition of reactionary critique contingent upon cultural trends characteristic of the late modern age. The archetypal narrative here is Max Weber's sociological account of a disenchanted modernity confined by the 'iron cage' of rationalizing systems (Gerth and Mills 2009: 196–264). Many have developed Weber's portrayal, including those who see in the contemporary world new systems of rationalized control emanating into a variety of social spheres as well as migrating from the west to the developing world (Ritzer 1996). Three lines of thought seem most relevant to the current discussion, commonly integrated into sociological debates about the transition from traditional to modern societies. These might be described as, firstly, the functional differentiation of social spheres – including the decoupling of traditional institutions concerned with education, health, religion and politics. A consequent tendency is the emergence of specialist providers whose purpose is defined in increasingly narrow terms and whose processes are segmented into discrete sub-divisions (Berger, Berger and Kellner 1974). Within the university context, a prime example would be modularization, which contains teaching and learning within relatively self-contained, discretely assessed courses. A second aspect of Weber's legacy that is particularly relevant here is the related proliferation of utilitarian habits of thought characterized by an instrumental rationality. Robert Bellah et al. (1985) theorized this as one dimension of western individualism in the late modern age, 'utilitarian individualism' being the tendency to forge identities in accordance with self-interest (emerging alongside 'expressive individualism', which foregrounds individual experience). While accounting for patterns in individual decision making, a more resonant definition for our purposes would also pay attention to how forms of instrumental rationality are embedded within institutional cultures, not least via bureaucratic systems of organization. A third aspect that extends Weber's model into a neo-liberal context is the growing tendency for the 'ends' of processes to be justified in economic terms. In university contexts, this includes the configuration of research so as to maximize the generation of external funding, but also the measurement of the success of university processes of teaching and learning according to cost–benefit analysis. On a deeper level is the complicit tendency to treat knowledge itself as a commodity, to be guarded, manipulated and negotiated in a way that maximizes 'return' (Kenway et al. 2006: 55). While these trends are manifest differently within the contexts in which Jevons and Collini are each working, they arguably proceed along the same trajectory. In other words, Collini is responding to the long-term amplification of the tendencies Jevons sees in embryonic form within his own industrial age.

Utilitarian habits of thought also inform assumptions within universities about accountability (Strathern 2000). For example, Collini calls attention to how, while freedom of intellectual enquiry is acknowledged by government policy makers to be essential to good scholarship, there is a concurrent tendency to intervene in university affairs. The overtures to academic freedom sound especially hollow when policy appears preoccupied with the question of how *useful* university activity really is. The language of utility is telling, and Collini is under no illusions about what is primarily meant by this: universities are increasingly measured by the extent to which their work serves the needs of the economy. This is what lies behind the recent emphasis on integrating skills that enhance 'employability' into undergraduate and postgraduate programmes, and informs the increasing prioritization of STEM subjects (science, technology, engineering and mathematics) at the expense of other areas of scholarship. Collini sees a tension here that reflects muddled thinking among policy makers, who while supporting a free market model that permits no measure of a university subject's worth beyond student demand, at the same time wish to preserve a privileged status for STEM subjects, whose economic value is presumably taken for granted. But Collini advances a more fundamental critique, calling into question the very criterion of economic value when used to justify university activity, a criterion he argues is presented in government policy documents – such as the recent Browne report on higher education funding (Browne 2010) – as if it were self-evident. Such is the pervasiveness of neo-liberal reasoning that arguments based on 'economic output' are not seen as in need of further justification. Collini takes a different view, pointing out that this assumption 'begs the question of what needs the economy serves' (2012: 110). If it enables us to do the things we think are important, as Collini puts it, we should decide what's important and adapt our economic strategies to the task of bringing this about. As it stands, we are in danger of simply spending money for the sake of generating more money.

But it is not simply the reduction of academic work to economic ends that Collini finds most objectionable; it is the instrumentalist reasoning that misrepresents and perverts the nature of university life. We have become uncomfortable, he argues, with the language of 'intrinsic goods', preferring instead to see the worth of an activity in measurable quantities. And yet the most important goals of a university are not quantifiable; they are not amenable to measurement, only to judgment by those competent to judge. Here he touches on a perhaps deep cultural tendency in English life that associates judgment with prejudice or snobbery. This tendency, at least in today's context, calls into suspicion human capacities that cannot be called to account with reference to a set of measurable outcomes. Moreover, an emphasis on measurable outcomes is morally validated by its advocates with reference to the values of transparency and fairness, making it difficult to contest without appearing self-interested or having something to hide. But as suggested by Jevons, such instrumentalist thinking is often distinguished by its tendency to disempower, rather than the opposite, for it reduces scholarly endeavour to a conveyer belt of skills and capital, and also denies the marginalized in society the vision of an irreducible higher learning so often enjoyed and coveted among the elite.

Collini also echoes Jevons in his wariness towards competition within educational contexts. Granted, Collini is talking about academic staff and Jevons is concerned with students, but they share a vision for intellectual enquiry that has co-operation at its heart. As Collini puts it, 'Cooperation and a sense of shared commitment to the enterprise is infinitely more fruitful' (2012: 135) than setting individuals against one another in a battle to the top (or, a battle to flee the bottom, as may well be the case). Collini expands on this by outlining his view of university work as essentially a creative task, about ideas and intellectual endeavour that is most effectively stimulated by co-operation and mutual, supportive engagement. This is a vision that would resonate with Jevons, the idealist champion of education as a source of enrichment and human flourishing, both at the level of the individual, and in its capacity to edify the group.

The collective and the individual in university education

While there is now abundant literature on the structural changes to the higher education sector that have come about in recent years, there is precious little on how these changes have affected the lives of university students. Does the commercialization of the sector encourage a more hard-headed ambition among undergraduates? Do they approach their university lives less as seekers after new knowledge, more as consumers keen to extract maximum advantage from their – now much more expensive – degree programmes? Or is there a residual idealism among arts and humanities students, perhaps, an ambition for a broadening of the mind that would warm the hearts of Jevons and Collini alike? Or are such students generally confined to the elite universities, comprised of upper middle class undergraduates who can afford to muse on the writings of Dickens or Coleridge, or debate the moral bankruptcy of the 'new left', precisely because they do not have to worry about their career chances after they graduate? According to this analysis, the visions of education promoted by Jevons and Collini are not only idealistic, they are also destined to be the preserve of the privileged few, an outcome that would be painfully ironic, given Jevons' ethical and political convictions.

Both Collini and Jevons present a vision of education that resists the elevation of the atomized individual and instead foregrounds the collective energies of the co-operating group. However, while both consistently affirm the *process* of education to be a collaborative one, neither offer a developed description of how the *outcomes* of education might be public, rather than private. Jevons' socialism leads him often to colour his impassioned speeches and writing with a vision for a better society, but this vision is often vague and as he is not aiming to develop a systematic sociology of education, his work lacks a concerted examination of the relationship between education and the social order. In this his work stands in contrast to his direct contemporary, sociologist Emile Durkheim, whose lectures on education examined the relationship between the French school system and the instantiation of broader social values (Durkheim 1956). Collini offers much more comment on how higher education interrelates with wider society, but while he conceives government influence over universities as a corporate, bureaucratized imposition, his understanding of how universities influence society very much focuses on the individual. In discussing students, his archetypes of choice are the employable graduate and the cultured scholar, each representing the anodyne and the enlightened in contemporary higher education respectively. Moreover, in reflecting on how universities might rescue something of value from the neo-liberal mire in which they find themselves, Collini has little to say about possible collectivist responses to society or novel methods of engagement that promote social change beyond the existentially inspired individual. The 'market model' reconfigures the student as consumer and higher education as a process of economic exchange (Sabri 2011), arguably frustrating the capacity of universities to build community, so it is unfortunate that Collini does not have more to say about possible strategies for retrieving a collective voice.

It is tempting to attribute this relative insularity to his Cambridge context, although I suspect it has more to do with how the disciplines of the humanities deal with issues of human identity. Again, a comparison with Jevons is instructive. The problem of the coherence of the self is one in which Jevons had a strong interest, and his book *Personality* (1913) grapples with the philosophical problems surrounding our understanding of the self, identity and personality. While acknowledging that any striving towards unity and coherence is imperfect in practice, Jevons' view of the self mirrors his view of society in so far as they point towards integration and co-operation rather than disintegration and fragmentation (Jevons 1913: 166). A framing influence here is Jevons' Christian faith, and his argument that society is properly integrative and participatory, a shared experience in which all must play their part, owes as much to his conviction that this emerges in Christian love for one's neighbour as it does to his communitarian political values. Jevons' thinking is also shaped by his understanding of evolution, which he takes to be the model along which societies develop, but not necessarily for the better; in other words, we cannot take it for granted that unfettered human evolution will lead to uniformly positive outcomes – as he says, 'evolution and progress are not identical' (Jevons 1896: 88). As a consequence, we need to be vigilant, and here his passionate convictions about education are put into context; sound and ethical educational processes are essential if we are to ensure that human evolution does not leave the poor impoverished and the lost without hope. This interventionist vision reflects Jevons' belief that education is about bringing about radical change – in individuals and in society – and that, for him, this ambition is inspired and validated by Christian teaching.

Collini's work on universities emerges from a different kind of stable. As a literature scholar, he is fully aware of the subtleties of language and the politics of representation, and makes self-conscious use of his skills in scrutinizing aspects of university life through a critical lens. His sensitivity to emerging complexities means he is also cautious in offering easy solutions to the problems he sees. In an amusing and perceptive essay on the 'useful' and the 'useless' in higher education, he observes how those arguing for a non-instrumentalist model are given to overstatement, seeming 'inexorably driven to ambitious phrases about the most general and most desirable human qualities, about a vision of a civilized community, about the ends of life' (Collini 2012: 52). His starting point in this essay is John Henry Newman's *Idea of a University* (Newman 1966), which is subjected to a sardonic analysis that leaves little doubt as to Collini's scepticism about both Newman's inflated and ponderous prose, and his argument for theology as the governing disciplinary jurisdiction within which all other subjects realize their significance. And yet Collini is not entirely dismissive of Newman's ambitious programme, and it is in this essay that his own perspective on how students might be transformed by university is most clearly expressed.

Collini is careful not to endorse a naïve vision – still often rehearsed by academics in the humanities – based around universities generating knowledge 'for its own sake' and hence representing a kind of irreducible value entirely untainted by objectives that lie outside of the 'pure' cultivation of the mind. He acknowledges the legitimate place of vocational training and is mindful of how even the most traditionally 'scholarly' disciplines are shaped by self-justifications that appeal to their 'usefulness'; he is not willing to jettison the language of utility altogether. And yet his attempts to characterize what is distinctive about the purpose of a university permit external ends only insofar as they refer to the expansion of an individual student's horizons. Part of this involves fostering a critical awareness of the contingency of different forms of knowledge, a hermeneutic of suspicion that generates skills in discernment and critical evaluation. A similar perspective is offered by former Archbishop of Canterbury Rowan Williams, who sees a major goal of universities as helping people to become 'intelligent citizens', enabled to exercise critical thinking and so more responsibly navigate 'the confused mass of propaganda and fashion that swirls around in the overpopulated information culture of our age' (Williams 2014: 38). Mike Higton, in his book *A Theology of Higher Education*, goes further in associating the cultivation of reason in universities with the development of virtue, which in turn contributes to the public good (Higton 2012). Adopting this understanding, it is easy to see how such an education could be a source of enrichment and empowerment for all people, whether faced with the common challenges of weighing up conflicting newspaper coverage, achieving a fair resolution to a neighbourly dispute, or deciding how to vote in an election. According to Collini, that which is learned within universities is indeed 'useful preparation for life' (Collini 2012: 56), but is distinctive insofar as the 'open ended quest for understanding has primacy over any application or intermediate outcome' (2012: 55). This language of 'open-endedness' coheres with assumptions about student learning that emphasize the broadening of the mind and the cultivation of cross-disciplinary awareness, and perhaps these are the kinds of outcomes that Collini imagines as taking place within universities when properly configured. In this, as in many other ways, Collini is crafting a counter-narrative to the functional differentiation of higher education alluded to earlier. While working within a sector structured around discrete and rationalized processes – from the modularization of degree programmes to their justification via specialist committees and audit trails – his instinct is to challenge boundaries rather than exist comfortably within them. Moreover, it is this challenge of boundaries – disciplinary, epistemological, even ontological – that he places at the heart of his vision for a university education. Students will ideally leave university with a learnt capacity to exercise such transgressive practice, to their advantage and to the credit of their universities. And while Collini does not use the language of empowerment, his argument for fostering in students a sense of the 'contingency and vulnerability of knowledge that is, in other settings, treated as so fixed and stable . . .' (2012: 57) hints at a vision for the emancipatory potential of higher education entirely in keeping with Jevons' own perspective. Where they differ is in their underlying teleological vision of higher education as a social good. For Jevons, this is essentially integrative, pointing to a model of society that has co-operation and mutual service at its heart; for Collini, by contrast, it is primarily disruptive, oriented to an unsettling of prevailing realities in the interests of human progress.

Given his tendency to conceive of the potential influence of universities primarily in terms of individuals, Collini may be accused of underestimating the power of universities to change society. Perhaps this is understandable given his jaded view of the current HE sector, and his essays often carry a tone of exasperation at a sector already deeply infected by a neo-liberal agenda. Put another way, it is difficult to read Collini without feeling the damage has already been done. But he does retain, as demonstrated above, a strong – if often implicit – emphasis on the individual student as a site of significant transformation. Collini's graduate is – if all goes to plan – at once enlightened, empowered and rendered autonomous by an education that has unsettled prior assumptions but replaced them with a keen intellectual awareness. Both Jevons and Collini share an understanding of education that foregrounds the interior, empowering experience of a profoundly personal learning, and while Jevons alone integrates Christian social teaching into his perspective, both assume a process that provokes the changing of minds, and, in consequence, the changing of identities. However, the university having been stripped of its capacity to change society, it is worth asking: does Collini *overestimate* the capacity of the university to transform the lives of individuals? In evoking an arguably nostalgic vision of the enlightened graduate, newly transformed following the rite of passage that is the university experience, does he risk resting his hopes on a powerful myth that is difficult to sustain against the realities of student life? A question impossible to answer in the abstract, at this point it is necessary to consider the available empirical research that has recently been undertaken into the lives of students.

Faith, identity and the student experience

Neither Jevons nor Collini are social scientists, and their reflections on the transformative potential of education operate on the level of ideas and broad reflections on the world around them, rather than on any concerted analysis of empirical data. Located firmly within the humanities, their preference is to deal in abstractions and also to privilege the cognitive and cerebral over the cultural or affective. Consequently, their treatments of education are compelling on account of their rhetorical elegance and conceptual nuance (not to mention their moral conviction), but they also lack an attentiveness to the perspectives and experiences of students. This is not meant as criticism – this is not what either of them set out to do – but it does raise the question of how empirical research might enrich our understanding of universities by bringing into conversation their astute commentary and the actual experiences of being at university among students who are on the receiving end of the processes Collini so persuasively critiques.

My focus in the discussion below is on students of faith, particularly Christian students, whose experiences of university present an empirical case study that, I would argue, benefits from being framed by the work of both Jevons and Collini, especially as it constitutes a lens through which arguments about the transformative power of university education might usefully be examined. Recent research into student faith in the UK highlights both the contentious status of religious groups represented in universities, as well as the public discourses that position religion as irrelevance, oddity or risk (Dinham and Jones 2012; Guest et al. 2013; Weller et al. 2011). Recent government policy intended to tackle so-called 'radicalization' among university students raises particular concerns about the treatment of Muslims (Brown and Saeed 2014) while also highlighting a broader tendency to conceive of religious students as passive subjects. While the neo-liberal rhetoric of the Browne report (2010) emphasizes students as empowered consumers, best placed to decide what they want from higher education, religious students are frequently portrayed in public fora as credulous dupes or as dangerously suggestible, their agency presumably flawed because they have clearly made the 'wrong' choices. Faced with such problematic assumptions, an empirically based consideration of how processes of influence proceed among students of faith becomes especially important.

The importance of a Christian context for Jevons has already been noted, as has his understanding of both society and self as properly integrated and participatory rather than atomized and self-serving. Collini does not share Jevons' framing hermeneutic of Christian love, but he does affirm an understanding of selfhood that assumes atomization is inimical to a healthy and enriching educational experience. Universities do their job best when fostering a capacity to see beyond immediate horizons and across parameters of intellectual possibility, always open to new insight and never ossified into fixed canons of meaning (Collini 2013).

In this respect Collini echoes other scholars who express concern about the instrumentalization of education and point to the growing tendency among both teachers and students to be assessment-led (Harris 2007; Hill and Kumar 2011). A consequence of measuring school and university education by quantifiably structured league tables, and of reducing education to economic advancement, is the danger that education becomes thoroughly compartmentalized. Knowledge is taught and learnt for the purposes of securing qualifications, resulting in an arguably impoverished learning experience, the problems of which Jevons was well aware. In the process, subject matter is divided into convenient digestible chunks and managed accordingly, and students are made less aware of the connections between them, and of the creative possibilities for thought that only occur when disciplinary and topical boundaries are crossed, subverted, questioned and challenged. Within university-based teaching about religion, there prevails a persistent assumption that personal faith has no place inside of the classroom and that to permit discussion of student experiences of faith would somehow undermine the 'objectivity' of university study (Fairweather 2012). This tendency reinforces compartmentalization by affirming a clear differentiation between commitment and knowledge (Flanagan 2001). According to this approach – pervasive in public universities in the USA and across the UK Higher Education sector – religion constitutes an object to be studied, while the religious convictions of students doing the studying ought to be 'bracketed out' and confined to non-academic contexts. As Fairweather highlights, this legacy of post-Enlightenment rationalism persists even in the discipline of social anthropology, in which the personal experiences of religious actors have long been acknowledged as central to a proper understanding of the religious phenomena they are assumed to embody. Permitting the faith lives of others into the classroom but not those of students themselves contributes to the 'othering' of faith communities and perpetuates a false polarization between 'religion' and the 'secular' (Fairweather 2012: 53). It also denies the university classroom a critical reflexivity that is defended and practised among academics undertaking social scientific research (Davies 1999). This secularization of the study of religion in universities has been criticized for not taking seriously the ways in which the perspectives of students – including their orientations to religion – shape the assumptions that frame the learning process. It similarly excludes the perspectives of university teachers, whose presentation of religious topics in the classroom may, as some recent research suggests, emerge as qualitatively distinct from how they conceptualize religion within their academic publications (Skeie 2015: 138). An approach that prevents such inter-subjective dimensions from being openly addressed in the classroom risks an impoverished presentation of religion and a disempowering experience of university education. It presumes a 'view from nowhere', preventing an honest conversation permitted to acknowledge the genuine differences between human actors, differences that, when critically addressed, can actually advance our understanding of religion.

So compartmentalization has at least two dimensions: the separation of disciplines and sub-disciplines into discrete bodies of knowledge, and the differentiation of student identities that positions personal religious convictions outside of the classroom. Both invite a challenging of intellectual boundaries of a kind that Collini seems to advocate. And yet it is precisely this crossing of intellectual boundaries, associated with a heightened awareness of the contingency of knowledge and the complexity of human meaning-making – to which the humanities are especially sensitive – that has persistently been seen as undermining the plausibility of religion. Sociologist Peter Berger has gone as far as suggesting that, not only is western style higher education a vehicle for secularization, but the humanities and social sciences are especially potent forces within this process (Berger 1999). It is the unremitting questioning of knowledge and its bases, something Collini sees as quintessential to both university life and the integrity of academic disciplines, that resonates with modes of thinking that encourage a critical perspective on religious truth, truth that, it is assumed, depends on foundationalist claims that cannot withstand this kind of analysis.

Aside from the assumptions and arguments of academics, this crossing of boundaries also provokes anxiety among Christian students who fear their university education will damage their faith. This is not helped by the general weakening of the liberal tradition within Anglicanism, of which Jevons was an advocate, so that intellectual enquiry as a means of enriching Christian faith is not a notion familiar to many of today's undergraduates. Indeed, as recent research has demonstrated, the most active and engaged Christian students are evangelicals (Guest et al. 2013). While this movement includes numerous variations and complexities, its dominant forms among students often privilege textual exposition of the Bible, leaving little room for contextual hermeneutics, and/or foreground charismatic worship and fellowship, favouring the experiential and subjective, with theological learning a secondary concern. In addition, Theology and Religious Studies as a subject area has suffered continued decline in recent years, with falling undergraduate applications leading to academic departments shrinking, merging or, in some cases, closing, and, in some quarters, a continued institutionalized scepticism about whether religion should be the proper concern of universities at all (Dinham and Jones 2012). Intellectual engagement with matters of faith within the context of university is often either peripheral to the culture of student churches, or is channelled into parallel curricula: Bible studies and discussion groups facilitated by local churches along lines in keeping with their own theological perspectives. The Christian Unions – long established as the most well-resourced and influential of student Christian organizations – run their own scheme for supporting students struggling with how to relate their faith to their studies. While such schemes may encourage intellectual engagement, it is an engagement whose boundaries and methods remain distinctive from those fostered within university degree programmes, often reflecting an underlying unease about the potential of university study to disrupt, challenge or undermine Christian faith. As might be expected, it is the evangelicals who are most concerned to address the interface between scholarship and faith as a challenge among Christian students.

And yet the evidence available suggests such anxieties might be misplaced, and that concerns among church leaders and evangelical organizations do not match the orientation to faith and study in evidence among the students themselves. Here I am drawing on research I undertook between 2009 and 2012 with Kristin Aune, Sonya Sharma and Rob Warner about the ways in which the experience of university shapes the lives of Christian undergraduate students (Guest et al. 2013). Notably, and keeping in mind my reservations about Jevons and Collini's intellectualist tendencies discussed earlier, the 'university experience' here is not restricted to classroom-based academic learning, but also includes the social experiences of university life (Sharma and Guest 2013). This approach is based on the observation that university encompasses a variety of human experiences that are mutually constitutive within complex processes of identity formation (Stevens, Armstrong and Arum 2008). It also responds to a discernible tendency in academic literature on student faith to treat students as atomized individuals, decontextualized from the institutional cultures that frame their experiences (Mayrl and Oeur 2009).

The 'Christianity and the University Experience' (CUE) project deployed a national survey covering 13 universities across England, supplemented by case studies including interviews with staff and students at five universities selected so as to be representative of the institutional variety of the HE sector. In order to avoid being led by doctrinal or practical assumptions about what properly counts as 'Christian', the survey was targeted at a random sample of all students and invited each respondent to identify the religious tradition to which they belonged. Allowing for sampling complications and taking into account comparative data, the proportion of self-identifying Christians we estimate at around 40 per cent to 45 per cent of the undergraduate population (a figure that reflects the proportion identified in the 2011 national census among young adults not working but in education) (Guest et al. 2013: 211–217). Among this population, there was significant diversity of belief and religious practice. Not surprisingly, those most active in church attendance and in local volunteering were the evangelical students, and this is matched by resource and influence filtered through university-based organizations like the Christian Unions. However, these evangelicals only constituted at most 20 per cent of the overall Christian student population, most of whom were more liberal in their morality and more uncertain in their commitment to core Christian doctrines. Around half of all Christian students never attended church during term-time; around a third never attended at all, regardless of context. Given self-identification was our method of ascertaining Christian identity, it is not surprising that a range of orientations was found, and this certainly includes a small minority who viewed their Christian identity in solely cultural, rather than religious, terms. Perhaps most strikingly, a significant majority – almost 75 per cent – when asked whether their religious identities had become stronger or weaker since they started their university career, said they had more or less stayed the same. This is mirrored in the very low proportion – 5 per cent – of students who reported a dramatic experience of conversion – either into *or out of* Christianity – since embarking on their university studies. Stability of faith identities was the norm (cf. Bäckström 1993), a far cry from the 'crisis narrative' that has, in the past, assumed faith and higher education exist in fierce opposition (Paton 1946).

This finding provides a clue to a broader tendency among Christian students, a tendency to keep their religious identities and their identities as learners in higher education markedly separate. Our survey allowed us to explore correlations between subject of degree programme and a range of other variables, including those related to religious belief, moral conviction and religious practice. There were no clear correlations between choice of degree and whether or not respondents self-identified as Christian, and subject choice could not be established as a predictor of responses to most questions about belief, morality or religious practice. An arguable exception relates to private prayer, with Christians studying physical science significantly more likely to say they never engaged in private prayer than students in medicine and allied subjects, social sciences or arts and humanities. One might attribute this to scepticism about an interventionist God or the supernatural more generally, although given it was medical students who were most likely to pray daily, the evidence does not point to a clear correlation between scientific training and scepticism about the act of prayer. Responses to a question about the relative authority of science and the Bible point in a different direction, with all four subject categories reasonably level in the degree to which they upheld creationism, intelligent design, evolution as the mechanism for divine creation, and the elevation of science above scripture respectively. The exception here was the social science students, who appeared significantly less keen on elevating science above scripture, but who included a correspondingly high proportion saying they were 'unsure' about this issue; social scientists were just as likely or unlikely to affirm creationism, intelligent design or divinely established evolution as students in other disciplines.

Interviews with students also suggested minimal engagement between the subject matter of their degree programmes and the beliefs and values they held to be essential to their Christian lives. Across subject areas, many Christian students did not seem to have considered how the new knowledge they had acquired might impact upon the assumptions they held as Christian believers – and this applies to fervently committed, church-attending Christians as well as those less engaged in conventional forms of Christian practice. The notable exception was students in Theology and Religious Studies, for whom a much more active engagement in how class-based learning might relate to their faith was in evidence, including reflection on meta-level questions such as how the faith orientations of lecturers might lead the class in a particular direction and if so, whether this was a legitimate part of the education process. For most Christian students, though, the encounter between scholarship and faith – something to be carefully managed according to evangelical organizations, but encouraged and celebrated according to figures like Jevons – features minimally in their reflections on their university experience. The compartmentalization of subject fields which some commentators fear is damaging the quality of higher education appears evident in the internally differentiated identities of Christian students, for whom religion is something they do in one segment of their lives, while study is something altogether separate, the two rarely being brought into conversation.

This is not a phenomenon restricted to the United Kingdom. Writing about the very different US higher education sector, Glanzer, Hill and Ream point to the 'disparity between the curricular and co-curricular as the reason why American college students have a reputation for vibrant religious practice, but not more advanced forms of religious knowledge both of their own and other religious traditions' (2014: 157). Jonathan Hill explores patterns of cognition and knowledge legitimation among young adults in the United States, focusing particularly on orientations to evolution and creationism, and argues for a clear distinction between learning about evolution and personal acceptance of it. He finds no evidence that attending college has any influence on whether young adults change their beliefs on these issues. Far more influential than formal education is stable involvement in religious subcultures of co-believers (Hill 2014). Another US study, Tim Clydesdale's *The First Year Out* (2007), identifies a pattern of compartmentalization among college students that presents an interesting angle on our present concerns. Clydesdale found that before embarking on their college education, students typically placed their religious identities in an 'identity lockbox', leaving them relatively unexamined and unquestioned during their first year. Religion was treated as something good to have, but chiefly as a resource to draw upon later in life; in effect, the relationship between religion and college was distinguished by a *lack* of interaction. Moreover, it was not only religious identities which were treated in this way; Clydesdale found students also putting aside concerns about gender, political, racial and civic identities in favour of 'daily life management' (2007: 2). They did not see their entry into a college education as an opportunity to examine their place in the wider world, but preferred to focus on more immediate concerns of relationships, personal gratifications and economic upkeep (2007: 2). In this sense, compartmentalization might be viewed not as a pattern of behavior that students simply learn by cultural osmosis, but as a deliberate strategy for coping with the pressures of young adult life, and there was clear evidence of this pattern in the CUE findings (Guest et al. 2013: 118). This is, perhaps, not a surprising discovery, and reflects the logic of arguments about modernization that point to a heightened social differentiation or even privatization of religion within some western contexts (Casanova 1994). That religion is reserved as separate from education both structurally and in the minds of individuals is arguably as understandable as the similar separation of religion from political or economic spheres of life. However, previous sociological discussion has tended to treat these consequences of differentiation as latent by-products of a broader modernization; their presence here as deliberate strategies deployed by individuals negotiating the challenges of university raises pressing questions about both the nature of religion and the character of higher education within contemporary Britain.

Concluding comment

Echoing the subversion of disciplinary boundaries that Douglas Davies has pursued so fruitfully during his academic career, my overall argument in this chapter is that student life is most effectively understood when public rhetoric about the purpose and status of universities is brought into critical dialogue with empirical investigation into the student experience. More specifically, a proper understanding of how religion is configured within universities cannot be separated from broader debates about the capacity of universities to shape the identities of their students. The work of Collini reveals common assumptions about how universities do and should function, but emerging debates about the status of universities in a neo-liberal age need to connect critique of institutional change with patterns of engagement among students themselves. We have considered Christian students as a case study, subjects of an influential narrative that positions them as vulnerable to a disruptive, secularizing encounter, but whose experiences suggest something different. The preceding discussion has raised far more questions than answers, but its exposure of a strategic compartmentalization among Christian undergraduates calls for further research into patterns of agency among the student body. Ongoing debates about radicalization highlight the need for a more sophisticated model of student identity than the passive one often rehearsed in government and media rhetoric (Guest 2015: 350–352).

I hope this discussion will continue, and conclude with a brief reflection on an issue that illustrates its potential benefits for wider academic discussion. It relates to the CUE project evidence of a strategic differentiation among Christian students, that deliberate process of keeping faith separate from learning that also finds evidence in US contexts. We might ask, does this suggest an impoverishment of the learning experience of higher education more generally, or just a profound curtailment of faith, which is apparently restricted to limited realms of interaction and thinking. Wider discussions about the instrumentalization of learning – teaching and learning 'to the exam' – might suggest the former, with matters of faith merely symptomatic of a wider tendency among students to prioritize the internalization of 'facts' over the forging of connections between new knowledge and pre-existing assumptions. In this sense, the study of religion in universities can be a case study in support of a more integrated learning experience, as Kieran Flanagan argues in calling for a legitimate place for reflexivity within undergraduate classes in the sociology of religion. It is in confronting and questioning the tensions between one's prior convictions and open observation of the religious 'other' that we achieve an appropriately nuanced and responsible understanding of religious identities (Flanagan 2001). Evidence from the CUE project suggests such reflexivity is lacking among many Christian students, and yet it is in abundant evidence among Christian students of Theology and Religious Studies, whose considered attempts to relate class-based learning to their personal orientations to religion mark a notable exception to the rule. Class-based proximity to religion as a focus of study appears to foster creative and thoughtful engagement rather than disillusionment, as some advocates of secularization theory might have us believe. By contrast, for Christian students in other disciplines such engagement appears to be fostered chiefly in 'alternative publics': within church home groups, Bible studies or friendship networks, reflecting the differentiation within education highlighted above. Further illumination of how these social clusters of reflexivity emerge and function might be afforded by future studies of student faith taking an ethnographic approach alert to the subtleties of meaning-making among the student population.

Note

1 I would like to thank Kristin Aune, Sonya Sharma and Rob Warner, with whom I collaborated on the 'Christianity and the University Experience' project whose research forms the basis of the final section of this chapter. I would also like to acknowledge an additional debt to Douglas Davies: our discussions about Jevons have been a great help in developing my understanding of his perspective on education.

References

Bäckström, A. (1993) 'To change by education: on stability and development in theological university students', *Scandinavian Journal of Educational Research* 37(3): 191–203.

Bellah, R. et al. (1985) *Habits of the Heart: Individualism and Commitment in American Life*. Berkeley, Los Angeles and London: University of California Press.

Berger, P. L. (1999) 'The desecularization of the world: a global overview', in Berger, P. L. (ed.) *The Desecularization of the World: Essays on the Resurgence of Religion in World Politics*. Washington: Ethics and Public Policy Center, Grand Rapids: William B. Eerdmans, pp. 1–18.

Berger, P. L., Berger, B. and Kellner, H. (1974) *The Homeless Mind: Modernization and Consciousness*. New York: Vintage Books.

Brown, K. E. and Saeed, T. (2014) 'Radicalization and counter-radicalization at British universities: Muslim encounters and alternatives', *Ethnic and Racial Studies* 38(11): 1952–1968.

Brown, R. (with H. Carasso) (2013) *Everything for Sale? The Marketisation of UK Higher Education*. London: Routledge.

Browne, Lord J. (2010) *Securing a Sustainable Future for Higher Education: An Independent Review of Higher Education Funding and Student Finance*. UK Government Report.

Casanova, J. (1994) *Public Religions in the Modern World*. Chicago and London: University of Chicago Press.

Clydesdale, T. (2007) *The First Year Out: Understanding American Teens after High School*. Chicago, IL: University of Chicago Press.

Collini, S. (2012) *What Are Universities For?* London: Penguin Books.

Collini, S. (2013) 'Sold out', *London Review of Books* 35(23): 1–22.

Davies, C. A. (1999) *Reflexive Ethnography: A Guide to Researching Selves and Others*. London: Routledge.

Davies, D. J. (1991) *Frank Byron Jevons, 1858–1936: An Evolutionary Realist*. Lewiston: Edwin Mellen Press.

Dinham, A. and Jones, S. H. (2012) 'Religion, public policy, and the academy: brokering public faith in a context of ambivalence?', *Journal of Contemporary Religion* 27(2): 185–201.

Durkheim, E. (1956) *Education and Sociology*. Glencoe, IL: The Free Press.

Fairweather, I. (2012) 'Faith and the student experience', in M. Guest and E. Arweck (eds), *Religion and Knowledge: Sociological Perspectives*. Aldershot: Ashgate, pp. 39–55.

Flanagan, K. (2001) 'Reflexivity, ethics and the teaching of the sociology of religion', *Sociology* 35(1): 1–19.

Gerth, H. H. and Mills, C. W. (eds) (2009) *From Max Weber: Essays in Sociology*. London: Routledge.

Giroux, H. (2014) *Neo-Liberalism's War on Higher Education*. Haymarket Books.

Guest, M. (2015) 'Religion and the cultures of higher education: student Christianity in the UK', in L. Beaman and L. Van Arragon (eds) *Issues in Religion and Education: Whose Religion?* Leiden: Brill, pp. 346–366.

Guest, M., Aune, K., Sharma, S. and Warner, R. (2013) *Christianity and the University Experience: Understanding Student Faith*. London: Bloomsbury.

Harris, S. (2007) *The Governance of Education: How Neo-Liberalism is Transforming Policy and Practice*. London: Continuum.

Higton, M. (2012) *A Theology of Higher Education*. Oxford: Oxford University Press.

Hill, D. and Kumar, R. (eds) (2011) *Global Neoliberalism and Education and its Consequences*. London: Routledge.

Hill, J. (2014) 'Rejecting evolution: the role of religion, education, and social networks', *Journal for the Scientific Study of Religion* 53(3): 575–594.

Jevons, F. B. (1896) *Introduction to the History of Religion*. London: Methuen & Co. Ltd.

Jevons, F. B. (1913) *Personality*. London: Methuen & Co. Ltd.

Kenway, J. et al. (2006) *Haunting the Knowledge Economy*. London and New York: Routledge.

McGettigan, A. (2013) *The Great University Gamble: Money, Markets and the Future of Higher Education*. Pluto.

Mayrl, D. and Oeur, F. (2009) 'Religion and higher education: current knowledge and directions for future research', *Journal for the Scientific Study of Religion* 48(2): 260–275.

Murphy, P. (2015) *Universities and Innovation Economies: The Creative Wasteland of Post-Industrial Society*. Aldershot: Ashgate.

Newman, J. H. (1966) *The Idea of a University*. New Haven, CT: Yale University Press.

Paton, D. M. (1946) *Religion in the University*. London: SCM Press.

Ritzer, G. (1996) *The McDonaldization of Society: An Investigation into the Changing Character of Contemporary Social Life*. Thousand Oaks: Pine Forge Press.

Sabri, D. (2011) 'What's wrong with "the student experience"?', *Discourse: Studies in the Cultural Politics of Education* 32(5): 657–667.

Sharma, S. and Guest, M. (2013) 'Navigating religion between university and home: Christian students' experiences in English universities', *Social & Cultural Geography* 14(1): 59–79.

Skeie, G. (2015) 'What does conceptualisation of religion have to do with religion in education?', in L. Beaman and L. Van Arragon (eds) *Issues in Religion and Education: Whose Religion?* Leiden: Brill, pp. 126–155.

Stevens, M. L., Armstrong, E. A. and Arum, R. (2008) "Sieve, incubator, temple, hub: empirical and theoretical advances in the sociology of higher education", *Annual Review of Sociology* 34: 127–151.

Strathern, M. (ed.) (2000) *Audit Cultures: Anthropological Studies in Accountability, Ethics and the Academy*. London: Routledge.

Weller, P., Hooley, T. and Moore, N. (2011) *Religion and Belief in Higher Education: The Experiences of Staff and Students*. London: Equality Challenge Unit.

Williams, R. (17th April 2014) 'No fooling about impact', *Times Higher Education*, p. 38.

13 A break from prose

Defying the boundaries of genre

Eleanor Nesbitt

Defying boundaries

This chapter, a clutch of poems, is contributed by one of Douglas Davies' first research students: he guided me in my investigation of 'Sikh Tradition in Nottingham' in 1979–1980. The poems, and preliminary reflection, are submitted as a gesture of support for Davies, the anthropologist-theologian, a transgressor of boundaries, and as a challenge to boundary-drawing more generally – especially against overly rigorous or unnoticed, and so unquestioned, boundary-drawing between one genre and another.

As an ethnographer, whose empirical contribution to religious studies has been institutionally based in religious education, within the wider framework of education, I have had frequent cause to reflect upon the drawing and crossing of the boundaries between disciplines. I have eavesdropped on debates about what constitutes a discipline, a field and a domain (see, for example, Piirto 2002: 432). The intrinsically multidisciplinary character of both education and religious studies provides a wealth of theoretical possibilities, as well as the constant hazard of woolliness. Conducting ethnographic research involves an ongoing debt to anthropology, while accepting on occasion the disciplinary aloofness of anthropologists. Engagement with religious studies means recurrent self-definition in relation to theology (see Ford 2005). Theology is characterized by Denise Cush as the 'clerical uncle' of 'big brother', religious studies and 'little sister', religious education (1999), and Kim Knott refers to theology as '"the other side" . . . theology, rather than religious studies' (2005: vii). However, encouragingly, there are increasing signs of a 'future in which theology and religious studies are pursued together' (Adams, Davies and Quash 2005: 211).

As it happens, an argument running through much of my work has been the need to unsettle some other boundaries. In company with Ron Geaves (1998), and more recently with Takhar and Jacobs (2011), I have, in part on the basis of data from my successive ethnographic investigations, challenged boundaries that are so widely assumed by religious educationists (though not by anthropologists [see Ballard 1999], or by all historians [see Oberoi 1994]) to separate off one 'world religion' from another (see for example Nesbitt 1990, 2012).

Meanwhile, the boundaries between genres are, at least in academia, even more strongly defined than boundaries between the disciplines, let alone the fuzzier delineations of fields and domains. So, to take an example, short stories and poems are unusual in peer-reviewed journals. (*The International Journal of Qualitative Studies in Education* is an exception in as much as it features poems.) Scholars obediently adhere to the stylistic norms for their monographs, reports and reviews. Many of them do, however, venture, alongside their academic writing, into other genres. So, one of my undergraduate supervisors, John Bowker, gave rein to his reasoning not only in his pioneering religious studies scholarship but also in his stories of the logical literalist Uncle Bolpenny for young children (1973). More famously, it is through his fictional evocation of Botswana and Edinburgh that bioethicist Alexander McCall-Smith finds his global audience. Within my own field of study (stretching as it does between the sociological and theological, the ethnographic and the textual), two recent novels have grown out of doctoral research: Hannah Bradby allowed data for her PhD thesis on Punjabi Glaswegians (1996, 2005b) to reincarnate as a novel, *Skinfull* (2005a). Alison Mukherjee (no date) shares insights into how and why the novel *Nirmal Babu's Bride* (2002) followed her doctoral thesis, *Biblical Bangla: An Examination of the Bengali Translations of the Fourth Book of Psalms* (2001).

Turning from fiction to poetry, one notes a contemporary move to validate poetry as a respectable medium for theology, and indeed a seasoned theologian's exhortation to colleagues in the twenty-first century to look to poetry as one way forward (Ford 2010), for '[P]oetry, and more widely the poetic imagination, is truth-bearing' (Guite 2010: 1). What is more, to quote Rowan Williams, 'poetry just is one of the refuges of the sacred in even the most secular environment; as obstinate and inconvenient to the managed society as (proper) theology' (2011: 22). With this encouragement in mind, five theologically alert members of a poetry workshop have published *Making Nothing Happen: Five Poets Explore Faith and Spirituality* (D'Costa et al. 2014).

Perhaps the theologians' capacity to honour poetry as a contemporary genre is unsurprising given the poetic content of the scriptures that are theology's foundation. If theology is understood as transcendent of another set of boundaries – those that demarcate 'faiths' and 'religions' – then not only the Psalms and Job but the Guru Granth Sahib and a wealth of Asian devotional poetry and epics add weight to calls for contemporary theology to engage with poetry as text, and they may also inspire experimentation with poetry as a potential contemporary medium for theology.

While theologians, and indeed religious educationists (Blaylock 2007), have made a case for poetry to further their project, I am waiting to hear specialists in religious studies arguing for this, although several scholars in the field admit to being poets. However, late-twentieth-century preoccupations with transparency, reflexivity and with the associated insider/outsider debate (McCutcheon 1999; Arweck and Stringer 2002) offer at least contact points between a religious studies scholar's poetic and academic enterprise. My investigation of the relationship between scholars' 'spiritual journeying and academic engagement' (Nesbitt 2010) not only introduced me to the interactions between my personal search for meaning and my study of Sikh and Hindu experience but also suggested to me the depth of integration between aspects of my life. Indeed it was my poems that expressed this integration and made it explicit to me. With regard to reflexivity, the impact of the field on the researcher may well find its expression in poetry. Moreover, with regard to ethnographic positioning as insider and/or outsider to the focus community, location or activity, the observers' poetry may afford valuable insights. The researcher's poems can provide insights no less for the researcher-poet than for readers of his or her reports.

Thus, for researchers in education, Jane Piirto has explored '[w]riting inferior poems as qualitative research'. She illustrates the value of poetic form with her own data-based poems, although these are, as she acknowledges, still too expository by poetic criteria:

> [T]he poem may convey a sense of empathy for the lives of the people being spoken about; it
> > also humanizes both the subject of the poem and the speaker of the poem . . . The research is
> > > treated as a work of art.

> (2002: 441)

Piirto's approach applies no less to religious studies than to education.

The poems: emotion, place and religious experience

Emotion provides a point of convergence between religion (if not religious studies) and poetry. While poetry is emotion recollected in tranquillity – at least according to William Wordsworth (1800) – religions entail a complex interplay of often intense emotion, as Davies' own work amply illustrates (2011, 2012). For emotion is 'generated in the interactions between self and society, self and symbol, and symbol and society' (Riis and Woodhead 2010: 7). Sarah Coakley's guest edition of *Modern Theology* provides recent discussions of the relationship between 'faith, rationality and the passions' (2011). Nor should it be overlooked that fieldwork, too, has an emotional aspect (Knowles 2006).

The four poems that follow span nearly 20 years of my religious studies career. They came into being in two continents and in religiously diverse and multi-layered settings. In each case I am, to differing degrees, both insider and outsider (see Dandelion's pertinent analysis – 1996: 37–50). As diagnostic tools the poems disclose to me retrospectively the ambiguities and shifts in my positioning and the experiences that affect me more deeply than religious buildings and behaviours. The first three poems spring from places: Glastonbury (a pilgrimage place in the English county of Somerset); the temple island of Elephanta (off the coast of India's financial capital, Mumbai); and – in Smethwick in the United Kingdom's post-industrial Midlands – a railway station and the gurdwara (Sikh place of worship) that is across the road from it. More specifically, the poems voice the deep dilemmas these places pose: the ambiguities of sacredness and the complexities of identity, indeed the emotional aspect of sacred place (Davies 2011). Perhaps they are an insider account of 'religious experience', those shining moments that seem less betrayed by poetry than by prose. For the fourth poem ('Synonyms') the subject is the nature of seeing, that crucial activity for the participant observer.

Smethwick, no less than Glastonbury and Elephanta, entails and evokes both journeying and a minor epiphany of arrival. Davies has written of the movement or journey motif in Christian tradition, in continuity with older Babylonian, Greek and Hebrew wandering and relocation (2004). To an unprecedented degree, twenty-first-century travellers move eclectically to sites of significance to others' both past and present as well as towards their own futures.

'Smethwick Rolfe Street' is more playful than the other three poems: its first line alludes to another poem that was sparked in a British railway station, Edward Thomas's poem 'Adlestrop' (no date), and there is a glancing reference to the meteoric rise of UK Punjabi poet, Daljit Nagra (2007). Then come the almost-rhymes (*langar* and hunger, *seva* and flavour) and the gruesome pun on *kirtan* (relying on its frequent mispronunciation by religious education teachers and others as 'curtain'), as well as the deliberately pedantic crossover to scholarly style by deploying footnotes. I am questioning the expectation that 'ethnic minority' vocabulary and subject matter are the preserve of 'ethnic minority' poets and articulating that 'individual plurality' and 'plural spirituality' which preoccupies some of my prose (Nesbitt 2009). One justification for contributing this poem to this volume is that it was under Davies' guidance in the University of Nottingham's Department of Theology that I conducted my first study of Sikh communities and my first fieldwork in gurdwaras. Davies had recently encountered Sikhs and their faith tradition on a stay in Punjab – hence his publication in Punjabi University's *Journal of Religious Studies* (1979).

Looking at these three poems together retrospectively invites me to reflect on religion and locality and to ponder what makes space 'sacred', and so the 'layering' of experience, story and physical construction. Glastonbury is deeply layered, a place of 'multiple meanings' (Bowman 2011) with many centuries of individuals' 'religious experience'; with retellings of associated story; with formal consecration; and successive construction of religious architecture. In Glastonbury's case, a dominant narrative tells of Joseph of Arimathea travelling, after Jesus' resurrection, to Glastonbury and 'planting' his staff which took root, flowered and grew into a tree. Indeed Jesus himself had allegedly come to Glastonbury with Joseph on an earlier visit.

The narrative is at once site-specific and a link to Christendom's universal salvific drama. Connections with the holy grail and King Arthur intensify the site's mythic allure for pilgrims and tourists (Bowman 1993). The abbey and the hagiography are historically underpinned by the earlier religious activity that Christians sought to erase, and they are in turn overlaid by recent and continuing 'Christianity, vernacular religion and alternative spirituality' (Bowman 2000). The 'ley lines' to which the poem refers are the (hypothetical) alignments claimed to link sites of particular cosmic energy.

On the temple island of Elephanta, too, religions met, as invading sixteenth century Catholic soldiers from Portugal used the rock-carved deities of the ancient indigenous tradition in their target practice. The Hindu and Buddhist iconography in the island's basalt caves has been dated by scholars to the fifth to eighth centuries of the common era. My poem refers to the very damaged sculpture of Nataraja (the dancing Shiva) in the Shiva cave.

The mystique of high places (such as the Tor at Glastonbury) and islands (Elephanta), and perhaps their remoteness and defensibility, predispose them to become centres of ritual and pilgrimage, which shades into tourism, and to be the focus of scholarly investigation and reflection. Both poems, 'Glastonbury' and 'Elephanta', allude to the ambivalent relationship between visiting as a devotee, as a scholar or as a sight-seer.

Smethwick's case is very different – urban, unsung, neither a tourist nor a pilgrim destination, nor the subject of study by scholars. Smethwick's once-thriving foundries sucked in labour from India's Punjab state in the 1950s and 1960s. The town, whose unremarkable places of worship had hitherto been Christian churches, became the site of one of Europe's largest gurdwaras (Sikh places of worship). Built (at 130 High Street) on the site of a church (a Congregational chapel), Guru Nanak Gurdwara is claimed to be the United Kingdom's largest gurdwara (http://www.gngsmethwick. com). Thus all three locations – Glastonbury, Elephanta and Smethwick – are, despite their evident dissimilarities, sites of 'inter-faith' encounter, or at least of a succession of religious clienteles, with varying degrees of accommodation and conflict. In each site the timeless moment is unconstrained by religious architecture or liturgical frameworks.

GLASTONBURY

(Visited by The British Association for the Study of Religions)

We were no new Age travellers,
Pagans, pilgrims, Christians on retreat
Or on the march, but academics
Visiting the field. So there, where ley lines meet
And Joseph walked and scholars theorise,
We left the bus and went our several ways
To ruined abbey, bookshops and the Tor –
Tourists now, happy, eager to explore,

But still constrained to analyse, impress,
And never free to risk not seeming wise
Or smart. And there was I, unable to express
Or comprehend the Torward pull, the purging
And the peace. Inwardly changed and mute,
Tranquil, ecstatic, free, I caught the bus and sat
And heard myself attempt to joke and chat.

(Nesbitt 1999: 12)

ELEPHANTA

'We Hindus do not worship broken images,'
explains the guide in Elephanta's pillared cave.
Chiselled from living rock, Shiva – long limbless –
dance your cosmic dance, subject for tourist snaps
and serious study, but not for worship.
In me, perplexed post-Protestant,
last of a line that loved a broken Lord
and shared fragmented bread,
wonder still wells afresh from broken stone.
With neither priest nor prayers
my worship springs, cleanses and heals
in roofless shrines and desecrated, awesome caves.

(Nesbitt 1999: 12)

SMETHWICK ROLFE STREET

Remembering Adlestrop I will be bold
and write of Smethwick Rolfe Street
that October Sunday when the clocks went back.
The bright low sun made paper silhouettes
of sturdy trees. Sycamore leaves – golden,
yellow, lime – spun pirouetting, trackwards
and a silver squirrel leapt, lightfoot,
along a gantry. Wind-in-tree sounds
softly washed the track.
A name like Dhillon, Dhanjal, Dhaliwal,
Nagra – not Nesbitt – would license me
to pun in Punglish,[1] Smethwick's mother tongue.
Punjabi metaphors drift from the gurdwara[2]
across the carriageway: hunger for langar,[3]
seva's[4] fulsome flavour, and a sangat (congregation)
washed by shimmering tides of hymns,
the kirtan, curtaining them from England –
traffic, graffiti, and a railway station
fleetingly wondrous as a woodland shrine.

SYNONYMS

Voyeur – that was the word you used,
deliberately derogatory,
demanding a denial.
You meant, I think,
that all I did was sneak
my fitful, furtive looks,
living vicariously and disengaged,
while others, hearty, honest, uninhibited,
dived into living.
Observer – that was the term I used
definitively for my daily role
as researcher, immersed
in others' lives,
recording and reporting,
fathoming unfathomable
individuality.
Seer – that was the metaphor
they used to pin –
in sarcasm and wonder –
on prophets, poets,
sightless bards,
those misfits like Tiresias,
so blessed and cursed
with vision.
Observant, voyeuristic,
may I some day see!

(Florance and Nesbitt 2011: 35)

As a theologian-anthropologist, Douglas Davies introduced me to a possible theoretical framework for my first period of fieldwork. He helped me to see as well as to observe, and for that I thank him. It was Davies too who set me firmly on the path of Sikh Studies which I continue to travel.

Notes

1 The spoken mix of Punjabi and English.
2 The Sikh place of worship.
3 Langar (rhyming with 'hunger') – the free, ample vegetarian spread for all.
4 Seva (pronounced 'savour') – voluntary service such as providing, preparing and serving langar.

References

Adams, N., Davies, O. and Quash, B. (2005) 'Fields of faith: an experiment in the study of theology and religions', in D. Ford, B. Quash and J. M. Soskice (eds)

Fields of Faith: Theology and Religious Studies for the Twenty-First Century. Cambridge: Cambridge University Press, pp. 207–221.

Arweck, E. and Stringer, M. (eds) (2002) *Theorizing Faith: The Insider/Outsider Problem in the Study of Ritual.* Birmingham: University of Birmingham Press.

Ballard, R. (1999) 'Panth, Kismet, Dharm te Qaum: continuity and change in four dimensions of Punjabi religion', in P. Singh and S. S. Thandi (eds) *Punjabi Identity in Global Context.* New Delhi: Oxford University Press, pp. 7–37.

Blaylock, L. (2007) *Spirited Poetry: Reflections about God, Life and Faith.* Norwich: Religious and Moral Education Press.

Bowker, J. (1973) *Uncle Bolpenny Tries Things Out.* London: Faber.

Bowman, M. (1993) 'Drawn to Glastonbury', in I. Reader and T. Walter (eds) *Pilgrimage in Popular Culture.* Basingstoke: MacMillan, pp. 29–62.

Bowman, M. (2000) 'More of the same? Christianity, vernacular religion and alternative spirituality in Glastonbury', in S. Sutcliffe and M. Bowman (eds) *Beyond the New Age: Exploring Alternative Spirituality.* Edinburgh: Edinburgh University Press, pp. 83–104.

Bowman, M. (2011) 'Understanding Glastonbury as a site of consumption', in G. Lynch, J. Mitchell and A. Strhan (eds) *Religion, Media and Culture: A Reader.* London: Routledge, pp. 11–22.

Bradby, H. (1996) *Cultural Strategies of Young Women of South Asian Origin in Glasgow, with Special Reference to Health,* unpublished PhD thesis, University of Glasgow.

Bradby, H. (2005a) *Skinfull.* London: Onlywomen Press.

Bradby, H. (2005b) 'Finding space in a tight-knit community – qualitative research with Glasgow Punjabis', in N. Hallowell, J. Lawton and S. Gregory (eds) *Reflections on Research: The Realities of Doing Research in the Social Sciences.* Maidenhead: Open University Press McGraw-Hill, pp. 49–51.

Coakley, S. (ed.) (2011) 'Introduction: faith, rationality and the passions', *Modern Theology* 27(2): 217–225.

Cush, D. (1999) 'Big brother, little sister and the clerical uncle: the relationship between religious studies, religious education and theology', *British Journal of Religious Education* 21(3): 137–145.

Dandelion, P. (1996) *A Sociological Analysis of the Theology of Quakers.* Lampeter: Edwin Mellen Press.

Davies, D. J. (1979) 'Models of religious communication', *Journal of Religious Studies,* Punjabi University 6(2).

Davies, D. J. (2004) 'Time, place and the Mormon sense of self' in S. Coleman and P. Collins (eds) *Religion, Identity and Change: Perspectives on Global Transformations.* Aldershot: Ashgate, pp. 107–118.

Davies, D. J. (2011) *Emotion, Identity, and Religion: Hope, Reciprocity and Otherness.* Oxford: Oxford University Press.

D'Costa, G., Nesbitt, E., Pryce, M., Shelton, R. and Slee, N. (2014) *Making Nothing Happen: Five Poets Explore Faith and Spirituality.* Aldershot: Ashgate.

Florance, I. and Nesbitt, E. (comp.) (2011) *Gemini Four.* Henley-on-Thames: OnlyConnect.

Ford, D. (2005) 'Introduction', in D. Ford, B. Quash, J. M. Soskice (eds) *Fields of Faith: Theology and Religious Studies for the Twenty-First Century.* Cambridge: Cambridge University Press.

Ford, D. (2010) 'Where is wise theological creativity to be found? thoughts on 25 years of modern theology and the twenty-first century prospect', *Modern Theology* 26(1): 67–75.

Geaves, R. (1998) 'The borders between religions: a challenge to the world religions approach to religious education', *British Journal of Religious Education* 21(1): 20–31.

Guite, M. (2010) *Faith, Hope and Poetry: Theology and the Poetic Imagination.* Aldershot: Ashgate.

Knott, K. (2005) *The Location of Religion: A Spatial Analysis.* London: Equinox.

Knowles, C. (2006) 'Handling your baggage in the field: reflections on research relationships', *International Journal of Social Research Methodology* 9(5): 393–404.

McCutcheon, R. T. (ed.) (1999) *The Insider/Outsider Problem in the Study of Religion: A Reader.* London: Cassell.

Mukherjee, A. (2001) *Biblical Bangla: An Examination of the Bengali Translations of the Fourth Book of the Psalms,* unpublished PhD thesis, University of Birmingham.

Mukherjee, A. (2002) *Nirmal Babu's Bride.* New Delhi: Indialog.

Mukherjee, A. (no date) 'From Biblical Bangla to Nirmal Babu's Bride: why the novel followed the thesis'. Available at: http://www.soas.ac.uk/literatures/satranslations/mukherjee.pdf (Accessed on 15 June 2012).

Nagra, D. (2007) *Look We Have Coming to Dover.* London: Faber & Faber.

Nesbitt, E. (1990) 'Pitfalls in religious taxonomy: Hindus and Sikhs, Valmikis and Ravidasis', *Religion Today* 6(1): 9–12, reprinted in J. Wolffe (ed.) *The Growth of Religious Diversity: Britain from 1945: A Reader.* London: Hodder for Open University, 1994.

Nesbitt, E. (1999) *Turn but a Stone.* Norwich: Hilton House.

Nesbitt, E. (2009) 'Building interfaith understanding', *The Friends Quarterly* 37(1): 15–27.

Nesbitt, E. (2010) 'Interrogating the experience of Quaker scholars in Hindu and Sikh studies: spiritual journeying and academic engagement', *Quaker Studies* 14(2): 134–158.

Nesbitt, E. (2012) 'Hinduism and Sikhism', in K. A. Jacobsen (ed.) *Brill's Encyclopaedia of Hinduism,* Volume 4. Leiden, Brill, pp. 573–587.

Oberoi, H. (1994) *The Construction of Religious Boundaries: Culture, Identity and Diversity in the Sikh Tradition.* New Delhi: Oxford University Press.

Piirto, J. (2002) 'The question of quality and qualifications: writing inferior poems as qualitative research', *International Journal of Qualitative Studies in Education* 15(4): 431–445.

Riis, O. and Woodhead, L. (2010) *A Sociology of Religious Emotion.* Oxford: Oxford University Press.

Takhar, O. K. and Jacobs, S. (2011) 'Confusing the issue: field visits as a strategy for deconstructing religious boundaries', *Discourse* (Subject Centre for Philosophical and Religious Studies) 10(2): 31–44.

Thomas, E. (no date) 'Adlestrop'. Available at: http://www.poemhunter.com/poem/adlestrop (Accessed on 15 October 2012).

Williams, R. (2011) in I. Florance and E. Nesbitt (comp.) *Gemini Four.* Henley-on-Thames: OnlyConnect, pp. 20–22.

Wordsworth, W. (1800) 'Preface to lyrical ballads'. Available at: http://www.bartleby.com/39/36.html (Accessed on 20 September 2012).

14 An inquisitive presence

Thinking with Douglas Davies on the study of religion

Michael J. Thate

An unsystematic appreciation

A natural ending for *Festschriften* might well be to offer a listing of the honoured author's written works or a kind of systematic review of their research. Though such approaches may well serve other collections, for this *Festschrift* in honour of a good friend and mentor, Douglas Davies, it is decidedly avoided for at least two reasons. First, from a former student's perspective, Douglas possesses that rare academic charm of being more interested in *good* ideas than merely having his own ideas parroted back to him. 'I know what I think', he would always tell students before essays were due; 'I want to know your best thoughts'. Moreover, he is a stimulating sounding board and an incredibly fruitful person to 'think with' on whatever topic of research one may be currently exploring. His office hours are frequented by students and scholars working in fields ranging from behavioural economics to government, classics to philosophy – all in order to discuss their current research with him. I could not help but think a systematic review of his work would utterly bore – or, worse, insult – the refined tastes of the inquisitive Welshman.

Second, throughout his writings, Davies often lambasts the 'systematic' or the 'consistent' in the field of religious studies. Each religious expression – be it framed by Mormonism or Sikhism, Christianity or Buddhism – 'is a distinctive world of its own' (Davies 1987: i). As such, religious phenomena are approached with an interest in the details of local developments extended into wider themes of concern as well as wider interests 'worked out in local developments' (Davies 1990: 7). George Steiner has written that our current cultural moment has 'embarked on a process of specialization from which it will never emerge' (2003: 176). This can be an unsettling reality to the tidy and neat presentations of academic work as any pretention to 'consistency' may well be a regional gloss within constructed boundaries of inquiry (compare the similarities with discussion of 'truth' and its instrumental 'proof' in Rorty 1982 and 2009). Davies himself has been an oft-traverser of disciplinary divides. Besides his dual expertise in anthropology and theology, he has also voyaged into joint projects ranging from classics to, notably, agriculture, as evidenced by his intriguing joint study with the Centre for Rural Studies at the Royal Agricultural College at Cirencester (Davies 1991). The study is a kind of extended reflection on the 1990 *Faith in the Countryside* report of the Archbishops' Commission on Rural Areas. The study engaged in five English Dioceses: Durham, Gloucester, Lincoln, Southwell and Truro. This range of inquiry models an embrace of complexity in all matters of religion which are themselves 'complex and demand serious reflection' (Davies 1991: 2). Within these diverse and complex fields, Davies is a self-styled 'inquisitive presence' (Davies 1987: i), and rather eclectic and instrumental in his usage of theory. Davies appears quite critical of 'theory for theory's sake' and cautious with respect to the subtleties of description which can function as their 'own form of interpretation' (see Davies and Guest 2007: 167; cf. 8–11). In all of his studies, 'several different approaches' are appropriated in order to provide 'a balanced view' of whatever topic is under analysis (e.g. Davies and Drury 1997: i). The drive for 'balance' takes precedence over the chimera of 'objectivity' as classifications of the latter are contingent upon 'social experience' (Davies 1984: 4; cf. Durkheim and Mauss 1967: 3–9).

Nevertheless, a significant aspect of the study of religion 'involves the construction of categories by which multitudinous data can be organized and understood'. Davies defines religion as a 'concept that refers to clusters of symbolic rituals that enshrine the prime values and beliefs of a group and intensify their associated emotions' (2011: 5). Elsewhere he follows Paul Tillich's definition of religion as 'being ultimately concerned about that which is and should be our ultimate concern' (1964: 40). He also follows, with critical alteration, Clifford Geertz's famous definition in 'Religion as a Cultural System' (1973: 90). Even here, however, there is a subtle anxiety apparent in Davies' work in his desire to arrive at 'appropriate categories' which are 'provided by the religions themselves' (Davies 1984: 14), while at the same time being aware of the bundled and messy nature of belief itself. There is a danger in imposing 'an artificial order on human experience' (Davies 2002a: 20) as life does not get lived according to some 'organizing blueprint' (Davies 2002a: 22). Moreover, 'life lived is not as life documented' (Davies 2002a: 20). Systems introduce the potential for over-interpretation, of seeking 'forms of meaning where it cannot be found', generating 'interpretation piled upon interpretation' (Davies 2002a: 115). Davies' approach is what he calls a 'cluster-approach' (2002a: 22). That is, most 'believers' have no system as such; 'only clusters of belief, clusters constructed through life experience, through influential individuals among family, friends, teachers, and priests' (Davies 2002: 23). These clusters tend to be 'partial, fragmentary, and changing' according to the shifting currents and needs of life (Davies 2002a: 119).

In lieu of a systematic review, then, what follows are a set of three clusters of ideas anchored in the expansive publications of Douglas Davies and appropriated for an entangled reading of the political together with the study of religion. *Meaning-making, identity* and *death* are read through Davies' oeuvre and illustrated by the Norwegian film, *Den brysomme mannen* (2006), as an experimental reading of the study of religion's subversive potentiality, viz., its ability as a *concept* to conceive of an alternative state of affairs. Much has been written lately on the harmful and negative aspects of religion – to which, of course, the study of religion must attend and listen. As Pascal observed, 'men never do evil so completely and cheerfully as when they do it from religious conviction' (1958: 265). But here we must be careful. It is not as easy as declaring *Religion Poisons Everything* (Hitchens 2009). Rather, it is that religion interfuses and is entangled with everything. It is difficult to think of any historical movement of 'good' or 'evil' where religion was not part of the equation, or, at least, not analysed from the perspective of the study of religion. Be they pogroms or poems, art or ideology, dig deep enough and you will find some veneer of religion. 'The challenge is to understand religion as it is – not just at its best but also its worst' (Prothero 2010: 7). Again, this is not to say that religion itself is 'good' or 'evil', nor that it is irreducibly human. (And perhaps we should question the assumption that 'religion' is a thing in itself.) But 'religion' does seem to show up around the fiendish compulsion characteristic of species to make things meaningful. It is therefore part of the composite and projection of who we are and how we make ourselves, and sits along the overlapping networks of identity matters, or, at least, it may be reflective of such matters. Though religion surely can carry the ugly freight of oppression and narrations of hegemony, it also remains a resource of subversive potential for groups living under domination to narrate and identify *themselves*. It allows for the polemical edge of identity resilience.

It is in this vein, then, that I would like to 'think with' some significant themes which are present in the work of Douglas Davies, illustrate them with the film *Den brysomme mannen*, and extend them into political and polemical contexts of identity construction as resilience and, indeed, a platform for potential resistance. I offer these brief and underdeveloped reflections – which are written in heart-felt honour of a man of vast mirth, generosity and wisdom – as an entrée into his wider work.

Meaning-making

A significant recurring motif in Davies' work is in the figuration of meaning-making. That is, the human drive for meaning and the human animal's mediation of that drive through a symbolic world (cf. Sayer 2011). Davies sees this as 'a kind of human instinct' (Davies 2011: 10). He calls 'the question of how the human drive for meaning might generate a sense of salvation' among the 'enduring themes' of his work (Davies 2011: v). His doctoral research centred on this theme and has been present throughout much of his later work (Davies 1984). Published in the mid-1980s, his first monograph represents a concerted effort to form meaning as a 'general concept powerful enough to match that of evolution' during the latter part of the nineteenth century (Davies 1984: 2). He assumes a general view of humanity as an 'animal engaged in creating significant realms of communication'. This model of meaning-making 'places mundane and supernatural concerns on a continuum of significance' (Davies 1984: 2). Tied in with his concept of 'meaning' are salvation processes which 'are as universal as the drive for meaning' (Davies 1984: 1). Salvation is seen as a term invested with a sense of meaning derived from a phenomenological context and becomes the term which best serves as a fulcrum upon which to engage in comparative study – in this instance, Sikhism and Mormonism. The question of 'what must I do to be saved' (cf. Acts 16:30) for Davies is thus seen as resting 'at the heart of the so-called world religions', and 'presumed to be present although unvoiced in these terms in every culture' (Davies 1984: 2). Salvation is therefore a kind of 'straddling term', pointing to patterns of meaning that extend across cultural boundaries (Davies 1987: 96; cf. Needham 1972).

The difficulty with this move is that it potentially reduces 'all religions as one' by in effect reading all religious traditions through the questions of one's confessional grammar – in this case, Anglicanism. Stephen Prothero (2010) has warned of the tendency amongst scholars of religion who construct, say, Daoism around the question of salvation and thereby miss-frame the discussion from the beginning with Christian questions. Though one would certainly want to quibble over Davies' rare slip in deeming such a term 'neutral' (see Davies 1984: 3), he is working with 'salvation' in a slightly different sense. He sees it as 'a form of self-perception involving a maximization of meaning in a world of competing explanatory schemes' (Davies 1984: 8). Yet still, the concept of 'meaning' itself is thought by some as bereft of meaning and an unhelpful term altogether (Ogden and Richards 1989). Noam Chomsky has spoken of meaning as a 'catch-all term for those aspects of language which linguistics [knows] very little about' (quoted in Ogden and Richards 1989: 158). Davies prefers the term, however, in its ability to 'provide a higher order of reference' by which genuine comparative studies can happen (Davies 1984: 5). Here he is near Wilhelm Dilthey's preoccupation with *Bedeutung* as 'a comprehensive category through which life can be understood' (Davies 1984: 6). He also sees meaning as a paradigm through which a 'potential unifying perspective' can be reintroduced into religious studies 'following the fragmented state of the field after the demise of evolutionary theories in the human sciences' (Davies 1984: 27). Davies thus sees, and perhaps signals, the swing from the 1880s to the 1980s in religious studies in terms of a conceptual transition from humans as evolving entities to humans as meaning-making creatures (Davies 1984: 155).

Though the term 'meaning' is deeply ambiguous in that it is socially contingent even in its definition, there remains intriguing potential. The study of religion is the study of the world made meaningful by varying communities of 'faith' where the 'ordinary world' is refigured with a 'sense of profound significance as passing moments are set within an immense sweep' of purpose (Davies 1987: 1). The 'basic accomplishment of any cultural orientation is its capacity to give symbolic order and meaning' (Kearl 1989: 24). Human reflection upon this 'meaning' transpires within a complex 'religious symbolism' (Davies 1990a: 9), funded by an aura of 'depth' – viz., a 'depth in humanity, depth in God, and depth in the divine-human relationships' (Davies 1991: 283; cf. de Lubac 1967: xii) – and enforced by and communicated through ritual (Rappaport 2008: 107–138; cf. Bell 2009). In principle, of course, symbols within a symbolic system carry differing forms and levels of meaning to participants within the relevant symbolic order (Smith 1976: 168; Sperber 1975). This variety, however, 'affords a pool of potential orientations available for different contexts' (Davies 2002a: 185; cf. Davies 2002: 247ff.). Moreover, the complex nature of 'belief' at both the practical level of the 'intricate combination of reason and emotion, set within the life context of each individual' (Davies and Drury 1997: 73), as well as the wider issue of how the flux of time affects 'the status of belief' (Davies and Drury 1997: 73), bears witness to the ambiguity and relativity of 'meaning' as an appropriate category for religious studies. Davies here is again near to Dilthey's notion of meaning as the totality of the knowing subject (see Davies 1984: 8). But perhaps we could (re)conceive meaning by appropriating Agamben's notion of *qualunque* – that 'whatever' of religious expression which coordinates local and wider convictions of the significant (de la Durantaye 2009). Agamben's *qualunque* is a kind of cheat which allows him to refer to that which is neither particular nor general, neither individual nor generic (1999). This fictive centre allows for the possibility of comparative study without necessarily reading, say, Buddhism through Catholicism or Islam through modern secularism. The 'straddling terms' of meaning and salvation allow for the terms themselves to be defined locally while also providing an overarching grammar that illuminates each symbolic system.

This understanding of meaning might also generate potentially creative theoretical thinking. Particularly fruitful is Davies' intriguing notion of symbolism as the outrage against 'ordinary experience' (Davies 2002a: 158), manifested in a 'heightening of ordinary processes of meaning-construction and human awareness' (Davies 2002a: 153). This is the transvaluation of 'reality' as 'ordinary forms of meaning' are translated into 'ultimate explanations' of the *meaningful* (Davies 2002a: 159). Here Davies follows Berger and Luckmann in their work on plausibility structures and insights into how the social basis for the suspension of doubt is inherent in the meaning-making process and the naming of 'reality' (Davies 2002a: 29; cf. Berger and Luckmann 1967; and Berger 1990). His analysis is also an extension of William James' conclusion to his study of religious experience in that 'religiosity is grounded in a basic uneasiness about life and in a consequent search for a resolution to wrongness' (Davies 2002a: 160–161). This quest for resolution is the 'ultimate concern' or ground from which a theory of religion could fruitfully emerge.

An intriguing illustration of these themes is present in the Norwegian film, *Den brysomme mannen* (*The Bothersome Man*) (2006), directed by Jens Lien and based upon the script of Per H. V. Schreiner. The film can be interpreted in any number of ways, but it is an insightful demonstration of the constructedness of 'meaning' – read as 'happiness' in the film – and the fragility of 'reality'. The film opens with the main character, Andreas, standing in a subway station next to two strangers who are kissing, eyes open, in a mechanical and grotesque manner. Andreas throws himself in front of an oncoming train and the scene goes black. After a couple of seconds the next scene is of Andreas being dropped off by a bus at a small gas station on the edge of wasteland. An elderly man puts up a 'welcome' sign and drives Andreas into a postmodern architectural city – a city with no problems – where he is thrust into a seemingly ideal existence. He is given an excellent job at a top firm, an exquisite apartment and meets a beautiful woman, Anne, with whom he eventually cohabits. This 'perfect' life, however, turns to the absurd as the intimate act of sex, for example, is portrayed as mechanical and repetitive. Even food, drink, and conversations seem to be devoid of any substance. Andreas appears to be the only person bothered by this hollow reality and seeks meaning in an affair with a co-worker named Ingeborg. The affair, however, proves to be just as perfunctory and absurd as everything else. The sense of unease grows in Andreas and he attempts to kill himself in what appears to be a return to the original scene as he again throws himself in front of an oncoming train. Even the pleasure of an ending, of death, however, is stolen from Andreas as he is forced to exist, almost Promethean-like, and returns to his former partner, Anna, who makes no comment on his absence or his bloodied and broken body.

Things begin to change, however, when he overhears beautiful music coming through the wall of a building. When Andreas investigates further he finds Hugo, a stranger he had earlier coincidentally met in a bar restroom and is himself bothered by the absurdness of the city, listening to the music through a crack in a wall. The two dig into the wall like fiends and just as they reach into a kitchen of a house which is cinematically presented as a higher dimension of reality – full of colour, tastes and smells – the police drag the two away. Andreas is thrown into the luggage compartment of the same bus which initially brought him into the city. The final scenes are claustrophobic and violent as Andreas is shown bouncing around the small and dark luggage compartment. He is cast out of the city and dropped off in a frigid, howling wilderness.

The three spaces represented in *Den brysomme mannen* as the 'city', the 'house' and the 'wilderness' illustrate the relationality of meaning-making – what we might provisionally call the super-plausible, the ordinary, and the Real. The 'city' is where most of life is lived and experienced – the ordinary. It is here where *perceived* reality is taken for granted *as Reality*. It is also a reality enforced and policed. Those who question it are labelled as 'bothersome' and punished or exiled. But from time to time cracks in the wall, as it were, emerge and music of a different register, tastes of a different sort, and smells of another fragrance awake us to the fictive reaches of the city's descriptive hegemony. These experiences heighten a sense of 'basic uneasiness' and dissatisfaction with life lived within the 'city' and its descriptive reach, and question the suspension of doubt that this 'reality' is in fact 'Reality'. The quest for a resolution to this 'basic uneasiness about life' transpires in the realm of the 'house' – the super-plausible (Davies 2011: 240–243; and Davies 2002a: 153). The house informs those within the city that there is a deeper sense, a deeper meaning, which results in a transvaluation (or reassessment) of reality and identity. The super-plausible renders established plausibility fragile as the house effectively renames the city as absurd. It is both the house *and* the city, however, which guard us from 'the Real' – the wilderness – that chaotic and formless dimension unmediated by any symbolic order, i.e. the realm of true meaninglessness (cf. Durkheim's notion of *anomie*). The super-plausible is the dimension from which possibilities for meaning 'escape' – or are 'saved' – in order to construct through a symbolic order a meaningful 'real' against the desert of the Real. Barbara Myerhoff states that loneliness and isolation are the 'other side of freedom' (1982: 132). True freedom from constructed senses of the real results in radical isolation and exile. (Here, if there were space, it would be worthwhile considering Lacan as a reader of Hegel and the notion of Being's emergence after 'division divides itself from itself' [Žižek 2012: 15; cf. Lacan 2007; Bailly 2009; Žižek 2007]).

Max Weber stated that 'every need for salvation is an expression of some distress' (Weber 1965: 107). The 'distress' in this instance is in Andreas' desire for authentic existence, existence grounded in the *being* of the house. Religion provides resources with which to assert the 'inadequacy of the everyday ordinariness of life', and offers a dual-layered critique of the 'ordinary' by pinpointing flaws and 'positing modes of redress' (Davies 2002a: 153; de Certeau 2011). This critique is carried out from a position of super-plausibility: a space from which 'a higher-order claim of meaning transcends the lower-order realm of failed plausibility in the everyday life-world' (Davies 2002a: 153), while also protecting us from the Real. As such, earthly powers and authority of every stripe are made fragile and fictive. The 'ordinary' world is thus unsettled and made strange by the looming disruption of the super-plausible, and thus responds with diverse modes of governmentality.

Identity

Co-implicated with the complexities and ambiguities of meaning-making are notions of identity, ritual, and myth. Identity, of course, is a complex idea in its own right (Davies 2011: 2; cf. Brooks 2011). Though reflections on ritual and myth may inform and help explicate identity (Lincoln 1999), there is a need for balance between 'outward, historical, and visible aspects' and an account 'of the inward and personal dynamics' of human experience, a balance especially pertinent within analyses of religious identity (Davies and Drury 1997: 3). What is more, the human self is a 'flux-confronted self' (Davies 1984: 8; cf. Taylor 1989), a self of 'inner-otherness' which can manifest itself in a sense of being a stranger to oneself (Davies 2002a: 29). Religion can prove an intensifying and potentially unifying force for identity in the way in which Hans Mol saw its obverse: viz., that humanity confers a 'sense of awe and a status of sacredness upon whatever gives [it] a strong sense of identity' (Davies 1984: 160; cf. Mol 1977; Mol 1978). Within the work of Douglas Davies, then, identity is presented as a 'negotiated sense of self developed over time through the emotions and moods that characterize feelings people have of themselves in relation to core values of their group' (Davies 2011: 5). Or, more generally, identity is understood in terms of 'the way people understand themselves in relation to other persons, to the world around them and to supernatural realms' (Davies 2002c: 4).

Instructive here is Davies' use of Tillich's notion of God as *Being* itself – the ground of being – and humanity as rooted in existence. Tillich was aware of the potential fragmentary effects of religion in its establishment of a distinct arena of activity wherein a life is caught between 'sacred' and 'secular' realms – between the 'house' and the 'city' in our illustration above. This is then the prime example of humanity's estrangement from its 'true being' (Tillich 1964: 42). Idolatry is the result when 'true being' is 'replaced by some lesser concern' (Davies and Drury 1997: 207). When the ground of being is replaced by 'broken cisterns' (cf. Jer 2:13), existence becomes fragmented. It is this fragmentation, this 'tragic estrangement from [humanity's] own ground and depth', that Tillich sees humanity attempting to overcome in its 'passionate longing for ultimate reality' (Tillich 1964: 8). Salvation is thus a kind of description of 'a quality of identity' (Davies 2002a: 145). It is the translation from a fragmented state of estranged existence into the 'other culture' of God (Davies 2002a: 26). I suggest that part of the category of religion's potency is in its ability to inform the 'flux-confronted-self' with sources for a unifying sense of self, anchored in this 'other culture' of God – the super-plausible – through *ritual* and *narration* (Brooks 2011: 139) amidst other competing narrations.

Within ritual we are confronted with a potential split between one's lived identity and a ritual, performative identity. When the Muslim, for example, performs an instance of the *salat*, or the Catholic attends Mass, or the Buddhist spins the prayer wheel, s/he is in a different state of consciousness, a place of an 'intensification of emotion' (Davies 2011: 38–40), or performing a different aspect of their identity than when, say, s/he purchases produce from the market. It is 'difficult to do justice to the way people feel and think when they are performing rituals' but it is fair to assume that there is a ritual identity which one 'enters' through the performance of the ritual itself (Davies and Drury 1997: 2–3; cf. Rappaport 2008: 72, 219). Rituals – be they worship or prayer or whatever – function as forms, patterns, of meaning-making and acts of identity centring (Davies and Drury 1997: 172). This occurs both at the individual and group levels as rituals bond core values of the group 'with its preferred emotions in response to life's reciprocal obligations and opportunities', by fostering identity through the giving of meaning and 'hope to life' (Davies 2011: 37; cf. Nussbaum 2013).

Though ritual introduces the potential threat of identity fissure, it acts as a kind of firewall against the assault of meaninglessness and other forms of 'identity depletion' (Davies 2011: ch. 3) while providing a communication system 'outside' a grammar of discursive articulation. As Davies enigmatically puts it, 'When philosophy fails ritual may succeed' (2002a: 15). In this sense, his approach evokes E. B. Tylor's division of ritual into performative and communicative functions (see Tylor 1958), although Davies' concern for the embodied aspect of human experience makes for a more subtle treatment. It also allows consideration of the participatory in ritual: the sense in which it embodies values and fosters a sense of what Victor Turner called *communitas* while providing an environment wherein potential fissures of identity are overcome, or, perhaps better stated, negotiated through *habitus* (Davies 2002a: 112, 124).

According to d'Aquili, ritual may be one of the few means available to humanity which 'solve[s] the ultimate problems and paradoxes of human existence' (d'Aquili et. al. 1979: 179). d'Aquili's proclamation may be a verging on hyperbole, but it also evokes more subtle analyses that present ritual in relation to the problem of the fragmented self, or, as Davies puts it, the 'flux-confronted-self', discussed earlier. His approach to ritual as an integrating medium is illuminated further when placed in conversation with the work of Paul Ricoeur. In his 1995 work, *Oneself as Another*, Ricoeur ponders the question of personal identity by first articulating *identity as sameness* and then *identity as selfhood* (Ricoeur 1995: 113–118). The latter explains how there can be an identity over time in the realms of promise making, for example. He concludes that 'I am the same person who made the promise 20 years ago who is now bound to keep it, even though there are few similarities (identity-sameness) left' (Reagan 1996: 50). Davies sees within a symbolic system a power that sustains identity as 'derived from the sense of time generated by ritual' (Davies 2002a: 187). It is within the 'ritual generation of time' (Davies 2002a: 184) where there is a 'transvaluation of time' (Davies 2002a: 192), and the fragmented self can be relocated into a whole *in time*. In other words, it is more than time that is out of joint. Ritual narrates the fragmented self into a meaningful whole even as it harmonizes the disjointed hours of lived experience. In this respect, Davies goes on to introduce the work of Nicolas Berdyaev, who 'affirmed the present as a time of spiritual awareness combining a desire to disintegrate the distinctions between past, present and future' so as to live what Berdyaev calls an 'eternal and integral present' (2002a: 198; cf. Berdyaev 1996). According to Davies' argument, the 'flux-confronted-self' is thus swept up into a transcendental consistency when engaged in ritual performances.

The ritual performance represents a group's participation in its narrated self and its related forms of 'myth' and 'history' amidst competing myths and histories. Davies sees myth and history as issues which must be taken together (see Davies and Drury 1997: 33 and more generally 33–62). By means of myth and history 'the world is made less strange, and a degree of order and certainty is brought to what otherwise might be seen as chaotic and dangerous' (Davies and Drury 1997: 33). Myth allows a 'picture of reality' to 'interpret the complexity of life' (Davies and Drury 1997: 33), and enshrine cultural values (Davies and Drury 1997: 58). This 'picture of reality' has been understood by Davies as 'sacred narrations' (Davies 2011: 42); narrations which 'compress complex ideas into easily remembered storylines and poignant symbols and motifs that become a paradigm, a model of and for' a view of the world (Davies 2011: 42). Davies is here following a tradition ranging from Victor Turner's 'root paradigm' (Turner 1974: 68), Rodney Needham's 'paradigmatic scene' (Needham 1982: 89), Robert Alter's 'type-scene' (Alter 2011: 50–51; cf. Arend 1933), and Ronald de Sousa's concept of 'paradigm scenarios' (de Sousa 1990: 182). Paradigmatic scenes, then, are viewed as 'commentaries upon life', which exhort while also 'judging and adding significant dimensions to the everyday life world' (Davies 2011: 240).

The late Peter Goldie suggested that though a 'narrative self' may be an inappropriate description of the identity process, a *narrative sense of self* is at the heart of meaning-making and identity (Goldie 2012; Brooks 2011). This narrative sense of self is funded by 'paradigmatic scenes' which are in themselves explanatory systems which can come into contact and competition with other explanatory systems (Davies 1984: 7; cf. Davies 2009a, 2009b). Constructions (Chalmers 2012), or, at least, explanations, of the world can trouble the poles of power's distribution. It is through the will to narrate oneself, and the grounding of one's ritual identity within the *mythos* of 'God', that the morality of the 'ordinary' is re-evaluated by the dynamics of the super-plausible.

To return to *Den brysomme mannen*, Andreas became 'bothersome' to the policing of the 'ordinary' at the level of his 'basic uneasiness about life'. His suspicion of the historicity, as it were, of the 'ordinary' as abnormal threatened the myth of the 'ordinary' at its core. The dimension of the super-plausible, the 'house', introduces a new calculus of valuation where the narrated sense of self is reintroduced as differentiated from colonial namings and narrations. The sheer absurdity and assertion of the 'ordinary' as meaningful – illustrated beautifully in Don Hertzfeldt's film, *The Meaningful Life* (2005) – is threatened by the super-plausible. The response of the 'ordinary' to this threat, as with the case of Andreas, leads to a form of marginalization manifested in exile or death. But even here, as we shall explore in the next section, power's punishments are met with the potentiality of subversion – or, what Régis Debray has described as the tendency 'to "positivize" extreme distress' through inverting its apparent meaning, thereby affirming an altogether different one (Debray 2004: 105).

Death, embodiment, and the body techniques of resilience

A significant amount of Davies' work has revolved around a bundle of issues related to death and dying (see 'Bibliography of published work by Douglas Davies' below). The study of death, particularly within the last decade of the twentieth century, 'has witnessed a quiet revolution' to which Davies' work has been a significant contribution (Bradbury 1999: 1). This contrasts with the so-called culture of avoidance from the 1940s through the later 1970s (see Jalland 2010: 11). Kellehear has warned that studying death 'is like gazing into a reflecting pool' where a purported sociology of death can mask auto-biography writ large (2007: 1; cf. Clark 1993; Kearl 1989: ix). Of particular interest in death studies, however, is the way in which death is represented 'as a result of social exchange' (Bradbury 1999: 188) – that negotiation of the living with the dying and the dying with death. Bradbury states further that there is a 'symbolism to gather by the armful if we only know where to look' (Bradbury 1999: 196). Somewhat related are Kearl's comments on the social functions of death (1989: 86–93). Expressions of grief or hope or consolation are 'mediated by culture' (Jalland 2010: 3), as are the 'meanings of our mortality' which are 'determined by a highly complex and changing social history' (Jalland 2010: 1; cf. Kearl 1989: 15). The 'facts of medieval death', for example, are 'Christian facts' (Binski 1996: 9), as the social imaginary of medieval Europe was, by and large, brushed with Christian colours. Images and depictions of the 'good death' as illustrated in the late fifteenth century *Ars moriendi* reveal how the 'good' is both socially contingent as well as impinging upon lived practice as framed by a Christian symbolic system (cf. Binski 1996). This example, however, could be charted across notions of *Romana mors* (a Roman death) and ideal types of 'Dying a Roman Death' (Edwards 2007: 1–8; cf. chs. 5 and 6), or warrior identities in Norse mythologies reinforced by views of the afterlife. Davies sees 'views of death rites as an adaptation to the fact of death, an adaptation underlying not only the major world religions but also local religious practice' (2002c: 1).

Early in his doctoral work, Davies, following Dilthey and Berger, saw 'death as a major force acting upon the construction of religious belief' (Davies 1984: 7). Other 'enduring themes' of his work have dealt with the 'human embodiment of cultural values' (Davies 2011: v), and emotions as 'focused feeling states of limited yet intense duration' (Davies 2011: 4). These 'moods of embodiment' imbue a sense of reality to that which is being communicated (Davies 2002a: 15), a 'sensed awareness of bodily life' as well as introducing a dynamic dimension of 'felt experience to formal classifications of the world and boundaries' (Davies 2002a: 97). Combining these themes, particularly with respect to how differing religious traditions shape 'certain patterns of emotion' (Davies 2011: 1), there is a potential to see approaches to death and death itself as not only religious acts but political ones as well (Kellehear 2007: 5). The capacity of 'religion' to 'explain and contain' – to manage – 'negative emotions' which may arise around death provides a fruitful field of comparative study where 'moral-somatics' are seen as a basis for human identity (Davies 2011: 211). Death 'is part of the environment to which all humans need to adapt' (2002c: 1). And, as with Foucault's notion of death as an opportunity for the transcendence of the 'dull monotony of life' in order to take on true subjectivity and individuality (see Miller 2000), Davies introduces the moral and somatic entanglement of the rituals of death as a site of complex contest.

In this sense, the body becomes 'a kind of natural symbol' (Davies 2002a: 35), and actions of the body 'a form of belief' (Davies 2002a: 41; cf. Brown 1988). Davies sees embodiment theory as a 'means of emphasizing the power of behaviour, especially in ritual contexts, to enshrine and express belief at one and the same time' (2002a: 41). The threat of death, or what Achilles Mbembe (2003) has termed the 'necropolitical actions of sovereign entities', can operate as an enforcer of 'social order' and the 'ultimate mechanism by which societies can establish the conformity of the populace' (Kearl 1989: 87). The body as symbol, however, can enact 'words against death' (Davies 2002c: 1), potentially even challenging the sovereignty of state-sponsored necropolitics by dying an 'offending death' (Davies 2002c: 211–213; and Davies 2001). An 'offending death' stirs 'demonstration against people in authority who are blamed for causing the death' itself or the circumstances which allowed the death of the innocent to occur and 'from whom some form of response and reparation is sought' (Davies 2002c: 211). As such, the body techniques and focused emotional states enforced by the 'ordinary' can be made fragile by those exiles and deaths informed by the super-plausible (cf. Mauss 1973). Sociologist Marcel Mauss recognized that there is no natural body behaviour – every bodily action reveals an imprint of learning or formation. Mauss, however, does not develop the political dynamic or potential wrapped up in such 'techniques'. Davies' work on 'offending death' and 'words against death' introduces a fascinating extension of Mauss in this respect. (Related and worth pursuing in their own right are religious acts of self-immolation within the political contexts of Mahayana Buddhism and Hinduism [Benn 2007; cf. Biggs 2005; on the role of the body within religious studies, see Coakley 1997].)

The power of the 'ordinary' exerted itself upon Andreas in two extreme ways within *Den brysomme mannen*. First, it robbed from Andreas the possibility of escape through suicide by forcing him back into the 'ordinary'. Second, the threat of the super-plausible was met by the policing of the 'ordinary', exiling Andreas into the wilderness of the Real. Precisely where the 'ordinary' was threatened – viz., at the level of alternative meaning-making – Andreas was thrust into the chaotic formlessness of the Real. The meaning informed by the super-plausible was marginalized through the exiling of Andreas into the formlessness of the Real. Yet even in this exilic state, the 'ordinary' cannot pretend to be the Real. Even in the ordinary's robbery of Andreas' defiance, his turned collar to the frigid winds of the desert of the Real are the embodiment of his 'words against death'.

Where *Den brysomme mannen* succeeds in demonstrating the remarkable power of the 'ordinary', Davies' notion of 'offending death' opens up possibilities for reading agency into those whom the 'ordinary' has marginalized through exile or death (cf. Thate 2013). If the actions of the body can be seen as 'forms of belief' (Davies 2002a: 41), the perception of actions done to the body might also be viewed as forms of belief informed by the super-plausible. The body as symbol, therefore, can enact not only 'words against death' (Davies 2002c: 1), but words against death and exile as the 'ordinary's' final marginalization of the self. In other words, necropolitics and the governmentality of death no longer have the final word. The religious and the political here are fused. Davies was right to read 'death as a major force acting upon the construction of religious belief' (Davies 1984: 7) and the embodiment of those beliefs. We could fruitfully extend his analysis to the treatment of religious beliefs and bodies as sources for and sites of subversive political acts.

Concluding reflections

In this chapter, I have attempted to engage with a set of three clusters of ideas anchored in the expansive publications of Douglas Davies. My aim has been to extend some major themes of his work – *meaning-making*, *identity* and *death* – into a conversation on the subversive potential of the study of religion. Other themes could have been usefully included (e.g. emotions), and the three themes covered could have been covered more thoroughly. These ranging reflections, however, are intended to be both entrée to and experimentation with the creative and effective force of his 'inquisitive presence' within the field of the study of religion these many years. At a time when the discipline of Religious Studies is becoming more and more introspective (and not a little defensive when it comes to funding decisions within University administration), appropriating the effusive and even prescient output of Douglas Davies along those points of convergence between the 'religious' and the 'political' may well model a provocative and fruitful way forward.

References

Agamben, G. (1999) *The Coming Community*. Translated by Michael Hardt. Minneapolis: University of Minnesota Press.

Alter, R. (2011 [1981]) *The Art of Biblical Narrative*. 2nd edition. New York: Basic Books.

Arend, W. (1933) *Die typischen Scenen bei Homer*. Berlin: Weidmannsche Buchhandlung.

Bailly, L. (2009) *Lacan: A Beginner's Guide*. New York: Oneworld.

Bell, C. (2009) *Ritual Theory, Ritual Practice*. Oxford: Oxford University Press.

Benn, J. (2007) *Burning for the Buddha: Self-Immolation in Chinese Buddhism*. Honolulu: University of Hawaii Press.

Berger, P. L. and Luckmann, T. (1967) *The Social Construction of Reality: A Treatise in the Sociology of Knowledge*. New York: Anchor.

Berger, P. (1990 [1967]) *The Sacred Canopy: Elements of a Sociological Theory of Religion*. New York: Anchor.

Berdyaev, N. (1996) *The Meaning of History*. London: Geoffrey Bles.

Biggs, M. (2005) 'Dying without killing: self-immolations, 1963–2002', in D. Gambetta (ed.) *Making Sense of Suicide Missions*. Oxford: Oxford University Press, pp. 173–208.

Binski, P. (1996) *Medieval Death: Ritual and Representation*. Ithaca: Cornell University Press.

Bradbury, M. (1999) *Representations of Death: A Social Psychological Perspective*. London: Routledge.

Brooks, P. (2011) *Enigmas of Identity*. Princeton: Princeton University Press.

Brown, P. (1988) *The Body and Society: Men, Women, and Sexual Renunciation in Early Christianity*. New York: Columbia University Press.

Chalmers, D. J. (2012) *Constructing the World*. Oxford: Oxford University Press.

Clark, D. (ed.) (1993) *The Sociology of Death*. Oxford: Blackwell.

Coakley, S. (ed.) (1997) *Religion and the Body*. Cambridge Studies in Religious Traditions 8. Cambridge: Cambridge University Press.

d'Aquili, D. G., Laughlin Jr., D. D. and McManus, J. (1979) *The Spectrum of Ritual*. New York: Columbia University Press.

de Certeau, M. (2011) *The Practice of Everyday Life*. Berkeley: University of California Press.

de la Durantaye, L. (2009) *Giorgio Agamben: A Critical Introduction*. Stanford: Stanford University Press.

Debray, R. (2004 [2001]) *God: An Itinerary*. Translated by Jeffrey Mehlman. New York: Verso.

de Lubac, H. (1967) *The Mystery of the Supernatural*. Translated by R. Sheed. London: Geoffrey Chapman.

de Sousa, R. (1990) *The Rational of Emotion*. Cambridge: MIT Press.

Durkheim E. and Mauss, M. (1967) *Primitive Classifications*. Translated by R. Needham. Chicago: University of Chicago Press.

Edwards, C. (2007) *Death in Ancient Rome*. New Haven: Yale University Press.

Geertz, C. (1973) *The Interpretation of Cultures*. New York: Basic Books.

Goldie, P. (2012) *The Mess Inside: Narrative, Emotion, and the Mind*. Oxford: Oxford University Press.

Hitchens, C. (2009) *God is Not Great: How Religion Poisons Everything*. New York: Twelve.

Jalland, P. (2010) *Death in War and Peace: Loss and Grief in England, 1914–1970*. Oxford: Oxford University Press.

Kearl, M. C. (1989) *Endings: A Sociology of Death*. Oxford: Oxford University Press.

Kellehear, A. (2007) *A Social History of Dying*. Cambridge: Cambridge University Press.

Lacan, J. (2007 [1966]) *Écrits*. Translated by B. Fink. New York: W. W. Norton.

Lincoln, B. (1999) *Theorizing Myth: Narrative, Ideology, and Scholarship*. Chicago: University of Chicago Press.

Mauss, M. (1973) 'Techniques of the body', *Economy and Society* 2: 70–88.

Mbembe, A. (2003) 'Necropolitics', *Public Culture*, 15(1): 11–40.

Miller, J. (2000) *The Passion of Michel Foucault*. Cambridge, MA: Harvard University Press.

Mol, H. (1977) *Identity and the Sacred: A Sketch for a New Social-Scientific Theory of Religion*. New York: Free Press.

Mol, H. (ed.) (1978) *Identity and Religion*. Thousand Oaks: Sage Publications.

Myerhoff, B. (1982) 'Rites of passage: process and paradox', in V. Turner *Celebration: Studies in Festivity and Ritual*. Washington, D.C.: Smithsonian Institution Press.

Needham, R. (1972) *Belief, Language and Experience*. Oxford: Blackwell.

Needham, R. (1982) *Circumstantial Deliveries*. Berkeley: University of California Press.

Nussbaum, M. C. (2013) *Political Emotions: Why Love Matters for Justice*. Belknapp Press; Cambridge, MA: Harvard University Press.

Ogden, C. K. and Richards, I. A. (1989) *The Meaning of Meaning*. New York: Mariner Books.

Pascal, B. (1958) *Pensées*. Translated by W. F. Trotter. New York: Dutton.

Prothero, S. (2010) *God is Not One: The Eight Rival Religions that Run the World and Why their Differences Matter*. New York: HarperOne.

Rappaport, R. A. (2008 [1999]) *Ritual and Religion in the Making of Humanity*. Cambridge: Cambridge University Press.

Reagan, C. E. (1996) *Paul Ricoeur: His Life and His Work*. Chicago: University of Chicago Press.

Ricoeur, P. (1995) *Oneself as Another*. Translated by K. Blamey. Chicago: University of Chicago Press.Rorty, R. (1982) *Consequences of Pragmatism*. Minneapolis: University of Minnesota Press.

Rorty, R. (2009 [1979]). *Philosophy and the Mirror of Nature*. Princeton: Princeton University Press.

Sayer, A. (2011) *Why Things Matter to People: Social Science Values and Ethical Life*. Cambridge, MA: Cambridge University Press.

Smith, W. C. (1976) 'Objectivity and the human sciences', in W. G. Oxtoby (ed.) *Religious Diversity*. New York: Harper and Row, pp. 81–102.

Sperber, D. (1975) *Rethinking Symbolism*. Cambridge: Cambridge University Press.

Steiner, G. (2003) *Lessons of the Masters*. The Charles Eliot Norton Lectures 2001–2002. Cambridge, MA: Harvard University Press.

Taylor, C. (1989) *Sources of the Self: The Making of the Modern Identity*. Cambridge, MA: Harvard University Press.

Thate, M. J. (2013) 'Identity construction as resistance: figuring hegemony, biopolitics, and martyrdom as an approach to Clement of Alexandria', in M. Vinzent (ed.) *Studia Patristica 66*. XIV. 18 vols. Leuven: Peeters, 14: 69–86.

Tillich, P. (1964) *Theology of Culture*. Oxford: Oxford University Press.

Turner, V. (1974) *Dramas, Fields and Metaphors*. Ithaca: Cornell University Press.

Tylor, E. B. (1958 [1871]) *Religion in Primitive Culture*. Part Two of *Primitive culture*. New York: Harper and Brothers.

Weber, M. (1965 [1922]) *The Sociology of Religion*. London: Metheun.

Žižek, S. (2007) *How to Read Lacan*. New York: W. W. Norton.

Žižek, S. (2012) *Less than Nothing: Hegel and the Shadow of Dialectical Materialism*. New York: Verso.

Bibliography of published work by Douglas Davies

The list that follows includes the items referenced in the foregoing essay but also adds further publications in order to furnish a comprehensive bibliography of Douglas Davies' published work from the beginning of his career up to 2015, when this volume was completed.

Books

Davies, D. (2015) *Mors Britannica: Life Style and Death Style in Britain Today*. Oxford: Oxford University Press.

Davies, D. and Warne, N. A. (eds) (2013) *Emotions and Religious Dynamics*. Farnham: Ashgate.

Davies, D. and Park, C. W. (eds) (2012a) *Emotion, Identity and Death: Mortality Across Disciplines*. Farnham: Ashgate.

Davies, D. and Rumble, H. (2012b) *Natural Burial: Traditional-Secular Spiritualities and Funeral Innovation*. London: Continuum.

Davies, D. (2011) *Emotion, Identity and Religion: Hope, Reciprocity, and Otherness*. Oxford: Oxford University Press.

Davies, D. (2010) *Joseph Smith, Jesus, and Satanic Opposition: Atonement, Evil and the Mormon Vision*. Farnham: Ashgate.

Davies, D. (2008) *The Theology of Death*. London: T&T Clark.

Davies, D. and Guest, M. (2007) *Bishops, Wives and Children: Spiritual Capital across the Generations*. Aldershot: Ashgate.

Davies, D. with Mates, L. (eds) (2005) *Encyclopedia of Cremation*. Aldershot: Ashgate.

Cameron, H., Davies, D. F. and Richter, P. (eds) (2005) *Studying Local Churches: A Handbook*. London: SCM Press.

Davies, D. (2004) *A Brief History of Death*. Oxford: Blackwell.

Davies, D. (2003) *An Introduction to Mormonism*. Cambridge: Cambridge University Press.

Davies, D. (2002) *Anthropology and Theology*. Oxford: Berg.

Davies, D. (2000a) *The Mormon Culture of Salvation: Force, Grace and Glory*. Aldershot: Ashgate.

Davies, D. (2000b) *Private Passions: Betraying Discipleship on the Journey to Jerusalem*. Norwich: Canterbury Press.

Davies, D. with Drury, C. (eds) (1997a) *Themes and Issues in Christianity*. London: Cassell.

Davies, D. (1997c) *Death, Ritual and Belief: The Rhetoric of Funerary Rites*. London: Cassell.

Davies, D. (ed.) (1996) *Mormon Identities in Transition*. London: Cassell.

Davies, D. and Shaw, A. (1995a) *Reusing Old Graves: A Report on Popular British Attitudes*. Crayford: Shaw & Sons.

Davies, D. (1995b) *British Crematoria in Public Profile*. Maidstone: Cremation Society of Great Britain.

Davies, D. (1991) *F.B. Jevons: An Evolutionary Realist*. New York: Edwin Mellon.

Davies. D. (1990) *Cremation Today and Tomorrow*. Nottingham: Grove Books.

Davies, D. (1987) *Mormon Spirituality: Latter Day Saints in Wales and Zion*. Nottingham: University of Nottingham Press.

Davies, D. (1986) *Studies in Pastoral Theology and Social Anthropology*. Birmingham: University of Birmingham Press.

Davies, D. (1984) *Meaning and Salvation in Religious Studies*. Leiden: Brill.

Essays and articles

Davies, D. (2013) 'Thriving through myth', in C. H. Cooke (ed.) *Spirituality, Theology and Mental Health*. London: SCM Press, pp. 160–177.

Davies, D. and Northam-Jones, D. (2012a) 'The sea of faith: exemplifying transformed retention', in M. Guest and E. Arweck (eds) *Religion and Knowledge, Sociological Perspectives*. Farnham: Ashgate, pp. 227–246.

Davies, D. (2012b) 'Changing British ritualization', in L. Woodhead and R. Catto (eds) *Religion and Change in Modern Britain*. London: Routledge, pp. 203–218.

Davies, D. (2010) 'Geographies of the spirit world', in J. Hockey, C. Komaromy, and K. Woodthorpe (eds) *The Matter of Death, Space, Place and Materiality*. London: Palgrave Macmillan, pp. 208–222.

Davies, D. (2009a) 'Memorable relations and paradigmatic scenes' *DISKUS* 10. Available at: http://basr.ac.uk/diskus_old/diskus10/davies.htm (accessed 22/10/16).

Davies, D. (2009a) 'Christ in Mormonism', in O. Hammer (ed.) *Alternative Christs*. Cambridge: Cambridge University Press, pp. 170–189.

Davies, D. (2009b). 'Superplausibility in life and death', in Anna Davidsson Bremborg et al. (eds) *Religionssociologi i brytningstider*. Lund, Sweden: Lund University Press, pp. 13–28.

Davies, D. (2009c) 'Visions, revelations and courage', in R. L. Nelson and T. L. Givens (eds) *Joseph Smith, Jr: Reappraisal after Two Centuries*. Oxford: Oxford University Press, pp. 119–142.

Davies, D. (2009d) 'Dying the Judeo-Christian tradition', in A. Kellehear (ed.) *The Study of Dying*. Cambridge: Cambridge University Press, pp. 233–252.

Davies, D. (2008a) 'Death, immortality and Sir James Frazer', *Mortality* 13(3): 287–296.

Davies, D. (2008b) 'Resurrection and immortality of the soul', in P. C. Jupp (ed.) *Death Our Future: Christian Theology and Funeral Practice*. London: Epworth Press, pp. 82–92.

Davies, D. (2008c) 'Cultural intensification: a theory for religion', in A. Day (ed.) *Religion and the Individual*. Aldershot: Ashgate, pp. 7–18.

Davies, D. (2007a) 'Mormon history, text, colour and rites', *Journal of Religious History* 31(3): 305–315.

Davies, D. (2007b) 'Mormonism', in J. R. Lewis and O. Hammer (eds) *The Invention of Sacred Tradition*. Cambridge: Cambridge University Press, pp. 56–75.

Davies, D. (2006a) 'Inner speech and religious traditions', in J. A. Beckford and J. Wallis (eds) *Theorizing Religion*. Aldershot: Ashgate, pp. 211–223.

Davies, D. (2006) 'Changing values and reposition cremation in society', *Pharos International* 72(1): 15–16.

Davies, D. (2006b) 'Altruism, ritual, welfare and practical theology', in Anne Birgitta Yeung (ed.) *Rajojen Ylityksia*. Helsinki: Suomalainen Teologinen Kirjallisuusseura, pp. 126–140.

Davies, D. (2005a) 'Death, grief and mourning reconsidered', *Thanatological Studies* 1: 27–36.

Davies, D. (2005b) 'Welfare, spirituality and the quality of life and place', in Anders Backstrom (ed.) *Welfare and Religion*. Diakonivetenskapliga institutes: Skrifterie, 10: 8–96.

Davies, D. (2005c) 'Forms of disposal', in K. Garces-Foley (ed.) *Death and Religion in a Changing World*. New York: M.E. Sharpe, pp. 228–245.

Davies, D. (2005d) 'Anglican soteriology: incarnation, worship and the property of mercy', in R. Keller and R. L. Millett (eds) *Salvation in Christ: Comparative Christian Views*. Provo, UT: Brigham Young University Press, pp. 53–67.

Davies, D. (2004a) 'Moral somatic relationships', *Tidsskrift for Kirke Religion Samfunn* 2(17): 97–105.

Davies, D. (2004b) 'Priests, parish and people: reconceiving a relationship', in M. J. Guest, K. Tusting and L. Woodhead (eds) *Congregational Studies in the UK*. Farnham: Ashgate, pp. 153–168.

Davies, D. (2004c) 'Time, place and Morman sense of self', in S. Colemand and P. Collins (eds) *Religion, identity and change*. Farnham: Ashgate, pp. 107–118.

Davies, D. (2004d) 'Purity, spirit, and reciprocity in the acts of the apostles', in L. Lawrence and M. Aguilar (eds) *Anthropology and Biblical Studies: Avenues of Approach*. Leiden: Deo Publishing, pp. 259–280.

Davies, D. (2003a) 'The sociology of wisdom', in J. A. Beckford and J. T. Richardson (eds) *Essays in Honour of Eileen Barker*. London: Routledge, pp. 205–216.

Davies, D. (2003b) 'The sociology of holiness: the power of being good', in S. C. Barton (ed.) *Holiness Past and Present*. London: T&T Clark, pp. 48–67.

Davies, D. (2002b) 'Ritual and cremation', in *Golders Green Crematorium*.

Davies, D. (2001a) 'Health, morality and sacrifice: the sociology of disasters', in R. K. Fenn (ed.) *Sociology of religion*. Oxford: Blackwell, pp. 404–417.

Davies, D. (2001b) 'Gestus manifests habitus: dress and the Mormon', in W. S. F. Keenan (ed.) *Dressed to Impress*. Oxford: Berg, pp. 123–140.

Davies, D. (2000a) 'Health, morality and sacrifice: the sociology of disasters', in R. Fenn (ed.) *Blackwell Companion to the Sociology of Religion*. Oxford: Blackwell, pp. 404–417.

Davies, D. (2000b) 'Robert Hertz: the social triumph over death', *Mortality* 5(1): 97–102.

Davies, D. (1999a) 'The week in mourning', in T. Walter (ed.) *The Mourning for Diana*. London: Berg, pp. 3–18.

Davies, D. (1999b) 'Implicit religion and inter-faith dialogue in human perspective', *Implicit Religion* 2(1): 17–24.

Davies, D. (1998) 'Popular reaction to the death of Princess Diana', *Expository Times* 109(6): 173–176.

Davies, D. (1997b) 'Theologies of disposal' and 'contemporary belief in life after death' in P. C. Jupp and T. Rogers (eds) *Interpreting Death, Christian Theology and Pastoral Practice*. London: Cassell, pp. 131–142.

Davies, D. (1996a) 'The sacred crematorium', *Mortality* 1(1): 83–94.

Davies, D. (1996b) 'The social facts of death', in G. Howarth and P. C. Jupp (eds) *Contemporary Issues in the Sociology of Death, Dying and Disposal*. London: Macmillan, pp. 17–29.

Davies, D. (1995a) 'Rebounding vitality: resurrection and spirit in Luke-Acts', in M. D. Carroll, D. Clines and P. Davies (eds) *The Bible in Human Society*. Sheffield: Sheffield Academic Press, pp. 205–223.

Davies, D. (1995b) 'William Robertson Smith and Frank Byron Jevons: faith and evolution', in W. Johnstone (ed.) *William Robertson Smith: Essays in Reassessment*. Sheffield: Sheffield Academic Press.

Davies, D. (1995c) 'Jural and mystical authority in religious: exploring a typology', *DISKUS* 3(2): 1–12.

Davies, D. (1993a) 'The dead at the Eucharist', *Modern Churchman* XXXIV(3): 24–32.

Davies, D. (1993b) 'Spirituality, churchmanship, and English Anglican Priests', *Journal of Empirical Theology* 6(1): 5–18.

Davies, D. (1992) 'Ashes and identity', *Report of 50th Conference of British Burial and Cremation Authorities*, pp. 79–87.

Davies, D. (1991) 'Pilgrimage in Mormon culture', in M. Jha. (ed.) *Social Anthropology of Pilgrimage*. New Delhi: Inter-India Press, pp. 310–325.

Davies, D. (1990) 'Cultural images and experience of cremation', *Resurgam* 33(3).

Davies, D. (1989) 'Mormon history, identity, faith community', in E. Tonkin (ed.) *History and Ethnicity*. London: Routledge, pp. 168–182.

Davies, D. (1988) 'The evocative symbolism of trees', in D. Cosgrove and S. Daniels (eds) *The Iconography of Landscape*. Cambridge: Cambridge University Press, pp. 32–42.

Davies, D. (1986) 'Person, power, and priesthood', in J. Fuller and P. Vaughn (eds) *Working for the Kingdom*. London: SPCK, pp. 93–101.

Davies, D. (1985a) 'Interpretation of sacrifice in Leviticus', in B. Lang (ed.) *Anthropological Approaches to the Old Testament*. London: SPCK & Fortress Press, pp. 151–162.

Davies, D. (1985b) 'F.B. Jevons', in J. E. Thomas and B. Elsey (eds) *International Biography of Adult Education*. Nottingham: University of Nottingham Press, pp. 285–288.

Davies, D. (1985c) 'The charismatic ethic and the spirit of post-industrialism', in D. Martin and P. Mullen (eds) *Strange Gifts?: A Guide to Charismatic Renewal*. Oxford: Blackwell, pp. 137–150.

Davies, D. (1985d) 'Symbolic thought and religious knowledge', *British Journal of Religious Education* 7(2): 75–80.

Davies, D. (1985e) 'Natural and Christian Priesthood in folk religiosity', *Anvil* 2(1): 43–54.

Davies, D. (1983) 'Evans-Pritchard, structuralism, and anthropological hermeneutics', *Renaissance and Modern Studies* 27(1): 85–101.

Davies, D. (1982) 'Sacrifice in theology and anthropology', *Scottish Journal of Theology* 35(4): 351–358.

Davies, D. (1979) 'Models of religious communication', *Journal of Religious Studies* 6(2): 55–60.

Davies, D. (1978) 'The notion of salvation in the comparative study of religion', *Religion* 8(1): 85–100.

Davies, D. (1973) 'Aspects of latter day saint eschatology', in M. Hill (ed.) *Sociological Yearbook of Religion in Britain*. London: SCM Press, pp. 122–135.

Epilogue
A response

Douglas Davies

It is a tremendous pleasure to respond to the chapters written by friends and colleagues in this celebratory volume that followed the considerable surprise of a day shortly before Christmas 2014 when most of these authors gathered for a kind of festive seminar in London. One by one, new faces appeared, bringing their association with different parts and places of my academic life. At the end of the day, the surprise promise of an ensuing volume of chapters from these friends and a few unable to be there at that event added its own interest. So, now, in the fortieth year of my university teaching, I have the challenge of commenting on a swathe of material that touches in one way or another on aspects of my own intellectual curiosity. In doing this I will certainly not rehearse what each author has gone to the trouble of presenting to us all, and I can happily leave critical response for specialists in the many fields covered here; this – selfishly perhaps – grants me the simple freedom of pointing at signposts, reminiscing and enjoying the company of my travelling companions. I will do this in the order in which the preceding chapters appear.

Seth Kunin bridges two of my academic locations having taught the anthropology of religion with me at Nottingham University for some years and, latterly, being one of the university officers here at Durham where he did much to forge an excellent arts and humanities faculty. Seth's American and British anthropological training and his intellectual interest in structuralism – embracing textual analysis of the Hebrew Bible, Rabbinic scholarship and ethnographic work on Crypto-Judaism – has provided an unusually strong foundation for a critical analysis of the American cultural base framing the text of the Book of Mormon. His chapter makes a most distinctive contribution to studies of this text by deploying a focused structuralist model to reveal a clearly American Scripture.

James Crossley, one of my former undergraduates at Nottingham's Department of Theology, encourages my own long-held sense of the importance of conceptual affinity by integrating specific concepts of money and death as expressions of cultural value and using them to analyse film, specifically Leone's American westerns. I recall my personal sense of amazement, that odd emotion aligned with 'having an idea', when I first saw how a money-motif runs through the Acts of the Apostles and could be used as one interpretative device for understanding the early Christian sect. To see James take this and relate it to 'words against death' and 'rebounding vitality' as part of an analysis of film is not only pleasing in a conceptual sense but now also sets me the task of watching the films he covers, and watching them in a way I have never watched any film before. That is the perfect circle of undergraduate to academic and of that academic to a colleague.

Grant Underwood comes to his chapter with a historian's training and full alertness to the growing contemporary Latter-day Saint (LDS) engagement with early Christian doctrinal debates. He extends an invitation to theologically minded readers to engage in some comparative theological studies of divine identities and their early cultural-philosophical matrix. In this he highlights scenes that demand such illumination if any serious cross-cultural engagement is to occur with the past and between diverse traditions of the present day. It is good to see my former Durham colleague David Brown and my present colleague Lewis Ayres' theological scholarship cited here. In reading Grant's chapter, the voice of my own Durham Patristics teacher of some forty years ago, Canon Professor H. E. W. Turner, kept its echoing reminder of Anglicanism's bridge-base in the Fathers as the English Reformation sought to make sense of the Bible amidst its own piety. Mormons, too, have their patterns of piety and, amidst these, Grant stands out as an open-hearted friend. I recall us once, in Utah, looking at a large painting of the return of the prodigal son. Doubtless, Grant had his own inner thoughts on this, mine included Karl Barth's 'Way of the Son of God into the Far Country' – and its ensuing Homecoming. Of such moments are bonds created and frames made, not least when turning from depicted narrative to the propositional analysis of 'Mormonism and the Fourth-Century Search for a Christian Doctrine of God'.

Christian Karner and David Parker's chapter stands as a firm reminder of that double locality within which residents seek to survive and, if possible, to flourish, while also being a focus for political forces and their exercise of control. Their exploration of the 'unsatisfactoriness of life' by means of long-term qualitative research captured in a locality study speaks its own validation. Time well spent in their Birmingham locale has revealed some of the dynamics of social change, including shifts in power-drives among religious groups. I have appreciated how some of my own rather theoretical generalizations on emotions, identity and religious groups, as well as the 'words against death' motif, have been given some cash value here. To see how Christian, as an insightfully creative former Nottingham student, has developed such a substantial academic career and a valuable research venture with David Parker brings its own pleasure. His reminder of my years spent on the St. Martin's Trust which encouraged some slight knowledge at least of parts of Birmingham remains as a clear spin-off of his locality study ethics.

Anders Bäckström and his chapter take us back a quarter of a century to student exchange between Nottingham and Uppsala Universities and on to research collaboration and friendship. This chapter discloses something of my colleague's encompassing grasp of the interplay of social processes and institutions and of how to integrate distinctive aspects of life – and here of death – within a sociological framework. We have, on numerous occasions, pondered the notion of 'quality time and quality places', and it is interesting to see that integration played out here. As Professor in the Sociology of Religion at Uppsala, Anders became highly influential in devising, obtaining funding for, and inviting research collaboration among European scholars. He was instrumental in drawing me into these networks where I came to be highly appreciative not only of the kind of theory-driven empirical work reflected in his chapter but also of the comparative base driven by cross-European case studies. To have been involved, for example, in sociological-theological issues surrounding the disestablishment of the Church of Sweden allowed me to begin to grasp something of the Swedish Lutheran world, itself so like and yet unlike the Church of England. Of the many events we have shared, as friends as well as academics, none left an impression stronger than a small informal party at the Bäckström home the year I received a doctorate, *honoris causa*, from Uppsala University – itself doubtless Anders' doing. Amidst this honour and its wonderful ritual celebrations, I was feeling pretty sorry for myself, being painfully plagued by quite severe shingles of the head, with one eye practically useless. Then, as we sat and chatted, one of Anders' sons appeared with a group of friends, all members of Sweden's most famous Orphei Drängar choir, and simply sang for me. If my ritual interests had not already been inspired enough by Uppsala's ceremonial life, this moment touched me by its complete unexpectedness, its echo of Wales, and its simple kindness.

Valerie DeMarinis is another Uppsala colleague, one who has also played a significant part in our Durham hosted project on 'Identity, Emotions, and Religious Communities' (Davies and Warne 2013). As an anthropologist with a deep interest in psychological processes and a firm sense of the power of ritual action, her chapter brings to sharp focus not only the all too human engagement with meaning-making, something that social scientists may well take too much for granted, but also the profound clinical relevance of such meaning-making for our existential well-being. Here a certain interdisciplinarity flows between psychology, clinical relationships, and the sociology and anthropology of religion. Its framing of ritual creates its own discipline of care for individuals whose life-circumstances may not guarantee coherence. Valerie's accounts of the two case studies that involved an invention of tradition highlight the deep personal dynamics of an individual life framed by the widely shared human capacity for effective ritual action. She shows us at a personal, microcosmic level, the power of myth-making for personal survival. To see some of my work used in relation to clinical psychology is gratifying not only because of the value I found both in the psychology I did as part of my original anthropology degree and in Michael Argyle's lectures on the psychology of religion I attended while engaged in my first research, but also because I have always found it intellectually difficult to follow Durkheim in a methodological split between psychological and anthropological-sociological domains.

Charles Watkins, in his reflection upon the Cedar of Lebanon, offers a chapter that I, for one, will reread many times. It brings a knowledge of this particular tree in which historical, mythical, biblical, botanical and geographical elements fuse with British locales. It brings alive its own distinctive form of cultural reflection, engendering an aesthetic excitement by describing the interplay of textual and literal travel with a sense of homeland. Whether on country-house estates or in civic cemeteries, we find a descriptive depth brought to the often relatively threadbare notion of 'reflexivity': a single phenomenon comes to bespeak British 'values' generated over time as the genius of distant places comes to local habitation. The illustrations serve as their own tutors to our taste and remind us that trees, like friendship, take time. I recall first meeting Charles when he came as a young lecturer to Nottingham University's geography department in the early 1990s and was, following an interview lunch that included myself, appointed as a resident tutor at Hugh Stewart Hall. There followed decades of dining and not a little celebration, including our membership of that university's Philoenic Society whose interest in the vine, rather than in Cedars, ranged far and wide. Without our conversations I would not have written my essay 'The Evocative Symbolism of Trees' (Davies 1988) and, in an undercurrent fashion, might not have been so predisposed to ponder Woodland Burial. Not only has Charles become a prolific scholar and leading figure in numerous British cultural circles, but he also succeeded me as warden of Nottingham University's Derby Hall, which he led in a most creative and convivial fashion. His allusion to my affinity with trees in general and to the *Araucaria* in particular takes me back to schooldays and to a deep interest in botany: it also reminds me of the large Monkey Puzzle planted at Hugh Stewart Hall, and to the four I currently have at home, all bought on the same day, and each of radically different height according to their positions in the garden and in pots. That says much about potential and context and, in retrospect, signals my good fortune in sharing with Charles something of a golden era of shared academic community within Nottingham's Halls that were far more than a 'system' of residence.

James Beckford's recollection of our first meeting at Bryan Wilson's seminars at All Souls College is clearly marked in my own memory, including post-seminar conviviality when my own academic milk-teeth were just about giving way to a firmer bite. Many moons have passed since then, with Jim's firm sociological concerns reminding numerous folk interested in the sociology of religion not to forget the wider social matrix, dynamics and change in their own overconcern with 'religion'. His chapter's concern with the interplay of numerous processes of development presents a critique of scholarship that might treat religious phenomena in a narrow fashion and as isolated from their broader spatial and temporal contexts.

The heeding of such advice would do much to ensure that the 'sociology of religion' might interest sociologists at large rather than appeal to a niche market. When Jim emphasizes that he is not documenting a 'resurgence' of religion – something that church leaders might often like to see – but is, rather, calling us to explore 'paradoxical aspects of rationalisation in late modernity', this is a clear invitation to avoid ready to hand explanations. With that in mind, I am particularly pleased to see him citing my notion of 'the charismatic ethic' which sought to typify 'the spirit of Post-industrialism' (Davies 1984). Its obvious echoing of Weber was, in its 1984 day, an attempt to set aspects of British charismatic behaviour in just such a wider social context. So, too, with Jim's pinpointing of my speculation over a Mormon ethic grounded in communal identity and in a theological-ethical dissonance between guaranteed endowments and personal fulfilment of obligation. These issues reflect my deep-seated interest in classical reciprocity theory – a point at which Weber's rationality and van Gennep's interpersonal pragmatics collide or potentially pervade each other. In conclusion, I should say that at our celebration seminar in London in 2014 I was entirely surprised to find that Jim had gone back and read my doctoral dissertation on *Meaning and Salvation in Religious Studies* and then engaged me in an utterly stimulating conversation, not least because he found themes in it of which I am not sure I was fully aware at the original time of writing.

David Martin's chapter also transports me to Wilson's All Souls seminars at which David made frequent appearances, always bringing with him broad sweeps of thought and diverse imagery – with musical expression seldom far away. This chapter is no exception, capturing much of his own wide intellectual interests so fully described in his many books and lectures. I found its focus of 'power' especially interesting because I had only just completed a book in which power, conceived in terms of social forces, manifested in diverse British elites and hierarchies, including the National Health Service as a potential contender with the Church of England as the medium for core cultural values of health and well-being, always recalling that, conceptually speaking, 'health' and 'salvation' lie close together. Drawing on my obedience to an early Durham teacher, the psychologist F.V. Smith, who advocated interdisciplinary promiscuity, I was also interested in David's engagement with 'power', having for years been impressed by how Gerardus van der Leeuw set out his phenomenology of religion as a phenomenology of power. Not only that, but when David turns to the notion of grace as 'a mixed case' encompassing divine mercy and the graciousness of monarchs, he touches directly on two issues that intrigue me. The first concerns the process whereby the drive for meaning becomes the need for salvation. That concern, especially when allied with David's emphasis upon narrative and charisma, also took me back a long way to thinking about the pool of potential orientations that Christianity in its many streams has made available to prophetic candidates a plenty. The second issue moves me much more in an anthropological direction to Rodney Needham's use of the dual sovereignty idiom to describe the complementarity between jural and mystical forms of authority, a perspective that offers a different idiom from that of grace as a mixed case. It also allows its own complementary approach to what David admirably describes in his way as the difference between the 'time-bombs secreted in the New Testament' – humility etc. – and elements so easily appropriated by dominant groups. There is so much one could say about these issues as, also, of the Pentecostal potential for generating a sense of authentic selfhood in erstwhile complex contexts. Indeed, one wonders to what extent contemporary discussion of radicalization of some Muslim youths could well be seen as a similar form of authentication. It cannot be accidental that today's popular references to 'cult' when describing this radicalization resembles the cult idiom deployed for the apparently disaffected youth of otherwise 'normal' American families in the 1960–1970s. Lest I extend comments on this chapter too far, let me highlight three cameos of many Martin experiences. One was of him as the external examiner of my old Oxford BLitt dissertation on *The Mormons of Merthyr-Tydfil*, a title he reminds me of from time to time, when the internal examiner, anthropologist Godfrey Lienhardt, was called from the viva, wearing gown and hood, to meet a visiting Dinka dignitary – David's face was a picture. The second occurred while he was delivering the Firth Lectures at Nottingham University, and called to meet me at Hugh Stewart Hall, but just as the delightful Georgian Senior Common Room was entirely dark for a slide-show dealing with wine and food. He peered in and left, I followed: he was amazed that 'the higher Hedonism had reached Nottingham!' My final cameo speaks the last word, for it was at Bryan Wilson's funeral in All Souls Chapel, 2004, when Eileen Barker, Karel Dobbelaere, Jim Beckford and I spoke appropriately of our various relationships with him. It was David who brought these good words to a close, speaking of his old friend at what was, avowedly, a secular ceremony, reminding us of the original function of that College as a place of prayer for the departed, and doing so in cordially generous words that flowed – stylistically though not in content – as if recited from The Book of Common Prayer.

Matthew Wood, one of my Nottingham doctoral postgraduates, has taken me back once more to that sense of haunting inevitably elicited by a book written some 30 years ago, itself the outcome of a doctoral thesis completed in 1979. Though given one devastating review at the time, I had confidence in it then, because the original doctoral examiners, Godfrey Lienhardt as an anthropologist and Trevor Ling as a historian and comparative religion scholar, had given it very solid acceptance. I have confidence in it still for pinpointing issues of meaning, embodiment and identity, and of the limits of reductionism given the creative capacity of individuals. Perhaps it was silly to make too much of the notion of the 'social person', but the motivation for avoiding nihilistic individualism on the one hand and an overly socialized self on the other remains valid.

One methodological conviction underlying that study has only deepened with the decades, viz., the advantage in seeking to cross-pollinate the many ideas and methods embedded in anthropology, sociology, psychology, the history and phenomenology of religion, and theology. Almost at random, I am delighted to see Philip Rieff, Ralph Dahrendorf, Dorothey Emmet, Reinhold Niehbuhr, George Steiner, Austin Farrer, Joachim Wach, David Schneider, Marshall Sahlins and others all contributing to a two-page spread (1984: 162–163). But, thinking now of Matt Wood's chapter and its own challenge to varieties of meaning, I am intrigued by his cluster of ideas expressed as the 'call to speak', 'calling research subjects to speak', and the 'elicitation and solicitation' associated with social scientific research. These are crucial concepts that remind me of several research contexts and catalyse one's reflection on them. Here I think, especially, of that double call to speak that may possess distinctive attributes for individuals possessing a religious 'vocation'. First, I am reminded of interviews conducted with a sizable group of retired Church of England bishops, part of the AHRC Project conducted by Mathew Guest and myself (Davies and Guest 2007). Here I comment on my own interviews, though I think Mathew would report similar experiences. I spoke with individual bishops, some who had been extremely well known in British society and some largely unknown. In doing so, I was speaking with men who had, themselves, been 'called to speak' in the most direct fashion through their ordination and consecration. They owned an official and traditional voice, though in choosing retired bishops we hoped that additional, and perhaps more relaxed, accents might emerge. This was often the case, not least in that distinctive phenomenon that sometimes emerges when an interview has progressed to a point of relative disjunction from formality to a personal informality, the point of tonal shift when one intuits that 'truth' is being spoken. This more intimate, 'between ourselves' moment is, of course, but one form of conversational behaviour known at crucial moments in everyday life. Second, I think of LDS individuals whether as young missionaries and their formal 'testimony' to the truth of their church, or at the LDS monthly 'Testimony' meetings where complex switching may occur between formally controlled diction and emotion pervaded speech of personal conviction. Beyond this, I also think of those more private settings with Saints one has known for a long time, or who are in distinctive life contexts, when the 'truthful' moment arises and one 'knows' that this person utterly embodies the faith or hosts partial or extensive disbelief. In such contexts, the very 'call to speak' that is foundational for the Mormon fosters or constrains what is or can be said.

Matt Wood has given us further pause for thought in a chapter that many young researchers will find invaluable. One of the joys of academic life, especially if we see it somewhat along Max Weber's view of knowledge as a vocational reality and, I would add, as its own form of friendship, is to think of Matt as a keen undergraduate, then as a doctoral student pursuing much field and intellectual work, sometimes while being quite physically unwell, and now as an established and creative scholar. At the time of writing Matt is, as many will know, profoundly ill. When we were recently together and, I suppose, 'called to speak', my conversational flow could, largely, only be met by Matt's ideas-full look: and perhaps such eyes conveyed what is really *vital*.

Hugh Goddard's question of where Islamic Studies should fit within contemporary British universities is valuable for its historical sketch of the last thirty or so years and for his own experience of teaching in this area at Nottingham and Edinburgh. Hugh is, as ever, both judicious and clear as to how Islamic Studies could, despite some current institutional constraints, and should be aligned with religious studies. In this I fully agree with him. His account of the long-running Philosophy and Phenomenology of Religion course at Nottingham prompts thoughts a legion. The foresight of Professor John Heywood-Thomas in developing the study of religion – and notably Islam – within what had been a typical theology department influenced generations of students, including Matthew Wood and Mathew Guest in this volume, staff as with Seth Kunin, as well as many clergy and a clutch of current ecclesiastical dignitaries. Hugh also mentions the RAF, and I well recall being with him while we held a contract for in-service training of their chaplains. His focus on a 'new paradigm' for Islamic Studies is potent, and much deserving of serious discussion, posing its own issue of how to frame with an academic and pedagogical rationale the factors of political-social and religious-ideological dynamics that pervade international politics and, just now, acts of terrorism. Hugh's specific focus on sensitivity is crucial; it is also typical of the man himself and, indirectly, raises the issue of the embodiment of modes of knowledge within academics and how this creates intellectual environments of friendship. I have already mentioned Nottingham's role here when speaking of Charles Watkins and Hall life; it was also profoundly true of the Nottingham Theology Department under John Heywood-Thomas where a small group of scholars from quite different disciplines worked most happily together and learned a great deal from each other. Sister Mary Charles Murray on Patristics and early Christian Art stands high in my thoughts and Hugh's. The theological polar difference between biblical scholars, the late Maurice Casey and Ed Ball, did not engulf bonhomie. Hugh and I have, over the last few years, had the benefit of each other's company at the funerals of both of these colleagues: a fact that reminds us all, younger and older, of our timeliness, and of the real value of sensitivity.

Mathew Guest's chapter brings its own personal pleasure, having known him since his undergraduate life and witnessed his progressive stages of teaching, administration and participation in research in the United Kingdom and beyond conducing, so far, to his current status as a reader and colleague at our Durham Department. Our joint work on several projects has always been intellectually stimulating, culminating in the AHRC-funded study of

Church of England Bishops and their families in which we sought to trace the transmission of values across generations (Davies and Guest 2007). Mathew's recent collaborative work on Christians in British universities has, again, amply exercised his empirical, qualitative and contextualizing skills as his chapter spells out in informative ways that are, perhaps, especially important for those of us working in theology and religious studies. That he frames his chapter's discussion of pedagogy, politics and religious dispositions with the work of Jevons and Collini in a cross-era comparison expresses much of my own interest in the comparative method whether involving historical periods or cultural-geographical distance. To see Collini, whose work I had not known until now, align with Jevons has given me the easy prompt to highlight serendipity within research, given that Jevons arrived on my desk by happy accident. Following a dinner conversation with Tom Whitworth, then Master of Hatfield College, Durham, and an incidental reference to his predecessor, we met some days later and he led me to a large chest where lay all of Jevons' literary remains. I was, then, a young resident tutor of St John's College, Durham, but almost immediately was appointed to a new lectureship at Nottingham University, and Dr Whitworth showed much trust in allowing me to take all the Jevons' papers with me. A subsequent short college fellowship back at St John's permitted some focused work on these leading to my biography of Jevons, published in 1991. Here, perhaps, I might advise any early-career scholar in the social sciences who might find opportunity to work on primary resources for a biography to do so, for it offers a quite different experience from that of analysis of ideas or of ethnography or other social survey ventures. In my experience it brought my life into touch with an earlier life, my thought with his, my days with his. Through this I experienced a kind of intellectual conversation and an understanding of Victorian-Edwardian perspectives that enhanced my preexisting interest in the early history of anthropology. Fortunately, it not only enhanced my joint interest in religion, society, and theology, but had the great advantage of being set in Durham, a place I had known a little and was, over the years, coming to understand in deeper ways. We often write much about 'space' and 'place' these days, and rightly so, but to reflect upon the life of someone in the place where they had their being and impact, albeit with a time lag, engages its own *genius loci*. Now, as a recent fellow of Hatfield College, it is hard not to dine under the portrait of someone whose thought one has pursued quite extensively without sensing an ongoing participation: the current fashion in death studies of speaking of 'continuing bonds' has relevance way beyond the realm of grief theory. If Collini, for example, could advocate 'transgressive practice', then he is of a heart with Jevons, and also with interdisciplinary promiscuity already mentioned above. To have come from classics into philosophy, to offer lectures on psychology, and to develop his own version of the history of religions in his day was no mean feat. Jevons was, I think, also the first to offer an English critical review of Durkheim's *Les Formes Élémentaires de la Vie*

Religieuse (1915). Much more significant was his work in bringing women students into Durham University and fostering St Cuthbert's Society as a welcoming college base for poorer students. In terms of social impact, he also, for example, knew how to address Durham miners on such themes as the advantages the coal owners made of them, only to twist the knife and ask if they, similarly, treated their wives badly. His classical knowledge of rhetoric ensured that he could set hearers on an apparently moral high ground only to sweep their feet from under them. As you will see, this individual significantly influenced my own thinking, not least when working on sociological ideas of salvation that would not divide 'primitives' from Presbyterians. So I thank Mathew for his judicious and informative chapter that challenges all of us in our university teaching and learning; but, even more than this, I thank him for collegiality and for unfailing help when needed.

Eleanor Nesbitt joined me, as a very early-career academic at Nottingham, to pursue some research on Sikh life in that city. It was shortly after I had begun to study aspects of Sikhism as an intentional engagement with an 'Indian tradition' that might complement my existing work on the 'American' tradition of Mormonism. A grant from Nottingham County Council to the university allowed for a research postgraduate in this field. Eleanor's appointment and subsequent career development, with its impact on Sikh Studies and education in the United Kingdom, shows the value of grant support for potentially significant topics: retrospectively, it also gratifies a supervisor. More recently it was excellent to have Eleanor as part of a Durham hosted project on 'Identity, Emotions, and Religious Communities' (Davies and Warne 2013). That project on emotions, along with various others touched upon in this volume, has allowed me to be just such a 'transgressor of boundaries' to which Eleanor refers and to engage in that 'interdisciplinary promiscuity' already alluded to when responding to David Martin's chapter. However, such boundary-bridging was far from common in the mid-late 1970s and early 1980s, a time when I was trying to understand and teach the study of religion. For biographical reasons, the issue of theology and religious studies was not, for me, one of kinship antipathies but more like twin studies. This was partly because both liturgy (and its theological hinterland) and ritual (with its anthropological hinterland) were familiar to me and tended to merge somewhere on the horizon, at a place devoid of immigration officers.

Certainly, of great help to me was having been able to begin to work out something of the dynamics of these areas within the relative ease of Nottingham's Department of Theology, working alongside John Heywood-Thomas who had studied with Paul Tillich in the United States and, accordingly perhaps, possessed a broad vision of 'culture' in relation to theological-philosophical thought. Moreover, just before that, I had every encouragement while reading theology as an anthropology postgraduate, from the indefatigable intellectualism of Old Testament scholar John Rogerson who was already engaged with Lévi-Strauss and other anthropologists interested in the Bible. That Eleanor should end her chapter saying that I had helped her 'to see' as well as to observe is among the most gratifying points, because I have long felt that 'seeing', not least as a phenomenological endeavour, let alone an anthropological necessity, is an art that develops over a lifetime. To have had these poems to consider has, quite clearly, been its own demonstration of Eleanor's competence in that art.

Michael Thate's concluding chapter is a strong reminder of numerous conversations whose open-ended shift to another subject is also evident in the first sentence of Michael's preface to the book version of his doctorate where he reminds us of Paul Valéry's 'revelation that poems are never finished, only abandoned', and that the same 'must be said of doctoral dissertations and academic monographs' (Thate 2013: vii). That book, entitled *Remembrance of Things Past?* is subtitled, 'Albert Schweitzer, the Anxiety of Influence, and the Untidy Jesus of Markan Memory'. While packed with all the apparatus of biblical and historical-critical scholarship surrounding 'the historical Jesus', it extends into theories of identity, memory, symbolism and of cultural context that would educate many a sociological researcher. Though I simply cannot recall how we first fell into conversation amidst the many disciplined ethos of Durham's Theology and Religion Department, it might well have been the link with Schweitzer, for his ethical revelation of 'reverence for life', not to mention his biography as such, has long helped foster my own convictions. In his chapter, Michael has clearly identified my own eclectic approach to the study of religion with its preference for thinking of clusters of belief and practice rather than of systematic formulations in people's lives, and he has appropriately pinpointed many other preferences, from the Weberian drive for meaning, through issues of super plausibility, to the 'words against death' motif and the 'theory of offending death'. In all of these, a biological sense of humans as adapting to their environment has played a more significant role than any particular philosophical or theological sense, with 'meaning-making' itself both an adaptation to existing environments and a creation of new ideological, theological, mythological environments in which devotees participate. As for 'salvation', while it often does involve an 'expression of some distress', as Michael rightly records Weber as saying, I tried in the 1984 monograph to argue for a notion of salvation not from any confessional standpoint but from that of the sociology of knowledge driven by human adaptations. I think this is even more theoretically important now, and in a chapter published recently I have considered how 'salvation' dropped out of religious studies discourse as UK interests shifted from 'world' or 'salvation religions' to issues of pagan and self-spirituality and the like. Rather than being superseded by the latter, I argue that 'salvation' as a concept ought not to be ignored even in terms of those phenomena, nor in terms of, for example, the National Health Service and its cradle to grave engagement with core cultural values of survival, illness and well-being (Davies 2015b).

As for the link between identity, the words against death motif and the theory of offending death, Michael's telling use of the Norwegian film *Den Brysomme Mannen* ('The Troublesome Man'), with its banal emotionlessness, could hardly be more appropriate when set against an invitation I accepted to Oslo to join some national and community leaders in a commemorative reflection a year after Anders Breivik killed so many young people on Utøya Island and in Oslo itself. I mention this event because it highlights for me the relationship between scholarly activities and potent theories on the one hand and, on the other, non-academic domains in which the emotional flows of death and grief hold prominence. At that commemorative event, which also presented results of local research on popular and national responses to the killings, we find an echo of Matthew Wood's earlier chapter title – the 'call to speak' – when thousands of Norwegians gathered to sing 'The Rainbow Nation', a song Breivik stated that he hated. Invoking Rodney Needham's use of the dual sovereignty theory of authority, I cautiously spoke in Oslo of the jural element pronouncing guilt in court while the mystical authority of the united voice of the people sang the utter unacceptability of such murder and cultural betrayal. It seemed to me that, in so doing, Norway sang words against offending death while affirming their civilized identity in a reverence for life that many societies would still find impossible to express (Davies 2015a).

Let me, in conclusion, thank each author for their chapter, for their variety of gentle criticism, for the time taken to respond to my own work, and above all for using this opportunity to express some of their new thinking and academic concerns. This must also be an opportunity to recall those many generations of undergraduate and postgraduate students who have, and continue to make, academic life worthwhile.

Let me thank Martha Middlemiss Lé Mon, in particular, for her part in planning this volume and its earlier celebratory seminar. We have known each other from her excellent undergraduate and master's degree work at Durham, and have collaborated on European research projects, often with a strong Uppsala base. It has been a delight to see her career, and family, develop. She is an excellent example of academic bridging between Britain, Sweden and beyond, as well as one integrating theological and more sociological perspectives.

There are, of course, many other postgraduates whose friendship, scholarship and research have sustained and invigorated me. Let me simply mention from very recent years Bosco Bae and Adam Powell. Both from the United States, they rapidly dispatched excellent doctorates, the former now knowing more about cognitive dissonance and identity theory than most, and the latter cross-fertilizing Patristics and Joseph Smith in a sociology of heresy while, almost as a sideline, completing much research and publication on Hans Mol's work. Mauro Properzi, an Italian American, previously of Brigham Young, Harvard and Cambridge Universities, completed a creative doctorate here at Durham on emotions and identity in Mormonism.

After further work at The Gregorian, he is currently assistant professor of religion at Brigham Young University. Jason Singh, also from the United States via Oxford, combined a vast amount of social science research to frame his narrative of people exiting religious group membership. As for Hannah Rumble, her AHRC collaborative doctoral award led to an excellent study of Natural Burial and whose time at Durham in anthropology, theology and religion inspired many and has so far continued to do so at Bath, Aberdeen and Exeter Universities.

I cannot end even this partial list, nor properly recall my time as a doctoral supervisor, without recalling my Korean friend Chang-Won Park, whose courage had him attend his viva while being much more ill than anyone appreciated. He largely recovered after months of hospitalization and serious operations and returned to Korea. We joint-edited *Emotion, Identity, and Death* (Davies and Park 2013), and his creative monograph *Cultural Blending in Korean Death Rites* was published in 2010 (Park 2010). His sudden death was deeply saddening, a loss to scholarship let alone a deep sadness for me. While he lived, he thought deeply and passionately as his focus turned from biblical to more social scientific studies, always with a sense of the interplay of Christian identity and the Confucian heritage that he treasured.

Life does, as we say, go on, and, personally speaking, I continue to love teaching at least as much as research as the close of academic year 2014–2015 marks my fortieth year of university endeavour. As I write this, I feel a little like a pioneer quite unsure as to the future. In the United Kingdom, at least, we now inhabit a period of academic social change where age-bands vanish and where older colleagues and acquaintances still ask if, or assume that, one has retired – a rumour quite untrue at the time of writing in July 2015! I am most grateful to Mathew Guest and to Martha Middlemiss Lé Mon for organizing, along with Grant Underwood, the London event lying behind this volume, and to Mathew and Martha for editing this book while I am still in harness and ploughing on.

References

Davies, D. J. (1984) 'The charismatic ethic and the spirit of post-industrialism', in D. Martin and P. Mullen (eds) *Strange Gifts*. Oxford: Blackwell, pp. 137–150.

Davies, D. J. (1988) 'The evocative symbolism of trees', in D. Cosgrove and S. Daniels (eds) *The Iconography of Landscape*. Cambridge: Cambridge University Press, pp. 32–41.

Davies, D. J. (2015a) 'Valuing emotion in tragedy', in A. Day and M. Lovheim (eds) *Modernity, Memory and Mutations*. Farnham: Ashgate, pp. 113–129.

Davies, D. J. (2015b) 'Salvation, death, and the nature of grace', in W. Dossett, H. Bacon and S. Knowles (eds) *Alternative Salvations: Engaging the Sacred and the Secular*. London: Bloomsbury, pp. 85–96.

Davies, D. J. and Guest, M. (2007) *Bishops, Wives and Children: Spiritual capital Across the Generations*. Farnham: Ashgate.

Davies, D. J. and Park, C. W. (eds) (2013) *Emotion, Identity, and Death*. Farnham: Ashgate.

Davies, D. J. and Warne, N. (eds) (2012) *Emotions and Religious Dynamics*. Farnham: Ashgate.

Durkheim, E. (1915) *Les Formes Élémentaires de la Vie Religieuse*. London: Allen and Unwin.

Park, C. W. (2010) *Cultural Blending in Korean Death Rites*. London: Continuum.

Thate, M. (2013) *Remembrance of Things Past? Albert Schweitzer, the Anxiety of Influence, and the Untidy Jesus of Markan Memory*. Tübingen: Mohr Siebeck.

Index

Note: *Italic* page numbers indicate tables and charts; **bold** indicate figures and illustrations. Davies' work is discussed throughout the text and is not fully itemized in the index.